THE RADIO EYE

Film and Media Studies Series

Film studies is the critical exploration of cinematic texts as art and entertainment, as well as the industries that produce them and the audiences that consume them. Although a medium barely one hundred years old, film is already transformed through the emergence of new media forms. Media studies is an interdisciplinary field that considers the nature and effects of mass media upon individuals and society and analyzes media content and representations. Despite changing modes of consumption—especially the proliferation of individuated viewing technologies—film has retained its cultural dominance into the 21st century, and it is this transformative moment that the WLU Press Film and Media Studies series addresses.

Our Film and Media Studies series includes topics such as identity, gender, sexuality, class, race, visuality, space, music, new media, aesthetics, genre, youth culture, popular culture, consumer culture, regional/national cinemas, film policy, film theory, and film history.

Wilfrid Laurier University Press invites submissions. For further information, please contact the Series editors, all of whom are in the Department of English and Film Studies at Wilfrid Laurier University:

Dr. Philippa Gates, Email: pgates@wlu.ca
Dr. Russell Kilbourn, Email: rkilbourn@wlu.ca
Dr. Ute Lischke, Email: ulischke@wlu.ca

75 University Avenue West
Waterloo, ON N2L 3C5
Canada
Phone: 519-884-0710
Fax: 519-884-8307

THE RADIO EYE

Cinema in the North Atlantic, 1958–1988

JERRY WHITE

Wilfrid Laurier University Press

LAURIER
Inspiring Lives.

This book has been published with the help of a grant from the Canadian Federation for the Humanities and Social Sciences, through the Aid to Scholarly Publications Programme, using funds provided by the Social Sciences and Humanities Research Council of Canada. We acknowledge the financial support of the Government of Canada through the Book Publishing Industry Development Program for our publishing activities. This work was supported by the Research Support Fund.

Canada

Canada Council for the Arts | Conseil des arts du Canada

ONTARIO ARTS COUNCIL
CONSEIL DES ARTS DE L'ONTARIO

Library and Archives Canada Cataloguing in Publication

White, Jerry, 1971–

The radio eye : cinema in the North Atlantic, 1958–1988 / Jerry White.

(Film and media studies series)
Includes bibliographical references and index.
Issued also in electronic format.
ISBN 978-1-55458-178-8 (hardcover). —ISBN 978-1-55458-614-1 (softcover)
ISBN 978-1-55458-212-9 (PDF). —ISBN 978-1-55458-299-0 (EPUB)

1. Motion pictures—Québec (Province)—History. 2. Motion pictures—Newfoundland and Labrador—History. 3. Motion pictures—Faroe Islands—History. 4. Motion pictures—Ireland—Gaeltacht—History. 5. Regionalism in motion pictures. 6. Vertov, Dziga, 1896–1954—Criticism and interpretation. I. Title. II. Series: Film and media studies series

P94.5.M55W55 2009 791.4309 C2009-903705-X

Cover design by Martyn Schmoll. Cover photo, showing Michel Brault filming *Pour la suite du monde* (1963), courtesy of Cinémathèque québécoise. Photo used with permission of the National Film Board of Canada. Background image courtesy of iStockphoto. Text design by Catharine Bonas-Taylor.

Paper printing 2018

Waterloo, Ontario, Canada
www.wlupress.wlu.ca

This book is printed on FSC recycled paper and is certified Ecologo. It is made from 100% post-consumer fibre, processed chlorine free, and manufactured using biogas energy.

Printed in Canada

FSC
www.fsc.org
RECYCLED
Paper made from recycled material
FSC® C103567

For 5 Victoria Street,
my most beloved North Atlantic stopover

CONTENTS

ACKNOWLEDGEMENTS

Acknowledgements in academic works are famously long-winded and self-indulgent. I promise to uphold that high standard here.

Research for this book was supported by a grant from the Social Sciences and Humanities Research Council of Canada (SSHRC), and it was indispensable. I am very grateful. It was also supported in its earliest stages by the Faculty of Arts of the University of Alberta, and I'm also very grateful for the faith they showed in what must have seemed a very quixotic project.

A lot of people have helped me along the way; I will go chapter by chapter.

Introduction: Thanks to Steve Gravestock (Toronto International Film Festival) for sharing his expertise on Icelandic cinema, Þórarinn Guðnason (Kvikmyndasafn Íslands / Icelandic Film Archive) for guiding me through the history of Icelandic cinema, and Laufey Guðjónsdóttir (Kvikmyndasjóður Íslands / Icelandic Film Fund) for chatting with me about Iceland's cinematic infrastructure.

Chapter 1: At Université Laval, Division des archives, I am grateful to Josée Pomminville, Sandra Morin, and James Lambert, for guiding me through the Fonds Pierre Perrault. The reproduction of the document from the Fonds Pierre Perrault in chapter 4 is by their kind permission. David Clandfield (New College, University of Toronto) invited me to contribute to the Pierre Perrault retrospective at the 2006 Toronto International Film Festival, and that got me started on a lot of this work. Daniel Laforest (University of Alberta) offered valuable feedback on the matter of Perrault as radio artist.

Chapter 2: I am grateful to Linda White at the Archives and Manuscripts Division of Memorial University of Newfoundland, and to the staff of their Centre for Newfoundland Studies. Darrell Varga (NSCAD University) provided precious feedback on an earlier version of this work, a shorter version of which appears in his book *Rain/Drizzle/Fog: Essays on Film and Television in Atlantic Canada* (University of Calgary Press, 2008). Tom Waugh (Concordia University) included me in his Challenge for Change workshop at the 2007 conference of the Film Studies Association of Canada, and that helped me focus a lot of my ideas about the roots of the Newfoundland Project.

Chapter 3: I published a sort of "what I did on my summer research trip in the Faroes" article in the online magazine *Synoptique* 9 (2005); thanks to Adam Rosaduik (Concordia University) for asking me to contribute this piece which, while chock full of errors, got me moving on this work. I am very grateful to Árni Conradsson for lending me his scrapbook of press cuttings related to Sjónvarpsfelagið í Havn and for making me copies of some of their programs; that material was invaluable. Jan Berg Jórgensen and Jóna Dalsgarð at Sjónvarp Føroya helped me find and make copies of key television programs. Zakaris Hansen, of the department of Faroese at Froðskaparsetur Føroya, helped me track down people involved in early Faroese television. Turið Sigurðardóttir, dean of Language and Literature and professor of Faroese at Froðskaparsetur Føroya, deserves special thanks; she has been of enormous help to me during my trips to the Faroes, a sort of intellectual lighthouse in a climate that was, at times, very foggy and windblown indeed. She also brought us to her sister Inga Rósa Joensen and to Undir Ryggi 13; hardly a day goes by when I don't think back to the happy days my family and I spent there, and we are all very grateful indeed.

Gaeltacht Introduction: I spent a very agreeable and enlightening afternoon chatting with An Comhairleoir Seosamh Ó Cuaig about the civil rights movement in the Gaeltacht; he was most hospitable and patient, and I thank him. Andrew Burke (University of Winnipeg) led me to *Raymond Williams on Television.*

Chapter 4: I presented a much shorter version of this chapter at the Constructions of Identity in Ireland and Quebec workshop at Concordia University in October 2006. Thanks to Michael Kenneally, Rhona Richman Kenneally, and Ron Rudin, all of Concordia, for inviting me. Thanks also to Desmond Fennell, for permission to reprint his Gaeltacht map and the image from his book *Heresies.*

Chapter 5: Ann Mitchell at the library of the National University of Ireland, Galway, made me feel very welcome and helped me find my way through their extensive collection of Irish-language newspapers. Miriam Allen and the staff at Galway Film Centre helped me copy video material. Ever since I became interested in the Gaeltacht, Bob Quinn has been a welcoming presence, a skeptical ear, a critical reader, and an all-around mensch, and I thank him heartily.

Chapter 6: My chats with Donncha Ó hÉallaithe made key parts of this project come together, and the access to his work from the Teilifís na Gaeltachta days was a godsend. Nuala Canny at the Stationery Office (Dublin) was good enough to send me a copy of a long-forgotten but for me key government report on Irish-language television. Thanks to Leila Doolan and Bob Quinn for permission to reprint their proposed Gaeltacht channel grid from *Sit Down and Be Counted.*

On matters of non-English-language proofreading and correction, I thank the following: Mary Haslam (Irish, French, Spanish), Randi Kúrberg (Faroese, Danish), Turið Sigurðardóttir (Icelandic). The Russian text was inserted by Dr. Peter G. Larson (University of Alberta). Pádraig Ó Siadhail (Saint Mary's University) provided invaluable feedback on matters of usage (and on the ideology of the Gaeltacht movement), and his corrections make me seem a lot smarter than I really am. I live in fear of the errors that remain, and emphasize that responsibility for them is mine alone.

Zoë Druick (Simon Fraser University) was the first to make it all the way through the manuscript, and her support and suggestions were just what the doctor had ordered. Thea Bowering and Celia Nicholls provided stellar research and editorial assistance.

On more general matters, I want to thank audiences at the annual conferences of the Film Studies Association of Canada (FSAC) and the Canadian Association for Irish Studies (CAIS), who have by now heard *a lot* of this material. CAIS has been especially important to me, serving, since the beginning of my academic career, as a sort of intellectual home base. Special thanks, then, to Jean Talman (St. Michael's College, University of Toronto) and Cecil Houston (University of Windsor), who have been my long-time mentors in that group, and to Danine Farquharson (Memorial University of Newfoundland) and Pádraig Ó Siadhail (Saint Mary's University), who have been my beloved partners in crime.

And Sara Daniels, as always, deserves the biggest thanks of all.

NOTES ON SOURCES AND LANGUAGE

None of the films and filmmakers that I deal with in this book is especially well known. But I would like readers to know, from the outset, that a lot of this work is very easily available. Going chapter by chapter:

Chapter 1: Subtitled versions of all of Pierre Perrault's films (except for the programs of *Au pays de Neufve-France*) are available on DVD at the website of the National Film Board of Canada / Office national du film du Canada (http://www.nfb.ca/boutique). *Au Pays de Neufve-France* was, in 1998, issued as a French-language box set on VHS, without subtitles, a set that included a CD of some of Perrualt's radio work; it can be found at http://www.onf.ca/collection/films/fiche/?id=33536. Most of these episodes are also available in an English version at http://www.nfb.ca. Perrault's Île-aux-Coudres trilogy has been subtitled in English and released as a box set by the NFB/ONF; see http://onf-nfb.gc.ca/eng/collection/film/?id=54873. Reel-to-reel tape copies of much of Perrault's radio work (including all the programs of *Au Pays de Neufve-France* and *Chroniques du terre et mer*) are held at the Fonds Pierre Perrault at Quebec City's Université Laval, Division des archives (http://www.archives.ulaval.ca).

Chapter 2: All of the films of the Newfoundland Project are available on DVD at the English-language website of the National Film Board of Canada, http://www.nfb.ca. VHS copies of the films shot by Memorial University of Newfoundland's Extension Service, as well as copies of their community television experiments, are held at Memorial University's Media and Data Centre, which is part of their Queen Elizabeth II Library (http://www.library.mun.ca/qeii/index.php).

Chapter 3: Availability of the broadcasts of Sjónvarpsfelagið í Havn is a real problem, and I deal with that directly in the chapter. But the Faroese television service, Sjónvarp Føroya, has an excellent archive of its own (post-1984) work. They allow viewing on site, and they will duplicate onto VHS or DVD most of the material they have broadcast, by special request and for a small fee. Contact Sjónvarp Føroya at 298-347-500 or http://www.svf.fo.

Chapter 4: Again, subtitled versions of all of Pierre Perrault's films are available from the French-language website of the NFB/ONF (http://www.onf.ca). *L'Acadie, l'Acadie?!?* is available with English subtitles as part of the box set "Michel Brault: Oeuvres 1958–1974 Works," which also includes an English-subtitled version of *Pour la suite du monde* (http://www.nfb.ca/collection/films/fiche/?id=53737).

Chapter 5: The community videos produced by Cinegael have not been formally archived; VHS copies are held by Bob Quinn, who can be contacted at admin@conamara.org. The 2004 film about that community video project, *Cinegael Paradiso*, was produced by Distinguished Features, which can be contacted at 353-1-668-2643 or mail@distinguishedfeatures.com; the sales agent for the film is High Point Film and Television, 44-20-7586-3686, info@highpointfeatures.com. Bob Quinn's *Atlantean* films and *Poitín* can be ordered on DVD at http://www.conamara.org/filmography.htm. VHS and 16 mm copies of his film *Caoineadh Airt Uí Laoire* are held at the Irish Film Archive (353-1-679-5744, http://www.irishfilm.ie/archive, or info@irishfilm.ie).

Chapter 6: Availability of the pirate broadcasts of Teilifís na Gaeltachta, like those of Sjónvarpsfelagið í Havn, is a real problem, and I deal with that directly in the chapter.

When I quote material, I offer an English version in the main text, and if this is a translation, I offer the original in an endnote. If a quotation is very short, I just give the original with the English translation next to it. Wherever possible, I have relied on published translations. If a citation makes no mention of an English-language translation, then the translation is my own. For the record, I used the following dictionaries in the preparation of this book:

Clari, Michela, et al. *Collins Robert Concise French Dictionary*. New York: HarperCollins, 2000.

Engelsk-Dansk / Dansk-Engelsk Ordbog. København [Copenhagen]: Gyldendals Røde Ordbøger, 2006.

Hólmarsson, Sverrir, Christopher Sanders, and John Tucker. *Íslensk-ensk orðabók / Concise Icelandic-English Dictionary*. Reykjavík: Iðunn, 2004.

Lea, Christine, and John Butt. *The Oxford Spanish Dictionary and Grammar*. Oxford: Oxford University Press, 1997.

Ó Dónaill, Niall. *Foclóir Gaeilge-Béarla*. Ed. Tomás de Bhaldraithe. Baile Átha Cliath [Dublin]: An Gúm, 1992.

Young, G. V. C., and Cynthia R. Clewer. *Føroysk-Ensk Orðabók / Faroese-English Dictionary*. Peel, Isle of Man: Mansk-Svenska Publishing, 1985.

For a few specific regional, archaic, or arcane references, I also had cause to consult the following:

Bergeron, Léandre. *Dictionnaire de la langue québécoise*. Montréal: Éditions TYPO, 1997.

Contri, Gianfranco. *Dizionario Faroese-Italiano/Føroysk-Italsk Orðabók*. Tórshavn: Føroya Fróðskaparfelag, 2004.

Dinneen, Rev. Patrick S. *Foclóir Gaedhilge agus Béarla*. Dublin: Irish Texts Society: 1965.

For material in German and Russian, I have relied entirely on published translations. The Russian text was inserted by Peter Larson, PhD candidate in Russian at the University of Alberta.

I want to make just a brief note on methodology. I spoke with a number of people responsible for these media projects, especially in the Faroe Islands and the Gaeltacht. By and large this was a matter of necessity; there is a real dearth of published information by or about these media experiments (especially in the case of the Faroes). This is not the case with the work of Pierre Perrault or the Newfoundland Project; Perrault wrote voraciously and gave a number of interviews (including a book-length one with Paul Warren), and much the same is true of Colin Low vis-à-vis the Newfoundland Project. Throughout the book, I have sought to balance textual analysis, contextual discussion, and the perspectives of practitioners. I just had to go to a few different kinds of places to find that third element.

INTRODUCTION

> Beyond merely *reflecting* or *restricting* public discussions, then—as a liberal or Marxist model might suggest—documentary programming may have *enabled* new forms of civic life.... In helping to develop new forms of public life in the age of mass communication, broadcast documentary was perhaps truer to the Griersonian democratic project than was documentary film itself.
>
> —David Hogarth, in the "Documentary and Canadian Radio" section of his book *Documentary Television in Canada* (34)

This book's title may create some unrealistic expectations. "The Radio-Eye" is a well-known concept in Film Studies, coined by Soviet filmmaker Dziga Vertov. This was closely related to his concept of the "Kino-Eye," which in a 1924 essay "Рождение 'Киноглаза'" [The Birth of the Kino-Eye] he described as:

> Not "filming life unawares" for the sake of "unaware," but in order to show people without masks, without makeup, to catch them through the eye of the camera in a moment when they are not acting, to read their thoughts, laid bare by the camera ... Kino-eye as the union of science with newsreel to further the battle for the communist decoding of the world, as an attempt to show the truth on the screen—Film-truth. (*Kino-Eye* 41)[1]

This notion of "film-truth" or "Kino-Pravda," the source of the term *cinéma vérité*,[2] seemed to achieve a new immediacy with the rise of radio technology. Indeed, David Hogarth has written of the way in which radio documentary of the pre-1940s period anticipated the rise of vérité, especially in Canada. He recalls how "the CBC made extensive efforts to reduce the weight of its sound recorders in preparation for the Royal Tour of 1939, developing much more portable equipment than the cumbersome camera units used by the NFB in its early (and even later) years. Though the days of the lightweight tape recorder had not yet arrived, some broadcast recording kits weighed only ten pounds and by the mid-1940s could fit into a knapsack" (24). Partially because it seemed to offer a new way of getting out of studios and into streets, radio was a technology that Vertov found very exciting. In a 1925 essay called "Киноправда и Радиоправда" [Kinopravda and Radiopravda], he wrote, "If, with respect to vision, our kinok-observers have recorded visible life phenomena with cameras, we must now talk about recording audible facts.... To artistic cinema we oppose kinopravda and kino-eye; to artistic radio broadcasts we oppose radiopravda and radio-ear" (*Kino-Eye* 56).[3] This figure of the "kinok," a filmmaker engaged with social reality and who completely rejects the traditional conception of an artist as somehow removed from society at large, is central to Vertov's thought and will appear frequently in my discussion of his work's relevance to the North Atlantic. This was very much in keeping with his ongoing desire to escape the shackles of the realist-illusionist, narrative feature film, and to make work that reflected everyday life of a transforming society. Such theorizing lead to formally experimental documentaries like *Шестая часть мира* [*A Sixth of the World*] (1926) or *Человек с киноаппаратом* [*Man with a Movie Camera*] (1929), documentaries that were very much of a piece with the theories of montage that were crucial to the state-funded Soviet avant-garde of the 1920s.

Furthermore, Vertov is enjoying something of a revival these days. This is driven in large part by the publication of Lev Manovich's 2001 book *The Language of New Media*. Manovich argues there that Vertov's work is a kind of prototype for the non-linear, associative sorts of interpretation, stating in the book's first pages that his 1929 film *Man with a Movie Camera* "will serve as our guide to the language of new media" (xiv) and going on to state that the film "is perhaps the most important example of a database imagination in media art" (xxiv, 239). This image of the database is key for Manovich, who also writes that "in the hands of Vertov, the database, this normally static and 'objective' form, becomes dynamic and subjective. More important, Vertov is able to achieve something new media designers and artists still have to learn—how to merge database and narrative into a new form" (xxviii, 243). Indeed, Manovich often writes of how far ahead of our own time Vertov seems, how modern he really is. He writes at one point about how *Man with a Movie Camera* is defined by "a very basic narrative that is also quintessentially modern—a camera moving through space recording whatever is in its way" (xxxii, 316). Thus for Manovich, Vertov's contemporary importance is the way in which his films merge story and document, data and narrative, into a single way of thinking, of moving through the world. This lack of distinction between fiction and documentary, this urge to use the camera in the world as you find it, is one of the defining characteristic of the films, videos, and television projects that I am discussing in this book. As much as he anticipates the "New Media" forms of the past few years, Vertov also anticipates the (indeed quintessentially modern) media experiments of Pierre Perrault, the Newfoundland Project, the Faroe Islands' Sjónvarpsfelagið í Havn, and the media militants of the Irish Gaeltacht.

Seth Feldman has summarized Manovich's importance to contemporary understanding of Vertov in ways that strongly set the scene for the sorts of arguments I will be unfolding in this book. Writing of the appropriation of the term cinéma vérité by French filmmakers Jean Rouch and Edgar Morin for their 1961 film *Chronique d'un été*, Feldman states:

> Theirs was a quintessentially modernist gesture, suggesting that technological progress had finally allowed the full realization of an earlier, less sophisticated, prototype for their work. Cinéma vérité, in other words, was what Vertov wanted to do but couldn't. In contrast, Manovich, in his use of Vertov, argues for what could be called a post-modern appropriation, one that links two of the great polar opposites of our time: the analogue and the digital. The digital world has not improved on the original ("improvement" in this sense being somewhat antithetical to the entire post-modern project). Rather the appropriation demonstrates an essential commonality between then and now. (45)

I am making a similar appropriation of Vertov here, although I hesitate to call it post-modern. Indeed, I am not seeking to link "two of the great polar opposites of our time." I am, however, insisting on the commonality between then and now, on commonality between Vertov's internationalist idealism (such a product of the 1920s); the fiercely anti-provincial regionalism that defines the ideology of the media-makers from Quebec, Newfoundland, the Faroe Islands, and the Irish-speaking[4] areas of Ireland (collectively known as the Gaeltacht) whose work from 1958 to 1988 forms the core of this book; and the globalized culture that has defined so much of the twenty-first century.

This book is thus about the *idea* of "Radio-Eye," of a form of cimema that is close to Vertov in spirit, although not connected to his work explicitly. Indeed, one slightly simpler way of explaining the project is to say that I am dealing with a group of filmmakers in the North Atlantic whose films seem closer to radio than to conventional cinema. I believe this to be true both in terms of form and in terms of the social place that these film and television experiments have. In many of the cases under examination, there is a very clear connection between video- or filmmaking and radio practice, sometimes via some shared experience (the Quebec filmmaker Pierre Perrault made quite a bit of work for radio, some of which I will discuss in the chapter devoted to his films and his television and radio programs), sometimes by way of common restlessness with linearity (I will argue that the films made on Newfoundland's Fogo Island are very close to the radio work done by Glenn Gould for the Canadian Broadcasting Corporation), and sometimes through a use of radio as a model (the agitation for television in Irish Gaelic was explicitly modelled after the agitation for the Irish-language radio station). The unifying argument of this book, then, is that between 1958 and 1988 the North Atlantic saw an exceptional amount of cinematic activity explicitly engaged with community-building, the politics of regionalism and/or minority nationalism, and the politics of language. Furthermore, this period also saw a significant amount of cinematic activity that stood outside of the commercial/feature-narrative tradition, frequently embracing a documentary containing fictional elements but in no way aspiring to the status of a film industry. This set of thematic concerns is, like a formal pattern that is primarily and unselfconsciously centred in a non-fictional mode of address while remaining open to certain elements of semi-fictional manipulation, a hallmark of much of radio practice. It is also, of course, a preview of the debates about globalization that so define discourse around communications media today.

Furthermore, radio is acting here almost as a metaphor, or at least as a sort of methodological ideal. Anticipating my desire to draw upon a certain idea of radio for cinema studies, David Hendy writes in *Cinema Journal*'s special section on "Sound Studies" that "those of us engaged in tracing radio's transmissions are, in some sense, always dealing in cultural history, simply because we have to. Sound carries, and it has never been possible to keep the airwaves segregated" (131). Indeed, the "integrated" quality of the airwaves is a defining characteristic of Pierre Perrault's work and that of the Gaeltacht media activists, who moved between film, radio, and television as though they were all part of the same cultural and political struggle, which of course they were. Furthermore, when the television pirates of the Faroe Islands were first ordered to cease their low-power "royndarsendingar" or test broadcasts, it was a law governing *radio* broadcasts that was used to shut them down.

This radio metaphor has as an aesthetic component, as well as an ethical one, and again, it is Hogarth who discusses this specifically in a Canadian context. A lot of the material that I discuss here is highly manipulated or constructed while also aspiring towards an intense form of realism. This paradox is, of course, at the heat of all of Vertov's work, but Hogarth argues that it is at the heart of radio as well. "During and after the war," he writes, "producers thus endeavoured to produce documentary 'facts' in the most effective radio form possible, and this generally involved not just obtaining location sounds but enhancing them with other types of material. Radio documentary evolved as an art as well as a science" (27). This combination of art and science is seminally Vertovian, and it is the sort of aesthetic that we will see recurring throughout this North Atlantic work. And this combination, Hogarth goes on to write, has an ethical component as well: "Broadcast documentary at least had the merit, in the view of its producers, of *attempting* to let its subjects speak—in however flawed and editorially compromised a way" (33–34). This North Atlantic work also emerges for the most part in the context of activist projects, projects that sought to decentralize mass communication and bring it closer to embattled communities. For Hogarth, it is radio that is the path-breaker for this approach to mass media; he writes that "the broadcast tradition is best seen not as a pale copy of documentary film or broadcast journalism but as an entirely distinct information form—an *alternative* documentary model for the television age" (35). That model, I hope to show, held a lot of sway in the North Atlantic from the fifties though the eighties, where the new forms of civic life that the epigraph to this chapter speaks of did indeed seem to emerge.

One element that all of these media-makers and media projects share is a sense of "in-between-ness" that defines the politics of so much radio practice. Pierre Perrault is the only figure in this book who did work in film, television, and radio. That is one of the reasons, of course, that the book begins with him. The way in which his work, like the work of everyone discussed in this book, tried to evoke a sense of collectivity that was deeply based in distinctive local textures is quite close to the historical work of radio. Michelle Hilmes has written that throughout its history, "radio's capacity for 'nationalized locality' made it a valuable medium for communication, discussion, and cultural cohesion across geographical boundaries" (11). That notion of "nationalized locality" is an excellent way of thinking of the cultural work of all of the projects that I am discussing here, despite the fact that none except Perrault's are based in radio itself. But Daina Augaitis and Dan Lander have written of "Radio's role in the development of nationhood, in Canada at least but in other countries as well" (1). Contextualizing more experimental approaches to the medium, they also note that "while many have held up radio's significant impact in articulating Canadian identity, nevertheless, a predominant feature of radio art is a resistance against state regulation of the airwaves and the many subtle and overt levels of control that have resulted" (1). The experimental projects that characterize this part of the North Atlantic's media history are quite notable in the way that they all embody these two seemingly contradictory paths of radio: the assertion of cultural and sometimes national identity and the resistance of state control. This is especially true of projects like the "royndarsendingar" or test broadcasts in the Faroe Islands and Teilifís na Gaeltachta in the Irish Gaeltacht, both of which were illegal, pirate broadcasts. But it's also true in more modest ways of the work of Pierre Perrault, the Newfoundland Project, and Cinegael, inasmuch as these projects were about advocating for or at least bringing to greater attention regions and cultural formations that had been marginalized by the cultural or political "centres" of their respective countries (Montreal/Quebec City for Perrault, St. John's/Ottawa for the Newfoundland Project, and Dublin for Cinegael). And yet, all of this work, from Perrault to the Newfoundland Project to the Faroes' Sjónvarpsfelagið í Havn to all of the media experiments of the Irish Gaeltacht, was also based in an attempt to assert cultural distinctiveness and identity, in a way that was very similar to the "significant impact in articulating Canadian identity" that Augaitis and Lander evoke. This push and pull between a desire to assert a distinctive cultural identity and skepticism of state formations is a characteristic element of the experiments of this part of the North Atlantic's media history, and it is a big part of what connects it, sometimes purely philosophically, to radio.

Defining "Cinema"

This book is subtitled *Cinema in the North Atlantic 1958–1988*, and a few words do seem in order as to how I understand the word "cinema." Although the term has colloquially become synonymous with the more intellectually ambitious forms of filmmaking (as opposed to the grubbier term "movies"), I would like to get away from that sense here. Rather, I think that cinema is reasonably understood as any form of moving-image arts. This is close, I suppose, to what has become known as "screen studies," a discipline that is generally understood to encompass scholarship on film, TV, computer-based media, and so on. Although it acknowledges that the term has "more aesthetic and artistic connotations" (and that in Europe it is synonymous with a movie theatre), Ira Konigsberg's *Film Dictionary* defines cinema first as "motion pictures in general" (48). That seems to quite easily, if implicitly, cover material like the television and video projects that I discuss alongside projects that originate on 16 mm film. More explicit still, and highly useful for my purposes here, is Laura U. Marks's discussion of the term in her 2000 book *The Skin of the Film: Intercultural Cinema and the Senses*, a work that deals with film, video, and television projects. She writes there that:

> It is important to establish a continuity between the media even while noting their formal, institutional, and perhaps ontological differences. Whether they are short experimental works or feature-length narratives, I choose to refer to all these works as cinema, because not only are they all time-based, audiovisual material, but also the word refers to the experience of an audience gathered in a theater. That these theaters are often drafty screening rooms in nonprofit galleries, and not the well-upholstered halls the term usually connotes, makes it a perverse pleasure to include these marginal viewing situations squarely inside the institution of cinema. (6)

As far as chilly discomfort goes, these non-profit galleries have got nothing on the drafty halls of the Connemara Gaeltacht, where the videos of Cinegael were screened as a run-up to attempts at pirate TV broadcasts, or those of the blustery Fogo Island, where footage was screened for the people about whom these films were made, to say nothing of the Faroe Islands, where the words "gale force" (*hvassur vindur* in Faroese) are used to describe the weather with startling frequency. These spaces make most "screening rooms in nonprofit galleries" seem positively luxurious in comparison. The work of early Faroese television associations is harder to characterize as based in "the experience of an audience gathered in a theater," although Marks's book also discusses work that, although having some life on the non-profit exhibition circuit, was really meant for broadcast (she discusses programs made by Nunavut's Inuit Broadcasting Corporation [16–17] as well as work by the United States' Independent Television Service [14]). Furthermore, an awareness of the relatively small number of TVs on the Faroes in the 1980s would lead one to believe that people were gathering around screens to watch these programs, and attendance at some of those gatherings was likely at least as numerous as some of the gallery screenings of avant-garde work that I have attended. From all reports these broadcasts were, at least at first, an event, just as much of an event as a screening held in an auditorium setting, especially on small islands such as Mykines, where, as a 1981 newspaper report pointed out, "there are at the moment two television sets."[5] While I understand the problems with conflating film and television, one of the goals of this book is to illustrate the degree to which the North Atlantic of the fifties, sixties, seventies, and eighties was home to a number of projects that did blur the boundaries between these media (Marks is trying to do something similar for a later period and a very formally different group of works).

Furthermore, while Quebec and Ireland are both home to relatively robust national cinemas (although this was less the case in Ireland during the period under discussion in this book), the works I discuss here—those of Pierre Perrault, and Gaeltacht-based media—exist almost entirely independently of the better-known (and more narrative) elements of their respective national cinemas. While there has been some narrative and documentary filmmaking in Newfoundland (Noreen Golfman has very succinctly outlined this history), the National Film Board of Canada's (NFB) Newfoundland Project does not seem to have had a tremendous effect outside of the media projects of Memorial University of Newfoundland. Although there have been a few films made in the Faroe Islands, there is no real national cinema to speak of, purely by virtue of the fact that these films can be counted on one hand. That said, the last two decades saw the emergence of two genuine auteurs, Teitur Árnason and Zakaris Hammar,[6] but both are connected strongly to the television service Sjónvarp Føroya, and their lyrical documentaries basically bear no resemblance to feature films like Nils Mamros' 1997 adaptation of the classic Faroese novel *Barbara* or even to Katrin Ottarsdóttir's low-budget Faroese road movie *Bye-Bye Blue Bird* (1999). This is all to say that this material—the work of Pierre Perrault, the Newfoundland Project, Sjónvarpsfelagið í Havn, and Gaeltacht media—is better understood in transnational terms than as part of their respective national cinemas. While I do believe in the continuing viability of the concept of the national cinema (and can certainly see why all of these projects belong in histories of their respective national cinemas), it is also clear that some of this work can be seen outside of this framework.[7] I strive to explain some of the local cultural and cinematic terrain in each chapter, and these sorts of concerns are certainly relevant. But the work I am discussing in this book does not generally illuminate much about the local state of narrative, feature-length filmmaking. However, this does not mean it should be left out of histories of the respective national cinemas, even though that has often been the case. Very much the opposite is actually true, and I will decry, in due course, the degree to which Perrault, the Newfoundland Project, and Cinegael have become marginal to the general understanding of the national cinemas of Quebec, Canada, and Ireland. Thus I am looking here at work that shares some connection to mainstream understandings of "cinema" but which is fundamentally different in important ways; similarly, the taxonomy I employ to group this work bears some connection to my understanding of the concept of national cinema but differs from that in important ways as well.

To a certain extent this duality can be explained through the work of Martinique writer Édouard Glissant. He has served as a shining example for a renewed Atlanticism, writing essays and novels that situate the ocean as a force that both unties and divides; following this view of the sea, he sees our globalizing world as a place defined both by mixture and difference. His best known phrase is likely "le monde se créolise" (*Introduction à une poétique du divers* 15), which provides a pithy summary of his world view. But Glissant has also written strongly about the role of small cultures and the way in which they provide a sort of "flesh of the world." Defining his notion of "Le Divers" in his 1997 book *Le discours antillais*, he writes that:

> *Le Divers* needs the presence of peoples, no longer as objects to be swallowed up, but with the intention to create new relationships.... You cannot become Trinidadian or Quebecois if you are not; but it is from now on true that if Trinidad and Quebec did not exist as accepted components of Diversity, something would be missing from the body of world culture—that today we would feel the loss. (*Caribbean Discourse* 99)[8]

Glissant's project is to both recognize the very real cultural differences that define the world (Trinidadians, Québécois), while still acknowledging their natures as complex composites, as projects that are put into relation with each other. He rejects the notion of métissage as obliterating these sorts of differences, writing in *Introduction à une poétique du divers* that "*métissage* would be determinism, while creolisation is, in relation to métissage, the producer of the unpredictable."[9] So it is not that I think that these works aren't really Québécois, or Newfoundlandish or Faroese or Irish, just because I am trying to create new relationships between them. Indeed, these projects are, as Marks and Glissant can show us, precursors to a globalized cinema, one that balances the specificity of both media and culture with the fluidity that inevitably emerges from the nomadic culture that has long been so common to maritime regions and which is now a key characteristic of globalized culture.

Defining the North Atlantic

"Atlantic History" is currently enjoying something of a revival. Long thought of as the intellectual underpinning of an "Atlanticist" foreign policy, it defined large portions of Cold War history, whether implicitly or explicitly. Some recent work on the region, though, has sought to shift the emphasis away from a "great powers" history and towards an understanding of the region as the site of colonial history and of an emerging post-colonial perception of culture. There's little doubt that this book shares more with the second group of intellectuals than with the first; some work associated with this latter-day shift, such as Édouard Glissant's writing on Caribbean culture and its relation to internationalism, is highly useful. But overall, this book is quite distinct from *both* schools. I am not sure that students of "Atlantic Studies" would immediately recognize its interests or perspectives.

For several generations, the notion of an Atlantic world has been a keystone of twentieth-century military history and political studies. The pathbreaking text here is Walter Lippmann's unsigned editorial for the *New Republic*, dated 17 February 1917 and titled "The Defense of the Atlantic World" (Bernard Bailyn states that the article is by Lippmann; see *Atlantic History* 6–7). This sets out a kind of internationalist approach to foreign policy that the magazine has, over the decades, continuously advocated. Arguing for the United States' entry into World War I, Lippman writes early in the article that "the war against Britain, France and Belgium is a war against the civilization of which we are a part" (59). He continued, "On the two shores of the Atlantic ocean there has grown up a profound web of interest which joins together the western world. Britain, France, Italy, even Spain, Belgium, Holland, the Scandinavian nations, and Pan-America are in the main one community in their deepest needs and their deepest purposes. They have a common interest in the ocean which unites them" (60). Bernard Bailyn, in his survey of Atlantic history, recalls how Forrest Davis, "a fellow journalist, published in 1941 *The Atlantic System*, a book-length commentary on Roosevelt and Churchill's 'Atlantic Charter,' in which he reviewed the history of Anglo-American relations and quoted Lippmann at length to argue the case for intervention" (7). Lippmann himself explored the concept in book-length WWII-era works such as *U.S. Foreign Policy* (1943) and *U.S. War Aims* (1944). This sort of work was, in turn, of tremendous influence during the Cold War period. As William O'Reilly writes, "The concept and vocabulary of Atlantic history emerged largely as a response to World Wars I and II, as a result of genuine academic interest but also as a form of shared interests by victorious states in incorporating their respective historical narratives into a shared hyper-narrative" (78). He also admits that "some critics see Atlantic history as little more than this: a 'NATO' history, which is a free world response to the Cold War" (78). This first enunciation of Atlantic Studies, based in military history and strategic studies and animated by the two World Wars and the Cold War, seemed to have little or no interest in cultural matters of any but the most superficial kind. Much the same has been true of key work in French, which even in its most romantic forms has a distinct geopolitical edge. Jean Buhler's 1951 travelogue *Sur les routes de l'Atlantique* is a very idealistic account of travels through Portugal and the Azores, and then through what he calls "le monde viking" of Iceland and the Faroes. But his chapter "Qu'est-ce la communauté Atlantique?" answers that question in mostly military terms (34–39). Paul Butel's monumental work *Histoire de l'Atlantique* (published in English as *The Atlantic*) has only one chapter devoted to the twentieth century, and its concerns are almost entirely economic and military. His section "Les mutations de l'Atlantique à la fin du xxe siècle" [Changes in the Atlantic at the End of the Twentieth Century] opens by stating "Whereas the North Atlantic saw its passenger traffic all but collapse with the sudden expansion of air traffic, its merchant traffic responded to the global boom in large-scale maritime commerce in the 1960s, before the oil crisis of 1973, and once this was over, continued to expand to reach its peak after the end of the 1970s" (*The Atlantic* 289).[10] This is as close as he comes to explaining the importance of twentieth-century Atlantic culture. This is true even of the lone book-length study of cinema and the North Atlantic, Ian Jarvie's 1992 work *Hollywood's Overseas Campaign: The North Atlantic Movie Trade, 1920–1950*, which is basically an economic history of the way in which Hollywood came to dominate European film markets in the post-WWI period (it is close in its concerns to Kristin Thompson's 1985 book *Exporting Entertainment: America in the World Film Market, 1907–1934*).

One important exception to this "great powers" trend in Atlantic Studies is the work of the cultural geographer E. Estyn Evans, whose writing on the culture and landscape of Ireland's northernmost province, Ulster, has always strongly emphasized its connections to other Atlantic regions (and which has thus challenged nationalist notions of an Ireland defined by a unified, Gaelic culture that was disrupted only by foreign invasion and settlement from Britain). Evans has also written that this sort of work tends to be dominated by geopolitical concerns; he stated in his 1961 Frazer Lecture "Atlantic Europe: The Pastoral Heritage" (reprinted in his book *Ireland and the Atlantic Heritage*) that:

> The term Atlantic Europe, in these days, has come to have implications of strategic, economic, and political co-operation in Western Europe, and it carries with it an ocean wind of freedom. My use of the term, similarly, for a more restricted part of the continent, is meant to imply that, despite physical and political fragmentation, the Atlantic ends of Europe have inherited many common features of economic, social and cultural life. (59)

Among these common features is a suspicion of authority and a general tendency towards rebelliousness. This is certainly visible in the work of Bob Quinn, whose Cinegael project is the subject of chapter 5 and whose own work on the culture of the Atlantic is strongly influenced by Evans and strongly influential on this book. Laying out that sentiment later in the essay, Evans sums up Quinn's own rebellious sensibilities when he observes, "The spirit of independence is notably strong in areas where the enjoyment of common pastoral rights is combined with the freedom of the sea: life on many smaller Atlantic islands offers a degree of freedom amounting to lawlessness" (70). Evans is also, like all of the cultural activists I am discussing here, keenly aware of the degree to which Atlantic culture is marked by an exceptional amount of dialogue between those watchwords of *globalization*, *margin*, and *centre*, or, to put it in terms more immediately connected to the concerns of this book, *high/islands* and *lowlands*. He states in that same Frazer Lecture that "the British Isles are distinctive among the regions of western Europe not only in being insular, but in having a fair balance, as compared say with Norway, France, or Spain, between the Atlantic-highland and continental-lowland zones. The two zones have been in constant interplay, and the resurgence of nationalism in the Atlantic-highland areas has fortunately not lead to their isolation" (72). This is all quite typical of the regions discussed in this book. We see a great deal of interplay between highlands and lowlands (I will try to show that Île-aux-Coudres is in constant dialogue with Montreal, just as Fogo Island is with St. John's, Tórshavn is with Mykines, or Connemara is with Dublin); we also see a strong presence or resurgence of nationalism or localism of one variety or another in all of these regions. Yet, as I will try to show, none of this has led to their cultural isolation; each of these media projects has quite explicit links to projects in one of the other regions, links that are in no way atypical for these very internationally open societies.

The recent work in Atlantic Studies based in literary and cultural studies has, for the most part, been animated by the history of the slave trade and colonial diasporas. The signature text here is clearly Paul Gilroy's 1993 book *The Black Atlantic: Modernity and Double Consciousness*. There he writes that:

> A concern with the Atlantic as a cultural and political system has been forced on black historiography and intellectual history by the economic and historical matrix in which plantation slavery—"capitalism with its clothes off"—was one special moment. The fractal patterns of cultural and political exchange and transformation that we try and specify through manifestly inadequate theoretical terms like creolisation and syncretism indicate how both ethnicities and

> political cultures have been made anew in ways that are significant not simply for the peoples of the Caribbean but for Europe, for Africa, especially Liberia and Sierra Leone, and of course, for black America. (15)

This vision of a renewed Atlantic Studies does try to move away from the instrumentalist approach that defined the "NATO history" paradigm and towards a more critical and culturally engaged model. No doubt such a cultural turn was long overdue, especially given the formative nature of the slave trade on the Atlantic world. Indeed, O'Reilly also notes that for some this turn is too little or too late: "Africanists, for example, find this newly found interest in the 'Atlantic' comic and condescending" (77).

Nevertheless, despite much idealism about internationalism, the geopolitical-military and the literary-cultural schools of Atlantic Studies share a tendency to centralize the United States–United Kingdom axis. In the shift from NATO history to globalization-informed cultural studies, an all-consuming interest in the most powerful member of NATO seems at times to have given way to an all-consuming interest in the most powerful producer of global culture. I exaggerate, but only slightly. Gilroy's work, for example, is certainly informed by writing and cultural production from the Caribbean and Europe, but his chapters are all organized around the cultural history of the United States and the United Kingdom. His chapter on black music deals mostly with the United States and the United Kingdom; the other chapters are on slave narratives, W. E. B. Du Bois, and Richard Wright, and all have international components but are centrally based in the culture of the United States.

My relative lack of interest in the culture of the United States is the part of this work which students of Atlantic Studies might find most foreign in the context of this emerging field. For while colonial history is certainly at issue in the discussions that will follow, as is the globalizing culture that has its base in the United States, I am interested in a different part of the Atlantic world, and a different part of Atlantic history, than that which has typically defined the interests of the field. Rather than focus on the paths between Europe and the United States via the Caribbean Sea—a trajectory that has defined quite a bit of work in the field—I have chosen a "Quebec to Ireland via the Gulf of St. Lawrence" trajectory. Rather than the "Middle Passage," I am focusing here on what is often known informally as the Atlantic Rim.

One crucial aspect of the organization of this book is both its progression from one side of the Atlantic to the other (from Quebec across Newfoundland and the Faroes to Ireland) and its focus on societies which are culturally and governmentally complex. Quebec is ostensibly one Canadian province among ten, but it has long constituted a sort of "nation within a nation," a status that was only in 2006 formally recognized by the Canadian Parliament. Newfoundland ostensibly has that same status as one Canadian province among ten, but it only joined Confederation in 1949, after a long history as a British dominion (sometimes self-governing, sometimes directly ruled); memories of this independent existence continue to strongly influence Newfoundland culture. The Faroe Islands are officially constituted as "a self-governing community within the Kingdom of Denmark" and in 1946 signed a home-rule agreement that granted their parliament control over almost everything except foreign policy and military matters; the fact that the Faroes are not part of the European Union while Denmark is gives a sense of how fluid even this first restriction is in practice. Ireland's Gaeltacht regions are small parts of the Republic of Ireland, parts that are not governed in any different way than the rest of the country (there is no home-rule agreement for the Gaeltacht)[11] but which have an enormous symbolic value because they are the location of the last vestiges of the language that was nearly wiped out in no small part because of nineteenth-century attempts to build a monolingually English-speaking United Kingdom. Thus all of these regions strongly resist easy equations between nation, state, and language.

To a certain extent these societies illustrate what, in his 1996 book *Modernity at Large*, Arjun Appadurai calls "culturalism," although that's not quite what we see here. Appadurai sees the rise of "culturalism" as a key part of globalization and, specifically, a key part of the recession of the nation-state that is part of that cultural condition. "Culturalism," he writes, "is the conscious mobilization of cultural differences in the service of a larger national or transnational politics. It is frequently associated with extraterritorial histories and memories, sometimes with refugee status and exile, and almost always with struggles for stronger recognition from existing nation-states or various transnational bodies" (15). Jürgen Habermas (a philosopher central to the conclusion of this book) writes of nationalism in similar terms: "the idea of the nation in its populist version has led to devastating acts of exclusion, to the expulsion of enemies of the state—and to the annihilation of the Jews. But in its culturalistic version, the idea of the nation also contributed to the creation of a mode of solidarity between persons who had until then remained strangers to one another" (*Postnational Constellation* 18).[12] Quebec, Newfoundland, the Faroes, and the Gaeltacht have all seen versions of populist, exclusionary nationalism (and this is particularly true of Quebec and Ireland), but these places are also the location of this Habermasian sense of nationalism as a creation of connections between strangers, connections that have very clearly been facilitated by the media projects this book discusses. Furthermore, we also find in each place "struggles for stronger recognition from existing nation-states or various transnational bodies," although extraterritorial histories and memories, like refugee status and exile, are present in this media history only occasionally.

Much the same is true of the other key part of Appadurai's argument, the connection between media and migration; that is actually what makes it most clear that this North Atlantic work is a preview of the present discourse surrounding globalization. He writes, "Implicit in this book is a theory of rupture that takes media and migration as its two major, and interconnected, diacritics and explores their joint effect on the *work of the imagination* as a constitutive feature of modern subjectivity" (3; emphasis in the original). This equation between media and migration as characteristic of a globalizing world figures quite explicitly in the work of Teilifís na Gaeltachta, which I discuss in chapter 6; it also strongly defines Bob Quinn's *Atlantean* project.

Indeed, Quinn has also embarked upon a very different sort of work than that discussed in chapter 5, making two films and writing two books that argue that Irish history should be understood in terms of its connection to the Atlantic; he also argues very forcefully against the very existence of a "Celtic" set of peoples or cultures. Quinn's *Atlantean* films, one three-part TV film from 1984 called *Atlantean* and a sequel from 1999 called *Atlantean 2: Navigato*, are essayistic works that focus on the areas around North Africa and eastern Russia, respectively, and try to argue that this is where the true roots of Irish culture are to be found. The tentative, deeply skeptical, and playful qualities of *Atlantean* have led Harvey O'Brien to claim that it is "the first truly postmodern Irish documentary" (201). The book that Quinn published in 1986 to accompany the film *Atlantean* is a fairly straightforward examination of the relevant arguments in archaeology and historical writing by way of advocating a rewritten Irish history that has the experience of the Atlantic world at its centre.

In 1999, Quinn published an updated edition of the book, called *The Atlantean Irish: Ireland's Oriental and Maritime Heritage*; its argument is more or less the same as the 1986 book, although the 1999 book is richly illustrated and more detailed. Furthermore, it is an ambitiously internationalist work, framing the Atlantic world as a site of intense circulation of and contact between cultures and languages. However, he sees this internationalism as being centred in marginal cultures, not the cultures of metropolitan centres. He sketches this out using Connemara, the Irish-speaking area where he has lived since the 1970s, as a sort of metaphor for the Atlantic experience that he wishes to recover:

> If the people of Conamara[13] could develop an unparalleled tradition of seamanship to overcome the apparent social disadvantage of their physical environment, could the same principle not apply on a larger scale to the entire Atlantic coast of Europe? If Conamara regarded intervening stretches of water not as insurmountable barriers to social intercourse but the very means of achieving this intercourse, could not the same principle apply on a larger scale? Just as the Irish-speaking minorities in Ireland constitute a cultural archipelago in a sea of English speakers (and are now united through the airwaves of Raidió na Gaeltachta), could not the "isolated" regions of Atlantic Europe constitute a similar archipelago, writ large? This would then include the Welsh, Bretons, Cornish, even the Galicians, in a unity that is much more solid than that that is normally suggested for them. I hope it is not too soon in my argument to point out that Morocco is also one such part of the Atlantic areas. (44–45)

Thus for Quinn, as for Appadurai, the crucial issue is the way in which small groups—Irish speakers listening to the Irish-language radio station for Quinn, "Muslim families ... listening to speeches by Islamic leaders on cassette tapes" for Appaduri (7)—use media in order to both sustain a cultural identity and participate in larger, often nomadic communities. Indeed, in a passage subsequent to the one quoted above, Quinn invokes "sociologist Michael D. Higgins," who wrote, "The migrant is the norm in coast parishes. The deviant is the person who does not move" (*The Atlantean Irish* 45).[14]

Back to the Sea

Overall, these film and broadcast projects are all defined by a kind of seafaring sensibility. I know how sentimental or romantic that sounds, and so I rush to point out that this seafaring metaphor has been centrally important—and wonderfully so—for many key texts in Atlantic Studies. Gilroy, for example, writes that:

> I have settled on the image of ships in motion across the spaces between Europe, America, Africa and the Caribbean as a central organising symbol for this enterprise and as my starting point. The image of the ship—a living, micro-cultural, micro-political system in motion—is especially important for historical and theoretical reasons that I hope will become clearer below. (4)

William Boelhower thinks along lines clearly influenced by this formulation of Gilroy's, writing of the image of the ship that "as the ship circulates, it creates an axis of linearization that allows us to follow the ways in which events and their frequency in space and time lead to the shoring up of a new world-system" (34). Ships are a crucial part of everyday life in the places I am discussing here. Pierre Perrault's most successful work arose from meditations on the poetic meanings of his beloved *goelettes* (small watercraft, very common to the Charlevoix area, that are a recurring motif of Perrault's work), boats are as important as automobiles for basic transportation on Fogo Island and in most of the Faroe Islands, and the architecture of boats and the history of sea navigation is a central part of the cultural-activist discourse of the Connemara Gaeltacht (a coastal area that includes many small islands). As in Gilroy's schema, these ships serve, and are organic parts of, living, micro-cultural, micro-political systems in motion.

The role of maps is equally important for Boelhower, and certainly a map-like consciousness is frequently present in these North Atlantic cinematic projects. At one point Boelhower writes that "we might say, ship is to map what discourse is to code" (35). In a very similar vein, the Connemara-based cartographer and artist Tim Robinson writes, in his 1992 essay "On the Cultivation of the Compass Rose," that "the 'topographical sensations' arising, for instance, from crossing a pass, completing the circuit of an island, or walking out to low water, are privileged moments of spatial awareness, able to bear the heavy vestments of symbolism" (*Setting Foot* 105). The discourse of the map emerges, in short, from the code of the journey (by foot for Robinson, by sea for Boelhower). This sort of approach to the philosophical or theoretical significance of maps is far more useful than previous work on mapping and cinema, and it will come up in particular in my discussion of the work of Pierre Perrault and his Irish comrade-in-ideas Desmond Fennell. Clearly, the key texts dealing with cinema and mapping are Sam Rhodie's *Promised Lands: Cinema, Geography, Modernism* and Tom Conley's *Cartographic Cinema*. Conley's book would seem to be the most relevant for my project here, and I do very much agree with his statement in that book's introduction that "a film, like a topographic projection, can be understood as an image that locates and patterns the imagination of its spectators. When it takes hold, a film encourages its public to think of the world in concert with its own articulation of space" (1). But relatively little of his book deals with theoretical concerns like this. Overall, I agree with José Teodoro's assessment that by spending most of the book talking about the presence of literal maps in films "Conley winds up obsessing over minutiae that, while undoubtedly contributing to the texture of the film in question, are minutiae nonetheless and not always representative of the cartographic significance the film may possess as a whole" (79). I feel similarly about Franco Moretti's work on maps and literature. He writes in his *Atlas of the European Novel* that "literary maps.... highlight the *ortgebunden*, place-bound nature of literary forms: each of them with its particular geography, its boundaries, its spatial taboos and favorite routes. And then, maps bring to light the *internal* logic of narrative: the semiotic domain around which a plot coalesces and self-organizes" (5). Like Conley, so far so good. But also like Conley, Moretti spends most of the book charting and graphing the geographical elements of various classic novels. Thus, like Conley, Morretti's approach strikes me as both too literal-minded in its tendency to look for examples of textual geography and too focused on already well-ploughed texts (works by Dickens, Austen, et al., which are about as canonical as Conley's primary examples of *Roma, città aperta* and *Boudu sauvé des eaux*). More theoretical writers such as Boelhower and Robinson, on the other hand, see mapping as more of an approach to meaning-making, a way by which certain kinds of linear activities (sailing, walking) reconcile themselves with a static, non-narrative image (a map), and through that process of reconciliation produce meaning that exists in neither a narrative travelogue nor a conventional map. This sort of dialectic approach—one that Vertov would recognize—is present throughout this North Atlantic cinematic work.

Other Routes Not Taken

I have structured this book in a very deliberate way. Each of the first three chapters of the "Islands" section—Pierre Perrault, the Newfoundland Project, Sjónvarpsfelagið í Havn—is directly linked to a chapter in the "Gaeltacht" section: Perrault connects to Desmond Fennell, the Newfoundland Project to the Cinegael project, and Sjónvarpsfelagið í Havn to Teilifís na Gaeltachta. I have done this to demonstrate a very real continuity in this part of the region's media history, and I believe that this structure is effective in binding the book's argument together and in preventing it from becoming a series of isolated case studies. But of course this kind of harmony almost always hides complexity. One roughly contemporary piece of North Atlantic culture is worth at least mentioning in some way: Icelandic cinema since the 1970s.

While there has been sporadic film production in Iceland since the silent period, until the 1980s most of it had been either amateur production or commercial ventures on the part of foreign companies. Erlendur Sveinsson's 1981 booklet *Kvikmyndir á Íslandi: 75 ára* identifies seven silent films made between

1918 and 1926, only one of which was made by an Icelander. It catalogues twenty-one more films made before 1980, fifteen of which were made by Icelanders; 1980 serves as an end date because that is the year the first film supported by the Icelandic Film Fund was released. That fund was created in 1978, as a result of what was officially known as the Lög um kvikmyndamál [the law on cinema]. This law, passed on 26 April 1978, was first announced by Vilhjálmur Hjálmarsson, who was then minister of culture, at a Reykjavík film festival (his remarks were published under his byline in the newspaper *Tíminn* on 5 February 1978). Section I of this law established the Icelandic Film Archive [Kvikmyndasafn Íslands]; Section II established the Film Fund [Kvikmyndasjóður] and specified an initial budget of ISK 30 million (currently about CDN$450,000).

That film fund was meant to support local filmmaking. Article 2.8 reads, "The intention of the Film Fund is to support Icelandic cinema as well as directing support or credit to film crews."[15] Thus the law is ambiguous about whether foreign film shoots that included Icelandic crews would be eligible for support. But Peter Cowie, even though he grumbles a bit that the initial budget for the fund was "less than half the cost of a single feature," writes that "this sum did however act as a trigger for a release of cinematic energy unequalled in the Nordic region since the establishment of the Swedish Film Institute in 1963" (80). Cowie notes that some of this is due to the fact that independent production companies "came forward," and their ability to come forward had to do with the presence of a television broadcaster in Iceland. Founded in 1966, RÚV had, in typical small cinema fashion, created the opportunity for a small pool of local technicians to emerge. Indeed, Chris Brögger, aware of the international enthusiasm for emerging cinemas that marked the 1970s, also sees this mostly as a matter of television producers wanting to move forward: "in the history of film there are many examples of domestic cinemas having risen from the ashes by creation of a law, but legislation on cinema grew stronger after the advent of television."[16] This situation is actually the exact reverse of what Pierre Véronneau describes in his history of early Quebec cinema: "It must be emphasized that most of these artisans moved to work for TV stations, or private companies that made series for them."[17] In Iceland, the traffic between television and private companies moved in precisely the opposite direction.

The law of 1999 established tax rebates for film production, a policy strategy that, in countries such as Ireland and Canada, has led not to the emergence of a local cinema but to the exploitation of local cinematic resources by Hollywood productions. However, the Icelandic experience has been quite different. The law creating the exemption does not differentiate between foreign or Icelandic productions, although it does mandate the creation of an Icelandic company or branch office for the purposes of the production (Article II.4.1).[18] It simply mandates, in Article 2, a 12 percent refund of any production costs for a production that spends at least 80 percent of its budget in Iceland, with allowances made if part of the budget is spent in the European Economic Area.[19] This has certainly led to the use of Iceland as a location for foreign film crews, but it has also led to the slow emergence of an Icelandic film community. Indeed, the law has an explicitly cultural mandate:

> In assessing whether a proportion of the production costs of a motion picture or television programme shall be reimbursed, the following conditions shall be fulfilled: (a) the production shall be suited for promoting Icelandic culture and the history and nature of Iceland (b) the production shall be suited for enhancing the experience, knowledge and artistic ambition of those involved.[20]

It is this second clause of the regulation that has led to some very interesting variations on the branch-plant experience so familiar to historians of Canadian cinema's tax-shelter years.[21] The law of 2003 updated this definition of the sort of films deserving support to the effect that "an Icelandic film is a film which is produced and sponsored by Icelandic parties or is a co-production of Icelandic and foreign parties. A project supported by the Icelandic Film Fund must have connections with Icelandic culture unless special cultural grounds exist for deciding otherwise."[22] This kind of explicitly cultural language seems to me unusual in a tax policy; more unusual still, though, is this sense that the definition of an Icelandic film, or a contribution to Icelandic culture, is negotiable. This is, of course, a clear echo of section 4(b) of the 1999 law, which allowed for enhancing the ambitions or knowledge of Icelanders.

Furthermore, local films' access to local screens, so long a key difficulty, if not *the* key difficulty in many debates around the policies of small countries (this is especially important in Canada), is practically a non-issue in Iceland. Part of this is the result of a small economy. One quirk of film exhibition in Iceland is that most theatres are owned by individuals or companies that also engage in distribution; there are no words in Icelandic for "Paramount decrees." Thus, there tends to be considerable incentive for any film with some distribution agreement to receive actual screen time. The Icelandic Film Fund has generally inserted within its production contracts a clause that requires companies to secure some Icelandic exhibition for any completed films. This clause is above and beyond the requirement that films be broadcast on television. Since there are fewer and fewer movie theatres of any description outside of, or indeed within, the capital city of Reykjavík, the access of the entire population of Iceland to Icelandic films is, in some ways, comparable to Canadians' access to Canadian films. Generally, you can't see Icelandic films in Grindavík, just as generally you can't see Canadian films in Peace River, Alberta. The crucial difference is that you can't see *any* films in Grindavík; at least in Peace River, you can, at the moment I am writing this, catch *The Da Vinci Code* and *X-Men 3: The Last Stand* at Cinema 72. In Iceland, so long as cinema is available, Icelandic cinema is available.

Thus the experience of Icelandic cinema has strong connections to the themes that I am tracing through this period of the media history of the North Atlantic. It is an example of the use of mass media in a "small language" in a country that only recently separated from a larger kingdom (it became independent of Denmark in 1944). The crucial difference is that it marks the establishment of a semi-commercial—if very small-scale—narrative film industry, and thus stands in vivid contrast to the work produced by Pierre Perrault, the Newfoundland Project, Sjónvarpsfelagið í Havn, Cinegael, or Teilifís na Gaeltachta. While the media projects that I deal with in this book are not fully exempt from commercial considerations, they all stand quite clearly outside of the systems of production and consumption of narrative that has defined conventional television and film. Bob Quinn, as part of his Cinegael group, produced independent narrative films such as *Poitín* (1977, which portrayed the deprivations of rural existence; poitín is an illegal, home-brewed liquor, the cultural equivalent of moonshine) or *The Bishop's Story* (1993, which dealt with an island priest having an affair with his housekeeper), which could sit comfortably alongside Icelandic films of the 1980s such as *Óðal ferðranna* (1980, which depicted the struggles of rural life in the wake of the failure of the co-operative movement). But those fiction films, despite the amount of attention they have received from historians of Irish film, are really the exception rather than the rule in Quinn's career, which has been largely devoted to documentary and community-based film, video, and television projects (although he has also worked in radio and theatre). Despite the way he has been represented by scholarly and more popular work about Irish cinema, he has more in common with the Newfoundland Project or Sjónvarpsfelagið í Havn than he does with Icelandic cinema.

I could have written a very different book about the cinema of this region, one that would have emphasized that narrative element of Quinn's work and the comparable narrative elements of the works emerging from each of these North Atlantic countries. Such a book would have likely replaced the Faroe Islands chapter with a chapter on Icelandic cinema, one that emphasized the work of Friðrik Þór Friðriksson (whose films, such as 1991's Oscar-nominated *Börn náttúrunnar / Children of Nature*, are well known on the festival circuit). It would have discussed not Pierre Perrault but the rise of Quebec's semi-independent narrative filmmakers such as Denys Arcand (whose 2003 film *Les Invasions Barbares* won the Oscar for Best Foreign Language Film). It would have discussed not the Newfoundland Project of Fogo Island but Newfoundland's CodCo group and the film and television projects they participated in (including Michael Jones and Andy Jones's 1986 hallucinatory "secession comedy" *The Adventure of Faustus Bidgood*). It would have discussed the rise of Irish cinema in terms of its feature-narrative filmmaking, with figures like Neil Jordan (1992's *The Crying Game*) or Jim Sheridan (1993's *In the Name of the Father*) at the centre and more independent voices like Bob Quinn (in his incarnation as a feature filmmaker), Pat Murphy (1982's *Maeve*, 1984's *Anne Devlin*, or 2000's *Nora*) or Margo Harkin (1990's *Hush-a-Bye-Baby*) at the margins. In seeking to discuss the "Vertov wing" of North Atlantic cinema deploying the metaphor of the Radio-Eye, this other part of the North Atlantic could be seen as the "Eisenstein and Pudovkin wing," inasmuch as it represents a group of films that are innovative in important ways but still, more or less, narrative-feature films. That could have been a very interesting book in its own right. I have not chosen the "Vertov wing" because the "Eistenstein and Pudovkin wing" is somehow compromised or less politically righteous or something like that; these are interesting films and filmmakers in their own right and are well worth further discussion.

But I have chosen the "Vertov wing" and the Radio-Eye of the North Atlantic for good reasons. Overall this part of the history of North Atlantic cinema is important in part because it provides an example of a group of media-makers, working independently of each other, who shared an interest in some of the issues that have become crucial to debates around globalization and culture. This period of the region's media history is like a dress rehearsal for the themes of globalization, as well as being an excellent example of Gilles Deleuze's hopes for a cinema of the "time-image," a cinematic practice where "the same transformation involves the cinema of fiction and the cinema of reality and blurs their differences: in the same movement, descriptions become pure, purely optical and sound, narrations falsifying and stories, simulations. The whole cinema becomes a free, indirect discourse, operating in reality" (*The Time-Image* 155).[23] This sort of cinematic utopia strongly recalls the sense of possibility that Lev Manovich located in Dziga Vertov's free movement between fiction and documentary, his creation of a cinema that moves through the world, making expression from whatever is in its path. And this North

Atlantic Radio-Eye is also internationalist in a strongly "culturalist" and equally strongly "creolized" way, a *creolité* that is partially expressed by this very oscillation between fiction and documentary. These seminally modern ideals are what define this period of the North Atlantic's media history, at its best moments. It is a part of international media history that is well worth a closer look.

Notes

1 "Не 'съемка врасплох' ради 'съемка врасплох', а ради того, чтобы показать людей без маски, без грима, схватить их глазом аппарата в момент неигры, прочесть их обнаженные киноаппаратом мысли ... 'Киноглаз' как смычка науки с кинохроникой в целях борьбы за коммунистическую расшифровку мира, как попытка показать правду на экране—киноправду" (*Stat'i, dnevniki, zamysly* 75).

2 *Cinéma vérité* generally refers to a style of documentary filmmaking where the filmmaker seems to be absent, there is no voice-over, and there is an emphasis on spontaneity and "life caught unawares." Jean Rouch is generally credited with coining the term, which was used to describe his film *Chronique d'un été* (1961) (it was used in the film's own voice-over and in its promotion). The French film historian Georges Sadoul also used the term in his discussion of the film, writing in his *Histoire du cinéma* that Rouch's "feature film was a passionate experience of "cinéma vérité," drawing on Vertov, whose camera-eye (and ear), interrogated a few men and women about their personal life and their worries" [long métrage fut un passionnante expérience de 'Cinéma vérité' se réclamant de Vertov où le caméra-œil (et oreille) interrogea quelques hommes et femmes sur leur vie personnelle et leur soucis] (515); see Sadoul, *Histore du cinéma* (Paris: Flammarion, 1962). Most scholars think of vérité as being less manipulated, more "candid" than *cinéma direct* or direct cinema, which is based on a similar aesthetic of spontaneity. However, historians of documentary have widely varying definitions of verité and direct, and I agree with William Rothman's position, who writes that "I find the distinction between 'cinema vérité' and 'direct cinema' prejudicial and unhelpful" (x). In clarifying these terms in the context of Jean Rouch's films, he could easily be writing about Pierre Perrault, Colin Low, or the media-makers of the Faroes and the Gaeltacht: "The distinction between 'cinéma vérité'—a cinematic practice in which the camera engages in provocation—and 'direct cinema'—a cinematic practice in which the camera refrains from being provocative—is rendered moot by the fact that it is the very presence of the camera, when it is doing its mysterious work, that constitutes the kind of 'provocation' that most interests Rouch.... observation is the camera's way of provoking its subject to manifest profound sides of themselves, the camera's way of participating" (87–88); see Rothman's *Documentary Film Classics* (Cambridge: Cambridge University Press, 1997).

3 "Если по отношению к зрению у нас кинонаблюдатели фиксировали киноаппаратами видимые жизненные явления, то здесь придется уже говорить о записи слышимых фактов ... 'Киноправду' и 'киноглаз' противопоставляем мы 'художественной кинематографии'; 'Радиоправду' и 'радиоухо' противопоставляем мы 'художественной радиопередаче'" (*Stat'i, dnevniki, zamysly* 86).

4 Irish Gaelic (Gaeilge) is usually just called "Irish"; the word "Gaelic" is generally understood to refer to Scottish Gaelic (Gàidhlig). The two languages are close to one another and are more or less mutually intelligible to native speakers (especially for native speakers of the Ulster dialect of Irish), but they are by no means the same. The relationship between the two is very much like that between Icelandic and Faroese.

5 "Tað eru í løtuni tvey sjónvarpstól í Mykinesi" ("Verðurfastir í Mykinesi" 1).

6 Zakaris Hammar worked for many years as a staff member of the Faroese television service Sjónvarp Føroya (SvF); he is based in Klaksvík, the second-largest city in the Faroes (population approximately 6,000). His work is quite poetic and lyrical, and it relies heavily on the rhythms of spoken language. This is most evident in a film he made about an old fisherman for the SvF show *Manna Millum*; it was first broadcast on 1 November 1992. Much the same is also true of Teitur Árnason's two documentaries *Burturhugur: Faroese Observations* and *Burturhugur: Observaciones de Cuba*. The former is shot on the very small and *very* hard-to-access island of Fugloy; the second, of course, is shot on Cuba. Both deal with the isolation of island culture in a gently patient and visually sophisticated way.

7 I have argued for the continued usefulness of the concept of the national cinema in the article "National Belonging: Renewing the Concept of National Cinema for a Global Culture," *The New Review of Film and Television Studies* 2:2 (Fall 2004), 211–32. I discuss there how filmmakers like Edgardo Cozarinsky or Raul Ruiz are genuinely transnational figures, but that even in these cases it is useful to know something about South American cinema (Cozarinsky started working in Argentina, Ruiz in Chile). Much the same applies to a filmmaker like Perrault in the context of Quebec cinema, or Quinn in the context of Irish cinema.

8 "Le Divers a besoin de la présence des peuples, non plus comme objet à sublimer, mais comme projet à mettre en relation.... On ne peut pas se faire trinidadien ni québécois, si on ne l'est pas; mais il est désormais vrai que si la Trinidad ou le Québec n'existaient pas comme composantes acceptées du Divers, il manquerait quelque chose à la chair du monde—et aujourd'hui nous connaîtrions ce manque" (*Le discours antillais* 327).

9 "le métissage ce serait le déterminisme, et la créolisation c'est, par rapport au métissage, le producteur d'imprévisible" (89).

10 "Alors que l'Atlantique Nord voyait pratiquement ruiner son trafic passagers avec l'expansion foudroyante du transport aérien, son trafic marchand répondit à l'essor mondial du grand commerce maritime dans les années 1960 avant la crise pétrolière de 1973, et, celle-ci passée, continuait à se développer pour atteindre un sommet dès la fin de la décennie 1970" (*Histoire de l'Atlantique* 300).

11 What the Gaeltacht does have, though, is Údarás na Gaeltachta, or the Gaeltacht Authority. This was a successor to the development agency known as Gaeltarra Éireann. Údarás na Gaeltachta has a twenty-member board, of which seventeen members are elected and three appointed by the minister responsible for the Gaeltacht. I am grateful to Mary Haslam for drawing my attention to the elected nature of Údarás.

12 "die Idee der Nation hat in ihrer völkischen Lesart zu verheerenden Exklusionen geführt, zum Ausschluß von Reichsfeinden—und zur Vernichtung der Juden. Aber in iher kulturalistischen Lesart hat sie auch dazu beigetragen, einen solidarischen Zusammenhang zwischen Personen zu stiften, die bis dahin Fremde füreinander gewesen sind" (*Postnationale Konstellation* 36).

13 Connemara is the widely used anglicization for the Irish word Conamara. Both Bob Quinn and Desmond Fennell use the word Conamara in their English- and Irish-language writing alike. Both words refer to an area of Galway which is, by and large, Irish-speaking and rural. Tim Robinson's works *Connemara: Part 1, Introduction and Gazetteer* and *Part 2, A One-Inch Map* (both Roundstone: Folding Landscapes, 1990) are an indispensible attempt to define and document the region. Despite the breathtaking detail of Robinson's map, the region's exact borders are not at all clear. Robinson writes in his essay "Space, Time and Connemara"(included in both the *Introduction and Gazetteer* and his anthology *Setting Foot on the Shores of Connemara*) that "*Ó Bhearna go Carna*, from Bearna to Carna, is the phrase favoured by Gaeilgeoirí [Irish-language learners] to delimit this linguistic homeland—but most Bearna people would direct you back westwards if you enquired for Connemara there, being close enough to Galway city to share its sense of Connemara as wilderness and westernness itself" (*Introduction* 5; *Setting Foot* 53–54).

14 Higgins was once a lecturer in politics and sociology at University College Galway (now National University of Ireland, Galway), but he is much better known as a politician for the Irish Labour Party. He was first appointed to the Irish Senate in 1973 and was elected to the Irish Dáil in 1981. As I discuss in the conclusion to this book, he became Minister for Arts, Culture and the Gaeltacht in 1993 as part of the "Rainbow Coalition" government, and his initiatives included the restoration of the Irish Film Board [Bord Scannán na hÉireann], the 1995 Green Paper on Broadcasting, and the creation of the Irish-language television station Teilifís na Gaeilge. He also appointed Bob Quinn to the Authority of Ireland's state-owned broadcaster RTÉ (Raidio Teilfís Éireann) in 1995. RTÉ's Authority acts as the broadcaster's board of directors and is appointed entirely by the minister responsible for the broadcaster.

15 "Tilgangur Kvikmyndasjóðs er að styrkja íslenska kvikmyndagerð með beinum fjárframlögum eða lánum til kvikmyndagerðarmanna" (reprinted in Brögger 90).

16 "Í sögu kvikmyndanna eru mörg dæmi um að innlend kvikmyndagerð hafi risið úr öskustó með setningu laga, en löggjöff um kvikmyndagerð hefur mjög vaxið fiskur um hrygg eftir tilkomu sjónvarps" (90).

17 "Il faut souligner que plusieurs de ces artisans passent au service de la télévision ou de ces compagnies privées qui réalisent des séries pour celle-ci" (45).

18 "A specific company shall be established in Iceland for the production; an Icelandic branch or agency of a company registered in another Member State of the European Economic Area shall be considered a specific company" [að stofnað sé sérstakt félag um framleiðsluna á Íslandi; íslenskt útibú eða umboðsskrifstofa félags sem skráð er í aðildarríki samningsins um Evrópska efnahagssvæðið telst sérstakt félag]. Note the distinction between the EU and the European Economic Area; the distinction is important, as Iceland, like Norway and Lichtenstein, is a member of the latter but not the former. The full text of this law is available at http://www.althingi.is/lagas/nuna/1999043.html; the official English translation can be found at http://eng.idnadarraduneyti.is/laws-and-regulations/nr/1162.

19 "When more than 80% of the total production cost of a motion picture or television programme incurs in Iceland, the reimbursement shall be calculated from the total production cost incurring within the European Economic Area" ["Nú fellur meira en 80% af heildarframleiðslukostnaði kvikmyndar eða sjónvarpsefnis til á Íslandi og skal þá endurgreiðsla reiknast af þeim heildarframleiðslukostnaði sem til fellur á Evrópska efnahagssvæðinu"]. Again, this is the official English translation, available at http://eng.idnadarraduneyti.is/laws-and-regulations/nr/1162; the Icelandic text can be found at http://www.althingi.is/lagas/nuna/1999043.html.

20 "Við mat á því hvort endurgreiða skuli hlutfall af framleiðslukostnaði kvikmyndar eða sjónvarpsefnis skal eftirfarandi skilyrðum vera fullnægt: (a) að viðkomandi framleiðsla sé til þess fallin að koma íslenskri menningu á framfæri og kynna sögu lands og náttúru, (b) að viðkomandi framleiðsla sé til þess fallin að stuðla að aukinni reynslu, þekkingu og listrænum metnaði þeirra sem að framleiðslunni standa." This is the official English translation of the law, and can be found at http://eng.idnadarraduneyti.is/laws-and-regulations/nr/1162; the Icelandic text can be found at http://www.althingi.is/altext/133/s/pdf/0095.pdf.

21 The 1970s and 1980s in Canada, and to a certain extent in Quebec, was the era of the Capital Cost Allowance program, a regime of tax shelters wherein the federal government gave producers highly lucrative tax breaks for filming in Canada and using a certain amount of Canadian personnel. What this often ended up meaning was that American producers came to Canada to make films set in the United States, starring and sometimes directed by Americans but with enough Canadians in bit parts and minor technical roles to qualify for the tax break. These were not, then, "Canadian" or "Québécois" films in any meaningful way; *Meatballs* (Ivan Reitman, 1979) and *Porky's* (Bob Clark, 1981) are seminal examples of the "tax shelter film," a *genre maudit* if ever there was one.

22 "Hlutverk Kvikmyndasjóðs er að efla íslenska kvikmyndagerð með fjárhagslegum stuðningi. Íslensk kvikmynd er kvikmynd sem unnin er og kostuð af íslenskum aðilum eða er samstarfsverkefni íslenskra og erlendra aðila. Verkefni sem styrkt eru af Kvikmyndasjóði skulu hafa íslenska menningarlega skírskotun nema sérstök menningarleg rök leiði til annars." This official English translation of the law is available at http://eng.menntamalaraduneyti.is/Acts/nr/2438; the Icelandic text can be found at http://brunnur.stjr.is/mrn/logogregl.nsf/nrar/reglugerdir2292003.

23 "C'est sous ces conditions de l'image-temps qu'une même transformation entraîne le cinéma de fiction et le cinéma de réalité, et brouille leur différances : dans le même mouvement, les descriptions deviennent pures, purement optiques et sonores, les narrations, falsifiantes [*sic*], les récits, des simulations. C'est tout le cinéma qui devient un discours indirect libre opérant dans la réalité" (*L'image-temps* 202).

PART 1

The Islands

mer à peine échappée à la terre où parfois îles, toutes îles, événements des archipels, cachent les villages d'hommes …

îles, toutes îles, que j'énumère, sonores!
île de La Demoiselle dans une baie des Belles-Amours!
île de Vieux Châteaux
île de la Tête à la Baleine
île du grand Mécatina
semis des îles Harrington
île aux Perroquets
îles Affligées
île du Défunt Français

îles, toute îles, sans nom que je décore
îles de la lune
île du soleil
île du dernier naufrage
île de la prochaine tempête
île des grandes échoueries

environment d'îles à reciter, à chanter, à parcourir, à légender, îles, toutes îles.

—Pierre Perrault, "mer de sable," in his collection *Toutes isles* (58–59)

1

Pierre Perrault

Perrault and [Jean-Pierre] Lefebvre: it's in Quebec that the most engaged forms of modern cinema today are born.
—Jean-Louis Comolli, "L'île, ou l'exemplarité d'un cinéma de combat"[1]

If René Allio feels more Marseillais on the French scene, I myself haven't really figured out how to be Québécois in a Canada where I'm not very comfortable, in a Canada where I feel excluded and even a foreigner. In a Canada that folklorizes me.
—Perrault, in interview with French filmmaker René Allio[2]

Of all the figures under discussion here, none are more closely tied to *both* cinema and radio than Pierre Perrault. Although he is best known for NFB-produced films such as *Pour la suite du monde* (1963) or *Un pays sans bon sens!* (1970), he actually got his start in media at Radio-Canada in the 1950s, writing text for the traditional music programs *Au bord de la rivière* and *Le chant des hommes*. "Not counting special shows, his radio credits list eleven series from 1955 to 1965,"[3] David Clandfield writes in his book *Pierre Perrault and the Poetic Documentary*, "among them *Poèmes et chansons* (1956) and *Ballades du temps précieux* (1961), which included material published in his first two collections of poetry" (4). The fact that this radio work intersects so closely with his work in *poetry* only brings him closer to Vertov, a filmmaker who, although certainly not without his propagandistic tendencies, made films with a sensibility closer to poetry than to prose.

Thus it is instructive to recover some of Perrault's identity as *cinéaste de la radio*. He was someone whose work was always informed not only by the rhythms and inflections of spoken language, but also by the play between spontaneity and a high level of construction that defines most radio practice. This is most clearly borne out, of course, by the relationship between his work that existed in both cinematic and radiophonic forms: *Au pays de Neufve-France* and *Pour la suite du monde*.[4] In both sets of work we see (and hear) an engagement with the emerging technologies of cinéma vérité as well as a desire to reconcile both the textual with the abstract and the representation of locality with a new form of Quebec nationalism. These are themes that recur throughout this period in the North Atlantic's media history: emerging technologies, their use in the representation of small or marginalized communities, and their frequent connection to the maintenance of small languages. Discussions of Perrault's work, which is is a well-known part of the history of Quebec cinema, very infrequently touch on his international importance. Focusing on his work in radio can help to make it clear why that broader context really is just as important as the Quebec one.

Monsieur Pierre Perrault, qui êtes-vous?[5]

Although he is not well known in the Anglophone world, Pierre Perrault is one of Quebec's real visionaries of the postwar period. His work in literature, radio, and film is quite well respected in Quebec, and he is also well known in France. As I indicated in the epigraph that opens this chapter, there was a time when his work was championed by the *Cahiers du cinéma* as being the leading edge of the cinéma engagé of the late 1960s (Comolli, a widely quoted figure in English-language film studies of the 1970s and 1980s, was writing in 1967). Furthermore, the French philosopher Gilles Deleuze talks quite a bit about Perrault in his work *Cinéma 2: L'image-temps*. Both the late-1960s *Cahiers* and Deleuze's books on cinema have been enormously influential on English-language film criticism, especially in North America; thus Perrault's status as an unknown in the Anglophone sphere of film criticism is somewhat puzzling (this has been ameliorated somewhat by David Clandfield's 2004 book *Pierre Perrault and the Poetic Documentary*, co-published by Indiana University Press and the Toronto International Film Festival). I will thus try to present some basics of his work before proceeding on to an analysis of its connection with radio, and, finally, to a discussion of its status (both geographically and ideologically) as a gateway to the cinema of the North Atlantic.

Perrault was originally from Montreal, where he had worked as a lawyer and developed a vocation as a poet; he was also married to Yolande Simard, a woman from the Charlevoix region of the north shore of the St. Lawrence River. She retained close family ties to the region, and Perrault credits her with introducing him to a landscape and a set of communities that would define his career as an artist. In a prose poem about Simard, contained in his book-length interview with Paul Warren (which David Clandfield calls "The Importance of Yolande" in the 2004 translation I quote here), Perrault writes:

> and it was my mother who taught me that I lived in a city ...
>
> but she was the one who taught me that I had a homeland! that my homeland had its language! that this language was poetry! and that this venturesome language had abounded in superlatives since the happy days of childhood as if it were only natural ...
>
> as if there were no other words too fine to tell of an unsung river ignored by literature ...[6] (Clandfield 167)

This is an interesting passage because it illustrates the degree to which, even though Perrault had a familial connection to the place, Charlevoix and the St. Lawrence were not simply about recovering a personal family history. Even when it is about Simard, the poem is drawn to the national ("j'avais un pays!"), the distinctive elements of that nation's culture ("mon pays avait un langage! que ce langage était poésie!") and that this culture has been marginalized by traditional notions of culture ("l'inédit d'un fleuve négligé des écritures"). Even when discussing his wife and her impact on him, the *territory*, ideas about "pays," and the way that the territory interacts with the language, are of equal significance. An interest in this interaction between territory and language lies at the core of his work.

This is most explicit in his most famous work, *Pour la suite du monde* (1963), which he co-directed with Michel Brault and Bernard Gosselin. This was Perrault's first major film, made after working in radio and writing the text for the radio and then television series *Au pays de Neufve-France* (1958–59). As I will discuss shortly, that series featured an episode on Charlevoix's Île-aux-Coudres, a small island in the St. Lawrence River where Perrault had spent time (he had made one episode of *Au pays de Neufve-France* there, entitled "La traverse d'hiver à l'Île-aux-Coudres"). He returned there in 1962 with a crew from the National Film Board of Canada that included the great cameraman Michel Brault. While there he convinced the islanders to revive a long-dormant whale hunt, one that used stakes jammed into the water as a sort of tidal whale trap. The resultant film, *Pour la suite du monde*, was widely acclaimed upon its release, showing in competition at the Cannes Film Festival (the first film from Canada to do so) and winning a special award at the 1964 Canadian Film

Awards. "This was the film that made Perrault's reputation," Clandfield writes. "It enabled Perrault to add filmmaking to his poetic career" (23). It became the first in a trilogy of films about the island (which also included 1967's *Le règne du jour* and 1968's *Les voitures d'eau*), and Perrault returned to the place again and again (especially in his 1970 film *Un pays sans bon sens!*, which I discuss in more detail in chapter 4).

As I will also discuss shortly, *Pour la suite du monde* is notable both for the degree to which Perrault was able to forge a new sort of relationship between subject and filmmaker, and for the degree to which it took advantage of then-emergent technologies of portable synch-sound gear; for both reasons, it is a crucial film in the emergence of cinéma vérité. Unsurprisingly, it figures centrally in French-language histories of the movement, both in France (such as Louis Marcorelles' 1970 *Élements pour un nouveau cinéma*, translated into English in 1973 as *Living Cinema*) and in Quebec (such as Gilles Marsolais' *L'aventure du cinéma direct*, first published in Paris in 1974 but reissued in Quebec several times thereafter; Guy Gauthier, Philippe Pilard, and Simone Suchet's 2003 book *Le documentaire passe au direct*, published by Montreal's VLB Éditeur, also puts the film in at the centre of its narrative of emergence). The film is, however, basically absent from the parallel English-language histories; Perrault's name does not appear at all in contemporary surveys such as Lewis Jacobs's 1971 *The Documentary Tradition* or Erik Barnouw's 1974 *Documentary*; the current situation is scarcely better, as his name is also absent from Brian Winston's otherwise invaluable 1995 book *Claiming the Real: The Documentary Film Revisited*, as well as being absent from Stella Bruzzi's 2000 *New Documentary: A Critical Introduction*, a book which devotes quite a bit of space to the Abraham Zapruder film of John F. Kennedy's assassination. I do think this constitutes a fairly serious hole in the English-language understanding of the transformation of documentary in the 1960s.

One element of this transformation that is lost as a result of Perrault's exclusion from these histories is quite important to the concerns of this book overall: the way in which cinema can be a force for the promotion of a spoken language and, specifically, the spoken languages of smaller national communities. In addition to framing him in the context of cinéma vérité or direct cinema, "cinéma de la parole" is a term that has been used to describe Perrault's unique style of documentary: a cinema of speech. "Of course you could say that I've made a cinema of speech" Perrault told Paul Warren in a book-length 1996 interview.[7] That cinéma de la parole was a result of Perrault's base in sound; it grew from work in radio, rather than photography or literature. "I can start by saying that I didn't come to the cinema via the cinema," Perrault told Peter Wintonick in the 1999 NFB documentary *Cinéma Vérité: Defining the Moment*. "I came to the cinema via the tape recorder."[8] Perrault was referring there to what he described to Paul Warren as "ma période magnétophone" (36), the period of the late 1950s when he was making radio series such as *Au pays de Neufve-France*. This is the period where his interest in speech took root, although it is not a period where "la parole" itself was as central as it would become in Perrault's later works.

Perrault himself has spoken at greater length of what he describes as *cinéma vécu*, "lived cinema." During a 1971 interview about his Île-aux-Coudres films he told Fr. Léo Bonneville, "I could have made a fiction-film and written a script. We opted for a document-film. I call that lived cinema. You can't write up in advance a year of living."[9] The "year of living" is an important part of the equation. Rather than parachuting into communities and taking some interesting footage, Perrault sought to live with the people he was making a film about, and thus to live the film that he was making.

Cinéma vécu and cinéma de la parole were, for Perrault, intimately connected. As he told Warren,

> I don't cite Eisenstein, Fellini, or Carné, but I do cite the island folk as an influence on my work. They taught me a language, a *chouenne*, a witty turn of phrase, navigation, a river of words and words for a river. And what they proposed to me was the great epic of the beluga. What a fantastic experience it was making a film with one's feet caught in the wrackweed of the mud flats when the tide is running in at terrifying speed!
>
> This way of using the tape recorder on the radio is not unusual. But I may have started a way of listening that gives as much importance to the story itself as to the language used to tell it. Because of Yolande in the first place, and then because of the people of the region, and finally because of the tape recorder, which allowed me to check things, experience them more deeply and appreciate the language, I came to realize that ... poetry was a way of taking possession of a country in the name of those who have been experiencing it in their lives. (Clandfield 171)[10]

Living the cinema, feeling the wrackweed and the mud during the shooting, is all made possible *because* Perrault is using the tape recorder in a way that is more typical of radio production. Thus, although Perrault eventually left radio more or less behind,[11] the lessons that he learned during his "période magnétophone" quite centrally define the philosophy of cinema that gives his entire body of work shape: the shape of a cinéma vécu.

This Perraultian combination of "la parole" and "le vécu" is important both for the history of documentary generally and for the sort of cinema that I am discussing in this book. Perrault's films offer a vision of cinéma vérité that both evokes and transcends the ethical issues that more famous films seemed unable to resolve, and does so in a way that eschews the more visceral and sometimes sensational aspects of those films. American works such as Frederick Wiseman's *Titicut Follies* (1967) or the Maysles brothers' *Gimme Shelter* (1970) endure as famous, illustrative examples of vérité partially because of the way that they emotionally batter the viewer with incredibly powerful images, such as the shot taken though the cell door of a naked man pacing and muttering in *Titicut Follies* or the images of a concertgoer being killed by a Hell's Angel (and of Mick Jagger watching and reacting to that footage) in *Gimme Shelter*. These sequences illustrate the raw power of the mobile, synchronized camera, and they also pose difficult ethical problems for filmmakers who were able to get closer to evolving, unpredictable situations as a result of that new mobility. In English Canada parallel examples are found in films such as Tanya Ballantine's *The Things I Cannot Change* (1966), where there is a sequence in which the man the film follows gets beaten up over an argument about a debt, or Allan King's *A Married Couple* (1969), where we witness (among many other instances of intense intimacy) an argument between the eponymous couple in their bed. Perrault's films, though, invoke this ethical quandary of how close a filmmaker can get to a subject by the way that he tries to fold himself fully into the life of whatever he is filming. His films use vérité's emphasis on spontaneity to centralize spoken language and its importance to the daily life of communities, rather than centralizing viscerally powerful images that often seem calculated to generate an emotional, even simplistic reaction. They are good examples of still-experimental cinematic technology being used to promote the survival of local cultural tradition in a way that emphasizes modernity though a self-aware cinematic practice that strips away all vestiges of the folkloric. The emergence of this sort of cinematic practice is the story of Pierre Perrault's career, and it is the story of this period of the North Atlantic's media history, too. Moreover, it is just as important as the mainstream English-language story about the emergence of cinéma vérité via a series of visceral, emotionally wrought, and sometimes just-shy-of-exploitative films.

Radio and Perrault, Radio and Quebec

It is in some ways natural that Perrault's filmmaking practice would emerge from radio. Part of this is a matter of his investment in the idea of a cinéma de la parole, since the degree to which a focus on speech is amenable to a formation in radio is not difficult to understand. But part of that is cultural, too; Perrault came from a culture, and especially a period, that was heavily invested in the social aspects of radio. His films have a sort of radiophonic ethic, and all of his films are quite centrally about that combination of the local and the national that Michelle Hilmes sees as central to radio.

Furthermore, radio has long played an important part in Quebec's culture. Greg Marc Nielsen argues throughout his book *Le Canada de Radio-Canada* (Société Radio-Canada is the name of the French-language service of the Canadian Broadcasting Corporation) that the place of radio is typical of the way in which although it "doesn't dominate the Québécois transindividual subject, we can nevertheless see a tendency towards the post-modern in the discourse of this period, a tendency that illustrates the doubled representation of 'staying traditional and progressive.'"[12] Mass media, and more specifically radio, is key to this tendency. One need not necessarily agree with Nielsen's assessment that this is all a nascent postmodernism to see that this duality of "restons traditionnels et progressifs" is crucial for understanding Quebec society of this period and Perrault's work generally. This paradox of a technologically advanced form being especially useful for the recuperation of tradition has also been evoked by Yves Lacroix, who writes specifically in the context of Perrault's work that "with the resurgence of oral text via the record, the radio and television ... we find ourselves somewhat in the situation—but reversed—of the medieval scribe."[13]

Thus, the crucial element of the cinema-radio interaction in 1950s and 1960s Quebec is a matter of language, not necessarily of technology. This rejection of technological determinism is a recurring theme of this book. It was especially important to the media activists of the Irish Gaeltacht whom I deal with in part 2, activists who were highly influenced by Raymond Williams's books *Communications* and *Television*, the latter of which was especially critical of the notion of technological determinism. Nielsen goes on to distinguish between Radio-Canada and private radio, writing that "the former produced works that were light (radio serials) and serious (radio plays), but not 'popular' works that reproduced daily language, despite being addressed to a 'popular' audience. Even though private radio brought to life certain 'popular' voices ... Radio-Canada tended to treat this voice, *joual*, as a negative object that needed correcting."[14] *Joual*, the highly inflected speech of working-class Montreal and Quebec City, is not the language of Perrault's work. But the point about Radio-Canada's disinterest in daily speech was a crucial part of what Pierre Perrault was seeking to correct. He was certainly trying to reproduce *la langue quotidienne*, although he was doing so for a language that was not part of his everyday life, or the everyday lives of most Québécois.

So while it may seem unusual for a film—especially works as visually distinctive *Au Pays de Neufve-France* and *Pour la suite du monde*—to exist in a "radio version," it is really no surprise in the context of a filmmaker like Perrualt, or for a society like Quebec. "The fictional cinema of this period is also marked by orality," Germain Lacasse writes of the 1940s and 1950s, "many films being adaptations of radio-serials."[15] By way of example of "radio films" Lacasse invokes narrative works like *Un homme et son péché* (1949), *Le curé du village* (1949), and *Séraphin* (1950), all of which, as explicitly commercial, formally conventional narrative films, are very different from Perrault's work.[16] But this does give a sense of the degree to which radio and cinema are, as with Perrault's oeuvre, quite intertwined in many aspects of Quebec cultural production. Perrault was beginning his work just at the end of the period when it was difficult to say anything about cinema or television without also discussing radio.

Au Pays de Neufve-France

Perrault's work in the early 1950s as a scriptwriter and host on folk-music radio programs was both abundant, and, judging from the holdings of the Fonds Pierre Perrault (held at Université Laval in Quebec City), fairly ephemeral. Some of these were ongoing series, some of them were specials. Unlike these programs, though, the radio version of his 1956 work *Au pays de Neufve-France* has been preserved in its entirety, and the 1958–59 television version is easily available on home video from the National Film Board of Canada. According to Céline Savard and James Lambert's register of the Fonds Pierre Perrault (specifically the note for P319/C6), it was broadcast on Radio-Canada in twenty-two episodes, from November 1956 to October 1957. It became a television series, directed by René Bonnière but with text by Perrault, in 1958, when it was produced by Crawley Films for Radio-Canada. The Île-aux-Coudres episode of the series became a direct source for *Pour la suite du monde*, by far Perrault's best-known film. It is the key work that lies between Perrault's "période magnétophone" and his emergence as a cinéaste.

"La traverse d'hiver à l'Île-aux-Coudres," which is the first episode of the television version of the series, most clearly signals this transition; there are, however, considerable differences between the episodes of the audio and television series that bear this title. The radio version (the episode of *Aux pays de Neufve France* called "La traverse à l'Île-aux-Coudres, la traverse de nuit," first broadcast on 20 February 1957) strongly evinces Perrault's experience as a radio presenter. Like the television programs, it opens with the music of Jacques Douai (heard throughout the programs) and text that is read in sharp, clear French by François Bertrand. There are also sections that feature interviews with islanders, and it is in this way that the program certainly anticipates a cinéma de la parole that would depend centrally on the rhythms of spoken language. But this is not quite in place yet; these interviews are a relatively small part of the program, which is made up mostly of Perrault's text. Early in the radio episode "La traverse d'hiver à l'Île-aux-Coudres," Perrault's text sets out his sense of the island as both linked to a traditional maritime economy and yet also marginalized and scrappy, having Bertrand say "to hunt the whale, you have to be rich and well-equipped; to hunt the seal, it's enough to be poor and brave."[17] This is followed by audio footage of an islander talking about hunting the seals, about how they would sometimes fall through the ice, and so on. The difference in linguistic register between Perrault's text and the islander's speech is enormous, and the listener's attention is very clearly drawn to the distinctiveness of the island French by virtue of its contrast with the voice of the narrator. This sort of dialectic—between standard French and island French, between the artifice of narrated text and the spontaneity of interview footage—defines the series. Furthermore, Perrault's text is still sprinkled with the distinctive language and attention to local landscapes and traditions that marks all of his work. As the text recalls at one point, "It's well-established work, this winter hunt across the ice, with two men, and a wooden boat, amidst the icefields, the slush [le frâsil], the great flight through ice and cold."[18] This passage is both preceded and followed by the voice of an islander talking about setting out across the ice as part of the seal hunt, looking for good spots, and so on. Nobody explains the meaning of words like "frâsil,"or the cultural importance of "goelettes," even though both come up with some frequency in the text. These words, specific to the *parole* of Île-aux-Coudres, convey the texture of life on the island, the degree to which it relies on locally distinctive boats to maintain everyday life (including economic life), the degree to which its landscape is defined by a word that is not really part of standard French ("frâsil" does not appear in *Collins Robert Concise French Dictionary*; Léandre Bergeron's *Dictionnaire de la langue québécoise* defines it as "small ice crystals floating on the surface of the water").[19] The speech that illuminates the life of the island is present here, even if it is only sometimes present in the form of an actual islander speaking. Yet this is far from surprising. Most radio documentary is defined by a fairly explicit duality between artifice and spontaneity, very rarely embracing the more clearly observational style of a then-emergent direct cinema, an aesthetic that would become Perrault's modus operandi. In this program, however, we can hear the distinctive elements of the life of Île-aux-Coudres and some of the language necessary to evoke it. But "la parole" as such is not yet at the centre of the work's aesthetic.

Traces of this aesthetic remain in the television version of "La traverse d'hiver." Clandfield writes of this television series in ways that are very close to what I have just said about the radio series: "It was a visit to the world of the other, a capture of silent images edited together beside a soundtrack that consisted of very little direct recording, but with music, sounds, and a commentary added later" (4–5). Obviously the radio series is not made up of "silent images," but generally Clandifeld is capturing an aesthetic here—one that relies only slightly on the actual speech of the islanders—that is certainly present in *Au Pays de Neufve-France*, both in its radio and television versions. The most famous part of the television episode "La traverse d'hiver à l'Île-aux-Coudres," and probably the most famous part of the entire television series, is when a group of men, Perrault among them, pull a boat across the semi-frozen river towards the island. And as with the radio series, there is some direct recording and some attention to the local language and landscape. Over images of the five men alternately rowing and hauling a small boat along a slushy, not-quite-frozen river, we also hear the word "frâsil" defined: "*le frâsil* is the in-between material that's neither ice nor water."[20] This is followed by images of an interview with Alexis Tremblay, a central figure in Perrault's Île-aux-Coudres films of the 1960s. Alexis, in David Clandfield's words, "describes, with great lucidity and in almost mythical terms, the techniques by which the passage could be achieved and the crew could arrive safely with boat and provisions intact" (5). This movement between speech and text, between the "Radio-Canada French" of François Bertrand and the island French of Alexis Tremblay, is certainly a significant part of the television version of *Au pays de Neufve-France*, as it was in the radio version.

What is different, though, is the presence of imagery that seeks to place the viewer closer to the action. Lacroix writes about this television version of *Neufve-France* that "for the first time with *Au pays de Neufve-France*, Perrault surrenders speech to the camera. The commentary here still means more than the image, but this only grounds or confirms the analysis."[21] It is important to recall here that Perrault wrote the text for these television films; they were directed by the French filmmaker René Bonnière (who went on to have a long career in Canada). One could also recall that Perrault told Bonneville in a 1983 interview with the Quebec film magazine *Séquences* that "an image remains on the surface of things. An image is simplistic."[22] I treasure that quote, for it is the images of the boat sliding across the *surface* of the St. Lawrence that distinguish the television version of *Au pays de Neufve-France* most clearly from its radio incarnation and set the stage most clearly for the films to follow. In the television version, there are five men, and the sense of the trek across the ice is slightly different and certainly more visceral. The sequence on the icefield of the St. Lawrence features quite a few instances of remarkable moving-camera. Early in the sequence, Alexis explains how the boat would roll back and forth; this is followed first by an extreme long shot of the boat being rowed across the ice by the men, then a close-up of Léopold Tremblay (Alexis's son, who will also figure quite centrally in the Île-aux-Coudres films) in the boat, and then a POV shot, outside the boat, as it rocks back and forth vertiginously; the screen becomes a roiling blur of white. While many of the shots that follow this are basically still or move only slightly to follow the boat, many of them are clearly shot from *le frâsil* itself, since there are several medium shots of the men rowing the boat through slushy ice. One sequence features a shot that begins right on the bow of the boat as it heads towards some ice (the angle in relation to the ice is thus quite low), which is followed by a continuity-maintaining cut to a medium shot of the boat ramming the ice and then men jumping out to haul it up. This low-angle POV shot is repeated several times, as is an equally visceral set-up taken from the boat's stern as it slides across the ice, a following boat visible in the distance. This movement between the long shots of conventional documentary and the kinetically subjective POV shots represents a shift towards the vérité aesthetics we will see in *Pour la suite du monde* five years later. This television work is not all the way to vérité yet, of course, because the sound over these images is non-synchronous; we are seeing an unfolding situation, but we are not *hearing* one. Lacroix acknowledges this as well, stating that even though Perrault concedes a bit to the image, it's still only there to illustrate and ground the commentary. And as with *Pour la suite du monde*, how much this visual sensibility has to do with Perrault himself is unclear, since it is Bonnière who is the director here. But also as with *Pour la suite du monde*, these images of movement, of subjectivity, are quite consistent with Perrault's notion of a cinéma vécu. The object of the filmmakers here is not simply to document a situation over which they have no control. Rather, they are helping to restage a now-dormant tradition, and to participate in its recitation (a term Clandfield uses frequently). The visible presence of Perrualt in the boat is part of signifying that lived recitation; putting the camera right into the boat, right onto the *frâsil*, is part of that recitation as well. The aesthetic of this episode of the television version of *Au pays de Neufve-France* is connected to Perrault's radio practice and even bears some of its limitations. But it also marks the emergence of a distinctly cinematic way of conceiving his cultural practice.

These sequences involving "le frâsil" are great examples of a distinctive part of the language of Île-aux-Coudres, being linked by Perrault to its *people* and their patterns of life. The radio series invokes the word in a way that conjures its meaning, but does not expand on it; the television series, however, *shows* us the word, re-enacts it, and gives it some cinematic life. And it is through this re-enactment that we see the emergence of a central part of Perrault's approach, an emergence that Clandfield goes on to discuss:

> However, the choice of the subject in *La traverse* does anticipate the future trajectory of Perrault's work. In order to cross over to the Île-aux-Coudres in the winter of 1958, it was no longer a matter of bringing a steel-runnered boat across a mixture of snow, slush, and ice by means of brute force and death-defying agility.... The running of the boats had been reduced to an olden-times exploit surviving as a competitive sport as many know who have seen it during the Quebec City Carnival and elsewhere. The film served to revive the exploit, to demonstrate it, and to recount it. This sequence of revival, demonstration and recital returns in his direct-cinema productions for the National Film Board, most notably with the beluga trap in *Pour la suite du monde* (1963) and the caribou hunt in *Le pays de la terre sans arbres* (1980). (5)

This aspect of performance, of demonstration, is linked not only to the recounting of "la parole," but also to the *experience* of "le vécu." A practice that evokes or describes is akin to where Perrault began in radio. As he moved towards cinema, he was trying to move towards a practice that recounted, that re*lived*. "Perrault was discovering the raw visual material for his NFB direct cinema," Clandfield writes. "Good contacts were being established ... the poetry was being discovered; rituals were being enacted. Recital was being localized" (6). I have tried to show that in addition to all of this, an aesthetic was being worked out as well, an aesthetic that was based in, but which moved past, radio.

Pour la suite du monde

Contacts were being established that would lead to the production of Perrault's most famous film, *Pour la suite du monde.* Quite a bit has been written on the film already; it is basically canonical in studies of both Quebec and Canadian cinema. There are, however, some important aspects of the film, related to my overall project in this book, which have not been widely discussed. Part of this is the presence of a radiophonic consciousness in the film; this is borne out by some discussion of the "radio version" of the film, broadcast between 1963 and 1964 as part of a series called *Chroniques de terre et de mer.* Part of the connection to this book, however, has to do with the highly complex matter of *Pour la suite du monde*'s authorship; this is the only chapter that deals with a single filmmaker, and I will try to show that this is not really as incongruous as it might seem.

Indeed, I hesitate slightly to include a section on "the work of Pierre Perrault" for two reasons. One is that another element of this period of the North Atlantic's media history is that none of its most important projects, except for Perrault's, can be identified by a single author; the following chapters are all about groups of people (the NFB's Newfoundland Project, Sjónvarpsfelagið í Havn, the Gaeltacht activists). But "the work of Pierre Perrault" is not as out of place here as it may seem. The degree to which Perrault is the author of these works has been the subject of considerable debate and, of course, a key element of cinéma vécu is the aspiration towards collaboration with the subjects of the film. "For the purposes of the present study the name Perrault is used as a sort of collective pseudonym," Michel Brûlé writes in his 1974 book *Pierre Perrault ou un cinéma national.*[23] Brûlé was acknowledging that filmmaking is always a collective experience, taking into account in this case both the islanders themselves and Perrault's co-directors, Michael Brault and Bernard Gosselin.

André Loiselle has offered the most forceful critique of the notion of Perrault as author of *Pour la suite du monde* and has done so partially by responding to that very statement of Brûlé's (he says Brûlé offers the pseudonym formulation "rather unconvincingly" [*Cinema as History*, 82]). Loiselle writes in his study of Michel Brault's films about how important it is to not relegate Brault to mere cameraman but recognize the degree to which he was responsible for key elements of the film. He writes that:

> *Pour la suite du monde* is thus the result of a collective effort, including the contributions of [Werner] Nold as editor, Marcel Carrière as sound recorder, and Bernard Gosselin as Brault's assistant cameraman. As [Gilles] Marsolais points

> out, without this group of skilled filmmakers, newcomer Perrault would have produced a talking-heads documentary in the old tradition that the Équipe Française was constantly trying to avoid. It is therefore thoroughly misguided to give credit only to Perrault for the production of the film. Yet many respected critics do just that. (*Cinema as History* 82)[24]

Loiselle identifies my own 2002 article on Perrault and Bob Quinn (published in *Cinema Journal* 42:2) as an example of this tendency, although if that means being mentioned in the same paragraph as Gilles Deleuze, Jean-Louis Comolli, and André S. Labarthe, I'll take it. Anyway, I do indeed take Loiselle's point, and there is little question that Brault needs to be acknowledged as a central collaborator on *Pour la suite du monde*. The logical response to this would be that it was Perrault whose contacts on Île-aux-Coudres made the film possible and whose philosophy of cinéma vécu clearly underwrites the film's patient, quotidian sensibilities. Loiselle is ready for this, though:

> While is it true that Perrault, the man of words, deserves credit for "discovering" the poetry of Tremblay, Harvey and the others, it is Brault who captured the rich context within which the lines are spoken.... The true power of *Pour la suite du monde* comes from the fact that the camera does not only show men speaking. It also shows those who listen, those who do not express themselves first through verbal language. (*Cinema as History* 83)[25]

That's a perfectly reasonable assessment of "the true power of *Pour la suite du monde*." Another assessment of its importance, though, would be that it is an example of a filmmaking practice that seeks to break down boundaries between subject and filmmaker, of a practice that is rooted in language, of a practice that seeks in marginalized communities an experience of modernity utterly at odds with the folkloric idealism that has too long defined their popular representation. This has little to do with the contributions of Brault's that Loiselle is trying to recover in his book on him. And in all fairness, Loiselle writes in the French version of his book that "for me, the distinction between Perrault and Brault is obviously not irrelevant. It's not a matter of denigrating the role of Perrault."[26]

And anyway, this authorship problem is hardly limited to *Pour la suite du monde*. If anything, it is more present in Perrault's radio works, where he was the *scripteur* rather than the *réalisateur*. Yves Lacroix tries to square that particular circle, writing that "radio is much more tied to the text than cinema." Tying this to the vexing question of who is the author of Perrault's radio works, he goes on to say that "it's the scriptwriter who conceives the broadcast. His text will be more or less respected as long as the director more or less agrees. In the happiest cases, the director becomes a 'chief technician' who faithfully executes that which the scriptwriter has conceived."[27] I have to say, though, that I find this quite unsatisfying; it is hardly instinctive that most radio directors are content to serve as chief technicians, and if Lacroix knows something I don't about the details of Radio-Canada's division of labour, he's not saying.

These are, of course, old problems in the discourse around film authorship, and I am struck by one solution offered by Leland Pogue and Robert Self. They engaged in 1986 (in the pages of *Cinema Journal*) in a debate about the book *Film Criticism: A Counter Theory*, which Pogue co-authored with William Cadbury, a book that was strongly under the influence of Monroe Beardsley, specifically his 1958 work *Aesthetics: Problems in the Philosophy of Criticism*. Beardsley, though, is most famous as the co-author (with W. K. Wimsatt) of the celebrated 1946 essay "The Intentional Fallacy,"[28] and *Film Criticism* also deals extensively with the problems of authorship (the five chapters that comprise part 2 are collectively called "Authorship, Meaning and Interpretation"). In this debate, Pogue tried to reject Self's use of Lacan and Self's characterization of Pogue's work with Cadbury as traditionally auteurist, writing that "the primary focus in *Film Criticism* is on 'criticism'; i.e., on the acts of viewing and interpreting and on the logic by which such acts take place and are defensible. Our view here is resolutely instrumental and pragmatic" (78). Robert Self responded that "Jacques Lacan is an authorial voice with power to shape the discourse of *Come Back to the 5 and Dime, Jimmy Dean, Jimmy Dean* for the viewer who knows his name. Monroe Beardsley is an author to be found throughout *3 Women* for the reader with ears to hear" (80). Similarly, Perrault is clearly an author to be found throughout *Pour la suite du monde*, for those with ears to hear. Nobody who knows the name of Michel Brault can fail to see his presence as an author in that same film. The acts of criticism that I am trying to perform in this book, though, are centred on an attempt to write a history of media experiments in the North Atlantic across three decades, experiments which include many works where Perrault can be understood as an author but only one work where Brault can be so understood.[29] Thus my privileging of Perrault (and the islanders along with him) as author of *Pour la suite du monde* (among other works) is resolutely pragmatic. It does not preclude an understanding Brault as an author of *Pour la suite du monde*, or Crawley Films as author of *Au pays de Neufve-France*. Such understandings could lead to really interesting works of criticism; Loiselle's two books on Brault *are* such works. But that is not the sort of criticism I am trying to perform here.

And, dare I say it, Dziga Vertov is, for those with eyes to see him and ears to hear him, an author here, too. I hesitate slightly here, for Perrault told Paul Warren in *Cinéatse de la parole* that "I saw a Vertov film a long time ago. I remember that his first name was Dziga. But I've almost totally forgotten his film."[30] He was responding to a question from Warren about Vertov's use of sound:

> In the years 1918–1919, he founded, in Moscow, *the hearing laboratory*. Some time beforehand, when he found himself at Moscow's central station, he was startled by the sounds, the noises and the multiple voices that came from everywhere simultaneously and which he took in with his ears for the first time in his life. He said that he had to capture the multiple voices of the new Russia. He made a recording machine to imprison the sounds. Then, in his laboratory, he delivered it to what he called *the montage of the things I hear*. Later, he got himself a camera and applied himself to the pursuit of images. Vertov moved, like you, from the heard to the viewed.[31]

Perrault takes this up a bit with Warren, but he makes it pretty clear that he doesn't feel a kinship with Vertov. Following Wimsatt and Beardsley, I'd like to say that "there is a difference between internal and external evidence for the meaning of a poem" (10), a difference between the internal evidence of Perrault's works themselves and the external evidence of his recollection that he doesn't remember anything about Vertov except that his first name was Dziga. Warren's sense of Perrault passing, like Vertov, "de l'ouïe à la vue" is part of this; it is clearly internal evidence that is leading him to see that passing. Furthermore, Vertov's belief that Radio-Eye was about "eliminating distance between people" (*Kino-Eye* 91)[32] connects strongly to Perrault's ideas about cinéma vécu and the connections among islanders themselves and between the islanders and the filmmakers. Perrault's progression from radio to cinema echoes the progression of Vertov's "kinok-observers," but in reverse. I mentioned in the introduction that Vertov had written in the 1925 essay "Kino-pravda and Radiopravda," "If, with respect to vision, our kinok-observers have recorded visible life with cameras, we must now talk about recording audible facts" (*Kino-Eye* 56).[33] With *Pour la suite du monde*, Perrault was now fully moving instead from recording audible facts to visible facts. But like Vertov, he did not lose track of the inseparable connection between the two.

One of the ways that Perrault kept faith with this connection was to produce radio programs based on his experiences making his Île-aux-Coudres films, all part of a series called *Chroniques de terre et de mer*. As Savard and Lambert document (in their notes for P319/C9.1–5) each of the episodes of the first series became episodes of the television version of *Au pays de Neufve-France*: *Le Jean Richard*, *Attiuk*, *Tête-à-la-Baleine*, *La Tabatière* (which became *L'Anse-Tabatière* in *Au pays de Neufve-France*), and *Les Diamants du Canada*. Savard and Lambert also indicate that there were thirty-nine episodes of the second series, which were broadcast on Radio-Canada from October 1963 to June 1964 (see the note for P319/C13.13). Their register also states that these radio programs were directed by Bernard Vanasse. It is the second series—whose episodes all open with the same music that *Pour la suite du monde* opens with—which fed directly into Perrault's most famous film. One of the episodes of this series is called simply "Pour la suite," and it contains some of the same material found in the film *Pour la suite du monde*. But the most important moments of *Pour la suite du monde* are actually found in an episode of this radio series called "La pêche à marsouin."[34]

Neither program is exactly a "radio version" of the film *Pour la suite du monde*; they follow certain elements of the film, and they *transpose* them for the radio. Both programs include written narration—something completely absent from the film *Pour la suite du monde* (except for the opening sequence, which features a reading from Jacques Cartier's journals), in keeping with the emerging ethic and aesthetic of cinéma vérité. This text, in these radio programs, is read by Perrault himself. "It was me, in search of a people, acted out by the mystery and directed by the prophets" is how Perrault opens the episode "La pêche à marsouin," by way of emphasizing the subjectivity of the quest.[35] This subjectivity tends to be emphasized visually in the film version, frequently via the use of stunning compositions rather than through this sort of poetic narration, which is a common element of the text of both *Au pays de Neufve-France* (in its radio and television forms) and *Chroniques de terre et de mer*.

One example of this crossover is where Alexis Tremblay rhapsodizes about the whale hunting. "It's the most exhilarating fishing," he says, "that makes men the most passionate. The most beautiful fishing you can do."[36] In the film *Pour la suite du monde*, there is an extreme close-up of Tremblay's face as he speaks these words; the camera seems to hover there, moving ever so slightly, giving a sense of breathless anticipation. This is followed by a series of images taken from inside a boat in the river (mostly close-ups and medium shots, although there are a few shots taken off the starboard of a neighbouring boat) as the hunters row out to set the traps. This is followed by another extreme close-up of Tremblay explaining the procedure for the hunt. This shot lasts for only a few seconds, though; Tremblay's voice remains, but the film cuts to images of the men on the beach. This is followed by synch-sound footage of getting the traps ready, including a striking shot of the water and the stakes, taken from a very low angle (the camera appears to be right on the surface of the beach). This sequence is concluded by footage of men arguing in a house about whether the hunt was started by "les sauvages" or "les immigrés." In the radio episode "La pêche au marsouin," Perrault's text starts by asking "What did we know of these men, and of their passion?" Then he plays those same words from Tremblay about how "c'est la pêche la plus enivrante," and then says himself, "Great things seek to be heard in the gap between the great words. Words traverse men by whistling like a tree filled by some god with air, the cold killed in its sleep, the beasts silent."[37] The argument about the origins of the hunt does not emerge until almost thirty minutes into this thirty-eight-minute radio program.

That is right before another sequence that is both in the radio program "La pêche à marsouin" and the film *Pour la suite du monde*. Alexis is asked by Perrault if he thinks the hunt will be revived. "I hope," he replies, "that it will return even when I'm gone, so that the young folks can see what the old folks invented."[38] In the film *Pour la suite du monde*, that last line, "pour que les jeunes voient ce que les vieux ont inventé," is placed over the most famous image of the film, an extreme long shot taken at dusk of a small boat against the fence of stakes in the river (that shot was on a Canada Post stamp in 1996 and, Loiselle is at pains to point out, was shot by Brault alone, without Perrault's presence [143/83]). But in the radio program "La pêche à marsouin," Perrault plays those same words of Alexis's and follows them with his own rapturous recitation, "He speaks, he speaks, he speaks, he speaks in the night! The sage and prophet Alexis, as if the future was something you could hold forth on at his age."[39]

Thus the difference here is between a lyrical sense of the photographic so typical of early vérité—lots of patient, often basically factual footage punctuated by visually striking images like the extreme close-up of Tremblay or the extreme low-angle shot of the river—and a more literary sense of the poetic, one that emphasizes the spaces between words, the way speech whistles through the trees. It is of course not surprising that cinema seems to centralize images while radio seems to emphasize speech; what is worth pointing out, though, is that both forms of this sequence emphasize poetry. Neither one is particularly linear, although both are in time-based media; neither one is purely about exposition, although there is plenty of that in both versions. This is entirely consistent with Perrault's overall modus operandi, which is cinematic but not *solely* cinematic. Yves Lacroix writes that *Chroniques de terre et de mer*, *Au pays de Neufve-France*, and Perrault's 1963 collection of short prose pieces, *Toutes Isles* (the source of the epigraph that opens this section on islands), "are different states of the same project."[40] That project is basically poetic, and also basically activist, one that presents traditional cultural forms (language, hunting rituals) in a context defined by modernity rather than folklore. "I was looking for a speech that would advance action," Perrault wrote in his 1967 "Discours sur la parole."[41] Gilles Deleuze understood what constituted this sort of action and how it connected to Perrault's cinéma vécu as well. As he wrote of Perrault in *Cinéma 2: L'image-temps*, "For Perrault, the concern is to belong to his dominated people, to rediscover a lost and repressed collective identity (*The Time-Image* 153).[42] We see chez Perrault a politically minded, progressive tension between modernity and tradition. We also see a desire to evoke the tension through a form that is neither narrative nor elliptical, one that is based in but not limited by radio, television, and film. And finally, we see a political sensibility that is underwritten by a certain sense of nationalism but also quite free of nationalist propaganda or didacticism. Indeed, on that last point, Deleuze writes that in Perrault's films, "This is no longer *Birth of a Nation*, but constitution and reconstitution of a people, where the filmmaker and his characters become others together from place to place, from person to person, from intercessor to intercessor" (*The Time-Image* 153).[43]

These are the recurring themes of this book. Both in terms of a linear chronology and a west-to-east geographic progression, *Au pays de Neufve-France*, *Pour la suite du monde*, and their radio companions are the place where we see these themes for the first time in that historical journey across this period of the region's media history. Like the St. Lawrence itself, the cinema of Pierre Perrault is the gateway to the North Atlantic.

Notes

1 "Perrault et Lefebvre: c'est au Québec que naissent aujourd'hui les formes les plus engagées du cinéma moderne" (58).

2 "Si René Allio se sent plutôt Marseillais dans le décor France, moi je ne réussis pas très bien à savoir comment on peut être Québécois dans un Canada où je ne suis pas très à l'aise, dans un Canada où je me sens exclu et même étranger. Dans un Canada qui me folklorise" (44).

3 This is roughly contemporary to the period generally known in Quebec as the "Révolution tranquille" or the Quiet Revolution. This is generally acknowledged to have begun in 1960 with the election of Jean Lesage's Liberal party, an election that followed the death of Premier Maurice Duplessis in 1959; Duplessis' Union Nationale had ruled Quebec since 1936 (with a brief period out of power during World War II). The degree to which this period has or has not been overstated as a turning point for Quebec culture, or whether pre-Quiet-Revolution Quebec really was an insular society dominated by the Catholic church, has been the subject of much debate

among historians. For a forceful, concise indictment of the tendency to overstate the illiberal essence of pre-Quiet-Revolution Quebec, see Claude Couture, *La loyauté d'un laïc: Pierre Elliott Trudeau et le liberalisme canadien* (Paris/Montréal: L'Harmattan, 1996), published in English as *Paddling with the Current: Pierre Elliott Trudeau, Étienne Parent, Liberalism, and Nationalism in Canada*, Vivian Bosley, trans. (Edmonton: University of Alberta Press, 1998). Writing of the inflation of the importance of the Quiet Revolution, Couture states in *Paddling with the Current* that "[Pierre] Trudeau has a teleological concept of the history of Quebec, including a moment of salvation and purification that allowed the society to start from scratch, throwing out wholesale its past—a past symbolized in particular by Duplessis. But as Borque, Duchastel, and Beauchemain (1994) have pointed out, Duplessism constituted a form of political discourse in which tradition and modernity were so tangled up that it was impossible to create an opposition between them. This idea, according to which a complex intertwining of features are categorized as ideal-types of tradition and modernity, could be applied to the western world in general, if not to any society" (104–5). For an invaluable survey and critique of these historical debates, see Ronald Rudin's *Making History in Twentieth-Century Quebec* (Toronto: University of Toronto Press, 1997). Rudin is critical of positions like Couture's, which he dubs "revisionist," borrowing the term from a movement in Irish historical writing that sought to construct Ireland as a "normal" country rather than one with a highly distinctive, and often embarrassingly violent, history. Many Quebec historians, Rudin argues, are comparably embarrassed by Quebec's distinctive and sometimes illiberal past, and are forever trying to construct its history as somehow "typical" or "normal."

4 I should specify here that the "radio version" of *Pour la suite du monde* is part of Perrault's 1962–63 radio series *Chroniques de terre et de mer, 2e série*, a series that was comprised of audio taken on Île-aux-Coudres. The second episode of this series is entitled "Pour la suite"; see Savard and Lambert's *Répertoire numérique détaillé du Fonds Pierre Perrault* P319/C13.3 for a note on that episode (this is the call number for the complete audio footage for this episode). The VHS collection of *Au pays de Neufve-France* also included a CD with an episode from *Chroniques de terre et de mer, 2e série* called "La peche au marsouin," which, as I discuss later in this chapter, has a "radio version" of key sequences of the film *Pour la suite du monde*. The Fonds Pierre Perrault call number for the complete recordings of *Chroniques de terre et de mer, 2e série* is P319/C13.13.

5 The first question that Fr. Léo Bonneville asks Perrault in his 1971 interview with him is "Monsieur Pierre Perrault, qui êtes-vous?" [Mr. Pierre Perrault, who are you?] Perrault replies: "For the moment, nothing! I was a lawyer.… After six years of university, after two years at St. Jacques Street, where it snowed like a blackout, I defrocked. Bravo. But I had to start over. The robes. The titles. I no longer had anything. Except my freedom. I become a 'radio author,' as Marcelle Barthe says, that is, less than nothing!" [Pour l'instant, rien! J'ai été avocat.… Après 6 ans d'université, après 2 ans de rue Saint-Jacques où il neige de la neige noire, j'ai défroqué. Bravo. Mais il fallait

recommencer à neuf. Le costume. Les titres. Je n'avais plus rien. Sauf ma liberté. Je suis devenu 'auteur radiophonique,' comme dit Marcelle Barthe, i,e, moins que rien! (672)].

6 "et c'est de ma mère qui j'ai appris que j'habitais une ville ... / mais c'est d'elle que j'ai appris que j'avais un pays! que mon pays avait un langage! que ce langage était poésie! et que cette poésie hasardeuse fréquentait le superlatif depuis belle enfance comme si rien n'était ... / comme si rien n'était trop beau pour dire l'inédit d'un fleuve négligé des écritures ..." (Warren 26).

7 "Bien sur on peut dire que j'ai fait un cinéma de la parole" (17–18).

8 "Je peux dire en commençant que je ne suis pas venu au cinéma par le cinéma. Je venais au cinéma par la magnétophone."

9 "J'aurais pu faire du cinéma-fiction et construire un scénario. Nous avons opté pour un cinéma-document. Moi j'appelle ça du cinéma vécu. On ne peut pas mettre sur papier à l'avance une année à vivre" (678).

10 "Je n'invoque ni Eisenstein, ni Fellini, ni Carné mais les gens de l'île. Ils m'ont appris un langage, un *chouenne*, une tournure d'esprit, la navigation, un fleuve de mots et les mots du fleuve. Et ils m'ont proposé la belle épopée du marsouin. Quel merveilleux cinéma que celui qu'on peut faire les pieds dans le varech des *battures* quand la mer monte à l'épouvante! Cette démarche radiophonique fondée sur le magnétophone n'est pas singulière. Mais j'ai peut-être inauguré une façon d'écouter qui se préoccupe autant du récit lui-même du langage qui le véhicule. Grâce à Yolande d'abord, grâce aux gens du pays, grâce enfin au magnétophone qui me permettait de vérifier, d'approfondir, de savourer le langage, j'ai enfin compris que ma mère était poésie ... et je n'en démords pas ... et que la poésie était une façon de prendre possession d'un pays au nom de ceux qui l'ont vécu" (Warren 33; ellipses in the original). Léandre Bergeron's *Dictionnaire de la langue québécoise* defines "chouenne" as "menterie, blague" [tall tale, joke] (131). Perrault has published a collection called *Chouennes: Poèmes 1961–1971* (Montréal: Éditions de l'Hexagone, 1975).

11 Perrault didn't leave radio behind completely. He had a few projects in the 1960s and 1970s: series such as *J'habite une ville* in 1965, *Gens de mon pays* in 1971, and *Visages de Montréal* in 1983. In 1984 he made, with Jean-Daniel Lafond, a thirteen-part series called *Avec bon vents naviguant*, a series that was linked to his two-part film *La Grande Allure*, which documented his transatlantic boat voyage to mark the 350th anniversary of the voyage of Jacques Cartier. For coverage of that radio series in the French press, see Louis Marcorelles, "Sur les traces de Jacques Cartier," *Le Monde*, 15 August 1984. In 1993 Perrault broadcast another thirteen-part series for Radio-Canada called *L'appel du nord*, about his voyage from Quebec City to Nansivik on the icebreaker *Pierre Radisson*. A book version of this was published, posthumously, in 1999, as *Le mal du nord*. It was awarded the Governor General's Award for nonfiction, and Perrault is the only author to have been so awarded posthumously (I mention the book briefly in chapter 4). A complete list of Perrault's radio works is found on pages 26–27 of the booklet published by the NFB in 1999 to accompany their box set of Perrault videos called "Le Fleuve" (it collected 1983's *Les voiles bas et en travers*,

both parts of 1984's *La Grande Allure*, and a 1999 interview with Perrault called *Pierre Perrault parle du fleuve*).

12 "ne domine pas le sujet transindividuel québécois des années cinquante, on discerne néanmoins une tendance à l'énoncé postmoderne dans le discours de l'époque, tendance qu'illustre la représentation dédoublée du 'restons traditionnels et progressifs'" (95).

13 "Avec le résurgence du texte oral par le disque, la radio et la télévision ... nous nous trouvons un peu dans la situation—mais inverse—du scripteur médiéval" ("Petite misère" 87).

14 "La première a produit des œuvres légères (radioroman) et sérieuses (radiothéâtre), mais non des œuvres 'populaire,' reproduisant la langue quotidienne, bien qu'elle se soit adressée à un public 'populaire.' Alors que la radio privée fait parler certains voix 'populaires' ... Radio-Canada a tendance à traiter cette voix, le joual, comme un objet négatif qu'il faut corriger" (107).

15 "Le cinéma de fiction de cette époque était marqué lui aussi par l'oralité, plusieurs films étant des adaptations de radio-romans" (52).

16 Quebec had a very small commercial film industry in the 1950s, producing 18 films between 1942 and 1953. The films Lacasse mentions are some of its best-known examples. The standard histories of this period of filmmaking in Quebec are Christiane Tremblay-Daviault's *Un cinéma orphelin: Structures mentales et sociales du cinéma québécois (1942–1953)* (Montréal: Québec/Amérique, 1981) and Pierre Véronneau's two-volume *Histoire du cinéma au Québec: Le succès est au film parlant français* and *Cinéma de l'époque duplessiste* (both Montréal: Cinémathèque québécoise, 1979).

17 "Pour chasser la baleine, il faut être riche, et bien équipé; pour chasser le loup marin il suffit d'être pauvre et courageux."

18 "C'est un vieux travail, cette chasse d'hiver à travers les glaces, à deux hommes, et un canot de bois, parmi la banquise, le frâsil, la grande fuite de la glace et du froid."

19 "Petits cristaux de glace flottant à la surface de l'eau" (235).

20 "Le frâsil c'est la matière intermédiaire, qui n'est ni glace, ni eau."

21 "Pour la première fois avec *Au pays de Neufve-France*, Perrault cède la parole à un camera. Le commentaire signifie ici encore plus que l'image mais celle-ci vient fonder ou confirmer l'analyse" ("À l'écoute" 34).

22 "Une image reste à la surface des choses. Une image est simpliste" (cited in Gauthier, Pilard, and Suchet 116).

23 "Pour les fins de la présente étude le nom Perrault est utilisé comme s'il agissait d'un pseudonyme collectif" (15).

24 Loiselle explains it somewhat differently in his 2005 French-language version of the book, *Le cinéma de Michel Brault*. "Gilles Marsolais signals that it's thanks, first of all, to Brault's suggestion to let go of the scripted dialogue, as well as to the technical genius of Brault on camera and Carrière on sound—and we could add Nold on editing and Bernard Gosselin, Brault's assistant cameraman, that the film moved beyond banal reportage." [Gilles Marsolais signale que c'est grâce, tout d'abord, à cette suggestion de Brault de laisser tomber les dialogues scénarisés, puis à l'ingéniosité

technique de Brault à la caméra et de Carrière au son—et on pourrait ajouter Nold au montage et Bernard Gosselin, assistant-caméraman de Brault—que le film a su dépasser le reportage banal (140).] He also quotes directly from Gilles Marsolais' 1997 book *L'aventure du cinéma direct revisitée* to explain how the NFB's Équipe Française wanted to get rid of ("liquider" is the word Marsolais uses) the traditional talking-heads documentary.

25 Again, *Le cinéma de Michel Brault* has it somewhat differently: "It's him [Perrault] who gave voice to Alexis and Grand-Louis, but it's Brault who is the poet of the image. However important, speech isn't the only aspect of the film that we should consider, and very much the opposite is the case.... The real power of *Pour la suite du monde* derives from the fact that the image doesn't only show those who speak, but also those of whom they speak and those who listen to the speech of others in order to discover their own speech." [C'est lui qui a donné voix à Alexis et Grand-Louis, mais c'est Brault qui est le poète de l'image. Toute importance qu'elle soit, la parole n'est pas le seul aspect du film qui vaille la peine d'être considéré, bien au contraire.... La puissance véritable de *Pour la suite du monde* résulte du fait que l'image ne vous montre pas seulement ceux qui parlent, mais aussi ceux qui dont on parle et ceux qui écoutent la parole des autres pour y découvrir leur propre parole (143)].

26 "Pour nous, la distinction entre Perrault et Brault n'est évidemment pas sans intérêt. Il ne s'agit pas de dénigrer le rôle de Perrault" (143).

27 "La radio est beaucoup plus liée au texte que le cinéma.... C'est le scripteur qui conçoit l'émission. Son texte sera plus ou moins respecté selon qu'il s'accorde plus ou moins avec le réalisateur. Dans le plus heureux des cas, le réalisateur devient un chef-technicien qui exécute fidèlement ce que le scripteur a conçu" ("Petite misère" 94).

28 This essay, originally published in the *Sewanee Review* in 1946, is found in Wimsatt's *The Verbal Icon: Studies in the Meaning of Poetry*. The cover of the 1954 paperback edition has only Wimsatt's name on it; the title page has the text "and two preliminary essays written in collaboration with Monroe C. Beardsley." Wimsatt's acknowledgements page mentions Beardsley, and he also refers in his introduction to "two essays which my friend Monroe Beardsley and I wrote to expose as fallacies two very prevalent approaches to the critical object, that by way of its origins in the mind of its maker, and that by way of its results in the mind of the audience" (xiii). The former refers to their concept of "the intentional fallacy" (the latter is the "affective fallacy"). Given that it is only Pogue and not Pogue *and Cadbury* who engaged with Self in this debate about *their* book, I think the degree to which ambiguities about co-authorship seem to hover around every imaginable element of this work is quite remarkable.

29 Perrault and Brault also co-directed the 1970 film *L'Acadie, l'Acadie?!?*, about Acadian student militants at the Université de Moncton. Loiselle returns to these ambiguities about co-authorship in his discussion of this film as well. As he writes in *Cinema as History*, "Like *Pour la suite du monde, L'Acadie* is in part Perrault's film and in part Brault's. Perrault's *L'Acadie* is about growing political awareness. Brault's

L'Acadie observes young people who are not *only* political agents, but also individuals with contradictory aspirations, personal issues and fears that do not all boil down to 'politics'" (127). He says something similar in *Le cinéma du Michel Brault* without invoking *Pour la suite du monde* directly, stating simply that this is really two films: "Perrault's film, about the Acadian students' *becoming aware*, and Brault's film, about the *students*, who aren't only political actors but also human beings with diverse experiences and sometimes ambivalent positions" [Le film de Perrault, sur la *prise de conscience* des étudiants acadiennes, et le film de Brault, sur les *étudiants*, qui ne sont pas que des agents politiques mais aussi des êtres humains avec des expériences diverses et des prises de positions parfois ambivalentes] (210, italics his). For what it's worth (and I fear the wrath of Beardsley's and Wimsatt's ghosts here), Brault told me in a 2002 conversation that it was more or less he who directed *Pour la suite du monde*; he also told me that this was not the case in the same way at all with *L'Acadie, l'Acadie?!?*

30 "J'ai vu il y a très longtemps un film de Vertov. Je me souviens qu'il se prénommait Dziga. Mais j'ai presque totalement oublié son film" (71).

31 "Dans les années 1918–1919, il a fondé, à Moscou, le *laboratoire de l'ouïe*. Quelques temps auparavant, alors qu'il se trouvait à la gare centrale de Moscou, il avait été frappé par les sons, les bruits et les voix multiples qui veinaient de partout à la fois et auxquels il prêtait l'oreille pour la première fois de sa vie. Il s'est dit qu'il fallait capter les voix plurielles de la Russie novelle. Il s'est fabriqué une machine à enregistrer pour emprisonner les sons. Puis, dans son laboratoire, il se livrait à ce qu'il appelait *le montage des j'entends*. Plus tard, il s'est procuré une caméra et s'est mis à la poursuite des images. Vertov est passé, comme toi, de l'ouïe à la vue" (71).

32 "говорит о 'радиоглазе' как об уничтожении расстояния между людьми..." (*Stat'i, dnevniki, zamysly* 115).

33 "Если по отношению к зрению у нас кинонаблюдатели фиксировали киноаппаратами видимые жизненные явления, то здесь придется уже говорить о записи слышимых фактов" (*Stat'i, dnevniki, zamysly* 86).

34 The NFB produced, in 1997, a box set of the complete television series *Au pays de Neufve-France*. This included a CD called "Émissions radiophoniques conçues par Pierre Perrault," which included the "Pêche à marsouin" episode of *Chronqiues de terre et de mer*, as well as the "Structure d'acier" episode of Perrault's series *J'habite une ville*. Both series have been preserved in their entirety and are available for consultation at the Fonds Pierre Perrault at Université Laval; the call numbers for the complete recordings are P319/C13.13 (*Chroniques*) and P/319/C14.6 (*J'habite*).

35 "C'était moi, à la recherche d'un peuple, interprété par le mystère et régenté par les prophètes."

36 "C'est la pêche la plus enivrante, qui donne le plus passion à l'homme. La pêche la plus belle qui peut se faire."

37 "Que savions nous des hommes, et de leur passion?... De grands choses cherchaient à être entendu à l'écart des grands mots. Les paroles traversaient les hommes en

sifflant comme un arbre investi par quelque dieu par l'air, le froid tué dans leur sommeils, les bêtes silencieux."

38 "Je souhaiterais qu'elle se retendra quand même que je suis parti, pour que les jeunes voient ce que les vieux ont inventé."

39 "Il parle, il parle, il parle, il parle dans la nuit! Le sage et le prophète Alexis, comme si l'avenir était un propos qu'on peut tenir à son âge."

40 "sont différents états d'une même entreprise" ("À l'écoute" 34).

41 "Je cherchais la parole qui fait avancer l'action" (32).

42 "Pour Perrault, il s'agit d'appartenir à son peuple dominé, et de retrouver une identité collective perdue, réprimée" (*L'image-temps* 199).

43 "Ce n'est plus *Naissance d'une nation*, mais constitution et reconstitution d'un peuple, où le cinéaste et ses personnages deviennent autres ensemble et l'un par l'autre, collectivité qui gagne de proche en proche, de lieu en lieu, de personne en personne, d'intercesseur en intercesseur" (*L'image-temps* 199–200).

2

The NFB's Newfoundland Project

"I go there not to make my film. I go there to make *their* film."[1]
—Pierre Perrault, on the Île-aux-Coudres films, in Peter Wintonick's 1999 NFB documentary *Cinéma Vérité: Defining the Moment*

"They were teachers, social workers, film-makers, and they were not only prepared to teach with film, they were also prepared to help ordinary people to make their own films. That bothered Grierson. That was carrying things too far."
—Colin Low, describing the filmmakers of Challenge for Change, in *John Grierson and the NFB* (111)

One of the more curious elements of the discussion around Colin Low's "Newfoundland Project" of 1967–69 is that hardly anyone has compared it with Pierre Perrault's Île-aux-Coudres films, despite their common origin at the NFB (albeit across the linguistic divide). There are several possible explanations for this, but the most important one, I believe, has to do with the way that these Newfoundland films have always been understood (by historians and by NFB administrators alike) as examples of process, not technique, as well as with a widespread inability to see the films as having any connections beyond their immediate environment. The NFB has certainly encouraged both tendencies, creating material surrounding the Newfoundland Project that is remarkable for its disdain of aesthetic considerations. I want to offer a modest corrective to this consensus and recover Low's Fogo Island films not only as examples of community-based media making (although that is an unquestionably important part of their identity) but as an aesthetically sophisticated form of non-narrative, poetic cinema. This kind of cinema, and these Fogo films, was very much in line with the work done by the NFB's elite Unit B of the 1960s and with that of Canada's liberal avant-garde generally (an avant-garde resident in government-funded institutions like the NFB or the CBC). It is a truism that form follows politics and vice versa. The Fogo Island films are actually quite wonderful examples of artworks that are as complex formally as they are politically; continually emphasizing the latter and ignoring the former really does a disservice both to the filmmakers and to their audience.

Fogo Island

Fogo is an island community off the eastern shore of Newfoundland. It has ten villages, many of which, at the time of the production of the Newfoundland films, had their own school boards (the amalgamation of school boards is a constantly recurring theme in these films). The island did, however, have an improvement committee, which was working to both found a fishing co-operative and attract fish processing onto the island itself. These efforts were due largely to the desperate economic straits in which Fogo found itself in the 1960s. The infrastructure on the island had deteriorated to such a point that the government in St. John's was considering evacuation and resettlement; many islanders felt that the government had begun to withhold services in an attempt to get people to move off on their own. The NFB saw this, then, as an opportunity to use film as a social catalyst, as a means to improve communication among the islanders and between the island and St. John's. Low wrote, in an untitled 1968 report to the NFB, that he "selected Fogo because: (1) It had many problems, social, economic, educational; (2) The policy of the government towards this area was being formulated. In effect its future was uncertain" (1). This opportunity to enable people to intervene in an evolving political situation did indeed seem to speak to the highest ideals of Challenge for Change, a program with which Fogo Island would be forever connected.

Challenge for Change

The Newfoundland Project was the flagship initiative of the Challenge for Change program, which the NFB began in 1967. The original mandate of the program was twofold: regionalization and increased collaboration between filmmakers and their subjects. Gary Evans, in his history of the NFB, *In the National Interest*, writes that the NFB "envisioned the project as a forerunner to initiating a regional production-distribution-advisory scheme, where films would be the catalyst to precipitate social action" (160). Although a few other films were produced during that first year of 1967 (such as *Encounter at Kwacha House–Halifax* and *PowWow at Duck Lake*), Gary Evans dismisses them as "not impressive cinematically" (163). I don't agree with this assesment. It's true inasmuch as *Encounter at Kwacha House–Halifax*, like *PowWow at Duck Lake*, is comprised mostly of interviews shot with hand-held cameras. But both films are treasure troves for those interested in the rhythms of spoken Canadian English; these filmmakers allow their subjects to speak at great length, in a way that only cinema (or perhaps radio) can accommodate. Although they are not exactly works of visionary innovation, the two pieces are cultural snapshots that have great value beyond their political content. That content is fascinating, though; participants in the discussion in Rex Tasker's *Encounter at Kwacha House–Halifax* dismiss Martin Luther King as an American liberal sell-out, and David Hughes's *PowWow at Duck Lake* centres on an extremely well-spoken teenager and a priest who are having a heated argument about the residential school experience. Yet I would admit that these first short films (they were nineteen and fourteen minutes long, respectively) were nowhere near as ambitious as the twenty-eight-film Newfoundland Project, the flagship of the Challenge for Change program.

Challenge for Change emerged from the controversy surrounding Tanya Ballantyne's 1966 film *The Things I Cannot Change*, and indeed surrounding the entire period of documentary film history of which this is a part. Ballantyne's film documented the domestic and economic troubles of an underclass Montreal family named the Baileys in the kind of detail that was quite uncommon in 1966. When the film was televised the family was horribly embarrassed. Gary Evans also recalls how "when John Grierson saw [the film] he hated it for revealing a person's private life without that person deciding that he or she be fully known. Colin Low agreed; the family was at a fundamental disadvantage because they were vulnerable and easy to exploit" (159). *The Things I Cannot Change* was a film whose fly-on-the-wall intimacy was made possible by the increased availability of lightweight camera gear and (perhaps more importantly) by portable synchronous sound recording equipment, and was thus part of the emerging aesthetic changes and ethical conundrums of cinéma vérité. Challenge for Change must be seen in the context of this technical-aesthetic revolution; lightweight sound gear created the ability of filmmakers to get close to their participants, but an ethical framework for this new technology was still emerging. "In the aftermath of *The Things I Cannot Change*," Janine Marchessault writes, "an ethical dimension was incorporated into the documentary process" (135). *Warrendale*, Allan King's portrait of a home for mentally ill youth also released in 1967, is part of the same attempt at an incorporation of ethics into technological change that would lead to filmmaking practice based in knowing, active collaboration between filmmakers and their subjects. Gradually, the aspiration of many Anglophone filmmakers became to make films *with* people, not simply *about* people. Low, like Perrault five years earlier, went to an island "pour faire *leur* film."

But strangely, there is very little in the literature on Canadian or Quebec film that compares Low and Perrault. The great Quebec filmmaker Jean Pierre Lefebvre wrote a rapturous article about Low in the Montreal film magazine *Objectif* in 1963, and while he didn't mention Perrault specifically (except for a brief invocation of *Pour la suite du monde* at the end of the essay), he noted that "if the real hero of Resnais' films is abstract memory, then the real hero of Low's films is "living memory," or concrete memory I could say."[2] Lefebvre could just as easily be talking about the key issues that separate Quebec filmmakers from their French cinematic cousins such as Resnais, and Perrault makes an especially good example of this transatlantic difference. The only other example of a Perrault–Low connection that I know of is found in the work of Pierre Pageau. In a 1986 essay, he compared, in terms of their treatment of historical narration, speech, nationalism, memory, and images of childhood, *Pour la suite du monde* and Low's 1957 film *City of Gold* (an examination of the Klondike gold rush that relied almost entirely on nineteenth-century photographs, which Low had re-photographed using an animation stand and thus integrating camera movement and reframing). The absence of the Fogo films from his formulations was baffling. But Pageau made up for lost time in 2006, writing in an essay called "Colin Low, un anglophone au Québec" that "the connections between Perrault's Île-aux-Coudres trilogy are more noticeable here; in effect, with this series of films on the inhabitants of Fogo Island, we rediscover the themes, the characters, and a usage of speech that evoke Perrault's films."[3] But even more important than Perrault's recurring interest in island communities or his cinéma de la parole was his notion of cinéma vécu, "lived cinema," as I discussed in chapter 1. Cinéma vécu's emphasis on choosing to spend time in a community over the exigencies of commercial filmmaking is key to the ethic of Challenge for Change and key to the program's desire to move away from a cinema that saw people and communities as fodder for exploitable images. Perrault's cinema, and especially his Île-aux-Coudres films (like his television and radio series *Au pays de Neufve-France*), depend on his investment in the community itself, his closeness to the participants, and his ability to live with them rather than simply appear and then disappear when the filming is done. He told Peter Wintonick, in the documentary *Cinéma*

Vérité, that "I become a participant, a collaborator; the islanders go along with me because they can clearly see that I have become a part of the island in a way."[4] Challenge for Change did not seek quite this level of integration for its filmmakers, an integration that was, in Perrault's case, partially the result of the family ties his wife, Yolande Simard, had to the Charlevoix region. But it was clear that they could not simply "parachute" themselves into such an isolated and tightly knit set of communities.

The involvement of Memorial University of Newfoundland's Extension Service, therefore, was instrumental. A 1968 report for the NFB entitled *Fogo Island Film and Community Development Project* states that:

> In effect it can be stated that this project reflects a logical culmination in the thinking and action of the Extension Service of Memorial University at St. John's, Newfoundland, and the Challenge for Change program....
>
> By the spring of 1967 the National Film Board and Memorial University were in the preliminary stages of negotiating a three-year agreement for collaboration in pioneering a new approach to film in community development. The first stage was launched in May, 1967, on Fogo Island. (1)

Donald Snowdon, as director of the Extension Service, was the lead on this connection; Low noted in his 1972 report *The Fogo Island Communication Experiment* that "Don Snowden of Memorial who had taken me to Fogo Island helped me understand some of the basic philosophy of community development" (2). But for Low and the Fogo project, Fred Earle, which the film *Introduction to Fogo Island* identifies as one of the Extension Service's community development officers, was the real insider. The opening voice-over of *Introduction to Fogo Island* states that Earle "was born and raised on Fogo Island. He knows, and is known, by all its people." The voice-over goes on to say that "we, as outsiders, felt that we could never go into such a community without the help of such a person." But Low's *The Fogo Island Communication Experiment* report is blunter (and this is characteristic of his writing inside and outside the NFB, both in English and in French): "I went to Fogo Island mainly because I was impressed by Fred Earle. I had an idea that if nothing more happened I could make a film about a fine community development worker who would help justify our involvement" (2). Earle is ever-present in these films, acting as a sort of Virgil to Low's Dante. It is his life (and his life's work) that makes it possible for Low and his collaborators to aspire towards a cinéma vécu.

The Fogo Process

These films were made with a very small crew, emphasizing flexibility and the unobtrusive integration of the filmmakers into the community. The 1968 NFB report *Fogo Island Film and Community Development Project* recalls that "after initial research in May [1967, Low] went to Fogo Island in late June to acquaint himself with the Island and at the same time to find subjects to be filmed. Only on August 1st, were a camera man, soundman, and assistant camera man assigned to Fogo Island. They filmed continuously for five weeks, accumulating over twenty hours of material" (5). D. B. Jones, in his history of the NFB, *Movies and Memoranda*, points out that "the shooting ratio of 4:1 was quite low for documentary" (162).

But the best-remembered element of the Newfoundland Project was its use of "feedback," the insistence on the part of the filmmakers that the islanders be shown raw footage and be given input into the final shape of the films. The opening voice-over of *Introduction to Fogo Island* states that "Challenge for Change is an experiment in the role of communications in social change. As part of this experiment, we filmed local people talking about the problems of a changing community, and played back these films in that community." In his 1972 *Fogo Island Communication Experiment* report, Low identified the use of "playback" and "communication loops between the community and government via film" as the two unique aspects of the project (1). Low, in his untitled 1968 report, states that "individuals must know that they could if they chose impose censorship on their material prior to its exhibition. Film would always be screened in advance for those people that are uncertain about their statements or their appearance during the filming" (3). Snowden's 1968 report to the U.S. Office of Economic Development (entitled *Film and Community Development*) makes the circular nature of the "feedback" more explicit. He has fifteen points that describe "The Newfoundland Experiment," and numbers four through nine are particularly illustrative of the core elements of the "Fogo Process":

4. People filmed are promised they will have first rights to edit for content, and this promise is kept.
5. After processing and editing for technical reasons, film is returned to the area as quickly as possible.
6. Local screenings are arranged—well advertised—in places convenient to the area's deprived people.
7. Screenings are arranged for the area's "power" people—whose planning, policies, or neglect affects the lives of the people already on film. The community

workers and film makers involved in the project must be available at screenings to explain, substantiate, reassure, suggest. "Power" people are not only those whose role is recognized as such, but those whose interest, time and help can be marshalled to alleviate the conditions of poverty, but who are not themselves poor.

8. Filmed responses may be made from the "power" people and attached to pertinent reels. Or the "power" people may choose to answer directly in public meetings.
9. Such filmed material is widely distributed among the area's people and may serve as an effective linkage point for mutual discussion and action, where this does not already exist. If possible, there should be participation at all screenings by community development workers, social and behavioural scientists, and the film maker. (6–7)

Low, in his *Fogo Island Communication Experiment* report, sums the process up similarly:

> In all, we filmed about twenty hours of material. Back in Montreal, we edited to six hours of cutting copy blocks on various themes, subjects, or personalities.... Three months after filming, we returned to the Island for playback of material. This was done in a different village every night for about a month and a half. Screenings usually included a general discussion. Fred Earle and Bill Nemtin of our NFB distribution staff were usually involved.... I have never been to more exciting film screenings. The appreciation was extensive, the discussions animated. We invited people to help edit the material, remove sections or add to it. In six hours of material, three minutes were removed because they were considered "unfair." (2–3)[5]

Appendix B of the *Fogo Island and Community Development Project* report lists each of these screenings and gives attendance figures. They were held from 22 November 1967 to 29 January 1968. There were thirty-nine screenings altogether, some with as many as three hundred people, and all with at least thirty.

This sort of filmmaking has strong Francophone roots. Pageau specifically mentions (in his 2006 article) how Jacques Leduc and François Dansereau had "fait du cinéma d'intervention sociale" (262). Low also told Pageau (in an interview as part of that same article) that "'it's Raymond Garceau who inspired us with his work in the Gaspé' ... referring to the making of twenty-six films as part of the ARDA (Rural and Agricultural Development) series."[6] This series was part of a modernization program sponsored by the federal government, one that sought to aid the development of a geographically marginal, maritime region; its connections to Fogo, then, are clear in terms of sociopolitics. But there are also strong connections cinematically. One film in the series, *L'Inventaire d'une colonie* (1964), serves as a sort of "résumé film" in the same way that *Introduction to Fogo Island* does; one very long take shot out of the window of a car slowly driving along the snow-covered dirt road of St-Octave looks almost exactly like the opening shots of *Introduction to Fogo Island*, which are shot out of a car as it ambles along Fogo's dirt road. *L'Inventaire d'une colonie*, like most of the films in the ARDA series, is also similar to the Fogo films in its use of "talking-head" interviews that engage with a wide variety of issues. Moreover, those issues are also close to those explored in the Fogo films, including such topics as the formation of co-operatives (one animated entry in the series, *L'Aménagement régional*, explicitly proposes that one way forward is to "consolider les coopératives"), the problems of welfare dependency, and the out-migration of young people (which is the central concern of an ARDA film called *Les Jeunes*). These Garceau films have occasional lyrical moments (such as the down-the-snowy-road travelling shot) but are for the most part drier in form than the Fogo films. Thus, it is hard to put Perrault aside when considering influences. In some ways, then, the Fogo films come up the middle between the poetic but still politicized sensibility of Perrault and the detail-oriented but still photographic sensibility of Garceau.

In terms of this sort of subject feedback, though, the clearest precursor is Jean Rouch's previously mentioned *Chronique d'un été* (1961). That film—made by a celebrated French ethnographic filmmaker who was encouraged by his friend Edgar Morin to examine his own "tribe," Parisians—concluded with the subjects of the film watching the rushes of their interviews and responding to them in the screening room. *Chronique d'un été* was photographed in part by a young Michel Brault, who would two years later co-direct, with Perrault, *Pour la suite du monde*, a film that has a strongly Rouchian sensibility.[7] And when I read this exchange between Perrault and Bonneville in their 1971 interview, I cannot help but think of the Fogo films:

> BONNEVILLE: Thus the film is also concerned with social contact.
>
> PERRAULT: We shouldn't leave it at that. We should say something else. I don't seek to make a point. I'm not a politician. But a lot of people have abused Île-aux-Coudres. We've been inconsiderate. We've neglected a great force.[8]

I discussed in the last chapter the way in which Perrault's films have been read (especially in France) as very political; that sense of politics, of *combat*, as Jean-Louis Comolli put it, is a crucial part of his films and a big part of what connects him to the other figures in this book. But it is also clear that Low has a much more concrete sense of himself as a political actor, as we can see from the very fact that he chose Fogo because the political and governmental situation was in flux. Nevertheless, like Perrault, and like Rouch, Low was interested in cinema because it allowed for social contact, for greater communication, and ultimately for a greater sense of community between people, in addition to *combat*. Like Perrault, Low saw that people in power had neglected and abused this island ("they were criminal in their indifference to people and were an example of political porkbarrelling I could not believe" he told D. B. Jones about Newfoundland politicians' previous attempts to resettle small communities [162]).

Gary Evans recounts how "Low's method became the model for most of the future Challenge for Change films" (164), and indeed this use of "feedback," this sense of film as a "social contact," is central to the philosophy of the program. Low was at pains in his 1972 *Fogo Island Communication Experiment* report to distinguish this sort of connection with groups of people, a connection made in the public sphere and with an aspiration for social change, from mere attention to liability considerations, writing that "there have been situations where film has been played back to subjects before the completion of a film in order to obtain permission to use the material. But never before had such a systematic effort been made to involve a complete community" (1). In his untitled 1968 report he wrote that these advance screenings "would contribute to the establishment of the confidence that is necessary for this kind of work" (3). This kind of confidence between subjects and filmmakers, and the freedom and agency that it can lead to, was the something which was lost when technology shifted again and the Challenge for Change program turned to small camcorders (then known as VTR technology, for Video Tape Recording). Indeed, Marchessault's critique of this later, video-based period of Challenge for Change is that "the interactivity and participation that video delivered instituted access without agency. It instituted a particular form of self-surveillance rather than transforming the actual institutional relations of production and knowledge" (141). In these Fogo films, access was less important than agency. And this really is the nub of the problem as far as how these films have been remembered.

Access or Aesthetics?

The aspect of this historical memory that seems to me the most problematic is that the Fogo films, like the work associated with Challenge for Change in general, have been discussed by historians and filmmakers alike purely in terms of process and not as a group of films. Marchessault writes of the video revolution of the 1970s that this electronic medium "redefined the film director's role. No longer an authorial agent, the director became a social animator whose chief function was to provide technical training to select communities" (139). But even in the celluloid era of the late 1960s, this writing was on the wall, as can be seen in the way in which the NFB and those involved in the Fogo films represented their work, and in turn by the way in which historians analyze the period, sometimes quite harshly.

Those attached to the Fogo films almost always insist that these films are about social change rather than about filmmaking. The 1972 booklet *Fogo Process in Communication* (published by Memorial University of Newfoundland [MUN]'s Extension Services) states simply that "it is crucially important to appreciate that the films are subsidiary to the purpose they serve and that the process deals with community action rather than film making" (8). In case there's even the slightest doubt about the utilitarian approach here, the booklet also states that "in this process, film is quite simply a tool, a means to an end and part of a total approach" (8). A booklet by Sandra Gwyn, ostensibly meant to document a workshop on the Fogo films (both the booklet and the workshop were entitled *Cinema as Catalyst*) states that "far more important than the films themselves, was the process of making them. More important still was the process of screening them, a month or so later, for the people of Fogo" (5). Even though Gwyn, in a rare cinephile lapse, writes that Low "became the D. W. Griffith of the Fogo Process" (5), cinematic considerations are basically absent from the internally generated discussion. Even Low himself seems to disown his non-narrative, poetic documentary roots, so celebrated in films like *Corral* (1954), *Universe* (1960), *Circle of the Sun* (1960), or the *Labyrinth* project (1967/79); Gwyn quotes him as saying, "I'd always been more interested in using [film] for poetic document. But in Newfoundland I discovered something very different" (5). Echoing this in a 1996 French-language anthology on documentary (*Le documentaire: Contestation et propagande*), Low writes in the section of his essay devoted to the Fogo project that "the 'artist' filmmaker and the 'social animator' filmmaker are two different people."[9]

Historians of the period have followed suit. As Thomas Waugh, summing up the frustrating nature of this discourse, writes, "There is a received wisdom that has accumulated over the years both in [Film Studies] and in the corridors of the NFB itself, that yes Challenge for Change / Société Nouvelle was indeed an interesting experiment, vindicated by its offshoots Studio D and Vidéographe, but practically flawed as well as ideologically and theoretically naive, and moreover no great shakes cinematically speaking" (11). Jones's assessment bears this out: "The Fogo *process* became more widely known than the films themselves," he wrote in his NFB history (164). And he deemed even this aspect of the Fogo project specifically something of a failure, writing that "the project was not a cost-effective model. Traditionally, films have seemed to make economic sense when used as mass communication.... And though the twenty-three films were produced at a cost comparable to what the Film Board spends on a typical one-hour television documentary, the amount of money represented no trifle and the audience differential was quite large" (164).

This consensus is further emphasized in the arguments about how the Fogo work should be distributed; nobody seemed to think that these films had any hope for wide distribution, any hope of being interesting to anyone not invested in these specific political situations. As Gary Evans writes, "The films were supposed to be a series of modules with relevance to Fogo Island and Newfoundland, but not much to the rest of the country" (164). Jones writes that "twenty-three films useful mainly to a small community of five thousand people constituted very expensive social change" (164). Fair play to these historians; they are only following the way in which the distribution was constructed by the filmmakers and administrators themselves. An NFB "Request for Funds" document dated 31 March 1968 (in which the question "The Production work covered by these finds has already been initiated" is answered in the affirmative and reference is made to "26 films varying from 1 to 3" reels and thus would seem to be for the core Fogo films) states, "The completed films will hopefully fill regional needs and will be released almost entirely for local distribution." An NFB internal memo from Bill Nemtin to "Distribution Representatives in field and H.Q." dated 3 October 1968 states that "when the Fogo material was being made we did not envisage that it would be distributed beyond that community," and explains that, rather than the film having relevance for areas other than Fogo, "More likely is the use of the films as examples of the Fogo Island process." Snowden writes in his 1968 report *Film and Community Development* that "some film which is very effective in the region has very little value for a broader distribution simply because it might be boring to a wider audience. Cinematic values and showmanship enter into a broader use of materials" (10). Barry de Ville's 1972 report called *Distributive Targets for the Fogo Island Films* holds out some hope for the wide distribution of Roger Hart's 1972 retrospective look at the project, *Memo from Fogo* (the report suggests it be shown on TV), but states that "such films as *Songs of Billy Cobb* [he means *The Songs of Chris Cobb*], *Children of Fogo*, and *When*

I Go... are obviously less comprehensive and, with the exception of *When I Go...* would suffer from relative antiquity and monochromatic listlessness in any general appeal to a potential viewing public" (2). Recounting a terrifying encounter at a seminar being given by John Grierson, Low recalls His Grey Eminence's response to watching one of the Fogo films, *Billy Crane Moves Away*:

> "What," Dr. Grierson wanted to know, "was the value of the film off Fogo Island? Was it good for television? Mass media? What did it say to Canada?" I was deflated. "What did it say to the world?"
>
> I had to admit that the film wasn't worth much outside the context of the situation—outside the mainland of Newfoundland. Billy Crane's accent was hard to understand. It had some specialized value in Ottawa, but it did not say much to farmers in Alberta, except that centralization and central decisions of government are not always right. ("Grierson and Challenge for Change" 114)

The only respites from this consensus regarding the films' utter parochialism, irrelevance, and, *in the NFB's own words,* "monochromatic listlessness," come from surprising places. One dissenting view on the aesthetics of the films comes from Snowden himself. Comparing the core Fogo films with the videos made on Fogo Island by Memorial's NFB-trained film unit (on which more shortly), Stephen Crocker recalls that "Snowden has described these projects as more 'information oriented' than the Fogo films which he characterized as 'impressionistic' and aesthetic in orientation, probably as a result of Colin Low's professional filmic interest" (134). Crocker also acknowledges the aesthetic quality of some of this material: "In addition to films that dealt with difficult social problems, there were also more lyrical films such as: *The Songs of Chris Cobb, Jim Decker's Party,* and *The Children of Fogo*" (127). Just to see the word "lyrical" in the discussion of the Fogo films feels like a revelation. Dissent regarding the irrelevance of the films to outsiders comes from the islanders themselves. In his untitled 1968 report, Low recalls that "during the filming, Fogo people everywhere asked me if their statements were going to be run off the Island. Many people were concerned that the statements receive a broad distribution" (8). In his *Fogo Island Communication Experiment* report, he recounts how, during the discussions in the villages that were so central to the "Fogo Process," "people continuously asked us to run the film off the Island—particularly to government" (3).

The sense that these films are purely instrumental with nothing to say to non-Newfoundlanders is a historical error of significant proportions. As Marchessault documents so vividly in her analysis of the Portapak era of Challenge for Change, access by no means equates to democratic action, *particularly* when we are talking about access to mass media. And anyway, access as such wasn't even the goal here. Grierson famously dismissed Challenge for Change as "eight millimetre films for eight millimetre minds" (quoted in Jones 159), presumably because he assumed that it would involve training people to use consumer-grade film equipment without much sophistication. As Low recalls in the epigraph of this chapter, training people to make their own films, training them to replace the artists of the NFB, was, for Grierson, carrying things too far. Jones (a diehard Griersonian in many ways) sees it as a betrayal of the NFB overall: "The shift in authority from filmmakers to 'the people' had aesthetic implications as well, not just for the program but for the whole Film Board" (168). But it is essential to understand that, at least when we are talking about the NFB's Newfoundland Project, this is not at all what happened. The program was not originally a media training program, along the lines either of the Portapak projects of the 1970s or the Super 8 projects launched in the high Arctic.[10] For these first Fogo films, *filmmakers* shot the footage, mixed the sound, and so on. Indeed, a 1974 report for UNESCO, prepared by H. Anthony Williamson (at that time head of community development for MUN's Extension Service) states clearly that "the actual filmmaking was in the hands of professionals" (2). These professionals were not simply there to show islanders how to turn on a camera. In this way, the introduction to Gwyn's *Cinema as Catalyst* is quite misleading as far as the Newfoundland Project goes, even if it does seem to confirm Grierson's worst fears about Challenge for Change overall. Claiming that film equipment was far too complex for most people to operate, Gwyn writes that "the arrival of cheaper and simpler equipment ... means that anyone can learn to be an operator in an hour.... Instead of writing a report explaining how Mrs. Snook got the road fixed, Tom O'Keefe can flick a switch and let Mrs. Snook tell about it herself" (1). Low, in the same essay where he distinguishes between "le cinéaste 'artiste' et le cinéaste 'animateur social'" implicitly acknowledges this. He writes of the islanders that "the people proved themselves very friendly, but modest regarding their capacity to contribute to the film."[11] Islanders were collaborating closely with filmmakers, but they were surely not *replacing* them. Low and his team brought a skill set quite a bit more complex than the ability to turn a camera to the "on" position.

Indeed, nothing will clarify this more quickly than a look at the films made by the Extension Service after the NFB had left. The booklet *Fogo Process in Communication* relates that "following the filming of Fogo, the National Film Board, at their Montreal headquarters, undertook the training of a Newfoundland crew to be attached the Extension Services Community Development

Division as a permanent film unit" (9). An untitled report for MUN's Extension Service, dated 6 January 1970, opens by saying, "Since April 1968, the National Film Board has trained five members of the [Extension Service's] Film Unit, processed film footage shot by us, transferred our sound, cut our negatives when requested to do so, and have made reversal prints of most of our footage. From time to time, the Board has advised us of specific technical problems and has provided further individual training on request" (1). Both that report and the *Fogo Process* booklet detail film projects undertaken by the Extension Service in Port-aux-Choix and on the Labrador coast, and projects on successful co-operatives in Prince Edward Island and British Columbia. The Port-aux-Choix films focused on two important figures: postmistress Olga Spence and the local priest, Father McGrath. *Olga Spence: Past, Present and Future* (1969)—which was one of two films the service made about Spence—is really just a talking-head documentary; although its opening images are of a snowy townscape, the rest of the film is entirely devoted to close-ups and medium shots of Olga Spence reminiscing about how life in Port-aux-Choix used to be and how difficult life is today. The composition here is awkward—the camera is set lower than it needs to be, and there is thus quite a bit of "dead space" in the upper half of the frame. There are also many needless zooms in and out on Spence. A similar, although much more intense, visual illiteracy defines the Father McGrath films, *Organizing Youth* (1968) and *Father McGrath and Students* (1969). *Organizing Youth*, which documents a discussion among McGrath and three teens, substitutes very jerky pans for sudden zooms and always puts its figures at the very edges of the frame, leaving enormous "dead space" in between. The compositions of *Father McGrath and Students* have to be seen to be believed; the camera is set too low, Olga-Spence style, and thus there is a plethora of dead space above, and while the figures are again on the very edges of the frame, this time there is incredibly loud and distracting floral wallpaper between them. Visual problems aside, these films also display no sense of concise organization. To be sure they were, in Snowden's words, more "information-oriented"—to a fault, I would argue. All three of these films are hopelessly bogged down by tiny details: the most minute aspects of welfare administration in the Olga Spence film, an argument about whether to pay a visiting band $60 or $90 that truly seems to go on forever in *Organizing Youth*, and an equally interminable argument about whether to exclude non-students from dances in *Father McGrath and Students*. These films evince the qualities of woodenness and parochialism that the NFB assumes that the Fogo films embody; it is *these* films that would have next to no interest outside their communities. But these films also make very clear the degree to which NFB filmmakers were bringing their signature visual and organizational skills to bear upon the material that that they recorded. These Extension Service films make it clear that the NFB filmmakers were not merely recording events as they found them, and they also make it clear that Low's mode here was far from purely instrumentalist.

Fogo and 1960s Canadian Nationalism

A purely instrumentalist understanding of the NFB's Fogo films is not only a matter of getting the aesthetics wrong, however; it also gets the politics of the films wrong. No film in the series illustrates this more vividly than the series' final, "résumé" film, *Winds of Fogo* (1969).

This is the only one of the Fogo films that is shot in colour, and it is one of the most poetic, and indeed the most visually oriented, pieces in the series. The original "Request for Funds" document proposing the film (then to be called *Journey to the Funks*) even has "General" written on the "Intended Audience" line, which is noteworthy in the context of the internal NFB understanding of the Fogo films. This is on one level an evocation of the life of William Wells (who is at the centre of *William Wells Talks about the Island*, where we mostly see him talking as he putters around his shed). *Winds of Fogo* spends time with Wells and his sons out on the sea. One of the most startling of these sea-bound sequences is an extreme long shot (which seems to be shot from another boat) of his boys undertaking a very dangerous disembarkation from a small boat onto the Grand Funk. There is also some mesmerizing footage of the boys working on the deck of the fishing boat as it rocks back and forth in the slightly choppy seas. The next sequence is a series of highly composed images of the boys building a boat in their garage (sequences that also feature a very sophisticated combination of synch, non-synch, and semi-synch sound). The film is also peppered with images of the waves crashing against shore near Wells's home, whose interiors Low also shows us (often in the form of images of quotidian objects such as sewing machines and fishbowls, bathed in soft light).

But the crowning sequence of the film comes at the end, which features images of kids flying kites as adults look on. One kite is made from a Canadian flag, at that time not quite three years old (having been approved by Parliament in 1964, it was officially ratified by the Queen in February 1965). Images where the kite shoots up through the air and then slowly rambles downward are graceful and kinetic, like so much in the film. Low has the younger Billy Wells say in the voice-over narration to this scene, "I like to make believe[12] …

teach my father ... you know ... wonderful flag. Oh-h-h...! *don't like the look of it, do you*? Not that he don't like the look of it, but he just don't like the flag. Oh, he still likes the Union Jack. All the old people are like that." Over a slow zoom out on the airborne Canadian flag, we hear the elder Wells say on voice-over, "I'd rather see the Union Jack. More colour. There's no blue." The younger Wells protests, "The sky is blue!" and his father responds, "Red White and Blue; I'll ever be true."

The politics here, obviously, are complex. The maple leaf flag which Low shows literally flying over Fogo replaced the Red Ensign, and that replacement spoke to an emerging post-British consciousness throughout English Canada (it is not clear if the elder Wells is talking about the Newfoundland or the Canadian variant of the Red Ensign or about the Union Jack itself). But the emergence of such an identity has special complexity in Newfoundland, whose historical ties to Britain are so different from the rest of Canada's. The province, after all, had joined Canada only in 1949, as the result of a referendum as divisive in its day as the more recent referenda on Quebec separatism. And yet, its ties to Britain had been the source of considerable strife, given the degree to which the pre-Confederation Newfoundland government had been both neglected and micromanaged by a distant London.[13] Thus, it is not entirely surprising that one of the last images of the film is the elder William Wells raising the Canadian flag on his fishing boat as he and his sons set out for the day. The message there seems clear: the new and modernity-oriented Canadian nationalism is the reality of present-day Newfoundland, even if it remains important to acknowledge that there is a different historical memory still alive on the island.

The fact that this historical memory is being evoked by the subjects of the film, subjects who are always speaking Newfoundland English, is also an important part of *Winds of Fogo* (and indeed of all the Fogo Island films). The film was released in 1969, when linguistic work around Newfoundland English was really starting to pick up speed. As G. M. Story and W. Kirwin recall, "By the early 1960s, G. M. Story, W. Kirwin and J. D. A. Widdowson were all three writing and publishing papers on Newfoundland speech more or less independently of one another.... In 1968 we agreed to join our forces and proceeded to draw up detailed proposals for the dictionary itself" ("Progress and Promise," 16). They also recall how they finally sent the work to press in 1982. It is an interesting piece of work, in that it is very invested in the idea of Newfoundland as a distinct Canadian society made up of a compound of elements, not simply some western version of Ireland. They state in the introduction that "much closer to the problem [of overlap of vocabulary between English-speaking communities] is the formulation by the editors of the *Dictionary of Canadianisms on Historical Principles* who define a 'Canadianism' as 'a word, expression, or meaning which is native to Canada or which is distinctively characteristic'" (xi). They also state that "there are occasional documentary references to monolingual and bilingual Irish-speaking fishermen working and settling in the island in the early years, but Irish seems never to have been established in Newfoundland and has had little influence on Newfoundland English independent of the development of Anglo-Irish parts of Ireland itself" (xv). So while they define Newfoundland as "one of the oldest overseas communities of the English speaking world" (xi), they are presenting it as part of Canada (and thus the dictionary is in essence documenting Canadianisms, not corrupted or anglicized Irish Gaelic).

This desire to balance difference and national cohesion, so clearly the subtext of this sequence of *Winds of Fogo* and so present in the work of this period around Newfoundland English, is absolutely of a piece with the ideology of Trudeau-era multiculturalism, a multiculturalism that emerged in no small part as a response to Quebec separatism, a much more threatening phenomenon for Canadian elites than lingering fondness for the Union Jack on Newfoundland. And Challenge for Change, with its desire to regionalize and to build stronger communities, and with its ability to work together with a French-language partner (the Francophone counterpart of the program, set up in 1969, was called Société Nouvelle), is classic Trudueau-era. Indeed, as Marchessault writes:

> It is well known that Trudeau's bicultural and multicultural policies were implemented to dissipate the burgeoning forces of the separatist movement in Quebec as well as the increasing demands of Canada's diverse ethnic and native communities. It is easy to see how Challenge for Change is entangled in that web of coercion and consent, technologies of domination and technologies of the self, which define the functioning of power in a liberal democratic state. (143)

No wonder, then, that the flagship program of Challenge for Change went to a place where a sense of nationalism was present but the Quebec separatist movement was strongly disliked. G. A. Rawlyk writes that most Newfoundland newspapers argued in 1967 that "Quebec nationalism threatened the very basis of Newfoundland's attachment to the federal state—the ability of Ottawa to redistribute the nation's wealth in the interest of its less fortunate parts. This, after all, the argument went on, was what Confederation was all about" (286).

For Newfoundlanders, it was not about accepting assimilation or absorption into a unified Canadian identity. This pragmatic approach to being part of Canada, so devoid of the sentimental patriotism that Quebec nationalists were reacting against, must have seemed, at the time, a perfect foil for separatism, a perfect way to dissipate that burgeoning force without having to oppose that movement's most emotionally affecting arguments about community or collective belonging.

This kite-flying sequence in *Winds of Fogo* is to my mind the most explicit example of an entanglement between coercion and consent to be found anywhere in the series, the clearest example of the way that the series takes Trudeau-era Canadian nationalism into a setting clearly inflected by the political discourse of Newfoundland. It acknowledges Newfoundland's status as a "distinct society" (I can feel the shudder of anxiety washing over the reader with the mere invocation of that term) not only by lingering on traditions of fishing and boat building, not only by extensive, cinéma-de-la-parole-style use of images of people speaking Newfoundland English, but also by focusing on *national* differences and on lingering connections to a different nation-state. And yet, these conflicts are resolved. The recently adopted symbol of Canadian modernity *does* fly over William Wells's fishing boat. Low shows that Newfoundlanders were, in the words of Raymond Blake's book about Newfoundland's integration into Confederation, Canadians at last. More importantly, there is no anger about the results of the 1949 referendum expressed in any of the Fogo films. In *Winds of Fogo* we see that differences, while not erased, are smoothed over as part of the work of a multicultural nation-state that recognizes how it has failed people materially but that clearly wants to do better.

This is quite consistent with the way that historians have explained Newfoundland's adjustment to Confederation. Rawlyk writes that, in 1967, "eighteen years as a Canadian province had not undermined the strong Newfoundland sense of community and close identification with the local perspective. Nor had it forged any strong emotional link with the rest of Canada" (282). But he also writes that, because standards of living had changed so much during this brief period, "in 1967, most Newfoundlanders wanted Ottawa to become even more powerful, and decried anything which threatened the federal power" (285). Raymond Blake recounts that, in the immediate post-1949 period, as Confederation came to be seen by most Newfoundlanders as a fact of life, "those who had demanded a return to self-government and fought against union quickly dropped their struggle and threw their support behind the union.... In their first electoral campaign, they promised to negotiate better terms with Ottawa rather than undo the union" (183). This combination of nationalism (really, of the "nationalized locality" Hilmes linked to radio) and federalism is one of the defining characteristics of the Newfoundland of Low's films. Fogo is shown here to be a distinct society and yet one that is now fully of a piece with Canada as a whole. The paradox of the cultural mosaic, the community of communities, seems resolved. *Winds of Fogo*'s optimistic Canadianism is a good example of what Blake argues was the perception of the inclusion of Newfoundland across Canada: "Confederation was an expression of a new mood felt throughout Canada.... Canadians expected a good life and welcomed the coming of the welfare state. Union with Newfoundland must be seen as an expression of this new-found confidence and ambition" (177–78), a confidence and ambition that would, in the 1960s, find expression in such things as a revitalized set of national symbols, such as the maple leaf and, a little later, a national anthem that made no reference to the monarchy.

Indeed, the ideology of *Winds of Fogo* is very close to the other film that Pierre Perrault co-directed with Michel Brault, *L'Acadie, l'Acadie?!?* (1971). The key moment in that film is when the group of Acadian students protesting the underfunding of the Université de Moncton crash a meeting of the Loyalist Society and sing, en masse, the French verse of *O Canada* (they are booed). Like the maple leaf flag in 1967, *O Canada* was in 1971 a symbol of a changing Canadian nationalism (it was at the time only an unofficial national anthem; *God Save the Queen* was the official anthem until 1980). This is a moment of the assertion of difference (Acadian solidarity, French lyrics in a sea of Anglophiles), but it is one that can be safely contained within the liberal multicultural Canadian state that was then emergent. *L'Acadie, l'Acadie?!?*, unlike *Winds of Fogo*, does include moments where participants express anger at the fate of a distinct North Atlantic society now incorporated into Canada. But most of the students in *L'Acadie, l'Acadie ?!?*, as the singing of *O Canada* suggests, are staunch federalists; the young separatist in the group is from Quebec, and Brault and Perrault show him to be a grouchy young idealist (Brault zooms in on him sitting and staring at the floor when the students rise for *O Canada*). This is the assessment of Quebec separatism that Rawlyk argues was the majority position in 1967 Newfoundland. Surveying the newspapers of that period, Rawlyk writes simply that "any empathy for Quebec's cultural and linguistic aims, in spite of perceived similarities in the emotional content of nationalist sentiments, was singularly lacking in Newofundland" (286). We can see that in *Winds of Fogo* very clearly; we can see it in *L'Acadie, l'Acadie ?!?* as well.

Rather than the populism or individualist empowerment that critics of Challenge for Change seemed to have feared, the politics of the series, as borne out so clearly by *Winds of Fogo*, are quite state-ist. This is in no way contradictory to its populist or empowerment-based mechanisms. "Low's notion of subject participation paralleled the liberal interpretation of cultural development," Marchessault writes, "and would play an essential role in the state promotion of community culture in Canada" (135). That *Winds of Fogo* walks this ideological tightrope so central to Canadian liberalism through the language of sound and image (the kite, the use of voice-over, the use of the Newfoundland-accented voice, the images of the otherworldly landscape of the Grand Funk) is entirely consistent with the way that all the Fogo films emphasize *both* the political and the visual, *both* communication and aesthetics, and refuse to sacrifice one for the other.

Readings

This is borne out simply by *looking* at the films, by trying to make sense of their visual language. This sounds obvious, banal. Alas, it is not. Arguing for the fundamental complexity of the Challenge for Change films, Waugh writes that he wants to "demonstrate the indispensable role of textual study in this process, of actually looking at the films and the videos" (9). He is almost alone in calling for such textual study. Indeed, he is very much opposed to scholars such as Jones, who writes, "The craft of filmmaking, developed laboriously over three decades at the Board, began to lose currency.... Challenge for Change, which sprang in part as a recoil from the aesthetics of self-expression, got rid of aesthetics, but not the self-expression" (168). I want to answer Waugh's call, and show that the Fogo films in no way got rid of aesthetics. Rather, these films made a significant contribution to political documentary filmmaking in Canada, as is borne out particularly well by several key Fogo films. They are excellent examples of the craft of filmmaking that had indeed been developed so laboriously at the NFB over so many years.

One crucial element of these films is their "vertical" structure, a concept that Low used to distinguish them from conventional documentary. The 1968 report *Fogo Island Film and Community Development Project* emphasizes the centrality of this, stating that "the major decision in editing was to cut the material vertically rather than horizontally. In other words, the films were based on personalities discussing a variety of issues, rather than an issue incorporating a variety of personalities" (8). Jones, drawing on an interview with Low, describes the approach in this way:

> The traditional documentary structure was, in Low's word, "horizontal," moving from one scene to another, cross-cutting between different points of view. Invariably, no matter how conscientiously the filmmaker tried to present a balanced, objective picture, the editing would introduce an element of bias. Any scene would invariably seem to be a comment on the one that preceded it. The "vertical" approach of expressing each point of view in a film of its own alleviated this problem. (162)

My interest here isn't in how the "vertical" approach alleviated the problem of bias. I don't accept that, and frankly neither does Low, who (some years before making the Fogo films) told Lefebvre, "It is in effect impossible to remain perfectly objective whatever the subject; you are always adding a personal point of view, and if it's not at the filming stage, then it's at the editing stage."[14] I understand how Low was trying to cut down on montage in the Fogo films and avoid crosscutting between views on specific issues. But as Low knows full well and clearly states to Lefebvre, point of view, editing, and any of the literally countless decisions that *every* filmmaker inevitably makes always lead to some sort of distortion, some sort of "point de vue personnel." It is somewhat disappointing to see him assuming a stance so much more naive than the one that he seemed so comfortable and confident with a few years earlier. All that said, this vertical or non-linear form really did represent an innovation in documentary structure. The Fogo films are unusual in the way that they simultaneously cohere and fragment, in the degree to which they are simultaneously linear and episodic.

The film *Introduction to Fogo Island* illustrates this structure vividly. The film begins didactically, with images of Fogo and a voice-over narration that introduces Fred Earle and explains the basics of the Fogo process. Even though the traditional documentary voice-over is present throughout the film, the film's imagery does not simply illustrate the soundtrack. Instead, there are a number of images that recur throughout the series. As the voice-over discusses how social and religious divisions persist, we see images from *A Wedding and a Party*, a 10-minute portrait that is part of the series. The aerial images that follow this recur in the film *Children of Fogo Island*. The sequence that follows uses footage that reappears in *Dan Roberts on Fishing*. Sequences that shortly follow those again use images from *A Wedding and a Party*. The film, then, is less of an introduction to the island—although in a way it is that—than it is an introduction to the *series*. The voice-over talks about the topics that will recur again and again: the divided school boards, the need to get a co-op started, the dependency of people on welfare payments, and so on. The imagery is also very heavy on material that we will literally see again and again. I would suggest, then, that rather than a "vertical" structure, the series has a circular structure, with *Introduction to Fogo Island* serving as the hub. A rough sense of chronological order can be established, since in some films—*The Merchant and the Teacher, Citizen Discussions, Jim Decker Builds a Longliner, Two Cabinet Ministers, The Fogo Island Improvement Committee*—there is discussion of the struggle to establish a co-operative, something we see actually happen in the film *The Founding of the Co-operatives*, which is basically a record of the meeting that sets up these co-ops (although even in this fairly dry film, there is a very lyrical opening sequence of men dry-docking boats, one that recalls the opening sequence of *Pour la suite du monde*). In this way, then, *The Founding of the Co-operatives* could be said to come "after" these other films. But other than this, these films are as completely independent from one another (you don't need to see any of them to understand any of the others) as they are interconnected (together they form a detailed portrait of the island, its landscape, its language, its economy, and its politics).

This non-linear structure even brings the films out of the realm of non-narrative cinema and seems closer to a medium like television (although I will argue at the end of this chapter that we are actually being brought closer to radio). Small wonder that the emphasis of the Challenge for Change project shifted to video and then community television in the 1970s; that form already seemed visible in the structure of this flagship project. Small wonder also, then, that the Newfoundland Project's greatest influence was felt in community TV circles. Crocker's discussion of the Fogo process takes its televisual quality for granted; it opens by saying that once the NFB and MUN had done their work, "this locally produced *televisual* image would then become a medium for communication with distant decision makers, such as governments and financial institutions. The Fogo Process … created a very effective *televisual* public space for addressing social and political concerns" (123, emphases mine). This was the influence that it had in Ireland; the community video experiments of the 1970s (the subject of chapter 5) that led eventually to the establishment of a TV station in Irish Gaelic (via a series of pirate TV broadcasts in Irish Gaelic, the subject of chapter 6) were strongly influenced by Challenge for Change. This televisual sensibility was also the reason for its influence in the United States. When Low and Snowden went to Farmersville, California, to act as consultants on the "War on Poverty," their efforts were written up in the *Washington Post*. There Michael Kernan quotes Herbert Kramer, public affairs director for the Office of Economic Opportunity, by way of explaining the Fogo Process: "Kramer said it 'doesn't have the drawbacks of Whitey's TV station.' It cannot be compared to the 'lily-white' TV man who goes into a ghetto for a documentary that may be effective or less than effective because the TV man may not know what it is like to be poor or black or uneducated" (4). Internationally, as domestically, the series tends to be remembered for procedural rather than cinematic reasons (the *Post* even uses the Billy Crane film to illustrate this, although it at least mentions some photographic consideration via the use of light: "The camera acts like a neighbor, looking at Billy while he talks, watching him coil some line and putter around his boat, but mostly just focusing on his rugged face in the gray Newfoundland light"). And internationally, as domestically, these procedures seemed to lend themselves to analogies with the less linear, more open-ended format of television.

But this is a different kind of television, one with a more complex sound-image relationship, for instance, than what one would expect from TV news. Even though *Introduction to Fogo Island*, for example, serves as something of a didactic hub for the series, the connection between sound and image is far from straightforward. Many times in the film there is a conflict between the two that approaches the dialectical. One of the most highly composed of these is a zoom in to a very tight close-up of a bride, who is wearing an elaborate veil; the narration over this image says, "In its problems of isolation, Fogo is a microcosm of all of Newfoundland, and perhaps of other encapsulated communities that are symbolic islands." This is, of course, not an image of isolation at all, but of intimacy. As the camera gently moves to reframe the image to include the groom, the voice-over says, "But Fogo is also an old community. It has been settled for almost three hundred years, and its people have a deep sense of history and tradition." Again, the wedding may be part of communal tradition on Fogo, but these are not *old* people we are seeing; their connection and the life they have yet to build together—in short, their youth—is precisely the point of this image, even though the sound is discussing something very different indeed. And the next sequence, which is also repeated from *A Wedding and a Party*, has narration that talks about how there is no future for young people on this island set over images of the bride and groom emerging from the church; again, the sound and image are in conflict, since this is an instantly recognizable image of celebration that is set to narration that is non-celebratory, to say the least.

I'm not trying to recover this as an example of Soviet-style contrapuntal filmmaking; the sound-image relationship here is not exactly comparable to Vertov's *Энтузиазм: Симфония Донбаса* [*Enthusiasm: Symphony of the Donbas*] (1930).[15] But nor is it simply a matter of voice conventionally or even lucidly illustrating image. The voice-over narration in *Introduction to Fogo*

Island, like that of *Winds of Fogo*, exists as a kind of companion piece to the imagery; it is connected (talk of the flag when the kite is flying in *Winds of Fogo*, talk of ceremony when we see images of a wedding in *Introduction to Fogo Island*) but it is different (it is the unseen Union Jack that we are actually hearing about in *Winds*; we are hearing about old people, not young people, over the images of a wedding in *Introduction*). Rather than assuming a passive viewer, a viewer who seeks only basic information—the viewer, in short, that seems to be assumed by all of those writers who so ignore any cinematic elements of these films—these films leave some space between their constituent elements, space for viewers to make some meaning, space for viewers to do some interpretive work. There is, then, something of Peter Wollen's "first avant-garde" (which he writes "can be loosely identified with the co-op movement," as opposed to the second avant-garde of Godard or Straub-Huillet [92]) in the Fogo project. Writing of this movement's connections to Cubist painting, Wollen points to "a semiotic shift, a changed concept and practice of sign and signification, which we can now see to have been the opening up of a space, a disjunction between signifier and signified" (95). Again, I'm not trying to claim these Fogo films as works of radical, fragmented aesthetics; the co-ops that Wollen is describing are pretty different from the co-ops that we hear about in these Newfoundland films. But these films do open up the space that he is talking about, abandoning both linear (or horizontal) form and facile sound-image relations in search of something different, in search of renewed connections between filmmakers, subjects, and viewers. This ethic of a search for the new is equally visible—and I do mean *visible*—in a number of the films themselves.

This is most evident in *Children of Fogo Island*, the most explicitly "poetic" of the Fogo films. It opens with aerial images of Fogo (again, the same images as in *Introduction to Fogo Island*) and is followed by hand-held, often zoom-laden images of boys carrying the large frame of a boat up some rocks. The sound is clearly wild, but it is non-synchronous (that is, none of the boys' chatter ever connects to any one boy's moving lips). This is a good indication of the way the film moves and is organized overall; there is documentary-style footage (characterized by hand-held imagery and sharp zooms), much of which is familiar from other Fogo films (the next sequence after the boys carrying the frame is a montage of children flying kites, strongly reminiscent of *Winds of Fogo*) and a pervading sense of montage privileged over continuity. This last point is the most important. Although there are sequences that feature long takes or are edited along lines that resemble continuity cutting (we see a long shot of boys sailing toy boats, then Low cuts to a slightly different angle of a long shot of the boys at play, then a series of close-ups of the boats, then a water-level shot of boys swimming nearby), among themselves the sequences do not cohere into anything linear. Indeed, Low moves back and forth between a few sets of imagery several times—the boys carrying the frame, kids walking on stilts, kids in a rowboat towing the boat that the frame seems to have become—in addition to using sequences that depict everyday life on the island or depict its landscape. Almost all of this is set to music; there are a few sequences that have the sort of semi-synch sound I described above, but not many. Overall, the object of the film is to create associations between these discrete sets of images: kids at play, the landscape of the island, and the rhythms of life in a place where boating is a core component of the everyday. Although this imagery does adopt the visual style of cinéma vérité, that form's emphasis on synch sound is missing. But other images are highly composed; one shot has the camera slowly panning along the frame of an old boat to reveal the bay between gaps in its planks. Another shot features a boat slowly floating from screen left to screen right in the foreground with a group of people working on another boat in the background; as an example of composition-in-depth and graceful horizontal motion it recalls both Lumière Brothers *actualités* and the famous sequence on board the boat at dusk in Jean Vigo's *L'Atalante* (1934). The next sequence—a montage of houses—also features some very highly composed shots of houses in soft, magic-hour light. But even the less composed vérité-style sequences have very real power. The next sequence, for instance, features the boys working on the frame sitting on some rocks, playing the harmonica, and jigging. The camera is often zooming and shaky, but there is also a sense of real intimacy and real connection, achieved largely though close-up. This sense of connection is a big part of what makes vérité affecting, and it's no wonder that its filmmakers were so often attracted to musical performance, to a kind of kinesis that adds an extra layer of excitement to this sort of intimacy.

It's precisely this element of vérité aesthetics that *Jim Decker's Party* and *A Wedding and a Party* draw upon. These are two fairly straightforward films; they document communal events using the kind of semi-synch sound I have already described. *Jim Decker's Party* opens with a shot of Fogo's landscape at night and then shifts to images of a man and a woman dancing to an accordion that we hear but whose player we do not immediately see (this first woman we see, though, is also a central participant in the discussions of *A Woman's Place* and *Discussion on Welfare*, films that are more or less "talking-head" or discussion films). The camera is always in motion during the dance sequences, weaving in and out of dancers in a crowded living room in a way that feels almost vertiginous. Much of the work is choppy—again, many sharp zooms and shaky movements—but it is a small marvel of vérité aesthetics in terms of the motion that it captures and the intimacy to which it aspires. One shot about midway through the film is quite wonderful; the lens zooms in just slightly and the dancers are all framed in a blur of bodies in motion; as they move in and out the musicians become visible as gaps momentarily appear. There's a very similar sense of energy and intimacy in *A Wedding and a Party*. The post-wedding party scenes (which also feature dancing) are not quite as kinetic as what we see in *Jim Decker's Party*; the filmmakers rely a bit more heavily on high-angle long shots than the close-ups of *Jim Decker's Party*. But the camera still zooms in and out of interesting compositions; early in the party sequence, the lens zooms in towards and essentially *through* the dancers, to reveal the bride, still wearing her veil, framed between people in motion in a sharply composed and vaguely melancholy image. Furthermore, this greater reliance on high-angle long shots is balanced by the images of the wedding, which feature a number of stunningly composed close-ups, shots that are so close as to become semi-abstract. Close-ups of candles and the cross at the head of the church are relatively short. But a shot of the bride's face, again bathed by the translucent fabric of the drawn veil, is *very* close; on the soundtrack we hear the priest reading the vows, and there is a moment of gentle disconnect between familiar-sounding material on a soundtrack and a more complex, expressionistic image. This is followed by an extreme close-up of the hands of the bride and groom as they exchange rings; again the unusual closeness of the image gives it a semi-abstract quality. Both of these films, then, operate on two levels. In one way, their titles truly say it all. But they do not say it all in the same way as do the titles of films like *Thoughts on Fogo and Norway*,[16] *Joe Kinsella on Education*, or even *Billy Crane Moves Away*. Those films do indeed have a sort of zero-degree quality that most observers have ascribed to the series overall, as they use the camera primarily to record people discussing issues important to the island. Instead, films like *Jim Decker's Party* or *A Wedding and a Party* document these communal events with sharp attention to the craft of documentary filmmaking and are very much part of the vérité lineage that engages with the capturing of musical performance, a lineage that includes such films as the NFB's own *Lonely Boy* (1960), D. A. Pennebaker's *Lambert, Hendricks & Co.* (1964), and Murray Lerner's *Festival* (1967), which features an incredibly visceral sequence with clog dancers that reminds me very much of what we see in a number of the Fogo films (such as *Children of Fogo*, *The Songs of Chris Cobb*, or *Jim Decker's Party*).

The title of *Dan Roberts on Fishing* might suggest that it runs along the lines of *Billy Crane Moves Away* or *Joe Kinsella on Education*, but that is not the case. The opening sequence is a montage of men working on fishing boats, and it was clearly shot from other boats or on the boats they document, since the camera sways gently back and forth with the sea; especially when the images are of one boat shot from another boat, the combination of gentle swaying is hypnotic. The next sequence is talking-head footage of Dan Roberts and a few other men (including Fred Earle) discussing the economics of fishing (we can also hear Low's voice asking questions off-screen); in this way the film is indeed *Billy Crane*–esque. But this sequence is, essentially, the long middle of the film. The end is, like the beginning, devoted to a montage (again with semi-synch sound) of work on these boats, and it takes on a rhythmic quality that Vertov would find familiar. This is especially true of a sequence where men move fish from the lower deck of the boat to the upper; the shot with one worker standing below deck is tight, very high-angle, and generally striking. On the soundtrack are the rhythmic sounds both of the shovelling of the fish and the putter of boat engines. The final sequence of the film (whose soundtrack is made up of a man singing and playing guitar, recalling *Children of Fogo Island*) features images of fish drying that, like so many other images in the Fogo series, make keen use of composition in depth to show how this fish work is inscribed on the landscape of the island. *McGraths at Home and Fishing* has a similar duality to it. It opens with a close-up of an old timer in a rocking chair, with Fred Earle off-screen asking him to sing one of the old songs. The lens zooms in and out as the old timer recalls a few of the songs he used to sing. After some hemming and hawing, he finally sings "Big Rock Candy Mountain." There follow several minutes of chat with the old timers about fishing, welfare, out-migration, and so on. So far we are pretty squarely in *Billy Crane* territory. But without warning, the film shifts from synch-sound images of old timers sitting around the house to shots of two men working on a small boat. The sound, though, is consistent, as one of the old timers rambles about not wanting to go on welfare and the difficulty of getting the money for a longliner together. Thus the film shifts into the more complex sound-image relationship so familiar from the other films and returns to the gentle bobbing rhythms that made *Dan Roberts on Fishing* so hypnotic. And as the film draws to a close it makes this shift wholesale. The voices of the old men are replaced on the soundtrack by guitar music and semi-synch sound of the men on the boat chattering, and there follow some stunningly composed images, including one *very* low-angle and close shot focused between a fisherman's legs as he pulls in a rope on his bobbing boat (a shot that really does seem taken right out of a Vertov film); the next shot retains this framing but moves back slightly; the shot after that reframes slightly again (although none of these would be characterized as jump-cuts). The time is again dusk, and a misty rain appears to be falling, giving all the imagery a certain grey glow. Waugh has highlighted this specific sequence as key to understanding Challenge for Change and key to its recovery from the historical purgatory in which it now exists. He writes that the film is remarkable for "using the simple, elegant device of cutting back and forth between conversation among family members in their homey kitchen and then action footage of their livelihood on their small vessel bobbing up and down in the swell of the richly luminous ocean," referring to the film as "this modestly confident 16mm black and white masterpiece" (10).

The ways in which the Fogo films sometimes draw upon and sometimes depart from cinéma vérité should not be ignored. Vérité was, by 1967, a highly international style that had, via its reliance on the then-cutting-edge technology of lightweight synch-sound gear, rewritten documentary aesthetics. By the 1970s it had become a sort of orthodoxy, easily integrated into television newscasts and other forms of commercial media. Laying out the task of his astonishingly internationalist book *L'Aventure du cinéma direct revistée*, Gilles Marsolais writes:

> It's mostly in the United States, in Canada, and in France that direct cinema was born and developed. Without listing all of the valuable films made in the cinema direct style in these countries … I want to outline here the principle landmarks of the "effervescent moment" (1958–1965) of this adventure and their immediate successors, until the arrival of the 1970s, which is to say the period when direct cinema broadens its scope and enters into the cinematic norms to the point of making its "difference" unnoticed—going as far even of being partially "recuperated" by the traditional cinema which it transforms from the inside.[17]

The Fogo films are very clearly part of this international "moment effervescent," and yet they are also aware of that moment's limitations. The films rely on vérité technology and aesthetics, but they are not bound by them. Low has no problem seeking other strategies, such as poetic montage, when the need arises, and has no problem mixing in "dashes" of vérité, sometimes mixed with non-synch sound (as we see in the dance sequence in *Children of Fogo Island*, or the boat-building and kite-flying sequences of *Winds of Fogo*). The excitement of a then-cutting edge element of media technology is clearly visible here, but so is a cooler rationalism, an ability to absorb the technical innovations of earlier breakthrough films while still integrating an older, less immediate but sometimes more aesthetically affecting form of documentary practice.

Another breakthrough in mass media that is in conversation with Trudeau-era Canadian nationalism that I evoked earlier as so central to the Fogo films is the radio work that Glenn Gould did for the CBC; it is this radio work which offers the most fruitful point of comparison to the Fogo films. Gould's best-known radio documentary was *The Idea of North* (1967), a meditation on the place of the north in Canadian identity that was mostly in the form of layered voices moving fluidly between signification and semi-abstract musicality (sometimes as many as five people are talking over one another). The fact that this was released in the year of the 100th anniversary of Confederation, which was also the year of Montreal's Expo 67, helps make its connection to an emerging Canadian modernity fairly clear. But two years later Gould broadcast a very similar radio documentary about Newfoundland, called *The Latecomers*. It opens with the sound of waves washing against the shore but is otherwise entirely comprised of layered voices. The discussions we hear are less economically detailed than those we hear in the Fogo films, and the overall thrust of the piece is much more philosophical. Gould wrote in the liner notes to the CD release of the programs that "it was obviously to be about the province-as-island, about the sea which keeps the mainland and the mainlanders at ferry-crossing's-length, about the problems of maintaining a minimally technologized style of life in a maximally technologized age" (6–7). Early in the program one of the voices says, "Work and duty? Yes, I do think so, very very much. As a matter of fact, I'm not thinking of it so much from the spiritual point of view but from the necessity of doing our best in the material sense. We can't do our best in the material sense unless we are tuned up, on the other side of life." This is a very different way of discussing work and material deprivation to be sure. But in both *The Latecomers* and the Fogo films, there is a pronounced push and pull between degree-zero signification and aesthetics (musical abstraction for Gould via layered voices, photographic or cinematic grace for Low via careful composition and affecting camera movements). These works strongly resist linearity, and they are both quite demanding if they are to be understood as wholes. Furthermore, they are both unmistakably born of an optimism about technology and the way that technology can be used, not simply as an individualist luxury, but as a means of understanding collective identities and landscapes. Northerners and northernness are the unmistakable preoccupations of both *City of Gold* (by far Low's most famous film, in large part because of its groundbreaking use of the animation stand) and Gould's *Idea of North*, just as Newfoundlanders and the North Atlantic experience are the unmistakable preoccupations of the Fogo films and *The Latecomers.*

But the modesty that Waugh evokes in *McGraths at Home and Fishing* is not an affliction that Gould ever suffered from; this quality has, I think, been the historical undoing of the Fogo films. Like the Challenge for Change program generally, these films were made by people motivated by an ethic of service, not personal expression. But in the case of the Fogo films, the formal sophistication that had marked all of Colin Low's films was inescapably present. This Newfoundland Project has clearly had considerable impact on less formally adventurous work, most famously on community television projects all over the world. But this really is only *part* of its contribution. By so forcefully disclaiming the aesthetic qualities of these films, a generation of well-intentioned filmmakers and historians have told only part of the cinematic story, and only part of the political story as well. It is well past time to look at these Fogo island films again, and perhaps to see them as though for the first time.

Notes

1 "Je vais pas là pour faire mon film. Je vais là pour faire *leur* film."

2 "Si le véritable héros des films de Renais est la mémoire abstraite, le véritable héros des films de Low est la "mémoire vivante," concrète pourrais-je dire" (33).

3 "Les liens entre la trilogie de l'Île-aux-Coudres de Pierre Perrault sont ici plus perceptibles; en effet, avec cette série de films sur les habitants de l'Île Fogo, nous retrouvons des thèmes, des personnages, une utilisation de la parole que nous rappellent les films de Perrault" (262).

4 "Je deviens participant, complice; les gens d'île sont allés avec moi parce ils voient bien que je fais parti de l'île en quelque sort."

5 Crocker, Jones, and Gary Evans all recall that only three minutes were excised, and all three state that this was because islanders objected to the questioner's tone of voice. See Crocker 128, Jones 162, and Gary Evans 164.

6 "C'est Raymond Garceau qui nous a inspiré par son travail en Gaspésie"; Colin Low fait référence à la réalisation de vingt-six films de la série ARDA (Aménagement rural et développement agricole, 1965–66)" (261).

7 Perrault told Bonneville that he saw similarities in techniques between his and Rouch's films, even though he felt opposed to Rouch (his French contemporary) because he believed Rouch filmed people in environments of *the filmmaker's* choosing, whereas Perrault preferred to go where people lived. See Bonneville 690.

8 "BONNEVILLE: Le film est donc aussi un contact social. PERRAULT: On ne doit pas en rester là. On doit dire autre chose. Je ne cherche pas à influencer. Je ne suis pas

politicien. Mais beaucoup de gens ont abusé de l'Île-aux-Coudres. On a été inconscient. On a négligé une grande force" (695).

9 "Le cinéaste 'artiste' et le cinéaste 'animateur social' sont deux personnes differentes" (70).

10 The NFB sent filmmakers to Arctic communities in the 1970s and trained local people in the use of Super 8 cameras. Some lovely work emerged from this project, especially Mosha Michael's short films *Natsik Hunting* (1975), *The Hunters / Asivaqtiin* (1977) and *Whale Hunting / Qilaluqaniatut* (1977).

11 "Les gens se montraient très amicaux, mais modeste quant à leurs capacités à contribuer au film" (70).

12 Wells's Newfoundland accent makes this sound indistinguishable from "I like the maple leaf"; the script of the film found in the NFB archives, however, has him saying "I like to make believe."

13 Roger Riendeau summarizes the history in this way: "After finally rejecting Confederation in 1894, Newfoundland remained a British colony with responsible government until it was granted Dominion status after World War I.... During the great depression, Newfoundland had to be rescued from bankruptcy by Britain, which suspended responsible government in 1934 and appointed a governor and commissioner to rule the island." In 1946 Britain offered to allow the island the chance to decide its future, and two referenda followed: one that proposed returning to Dominion status, Confederation within Canada, or retaining rule by the commission (the results were 44%, 41%, and 15%, respectively), and a second that proposed either Dominion status or Confederation within Canada (which favoured Confederation, 53% to 47%). On all this, see Riendeau 244. G. A. Rawlyk sees the relationship with Britain in similar terms, writing of Britain's role that "though anxious to be rid of Newfoundland, the Labour government recognized the colony's vulnerability. Of two possibilities opened up by Newfoundland's post-War re-orientation, economic or political union with the United States or with Canada, the British government preferred the latter option and worked assiduously towards achieving that end" (70).

14 "Il est en effet impossible de demeurer parfaitement objectif face à un sujet quelconque, on y ajoute toujours un point de vue personnel, et si ce n'est pas au stade des prises de vue, c'est à celui du montage" (34).

15 *Enthusiasm*, which was also known as *Symphony of the Donbas*, was Vertov's first sound film. Its subject matter recalls the better-known *Man with a Movie Camera* (1929): industrial images, everyday life in the Soviet Union, and so on. But *Enthusiasm* has an extremely complex sound–image relationship, with the sound moving in and out of synchronous and indeed mimetic functions very freely. For some discussion of the film, see Vertov's essays "Let's Discuss Ukrainfilm's First Sound Film: *Symphony of the Donbas*"and "First Steps," in *Kino-Eye*, 106–15. The film has recently been released on DVD by the Austrian Film Museum, and can be purchased at http://www.filmmuseum.at.

16 Although this seems like one of the series' more innocuous "talking head" films, there is clearly a backstory here. The film is a record of a conversation between Fred

Earle and Cato Wadel on differences between the fisheries of Norway and Newfoundland; there is talk of co-operatives, centralized fish processing, guaranteed minimums, and so on. But a letter from T. J. Bindon to Bruce Pilgrim dated 12 September 1969 (held at MUN's Centre for Newfoundland Studies) speaks suspiciously about "Cato Wadel's sociological report on Fogo Island." Bindon goes on to write that "Mr. Wadel is a Norwegian professor of Sociology and his research on Fogo Island was bankrolled by the Extension Service. He claims he wrote the entire manuscript himself, with the exception of the attached portion dealing with the Film Project. He was assisted in the final writing of this by a MUN student, which might account for the penciled notes." A postscript to the letter states "Mr. Snowden disagrees with the film comments while still holding Cato Wadel in very high esteem. He argues that a man who can write two hundred good manuscripts is entitled to one 'boob.' Ironically, his 'boob' had to be the Fogo Film Project." Cato Wadel's report on Fogo Island has a chapter on the Newfoundland film project; the copy that is held at Memorial University's Centre for Newfoundland Studies, however, is missing that chapter, with a note to that effect written in pencil on the table of contents page.

17 "C'est principalement aux États-Unis, au Canada et en France que le cinéma direct est né est s'est épanoui. Sans répertorier tous les films valables faits en direct dans ces pays respectifs … nous repérons ici les principaux jalons du 'moment effervescent' (1958–1965) de cette aventure et leurs suites immédiates jusqu'au tournant des années 70, c'est-à-dire jusqu'à ce jour où le direct étendra ses ramifications et entra dans les mœurs cinématographiques au point du faire oublier sa 'différence'—allant même jusqu'à être partiellement 'récupéré' par le cinéma traditionnelle qu'il transforme de l'intérieur" (63–64).

3

Sjónvarpsfelagið í Havn

In 1950 I was living in St. John's and I had made the acquaintance of Duke, a young American boy who lived on the American Armed Forces base Fort Pepperell. In the corner of his living room I saw a wooden box with a glass window and some buttons on it. I asked "what is it?" He replied, "It's a television set." I then asked "What does it do?" And he went on to tell me that it brings all kinds of things into your living room—moving pictures—movies, entertainment, sports and events from all over the world. I said, "That's fantastic! Let me see it!" He said "I can't because there is no television in Newfoundland."

—Charlie Callahan, Memorial University of Newfoundland's Extension Service (recounted in Extension Service's *Community Television Conference Report* 17)

Another matter is that the percentage of imported programs is very high. Fifty percent of RTÉ broadcast comes from the United States and England, and 4 percent comes from other countries.

—Maolsheachlainn Ó Caollaí, "Teilifís—Fórsa Láidir inár Saol," *Inniu* 13 June 1975[1]

The Faroe Islands, which lie halfway between Scotland and Iceland and are constituted as a "self-governing region within the Kingdom of Denmark" (and thus have the same status as Greenland), were the last European society to get television. Their distance from the European mainland may preclude some from thinking of them as a "European society," but at any rate, a European language is indigenous to the Faroe Islands. Faroese is an insular-Scandinavian language, closely related to Icelandic and fairly distant from Danish (which all Faroese children learn at school). As "small languages" go, Faroese is relatively strong. I'll discuss that in more detail in chapter 6, by way of a contrast with Irish Gaelic. Suffice it for now to quote Jóhan Hendrik W. Poulsen, one of the Faroes' most distinguished scholars, on the matter of the language's historical evolution: "From having been a pariah in its own land, without official standing, for several centuries the spoken language of about 5,000 people, Faroese has made its mark as the official language of the country, the spoken and written language of about 50,000 Faroese" ("Danish Interference in Faroese," in *Mal í Mæti* 249–50). Faroese is also unusual among "small languages" in the degree to which those responsible for its maintenance (including Poulsen, who was for many years chair of Føroyska Málnevndin, the Faroese language committee, based in the Faroes' capital city of Tórshavn) have created neologisms for modern objects and concepts that are now *actually* in everyday use without resorting to English loan-words, although some of these news words are borrowed from Icelandic.[2] "Sjónvarp" is one example of such an Icelandic borrowing: that's the word for television.

One way to examine this late introduction of television to the Faroe Islands would be to investigate the ways in which it changed the life of a relatively insular society. This is a fairly well-played method in anthropology, and as a method it is by no means limited to television. Studies of the effects of the introduction of radio, of film, or of running water for that matter to isolated societies offer a chance to replay a familiar narrative of the fall from communal solidarity into modernity. Not all studies of this sort come to the same sorts of romantic conclusions about the old ways of life being forever lost because of radio/television/cinema/plumbing being introduced into a remote outpost, but there is a way in which this narrative of the fall has come to define studies of the introduction of communications technology even when they consciously try to avoid it.

The experience of the Faroe Islands, on the other hand, is an example of a highly gradual introduction of television into a national community, one that offered considerable opportunity for locally based planning, debate, and experimentation: no less than eleven years elapsed between the first plans and the first broadcasts, the debate leading up to those broadcasts was vigorous, and the energy that these debates produced bore some surprising fruit in terms of the spread of the medium. But there were other surprises too. Indeed, despite this very gradual, very thoughtful introduction of television on the part of highly engaged activists, there is a sense in which the medium got away from them. The television that actually emerged from these sometimes quite experimental projects was Faroese almost in name only. Despite the localism that defined its formations, Faroese television never existed, as far as I can tell, as much more than a shadow of a truly local, or even truly national, broadcast project. In terms of its planning, and in terms of many aspects of its execution, it was a model for other small countries and other small language groups; the degree to which it was indeed a model for television in Irish Gaelic is the subject of most of chapter 6. But its actual record of making Faroese television is quite mixed, and the degree to which this foreshadowed television in Irish Gaelic is dealt with in the conclusion.

Pre-TV

Part of what makes Faroese television unusual is its origins not as a private, for-profit enterprise, or even as a national state-funded service, but as a group of non-profit organizations that at first had no real government connections except for the obligation to follow regulations, which got in their way as often as not. These origins are closer to the way that small national cinemas emerged in the 1950s and 1960s; interested individuals formed a group that sometimes received support and sometimes received trouble from the government. Faroese television is thus an important model not only for those who would blur the lines between film and TV, but also for those who would use television for communitarian ends, seeking to escape the coercion of state forces. These origins seemed to offer a fairly original model for television: neither state-ist nor capitalist. They seemed, in short, to be headed towards the emergence of a Faroese television defined (albeit never explicitly) by the idealism of Jürgen Habermas's public sphere, a television service that simulated a place of open exchange where (as Habermas wrote) "the sphere of private people come together as a public" (*Structural Transformation* 27).[3] While that was not what Sjónvarpsfelagið í Havn turned out to be at all, it's not clear that this was what it was ever meant to be.

The story begins, more or less, in 1967. On 18 March of that year, the front-page headline of the newspaper *14. September*[4] was "Skulu vit hava danskt fjarsýn?" [Should we have Danish television?]. This headline was significant for two reasons. One was that it illustrated the degree to which "television in the Faroe Islands" was, from the very beginning, synonymous with "dansk fjarsýn" [Danish television]; television produced in the Faroe Islands, in Faroese, does not initially enter into the equation at all. Moreover, this is emphasized by the fact that the headline uses the Danish word for television, "fjarsýn," and not the Faroese word, "Sjónvarp"; this appeared, furthermore, in the Faroese newspaper whose politics were most reliably pro-independence. This article was reporting on a debate in the Faroese parliament (called the Løgting) about whether the Faroes should get television, and the benefits of preventing the domination from foreign providers: Danish TV, it seems, might be better than foreign TV. What followed shortly from these debates was a series of "royndarsendingar," or test broadcasts. These were experimental broadcasts, staged by Halgir Lindberg and Árni Joensen[5] and done quite outside of any official mandate. A front-page notice in the 2 September 1967 issue of *14. September* announced the beginning of these experiments, stating that "this is a test of the possibility of and an attempt to generate interest in the establishment of Faroese television, having ourselves a feasible broadcast station and the intention to create legal broadcasts in Tórshavn."[6] It was signed by Halgir Lindberg and Árni Joensen, and included a listing of what they would be showing on both Saturday 2 and Sunday 3 September: music at 8 p.m., and an American documentary called *Little Rock* at 9 p.m. They continued these broadcasts every week for several months, transmitting very similar sorts of material. Joensen recalled in our 6 August 2007 conversation that Danish television had sent them some material, and that he was also broadcasting 16 mm films that had been lent by embassies. This televisual experiment lasted until, as the front-page headline of *14. September* declared on 2 December 1967, "Løgmaður steðgar royndarsjónvarpinum" [Faroese Prime Minister stops television tests]. That article (the author is unknown; all of the newspapers in the Faroes published only unsigned reporting at that time) is mostly an interview with Joensen, who gives the technical details of the test broadcasts (first broadcast on a 10-watt transmitter, then on a 70-watt, at a cost of 60,000 kronur [now about CDN$12,000], etc.), but it also reproduces a letter that Peter M. Darn (the minister responsible for radio) sent to Halgir Lindberg, quoting the law restricting radio broadcasts to those of Útvarp Føroya, the national radio service: "According to article 1 of bill #23 from 28 March 1956, the Løgting has the sole right to create radio in the Faroe Islands with the foundation of Útvarp Føroya, and therefore it is parliament's responsibility to make you aware that your broadcasts have broken the relevant law, and that you must immediately halt broadcasts outside of Útvarp Føroya."[7]

But they were not down for long. The front-page headline of the 13 December 1967 issue of the Faroese newspaper *Sosialurin* read simply "Sjónvarpsfundur" [Television meeting]. That article reported on a meeting held to form a group committed to establishing a television station in the Faroe Islands. The author rattled off the names of the people who would be responsible for the group, and then stated, "What future intentions big countries have it is hard to say, but it is not impossible to think that in a few years we can have access to television broadcasting from outside."[8] Like assumptions of Danish centrality in those first articles about Faroese television, this would prove to be prophetic in ways the author clearly did not at that time understand.

The group that emerged from that meeting, Sjónvarpsfelagið í Havn[9] [Tórshavn Television Association], was founded in 1968. Árni Joensen's letter to the editor of *Sosialurin* published on 11 February 1968 identified the members as Daniel Magnussen, J. P. Gregoriussen, Hilmar Johansen, Kjartan Mohr, and Árni Joensen, with Halgir Lindberg and Hanna Liserg as deputy members. Sjónvarpsfelagið í Havn requested that the Faroese parliament grant them permission to make regular broadcasts, but the proposal was defeated. *Sosialurin* recalled in an 11 January 1978 article that "Sjónvarpsfelagið was founded in 1967. That year the association also had negotiations with the Faroese government about getting permission to do test broadcasts. They were not successful."[10] Joensen told me during our August 2007 conversation that during this period of inactivity he was circulating tapes among groups of people. At first this sounded like the Irish-language video project Cinegael, which, as I will discuss in chapter 5, made videos not for broadcast but for exhibition at town halls, small theatres, and so on. Those were videos of local events, though, and were always described by that group's animator, Bob Quinn, as a closed-circuit local television. The tapes that Joensen was circulating, on the other hand, were not local at all; he told me that they were mostly football matches and films from Danish, Swedish, and British TV. The sense that the experience of Sjónvarpsfelagið í Havn is similar to the Irish Gaelic television activism until you dig a bit deeper is a recurring theme in my research. At any rate, the tide began to turn in the mid-1970s. Finally, on 11 January 1978, came the headline in *Sosialurin* that everyone in the association had been waiting for: "Sjónvarpsfelagið vil hava sendiloyvi" [Television association wants broadcasting permission].

Initially, Faroese televisual aspriations were local in scope. On 11 February 1978, an article in the newspaper *14. September* reported that "the Tórshavn town council last night gave consent for the council to call upon the national [Faroese] government to give Sjónvarpsfelagið, or the council in co-operation with Sjónvarpsfelagið, permission to broadcast television locally in Tórshavn."[11] *Sosialurin*'s front-page headline of the same day was "Býráðið vil hava sjónvarp í Havnini" [Town council wants television in Tórshavn].

Within a month, television was starting to appear all over the Faroes. The newspaper coverage bears out the slow but steady emergence of a system to broadcast over all eighteen islands. This system was comprised of private organizations, all of which, like Sjónvarpsfelagið í Havn, were authorized by the Faroese government and the Post- og telegrafverkinum [Department of Post and Telegraphs] to broadcast. The first place outside of Tórshavn to get signals appears to have been the "second city" of the Faroes, Klaksvík (with a population of 6,000, it is roughly a third the size of Tórshavn), with *14. September* reporting in an 11 March 1978 article that "television broadcasts are now going out in Klaksvík."[12] A number of other private organizations began to arise once Sjónvarpsfelagið í Havn actually started broadcasting in 1979, organizations from all over the Faroes. *Sosialurin* reported on 15 September 1979 the formation of Tvøroyrar sjónvarpsfelags [the Tvøroyi television association] in the village of Tvøroyri on the southernmost island of Suðuroy ("Hava fingið loyvi at sjónvarpa á Tvøroyi" 4). On 13 February 1980 *Sosialurin* reported that "now there are thirty television sets in Skálavík, out of a total of seventy households,"[13] and this village on the not-quite-as-southern island of Sándoy was now able to get signals from an antenna in Støðlafjalli. On 28 January 1981 a front-page *Sosialurin* article reported "Television is coming to Mykines," famously one of the most inaccessible of the Faroe Islands.[14] The article went on to give the impression that a piggyback system of antennas was developing, stating that "this was broadcast from Tórshavn, taken from the antenna on Sandoy." The article also notes: "There are at the moment two television sets on Mykines."[15] The statistical yearbooks for the Faroe Islands tell a similar story. *Ársfrágreiðing 1979* (the first such yearbook to appear in Faroese; previous publications had been in Danish) reports that Klaksvík and Eysturoy (the large island between the cities of Tórshavn and Klaksvík) had set up television associations and that permission had been given to groups in Tvøroyri, Vágur (a town on the island of Suðuroy), and Vestmanna (Føroya Landsstýri 270). *Ársfrágreiðing 1980* adds the village of Eiði and the islands of Vágar and Sandoy to the list of communities getting television associations (Føroya Landsstýri 283). When I spoke on 9 July 2004 with Jógvan Asbjørn Skaale, a former head of Sjónvarpsfelagið í Havn and the first director of its successor public service, Sjónvarp Føroya, he dryly quipped that "it spread like a disease."

But before the spread of the associations, indeed before any signals were sent *anywhere* in the Faroes, there was a very spirited debate about the role that this new medium should play in Faroese society. From 18 February to 27 May 1978, *Sosialurin* published articles by eight different people giving widely differing opinions on whether the Faroes should welcome television and how it should or should not be used. The first to weigh in was Dánjal Pauli Danielsen, who had been taking the lead role as to the government's position on the matter. Others included Martin Fjallstein, an author who had already criticized proposals to introduce TV in the pages of *14. September* (especially on 25 January

1978); J. Karter Højgaard, then director of Sjónvarpsfelagið í Havn; journalist Johann Mortensen; the Christian missionary Henry Andreassen; Jógvan Arge, then director of Útvarp Føroya, the national radio service; Tormóður Dahl, an "industrial consultant" [ídnaðarráðgevari]; and Andrias Højgaard, at that time the rector of the teacher's college. And the opinions on offer were truly all over the map. Dahl's essay of 15 and 22 April seems to me the most eccentric: a two-part piece probably running around 10,000 words altogether that opens by quoting Goethe (in untranslated German) and features a section called "Sjónvarp og epilepsy" [Television and epilepsy] (he had already published a piece in *14. September* on 18 February 1978 that claimed that the radiation from television's beams was dangerous and that television caused nearsightedness and nervousness in children ["Um sjónvarp, tey gomlu á bygd" 7]). Both Danielsen and J. Karter Højgaard, probably the ones closest to the operational details of Sjónvarpsfelagið í Havn, speak to the inevitability of the spread of the "disease" (in Skaale's if not Dahl's sense of the word) with Danielsen pointing out in his 25 February article that "Sjónvarpsfelagið estimates that there are 600 television sets in the country, mostly in Tórshavn"[16] and J. Karter Højgaard trying to head off opponents of the television proposals by writing in his 11 March article that "they must avoid being unreasonable to those who have not thought to buy a video-cassette television set."[17] Fjallstein, though, argued that for a society like the Faroes television was both counterintuitive ("No instinct demands television") and indulgent ("We have no need of television. Television is a luxury that we permit ourselves").[18] This *Sosialurin* debate was, in short, an attempt to capture the opinions of a fairly wide swath of the Faroese intelligentsia, not just specialists in media or technology (admittedly, the all-male quality of the panel takes away from any claim to comprehensiveness that I might try to make here). This was all before anyone had actually received permission to broadcast anything outside of Tórshavn.

This debate clearly illustrates the degree to which television was being framed by the Faroese media as a public institution, not as something meant to enable a withdrawal from the public into an existence of completely domestic consumption of images. The two-month-long debate in the pages of *Sosialurin* gives the sense that there is something significant at stake here, that television will have an impact on the Faroese collectively and not be merely the introduction of another material good that people could choose whether to indulge in or not. For *Sosialurin*, and for many Faroese intellectuals, this wasn't like the sudden availability of a new sort of sofa; this was social, rather than domestic.

But Faroese ethnologist Eyðun Andreassen has argued that there was, beneath this talk of epilepsy and collective instincts, a decidedly domestic *and* international quality to the cultural transformation that the introduction of TV was part of. He states in his 1992 book *Folkelig offentlighed* that "television came to the Faroes 'as a part of general development' and not as the result of any 'popular demand.'"[19] In the book's English-language summary (which is at the end of this otherwise Danish-language monograph) he writes:

> I have indicated the factors which directly broadened people's consciousness prior to the introduction of TV, and which, as it were, prepared the way for this medium in people's consciousness: Danish magazines introduced people to the TV-world many years before the question of Faroese TV was thought of; travelling abroad, particularly to Denmark, made people aware of the presence of TV in the sitting-room; the import of standard houses, and furniture designed with the TV set as the natural centre of family life increased, which, again, influenced the local building style and the arrangements of rooms; and influences on fashions by TV and other cultural industries were noticeable. As a conclusion, one could observe a remarkable impact on everyday life from a not yet existing TV. (308–9)

He had introduced a similar argument about the impact of the material object of the television set on domestic life in the 1970s, when, according to an article in the 4 August 1979 issue of *Sosialurin* ("Føroyingur fingið halva" 3), he had been working at the universities of Oslo and Copenhagen. Indeed, that article features a Faroese-language dry run of some of these theories; it includes a photo of a house being built that carries the caption "Youth centre in Húsavík. How active will this be, when every house has got a television set?"[20]

Andreassen's approach is closely in keeping with the mainstreams in Anglo-American discussions of television (an academic field which was, in 1992, still relatively emergent). "A textual study of television," writes John Fiske in the seminal (although now slightly dated) *Television Culture*, "involves three foci: the formal qualities of television programs and their flow; the intertextual relations of television within itself, with other media, and with conversation; and the study of socially situated readers in and the process of reading" (16). These are the sorts of concerns that we find throughout *Folkelig offentlighed*. The passage just quoted seems most engaged with the second focus, engaging with the intertextual relations between television and other media such as popular Danish magazines (which are very widely available in the Faroes). But it is also very clearly engaged with the reading and meaning-making processes of readers socially situated in the pre-television Faroe Islands. An engagement with formal elements is certainly present in Andreassen, although (perhaps in keeping with his primarily sociological/ethnographic engagement) it is the least dominant aspect. This sort of approach strikes me as a rebuke to the more idealistic vision of the medium that one encounters in publications such as *Sosialurin* or *14. September* during this period. I tend to favour the socialist-communalist assumptions that those newspapers make about television's role over Andreassen's more materialist analysis, if for no other reason than the fact that economic stakes involved in a television service for 50,000 people are, in the world view of mass consumer capitalism, so incredibly small that it is difficult to see how outside forces would stand to gain by imposing their products, cultural-imperialism-style. There must have been some sort of "folkekrav," some sort of collective desire to at least explore the possibilities television appeared to offer. The idea that Faroese television was caught up in a global, presumably American-led system of capitalist production and consumption does not strike me as very compelling because of the incredibly small scale of the operation.

Furthermore, the first Faroese television broadcasts were free of advertising. Sjónvarpsfelagið í Havn was initially funded by the state, first via a tax regime and then via a television licensing system. In order to get the broadcasts underway, though, the government needed to create some sort of start-up fund. This was initially done via a system of taxation. Jørgen Poulsen, in his book *TV og den færøske kulturs fremtid*, explains the proposal passed on 27 May 1968 (which was tagged as Forslag 58/1968) as "a proposal introduced for tax on TV equipment of 300 kronur per set plus 30 percent of the worth."[21] Eventually, though, the funding was based on the numbers of televisions the government assumed were in the country and would be bought over the course of the first two to four years of the broadcasts. Annette Schäfer Hansen and Ulrik Schack, in their booklet *Sjónvarp Føroya*, describe it as follows:

> The television station will become financed through licences. They calculate that in the first year there will be 9,000 viewers, and thus there will be 11,000 television sets imported from 1976 to 1983, and licences will be set at 715 kronur. By this they will get a total of 6,435,000 kronur, which is the amount with which Asbjørn Skaale has to juggle.[22]

By televisual standards a budget of 6 million kronur—approximately CDN$1.2 million—is miniscule indeed, particularly given the fact that this was meant to last *seven years*. That amount of money would barely support a small newspaper for that long. Furthermore, the lack of advertising—a debate that was laid out in articles in *Sosialurin* on 11 and 29 April 1981 ("Sendið lýsingar" and "Neyvan rætt")—tags Faroese television very clearly as a non-commercial venture, one that isn't part of the global sea of mass media in quite same way as, say, Danish magazines, which do rely on advertising to survive.

This more materialist approach is helpful, though, for the way in which it leads to a focus on the fact that, as in Newfoundland in the 1950s, in the Faroe Islands there were television sets but no television signals. It's all well and good to engage in a wide-ranging debate and to put in place policies to secure some sustainable funding, but without the presence of a *material object*, a television set, it all means nothing. And the number of televisions in the Faroes is a recurring topic in the media coverage leading up to the first broadcasts. The sense of these articles is that the question of whether there would be enough presence of the basic technology to support this experiment was a real worry. During our July 2004 conversation, Jógvan Asbjørn Skaale tried to explain the somewhat counterintuitive presence of television in the Faroe Islands as a product of the migration of students back and forth from Denmark. He told me that there was a glut of televisions in the Faroes because Faroese studying in Copenhagen would buy them, suddenly find themselves unable to sell them when they were leaving because of the massive changeover to colour in the early 1970s, and toss them in the sea box that they were renting to get the rest of their possessions back home. "For seven years, lots of televisions in the Faroes," he told me dryly. "But no television." Skaale's explanation is not only close to Charlie Callahan's reminiscence which forms this chapter's first epigraph; it's also not far off of Andreassen's assessments in the way that it points to the way common experiences of Faroese life—the need to spend some time in Denmark, the way in which that sort of travel broadens one's consciousness—partially explain the rise of a communications technology.

Furthermore, in all fairness, Andreassen's materialist approach helps to hold in check the temptation to read the *Sosialurin–14. September* debates as aloof from any connection to commerce. Consumer capitalism, partially in the form of mass-media-driven expectations, was clearly playing some sort of role in the push towards a Faroese television service. There is, for example, considerable exchange between the need to create a new desire to purchase televisions and the discourse of, say, *Sosialurin*. An article in the 7 February 1979 issue of *Sosialurin* ("Sjónvarpssendarin kemur um hálvan") did a rundown of where TV sets and antennas could be bought and at what cost, and it stated that "there are many people who already have bought TV sets. Some of them are old sets, and bought in Denmark, and some are new sets, some of which you can get in the Faroes."[23] Advertisements for those newer television sets began to appear in that same newspaper on 10 March 1979 and ran fairly regularly thereafter. On 4 April 1979 (two days before the first fully regulated TV signals were sent), Phillips Television ran an ad in *Sosialurin* for its new television sets, with copy entirely in Faroese (they were being sold by the local store Martsein). In turn, *Sosialurin* reported on 7 April 1979 that "tomorrow and Sunday between 2 p.m. and 9 p.m., Phillips will have an exhibition of televisions at the Hotel Hafnia. Four men from Phillips Enterprises in Denmark will come to the Faroes for this meeting. They will have with them the most modern televisions sets and tape recorders for television [VCRs] to be found on the market."[24] Really, then, I agree with Andreassen that the desire for television was interlinked to discourses of print culture. It's just that I am focusing here on Faroese newspapers, not popular Danish magazines.

This pre-television period is important to Faroese media history because of the way in which television was introduced to a society that had had plenty of time to think about it. The debates, all-male though they may have been—were vigorous and wide-ranging. The public nature of the TV service—although indeed caught up, like the newspapers that published those debates, with consumer capitalism—was never questioned. The Faroes seemed to have run the lead-up to television in such a way that it would seem logical to expect a locally rooted, flexible, and responsive TV service, one that was very much in line with, say, the relationship that the Challenge for Change filmmakers sought to have with their communities. In the end, it was only occasionally that and was, for the most part, something very different indeed.

Sendiloyvi

Full permission to broadcast television signals came on 9 November 1978; *14. September* published an article that day with the headline "National [Faroese] government gives television association broadcasting permission" [Landsstýrið givið Sjónvarpsfelagnum sendiloyvi (4)]. On 7 March 1979 *Sosialurin* published the somewhat giddy headline "Television broadcasts are coming on the 20th of April!!" [Sjónvarpssendarin kemur 20. apríl!! (2)]. The government's statistical summary *Ársfrágreiðing 1979* reported that "Sjónvarpsfelagið í Tórshavn ... was the first to broadcast programs regularly, starting from 6 April 1979,"[25] and the front-page headline of the 11 April 1979 issue of *Sosialurin* was "Television broadcasts now regular" [Sjónvarp sendi nú reguliga]. These first fully legal broadcasts from Tórshavn could also be seen on the neighbouring islands of Nólsoy and Eysturoy, according to a 21 April 1979 *Sosialurin* article with the title "Television to those on Eysturoy, the northern islands—price 100,000 kronur."[26] According to the television listings that *Sosialurin* started to run on 7 April 1979, this was the first lineup:

Saturday the 7th

3:00–5:00 p.m.	Badminton, All England Competition
8:00 p.m.	Émil from Lønneberg
8:30 p.m.	Grand Prix Tune 1979
10:15 p.m.	Richie Brockleman

Sunday the 8th

3:00 p.m.	Worship service in Nykøbing F. church
4:20 p.m.	Sea of Birds
8:00 p.m.	Journey with Tigris, part 4
8:49 p.m.	The Hunt for Dr. Mengele
9:44 p.m.	Off[27]

This little television listing is a surprisingly complex text nationally and linguistically. Obviously some of this programming is Danish (such as the church service from the Danish city of Nykøbing, or *Melodi Grand Prix*, which is a Danish musical program and part of the Eurovision Song Contest) and some of it is British (such as the badminton, or the 1978 British television documentary *The Hunt for Dr. Mengele*). There's even a dash of Swedish here; *Emil frá Lønneberg* is an adaptation of the Swedish children's book by Astrid Lindgren. The origin of some of the other material is harder to make out, such as the *Fuglasjógvurin* [Sea of Birds] program, which could very well have been in Faroese, or which could have been a rebroadcast Danish- or English-language nature program.

Indeed, material in Faroese accounts for a very small amount of Sjónvarpsfelagið í Havn's broadcasting history. This is borne out by the information contained in the annual statistical yearbooks published by the Faroese government. *Ársfrágreiðing 1979* gives breakdowns only in terms of genres (children's programming, religious programming, etc.), and gives no information about country of origin or language of programs. But the *Ársfrágreiðing* reports from 1980 onward specify the amount of material being broadcast that had also been produced by Sjónvarpsfelagið í Havn. Derived from data in Føroya Landsstýri's *Ársfrágreiðing* reports for 1980–83, Table 3.1 details the breakdown of the Sjónvarpsfelagið í Havn broadcasting content over its lifespan, except for its first year.

TABLE 3.1

Year	Total hours broadcast	Total hours produced by Sjónvarpsfelagið í Havn	Percentage of Sjónvarpsfelagið í Havn material broadcast
1980	990	56	5.6
1981	1023	87	8.5
1982	1255	87	6.9
1983	1314	94	7.1

Thus, between 1980 and 1983—almost the entire lifespan of Sjónvarpsfelagið í Havn—4,582 hours were broadcast, of which 324 hours were produced by them, for a total of 7 percent Sjónvarpsfelagið í Havn production and 93 percent from other sources.[28]

A big part of the problem could have been the fact that satellite TV was already present in the Faroes. During our July 2004 conversation, Skaale told me about the rush to get Sjónvarpsfelagið í Havn broadcasting before satellite became widely available, thus taking the pressure off of the Faroese government to fund a television service. "If the satellites came before we got started," he said, "we would *never* get them to pay for it." In the 1980s, though, satellite dishes did begin to appear in the Faroe Islands. These could receive signals from the Nordsat network which, despite the pan-Nordic sounding name, transmitted quite a bit of American television. A Swedish cartoon reprinted in *Sosialurin* on 12 July 1980 satirizes the way that Nordsat created the illusion that subsribers were getting television from all Nordic countries even though the selection of programming was actually quite limited (see Figure 3.1). In the English-language summary of her 1998 book *Børn med tv* (published by the Nordic Council), Jette Forchhammer writes that "prior to the setting up of the official Faroese service, providers [such as Sjónvarpsfelagið í Havn] were forced to face serious international competition, as during the 1980s the population gained access to satellite-TV, and the landscape was soon dotted with the familiar satellite 'dishes'" (17). This may very well have put pressure on groups like Sjónvarpsfelagið í Havn to "bring people in" via the broadcast of popular foreign programs, the likes of which were, to some extent, available on satellite. But the more I look at the history of this project to bring television to the Faroes, the more I get the sense that this presence of foreign television was not really perceived as a problem as such. Nor was the lack of Faroese-produced programming.

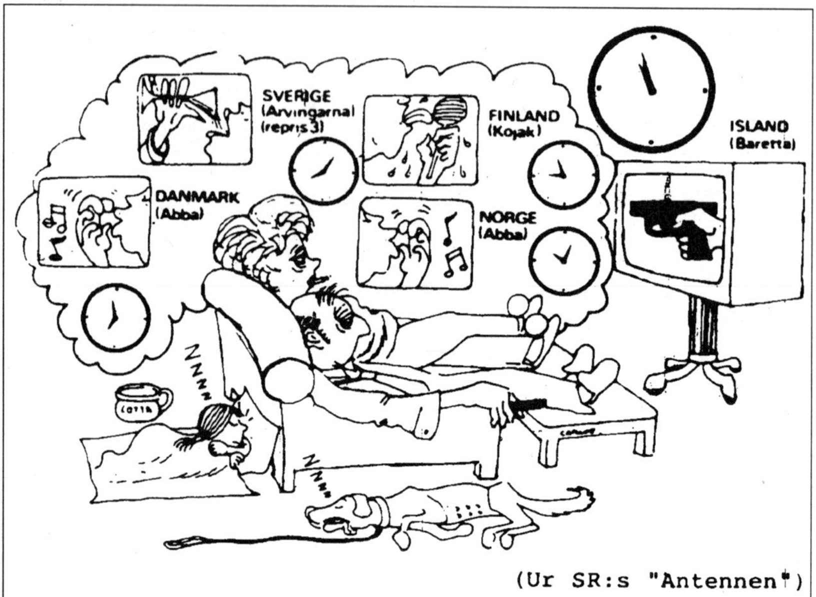

Nú fáa føroyingar kanska føroyskt sjónvarp, og um nøkur ár kunnu teir taka fleiri lond frá Nordsat, um hann verður veruleiki

FIGURE 3.1 A Swedish cartoon reprinted in *Sosialurin*, 12 July 1980, p. 9. The Faroese-language caption translates as "Now perhaps the Faroes can have Faroese television, and after some years could get programs from other countries from Nordsat, if that works out."

Is There a Text in This History?

Conclusions about the precise effect that competition from satellite TV had on the broadcast choices made by Sjónvarpsfelagið í Havn are necessarily speculative. Indeed, there is a large historical problem at the centre of this discussion: the fact that material (both written and audiovisual) connected to Sjónvarpsfelagið í Havn has not been very thoroughly archived. Bits and pieces of programs and documents are out there: some are held by Sjónvarp Føroya, the public television service that was created in 1984 and which replaced Sjónvarpsfelagið í Havn. Some material is in the possession of various people who were involved with the associations. But the legacy of Sjónvarpsfelagið í Havn has not been preserved in a way that is comprehensive or generally accessible.

The archival situation for the video texts of this material, as for its Irish-language counterpart projects such as Cinegael or Teilifís na Gaeltachta, is quite tricky. As I will discuss in chapter 5, the programs produced by Bob

Quinn's Cinegael project have been kept; indeed, they are excerpted in a television film about the project, 2004's *Cinegael Paradiso*. But the only remaining copies of them are on decades-old VHS tapes whose only identifiers are handwritten codes like "6A." These tapes are stored in Quinn's garage in Béal an Daingin (a garage that is actually quite a treasure trove of films, videos, and photographs relating to life in Connemara since the 1960s). Quinn was very generous about letting me watch the Cinegael material (among other films and videos) at his house and didn't mind at all that I made copies. But this is clearly a less-than-ideal archiving situation, if for no other reason than the fact that videotape in any format decays very badly if it is not stored under precise conditions. As I will discuss in chapter 6, the Teilifís na Gaeltachta broadcasts were staged illegally, and the only remaining copy of them is a VHS tape (now also decades old) in the possession of Donncha Ó hÉallaithe. He also let me watch it at his house, also in the Connemara Gaeltacht, just down the road from Quinn (although he didn't want me to make a copy). The archival situation of Sjónvarpsfelagið í Havn is comparably informal. For the most part, I saw Sjónvarpsfelagið í Havn programs by tracking down specific individuals, such as Árni Joensen, who had copies of some of the material (including a broadcast from the Norönna ferry, on which more later) and who was kind enough to make me copies.

Television is, by its nature, an ephemeral medium, but of course this is deceptive. Many countries have television archives (the United Kingdom, for example), and almost all public and private television networks maintain archives of their own. In a way, the Faroes are no exception. The now-public television service Sjónvarp Føroya (SvF) does indeed have an archive of its programs. Many of the earliest ones are on U-Matic (three-quarter-inch) video, and these tapes are so delicate that their custodians will not allow them to be played except in order to digitize them; Margaret Compton calls U-Matic "one of the most ubiquitous and simultaneously most endangered broadcast formats in archives due to its inherent fragility—it was never designed to be stored long term" (130). But those programs are present in the archives, unstable though they may be, and they are catalogued. This isn't immediately apparent to a prospective researcher, however. During my first research visit to the Faroes in 2004 the staff at SvF was unable to shed any light on my inquiries into the era before public service; any question I asked about what had gone on in the late 1970s or early 1980s was always met with a friendly clarification that SvF only started broadcasting in 1984. The staff I spoke with considered Sjónvarpsfelagið í Havn to be basically extracurricular, outside their field of responsibility. During my second visit in 2007 the archivist told me that they had some of the material shot by Sjónvarpsfelagið í Havn, mostly raw footage of interviews. She estimated they had about fifty interviews and said that many of them were on U-Matic tape and thus, as I had heard in 2004, inaccessible except in order to be (someday) digitized. After a bit of pushing, SvF's archivists did locate a fair bit of material (although some of it was on the less accessible three-quarter-inch format). What actually did the trick was when Hjalti Skaale, who knew where this material was, spoke with the SvF archivists and got them to print out catalogue information. SvF also made me some dubs of programs, including one called *Sjónvarpsfelagið*, which was the last transmission by Sjónvarpsfelagið í Havn (SvF records show that it was broadcast on 31 March 1984) and was a sort of history of their work, featuring clips from newspapers and excerpts from broadcasts. So the material is there, but it is not at all easy to access.

To be fair to Sjónvarp Føroya, most of the programs produced during their existence are very easily available. Indeed, during my visits to the Faroes, the staff at SvF have extended every possible courtesy, allowing me to watch work from as far back as 1985 (I viewed *Havnar Myndir*, a program that placed old photographs and contemporary video footage over text from the Faroese novelist William Heinesen[29] and was the first production that used SvF's mobile studio) and later making me dubs of material in which I was particularly interested.

In part, these difficulties recall the problems that scholars of early cinema face. A great deal of historical work done on early cinema relies on the sorts of newspaper accounts that I have been quoting from here. The work of the Montreal-based group GRAFICS (Groupe de recherche sur l'avènement et la formation des institutions cinématographiques et scénique) is an excellent example. They have compiled a complete filmography for the province of Quebec from 1897 to 1930 entitled *Filmographie des "vues" tournées au Québec au temps de muet (1897–1930)*.[30] The fact is, though, that the majority of the prints of films made before 1915 do not exist anymore. Thus the GRAFICS researchers, like many scholars of this period, have relied on newspaper accounts as well as the internal and promotional documents of the production companies, inasmuch as these survive, to reconstruct the cinematic landscape of the period. The work that has emerged from *Filmographie* has been invaluable for researchers of early cinema (and especially early cinema in Canada), and a companion project for the province of Ontario is under way. But the *textual* quality of these works of research is inevitably limited, simply because the texts themselves, the 35 mm film prints, have, for the most part, turned to dust.

These archival issues are an important part of the reason that any history of Sjónvarpsfelagið í Havn is likely to wind up neglecting, or at least paying less attention to, the actual programs that the group produced themselves, but there are other reasons for that as well. Speaking with Joensen and Hjalti Skaale in August 2007, it became clear that the broadcast of locally produced material was not a tremendous priority for Sjónvarpsfelagið í Havn. Jógvan Asbjørn Skaale spoke very passionately with me in July 2004 about his desire to create interesting programs in Faroese and could even describe in astonishing detail the breakdown for series that do not, as far as I can establish, exist anymore. He talked, for example, about a group from Sjónvarpsfelagið í Havn going to the island of Kalsoy and spending three days making a program about the village of Trøllanes, a program which, in all, was comprised of nine thirty-minute segments. He was able to describe, from memory, every episode in this series.[31] But Hjalti Skaale was much more pragmatic, telling me that Sjónvarpsfelagið í Havn wanted to create Faroese programming, but the expense and the time involved rendered this, for the most part, impractical. Overall he didn't seem terribly invested in the actual programs that the group had made, remembering them mostly as interviews with prominent Faroese writers and artists and the occasional "man on the street"-type interviews. For him, the challenges from this period seemed to be largely organizational or political, centred on the creation of a television station based in the Faroes. Joensen was more pragmatic still, and told me that for him, this was a technical challenge, not a linguistic, cultural, or national one. He told me very plainly that he assumed that most people watching Sjónvarpsfelagið í Havn considered it primarily a means of entertainment. Thus the fact that it was, for the most part, broadcasting foreign material, was a complete non-issue for him.

Nevertheless, the material that does survive is interesting, not only for its local importance but for the way that it very neatly synchs up with early video and TV produced in Irish Gaelic, material that is the subject of chapters 5 and 6. As I will discuss in chapter 5, Bob Quinn, the Irish-language filmmaker and activist, wrote of the skeptics of a more local Irish television that "their enemy will not be uniformity, but amateurism—the Celtic thing. Initially, the quality may be extremely tatty. But this must be risked" (Dowling, Doolan, and Quinn 381). This was, without a doubt, a risk that Sjónvarpsfelagið í Havn was willing to take as well. That was the impression I got from the material I was able to view, at any rate. Thus I want to briefly discuss two works, *Mykines* (1981) and *Flaggskip okkara: Norrøna* (1983), that were produced by Sjónvarpsfelagið í Havn. I don't want to make any argument for their quality as lost cinematic gems; the visual quality of both pieces is, as Bob Quinn would say, extremely tatty. And yet, they are worth looking at, if for no other reason than the fact that they offer glimpses of some of the first televisual images that the Faroese had of their own experience.

Mykines is the shorter of these two pieces and the more compact in terms of subject matter. It is essentially, a document of a trip to that most isolated of the Faroe Islands. There is a certain emphasis on the landscape here. The piece is bookended by images shot out of a helicopter (and these are very long takes), and there are several interview sequences where people point out unusual aspects of the topography over a (sometimes jerkily) moving camera. One particularly interesting example of this comes about eighteen minutes in, where an interviewee points out the other islands that can be seen on this exceptionally clear day, as the camera pans across them: Hestur, Sandoy, Skúvoy, Stóra Dímun, and the uninhabited Lítlu Dímun. There are also images of everyday life on the island: another very long take, for example, documents the loading and then departure of the ferry at the quay. This is quite a visually compelling composition. The image is an extreme long shot from a very high angle; as the ferry sails off from screen left to screen right and then arcs left again, there is quite a bit of very different movement as people shuffle off towards the left and the right at the bottom third of the image. The shot reminds me of a Lumière *actualité*, with its multiple planes of differing movement and its sense of just where to place the camera. Also like those Lumière films, *Mykines* is above all a portrait and has no narrative quality whatever. This moment of compositional grace is, though, an exception. The video is very grainy, and the camera work tends to be very bumpy. Furthermore, the entire piece is edited in-camera (both Jógvan Asbjørn Skaale and Árni Joensen told me they had no editing equipment at the time; Joensen told me they acquired such equipment around 1983). On one hand this leads to a strategy of sometimes hypnotically long takes, but the staticky breaks between sequences are quite disruptive. The piece is, thus, like the works of Bob Quinn's Cinegael project: a thoroughly low-end attempt to use an emerging technology in a way that both projects a local set of imagery and ignores completely the standards of technical perfection that were customary in the television industry.

Much the same could be said of *Flaggskip okkara: Norrøna* [Our Flagship: Norröna].[32] The Norröna is the ferry that runs between Iceland, the Faroes, and Scotland. It is a real presence in the life of Tórshavn, especially during the summer as it pulls into the port and discharges tourists with considerable regularity, in addition to providing a link between Iceland and the Faroes that has greatly increased the cultural connections between the two places. This was actually one of the higher-profile of Sjónvarpsfelagið í Havn's productions. The front-page story of *Sosialurin* for 21 June 1983 has the headline "Norröna on television" [Norröna í Sjónvarpinum]. This article reported that "the television crew sails on board and accompanies the ship, first to Scrabster in Scotland and then sailing to Seyðisfjörður in Iceland."[33] The article also featured photos of Árni Joensen and Herman Jacobsen, with captions explaining that Joensen was responsible for the technical aspects of the remote broadcast while Jacobsen was responsible for "the editorial aspects of a broadcast of seventy-three minutes."[34] This is a slightly more polished production, featuring an opening montage of the Norröna sailing into Tórshavn harbour, with a voice-over narration explaining what the ship is (it gives some vital statistics) and generally waxing poetic. The staticky interruptions between shots are absent here, although they reappear elsewhere in the piece. For the most part, *Flaggskip okkara: Norrøna* is a series of interviews with people on the Norröna (passengers, the bartender, members of the bridge crew) and in the communities that it visits. Indeed, the piece is quite diverse linguistically; when the ship lands in Scrabster, there is an interview with a local businessman conducted entirely in English, and when they land in Seyðisfjörður there is an interview with two men speaking Icelandic. Like *Mykines*, there is a certain emphasis here on landscape, with some shots panning across the Scottish hills. And there is, like *Mykines*, quite a stirring image of approach; as the Norröna sails into Seyðisfjörður, it is followed by small fishing boats which carry young kids waving Faroese flags. Overall, then, the piece is a very succinct evocation of the transnational elements of Faroese life: the strong connections with Iceland (where the language is, more or less, mutually intelligible with Faroese) and the sense that Scotland is near enough geographically and close enough culturally to be an important link (although separated by language). It is also a sort of tribute to the ship as the essential element of Faroese transport. These elements are, to a certain extent, disguised underneath a not-terribly-innovative documentary about a big boat. But it does strike me as important to Sjónvarpsfelagið í Havn's history because of its ambition, both technically (some editing was done, and appears to have been done on the ship) and culturally (the Norröna is an indisputably central part of the rhythms of the Faroese capital).

I take Árni Joensen and Hjalti Skaale's point, though, that the production of their own material was not really central to the project of Sjónvarpsfelagið í Havn. The material I have been able to see is interesting, but it is certainly not revelatory in the way that the Fogo Island films are, nor is it linked to an ongoing project of local cultural production in the way that the Teilifís na Gaeltachta broadcasts are. Indeed, this material gives the vague sense that television *in Faroese* is more or less marginal to understanding Sjónvarpsfelagið í Havn overall. It was only occasionally (although sometimes interestingly) a venue for the production of televisual work in Faroese. It was, first and foremost, a *broadcaster*.

Public Service Days

It was only once a public service got started that steps were taken to try to improve the Faroese televisual situation, both institutionally and linguistically. The primary motivator here was likely the legislation that created Sjónvarp Føroya, which had strong language about the degree to which the station was expected to contribute to Faroese culture. There is also a sense in some of this discourse that the national radio station, Útvarp Føroya, was a far more successful operation. This had been clear for some while, with the front-page story in *Sosialurin*'s 14 February 1981 issue noting that "Eyðun Andreasen takes the example of news broadcasting on the radio as proof that in reality we similarly want Faroese broadcast on the television."[35] As with all of the media I discuss in this book, then, the questions about the role and the future of television in the Faroes do come back to radio. And as with the project that Faroese television most strongly influenced, television in Irish Gaelic, this comparison is often couched in terms that emphasize radio's successes and television's unrealized aspirations.

On 21 May 1982, the Faroese government passed Løgtingslóg 77, also known as *Løgtingslóg um sjónvarp*; this was the law that created the public television service called Sjónvarp Føroya (it is reprinted as appendix 1 in Hansen and Schack, and that is what I am quoting here). Article 1.4 gave it a sort of mission statement, which reads, "Sjónvarp Føroya strives to have the objective, factual, and informative news and other broadcasts which preserve and nurture Faroese culture, beliefs, and morals."[36] This is similar to the NFB's mandate to "interpret Canada to Canadians and the world," inasmuch as it is too vague to mean anything very specific but nationalist enough to give a sense that the organization needs to keep its eyes on the home field. The text of the law itself makes no specific mention of how much Faroese-language content is to be broadcast on SvF, but the message seems fairly clear: this was to be a Faroese station, not a platform for recycled American and Danish television. Those responsible for SvF—including Skaale, who became its first director—seem to have taken this seriously, at least judging from the statistics. Føroya Landsstýri's *Ársfrágreiðing fyri Føroyar 1984* reports that in the first full year of SvF's existence 789 hours were broadcast, of which 144, or 18 percent, was

Faroese-language material (327). Their *Ársfrágreiðing fyri Føroyar 1985* reports that 1,203 hours were broadcast in total, of which 318, or 26 percent, were in Faroese (303). In 1987, a year that is (as I'll discuss in chapter 6) important for the comparative work I am trying to do in this book, Føroya Landsstýri's *Ársfrágreiðing fyri Føroyar 1987* reports that a total of 1,560 hours were broadcast, of which 353 were in Faroese and 80 were subtitled, making a total of 27 percent of Faroese-language material (290). In 1990, another year that is (again, as we'll see in chapter 6) interesting from a comparative standpoint, 35 percent of broadcast material was Faroese-language (Føroya Landsstýri, *Árbók fyri Føroyar 1990* 388). Thus from 1980 to 1990 the amount of material in Faroese had increased fivefold. This is a success story, if you want to emphasize that multiple of five. But another way to read this progression would be to point out that after a decade of work and millions of kronur spent under two different televisual regimes, 70 percent of the material on the Faroese national television service was still in a foreign language. For me, this is more difficult to understand as a success.

The period directly following the establishment of SvF also saw some renewal of the television debate in the pages of *Sosialurin*; two of the sharpest commentators were none other than Eyðun Andreassen and Jóhan W. Hendrik Poulsen. In an article by Dagny Joensen of 24 May 1984, Andreassen expressed concern about the unfair competition represented by shows like *Dallas* (which, according to *Sosialurin*'s TV listings, Sjónvarpsfelagið í Havn had started airing on 30 January 1981), writing that "our niche in television could be programs that we cannot get elsewhere! We should neither set great demands for technical quality, nor edit foreign broadcasts. Thus we should stress the establishment of relevant Faroese documentaries, which people here are interested in."[37] This was in keeping with previous critiques he had made in the newspaper about the impact television could have on Faroese culture and the importance of having the Faroese language—and especially Faroese-language news—be an important part of the station. Poulsen had voiced similar sentiments a week earlier, in an interview that bore the headline "It's not just a question of money" [Ikki bert spurningur um pening]. His concern, like Andreassen's, was cultural, although he was more primarily concerned about language, especially the emerging status of Faroese as a minority language on television despite its clear majority status in the nation as a whole. He was clearly thinking of Faroese's status when he said to Dagny Joensen, "If all broadcasts are in a foreign language, night after night, then that must have an effect on language consciousness."[38] That's not to say he was entirely hostile towards the enterprise; indeed, he saw the possibilities that television held for the development of the language. "It's quite necessary that as many broadcasts as possible are in Faroese," he said in that same interview, "and then that foreign broadcasts are sent with subtitles, so that the language can become stronger and more flexible."[39]

Years later both Andreassen and Poulsen would be quite clear that, in retrospect, the introduction of television was not an entirely negative experience. Recalling how there was concern that television would displace communal activities, Andreassen wrote in *Folkelig offentlighed* that "I shared this apprehension at the time TV was introduced, but for the time being I can say that so far this apprehension has been unfounded" (311); this was eight years after the introduction of SvF in 1984 and twelve years after the first broadcasts of Sjónvarpsfelagið í Havn. But Poulsen, writing in 1994 (two years after *Folkelig offentlighed*) in that "Danish Interference" article that I quoted at the beginning of this chapter (which was reprinted in his book *Mál í Mæti*), said:

> Even though Sjónvarp Førorya (the Faroese television service) is a completely Faroese institution and does its best to produce programmes in Faroese, it has neither the money nor the personnel to fill out the whole range of programmes with Faroese material. It therefore resorts to a considerable degree to showing cheap or even free Danish programmes, also for children, often without furnishing them with Faroese subtitles or speech. (255)

I can sense Poulsen's desire to be supportive here, a desire that I share. But his sense that the television, in 1994, remained dominated by non-Faroese material is equally unmistakable. Sjónvarpsfelagið í Havn was "completely Faroese" in more or less the same way that SvF was; both were (and SvF still is) run by a Faroese staff, with funds from the Faroese state, and broadcast mostly non-Faroese material. As institutions, both SvF and Sjónvarpsfelagið í Havn were models of local control. As creators of material for broadcast, they have been something else entirely.

Conclusion

As Hansen and Schack's booklet *Sjónvarp Føroya* recounts, "Asbørn Skaal hoped that the running of their own productions would cover 15 to 20 percent of the programming."[40] The cold reality of the annual statistical reports document very clearly that Skaale did not achieve even half of the low end of this goal during the Sjónvarpsfelagið í Havn period. This centrality of foreign programming throughout its time on air really is the nub of the problem of Sjónvarpsfelagið í Havn, the problem of its legacy. Yet this is very rarely presented as a problem in the Faroese context. The people involved with Sjónvarpsfelagið í Havn with whom I spoke were nonchalant about it. Boði Godtfred, in his 1980 MA thesis on a then-emergent Faroese television, was equally nonchalant, writing coolly, "All the programming broadcast by the societies was taped from Radio Denmark, with the exception of some broadcasts by Sjónvarpsfelagið í Havn made with a single semi-professional video camera."[41] Godtfred is far more concerned about the copyright problems that this taping and broadcast created. The very small amount of "semi-professional" programming in Faroese is *considerably* smaller than the amount of Irish programming that Maolsheachlainn Ó Caollaí thought was such clear and pitiable evidence of the degree to which RTÉ (Raidió Telifís Éireann, Ireland's state-owned broadcaster) had succumbed to cultural imperialism (as I will discuss in the next chapter). Even well into the history of the public service, the percentage of Faroese-produced material still totalled far less than the 50 percent that Ó Caollaí considered such a shortcoming for Irish television.

And yet, the example of the Faroes has been important for many small-language activists, and the example of Faroese television was, as I will discuss in chapter 6, very important to the activists trying to set up television in Irish Gaelic. In some ways, it is not hard to see why. Sjónvarpsfelagið í Havn, like the television associations on the other islands, was a grassroots operation that was run in a non-commercial way and merely sought to bring a crucial part of modern communications technology to the Faroes. Indeed, these groups are part of a very interesting negotiation with modernity that was going in the Faroes in the 1960s and 1970s. This is a period marked by a strong socialist (or at the very least social-democratic) movement, a movement that was comprised of *both* pro-independence and pro-union elements and thus avoided the sentimental nationalism that socialist or social-democratic parties in small countries can so easily lean towards. Indeed, the pages of *Sosialurin* indicate very clearly that the movement was very aware of *international* developments; reading through the paper in this period, one comes across long, detailed articles about the culture not only of Scandinavian neighbours like Sweden, but also of Switzerland, and of Israel, Yugoslavia, and other "peripheral" socialist countries as well, all just in the year 1967. I will discuss in chapter 4 how the examples of both Israel and Switzerland were very important indeed to Desmond Fennell, an Irish intellectual who, as I'll discuss in chapter 6, encouraged language activists to "take the Faroes, for example." Moreover, one also comes across a great deal of debate in a variety of venues about the role of television in a changing Faroese society. Looking back on this period, it is very easy to develop a romantic sense that it was the site of a model "public sphere," one that looked both inward and outward, one that was both protective of tradition and language and engaged with the meanings and possibilities of communications technology. It would seem that this television could serve as an example where, as Habermas writes, the people "claimed the public sphere regulated from above against the public authorities themselves, to engage them in a debate over the general rules governing relations in the basically privatized but publicly relevant sphere of commodity exchange and social labor" (*Structural Transformation* 27).[42] That certainly seemed to be the case with the original "royndarsendingar," which both challenged the state authorities (who shut them down because they seemed to violate the law about radio broadcast) and began a long and often very highly engaged debate about the role television could play in Faroese society.

I realize that this is romantic, and I have tried to indicate as much by acknowledging not only Andreassen's argument that this debate over television had to do with the wide circulation of mass-market Danish magazines but also my own sense that the coverage *Sosialurin* was giving to television dovetails with the advertising that was starting to appear in its pages. Indeed, in the conclusion to this book I will discuss more explicitly the degree to which scholars of Irish-language media argue that television very rarely acts as a genuinely Habermasian public sphere. But it is still hard not to be struck by the degree to which people acting sometimes collectively, sometimes independently, and generally apart from—although with the support of—the state tried to wrestle with the complexity of an emerging modernity.

Thus we arrive at the nub of the problem. Does the fact that there was never much Faroese on Faroese television mean that it was not a successful venture? For the language activists of the Irish Gaeltacht, getting a station in Irish Gaelic was an important goal, but it was just as important (as I will discuss in chapter 6 especially) that this station be locally controlled. "It was local before it was Irish," Seosamh Ó Tuairisc said about the campaign for an Irish-language radio station in the 1960s. "In fact it was local and it just happened that the people spoke Irish" (qtd. in Hourigan, "A Comparison" 148). Faroese television was local for sure. It was centred in Tórshavn and, in the pre-SvF days, made up of a network of associations based on a number of other islands and frequently in very small communities; none of these groups answered to anyone in the ostensible metropolitan centre of Copenhagen. Moreover, the technical and political goals that those who were involved with the project set themselves—for example, the establishment of a publicly operated system that could broadcast reliably over all of the islands—were achieved. Sjónvarp Føroya *was* established; every Faroese person could expect to be able to see it.

What they could not expect was to be able to hear much Faroese, or to see a majority of Faroese-produced programs, on that station. While this was no doubt a disappointment for some, following the historical record it seems that few people (even language activists like Jóhan Hendrik W. Poulsen) seem to have seen this as a fatal flaw. Sjónvarpsfelagið í Havn was successful then, in accomplishing its own goals. What is less clear is whether it was successful in accomplishing the goals central to the Irish-language-television movement. The seeming connection between these projects, and their considerable distance in actuality, will be the subject of chapter 6.

Notes

1 "Ábhar eile is ea an céatadán an-ard de na cláir a allmhairítear. Ó Mheiriceá agus Sasana a thagann 50% dá gcraolann RTÉ, agus ó thíortha eile a thagann 4%" (7).

2 Poulsen has a passion for the country's connection to Iceland that is in no way atypical; Iceland has been a kind of role model for the nationalist Faroese intelligentsia. In 1946, just after the British ended their wartime occupation of the Faroe Islands, the Faroes voted to separate from Denmark (which had been occupied by the Nazis and was thus cut off from the British-occupied Faroes entirely) in a very close decision. The Danish government of the day, citing polling irregularities and very low participation rates, did not accept the result; an election in the Faroes shortly followed and unionist parties consolidated a majority. A home-rule agreement was successfully negotiated with Denmark in 1948. (This is all explained very concisely in Jonathan Wylie's *The Faroe Islands: Interpretations of History*, 227n25.) Iceland, however, which was also a Danish possession going back many centuries, gained its independence in 1944, as the war was winding down. This sense that Iceland achieved what the Faroes only narrowly missed is present in a lot of the discussion around Faroese independence. On a more linguistic note, though, Poulsen writes in the "Danish Interference" article quoted earlier that "we must not forget the example of Icelandic, absolutely the most important factor in coming so far in the realization of what was once regarded as impossible. From the Icelandic language maintenance we learned strategies in language planning and the art of creating new words from native language material. Indeed, in a great many cases, we were able to adopt the new formations directly, or with necessary alteration to Faroese phonology" (250).

3 "die Sphäre der zum Publikum versammelten Privatleute begreifen" (*Strukturwandel der Öffentlichkeit* 38).

4 There are currently two large newspapers in the Faroes: *Sosialurin*, founded in 1927, and *Dimmalætting*, founded in 1878, both of which published two or three issues a week during this period (and both of which currently publish five issues a week). During the period under discussion in this chapter there were several other newspapers; these included *14. September*, founded in 1947. All of these are Faroese-language publications, although quotations and essays in Danish do occasionally appear in all

three. *Dimmalætting* has historically been a "unionist" newspaper, inasmuch as it has favoured retaining ties between the Faroes and Denmark; its politics have generally been liberal. *14. September* was aligned with the independence movement, and politically was both socialist and centrist; it was close to (although not actually owned by) Tjóðveldisfloksins, the Faroese Republican Party, whose membership also was (and remains) fairly diverse politically but united on the matter of independence. *Sosialurin* was until recently a similar sort of socialist newspaper. It was founded and, for most of the period under discussion here, owned by Føroya Javnaðarflokkur, the Faroese Social-Democratic Party; the paper had *both* unionists and nationalists under its wing, as both political camps had socialist elements (although Føroya Javnaðarflokkur is a unionist party). *Sosialurin* was sold in 1983 and is today basically apolitical; *Dimmalætting* is now by far the Faroes' largest newspaper (it also owns the largest printing press in the country) and retains its unionist character and more or less liberal outlook; *14. September* ceased publication in 1994. For an overview of the history of Faroese newspapers, see Arnbjørn Ó. Dalsgarð, *Føroysk blaðsøga 1852–2002* (Vestmanna: Sprotin, 2002).

5 Joensen now goes by Árni Conradsson. He changed his name, as many Faroese have, to follow the traditional patrilineal or matrilineal naming system that is also in use in Iceland. This system had been in use in the Faroes for centuries, but in 1832 the Danish government introduced laws compelling Faroese families to adopt a common surname. In 1992 the Faroese parliament passed a law making it easier for people to change back to the older system (and making it harder to give a baby a name not approved as Faroese by Navnanevndin, the national names committee).

6 "Sum ein roynd at kanna møguleikarnar og fyri at skapa áhuga fyri at seta á stovn føroyskt sjónvarp, hava vit gjørt eina sendistøð, og ætlanin er at fara undir regluligar sendingar í Havn" (Lindberg and Joensen 1).

7 "Eftir §1 í løgtingslóg nr. 23 frá 28. marts 1956 hevur løgtingið einarætt at hava útvarp í Føroyum við støðini Útvarp Føroya, og er tað tí skylda landsstýrisins at gera tygum vart við, at tygum við sendingunum hava brotið galdandi lóg, og at tygum tí beinanvegin mugu halda uppat við sendingunum uttan um Útvarp Føroya."

8 "Hvørjar framtíðarætlanir tey stóru londini hava er ilt at siga, men tað er ikki ómøguligt at vit um fá ár kunnu hava høvi til at taka ímóti sjónvarpssendingum uttan ífrá."

9 "Havn" is the way that Tórshavn is generally referred to in Faroese; it is the word for harbour (Tórshavn literally means "Thor's Harbour"). The full word "Tórshavn" is occasionally used, but it is unusual. This is a bit like the use of "New York" for "New York City" or "Quebec" for "Quebec City."

10 "Sjónvarpsfelagið varð stovnað í 1967. Felagið hevði eisini samráðingar við landsstýrið hetta árið um at fáa loyvi at fara undir royndarsjónvarp. Hetta eydnaðist ikki" ("Sjónvarpsmálið lagt fyri" 1). Jørgen Poulsen's book *TV og den færøske kulturs fremtid* has a slightly different timeline, pegging Sjónvarpsfelagið í Havn's foundation at 1968–69. He writes, "1968–69: The television association (Sjónvarpsfelagið) starts with the purpose of working towards the introduction of television in the Faroes, but the issue causes problems (presumably because of high cost) and the association is not

revived until 1975" [1968–69: TV-foreningen (Sjónvarpsfelagið) starter med det formål at virke for indførelsen af TV på Færøerne, men spørgsmålet er for vanskelgit (antageligt for dyrt) og foreningen liver først op igen i 1975 (32)].

11 "Á býráðsfundi í Havn hóskvøldið samtykti Býráðið at heita á landsstýrið um at geva Sjónvarpsfelagnum ella Býráðnum í samstarvi við Sjónvarpsfelagið, loyvi til lokalar sjónvarpssendingar í Havn" ("Býráðið í Havn" 3).

12 "Sjónvarpssendingar fara nú fram í Klaksvík" ("Sjónvarpssendingar í Klaksvík" 11).

13 "nú eru útvið 30 sjónvarpstól í Skálavík, sum telur 70 húsarhald" ("Næstan annaðhvørt hús sjónvarp" 5).

14 "Sjónvarp er komið til Mykinesar." One of the most famous Faroese novels, Jørgen-Frantz Jacobsen's 1939 work *Barbara* (which is actually written in Danish, and has been translated into English by the late Canadian scholar and poet George Johnston), has as its climax a situation where the eponymous protagonist's husband, a Danish minister, is stranded on Mykines for almost two weeks and leaves her, she believes, bereft. This leads her in turn to run off with her lover. The storms that the island is subject to, combined with the very small quay, still make it extremely difficult to get boats in and out; contemporary visitors are generally warned that they should be prepared to be stranded there for days at a time.

15 "Hetta vóru sendingar úr Havn, sum tey kundu taka frá antennuni í Sandoynni.... Tað eru í løtuni tvey sjónvarpstól í Mykinesi" ("Verðurfastir í Mykinesi" 1).

16 "Sjónvarpsfelagið metir at eini 600 tól í landinum, mest í Havn" (7).

17 "Tað má haldast at vera órímiligt, at tey, ið ikki hava ráð at keypa videokassettu sjónvarpstól" (6).

18 "Eingi instinct krevja sjónvarp.... Okkum er ikki tørvur á sjónvarpi. Sjónvarp er eitt luksus vit loyva okkum eins" (6).

19 "TV kom til Færøerne 'som et led i den almindelige udvikling' og ikke som resultat af noget 'folkekrav'" (255).

20 "Ungdómshúsið í Húsavík. Hvussu verður virksemi her, tá hvørt hús hevur fingið sjónvarpstól?" ("Føroyingur fingið halva" 3).

21 "Forslag om afgift på indførelse af TV-apparater på 300 kr. pr. apparat + 30% af værdien" (31).

22 "Fjersynsstationen vil blive financieret gennem licens. Man regner med, at der det første år vil blive 9000 seere, idet der importeres 11.000 TV-apparater fra 1976-83, og licensen vil blive sat til 715 kr. Herved kommer man til tallet 6.435.000,00 kr., som er det beløb, Asbjørn Skaal [*sic*] har at jonglere med" (34).

23 "Tað eru nógv folk, sum longu, hava keypt sjónvarpastól. Hetta eru partvíst gomul tól, sum eru keypt úr Danmark og partvíst nýggj tól, sum eru at fáa í Føoyum [*sic*]" (3).

24 "Í dag og sunnudagin millum klokkan 14 og 21 hevur Phillips framsýning av sjónvarpstólum á Hafnia. Í hesum sambandi eru fýra mans frá Phillipsfyritøkuni í Danmark komnir til Føroya.... Við sær hava teir tey mest nútímans litsjónvarpstól og bandupptakarar til sjónvarp, sum finnast á marknaðinum" ("Philips byrjar" 4).

25 "Sjónvarpsfelagið í Tórshavn ... fór sum tað fyrsta undir reglugligar sendingar 6. apríl 1979" (Føroya Landsstýri 270).

26 "Sjónvarp til eysturoyingar og norðoyingar—prísurin 100.000 kr" (3).

27 "**Leygardagin** 7: 15–17: Badminton: All England kappingini; 20.00: Émil frá Lønnebergi; 20.30: Melodi Grand Prix 1979; 22.15: Richie Brockleman. **Sunnudagin 8:** 15.00: Gudstænasta í Nykøbing F. Kirkju; 16.20: Fuglasjógvurin; 20.00: Ferðin við Tigris, 4; 20.49: Jagstranin av Dr. Mengele; 21.44: Ikk" (*Sosialurin* 7 April 1979: 19).

28 Throughout this analysis, I am conflating "program produced by Sjónvarpsfelagið í Havn" with "program in Faroese." While there is an outside possibility that some of the programs Sjónvarpsfelagið í Havn produced might have been in Danish (although that seems unlikely), the chance of anyone else producing material in Faroese seems so remote as to be negligible. Sjónvarpsfelagið í Havn did not, at this time, add Faroese subtitles to material. Its public-service successor SvF sometimes did do that, and that is reflected in their *Ársfrágreiðing* summaries, which are explicit about number of hours *of Faroese* that are broadcast each year. This is all to say that the numbers here reflect the most optimistic estimate possible of the amount of Faroese on the air during the Sjónvarpsfelagið í Havn period.

29 William Heinesen is probably the Faroes' most renowned novelist; his most famous work is *De fortabte Spillemænd* (1950, translated into English as *The Lost Musicians*). Like his cousin Jørgen-Frantz Jacobsen, he wrote in Danish, and he famously wrote to the Nobel committee that he did not wish to be nominated for the prize, since if a Faroese novelist was to be so honoured it should be a novelist who wrote in Faroese. Heinesen probably had Heðin Brú in mind, who, with Heinesen and Jacobsen, forms the "big three" of twentieth-century Faroese literature, and whose 1940 novel *Feðgar á ferð* (translated into English as *The Old Man and His Sons*) is the most renowned twentieth-century novel in Faroese (although not the most widely acclaimed Faroese novel, which is probably either Jacobsen's *Barbara* or Heinesen's *De fortabte Spillemænd*). An introduction to all three novelists can be found in Hedin Brønner, *Three Faroese Novelists* (New York: Twayne, 1973).

30 Available at http://cri.histart.umontreal.ca/grafics/fr/filmo/default.asp.

31 The series, he said, was just called *Kalsoy* (named for the island), and he gave me the breakdown as follows:

> Episode 1: About farmer Jógvan Joensen, who discusses the village's history and place names.
>
> Episode 2: About the post boat which travelled in and out of Kalsoy; Joensen did the voice-over.
>
> Episode 3: About Joensen travelling from Trøllanes to Mikladalur along a very treacherous path.
>
> Episode 4: Interviews with old men (in their eighties) in the village of Trøllanes, about its history.
>
> Episode 5: An interview with an old man (in his nineties) about the history of Trøllanes.
>
> Episodes 6 and 7: More interviews with old men, this time in the village of Húsar.
>
> Episode 8: Interview in the village of Syðradalur with a man whose ancestors were from there.

Episode 9: About a voyage in a small speedboat to Blankaskáli, a village that had been abandoned for the last hundred years and whose houses were moved to Syðradalur. Interviews were conducted in the abandoned village.

He told me that they shot in July but did not broadcast the series until November and December of 1979. "We waited until the dark times came," he (again, very dryly) said of the decision to delay airing the series until the season where days in the Faroes are *very* short. "It made the picture look better than it was."

32 The Faroese character ø is sometimes rendered as ö. *Flagsskip okkara: Norrøna* is the title that appears on the screen of this video, but "Norröna" is the name that is written (and is still written) on the ship's hull.

33 "Síðani fara sjónvarpsmenninir umborð og fylgja við skipinum—fyrst til Scrabster í Skotlandi og siðani til Seyðisfjarðar í Íslandi."

34 "redaktionella partinum í sendingini uppá ein tíma og trettan minuttir"

35 "Eyðun Andreasen [*sic*] tók dømið við tíðindasendingunum í Útvarpinum sum eitt prógv um, at vit veruliga eisini ynskja føroyskar sendingar í sjónvarpinum" ("Eitt alment føroyskt sjónvarp").

36 "Sjónvarp Föroya hevur til endamáls at hava objektivan, sakligan og upplýsandi tíðindaflutning og sendingar annars, ið varðveita og fjálga um föroyska mentan, ártrúnað og siðlæru" (61).

37 "Ein táttur har sjónvarpið kann gera seg galdandi er við at gera sendingar, sum vit ikki kunnu fáa aðrastaðni! Heldur ikki eiga vit at seta so stór krøv til teknisku góðskuna, ella at nýta tíð til at kuta útlendskar sendingar. Her átti dentur at verið lagdur á at gera føroyskar aktuellar sendingar, sum folk her hava áhuga fyri" (Dagny Joensen, "Leggið dent" 8).

38 "Um nú allar sendingar verða á fremmandum máli, kvøld eftir kvøld, kann tað ikki annað enn fáa ávirkan á mál tilvitið hjá folki" (Dagny Joensen, "Ikki bert" 16).

39 "Tað er alneyðugt at so nógvar sendingar sum gjørligt verða føroyskar harnæst at útlendskar sendingar verða tekstaðar, so málið kann mennast og mýkjast" (Dagny Joensen, "Ikki bert" 16).

40 "Asbørn Skaal [*sic*] håber på, at egenproduktionerne i løbet af et par år vil dække 15 til 20% af programfladen" (40).

41 "Alle programmer som foreningerne sender er tappet fra Danmarks Radio, med undtagelse af nogle få udsendelser som Fjernsynforeningen i Tórshavn laver med et enkelt semiprofessionelt video-kamera" (55).

42 "reglementierte Öffentlichkeit alsbald gegen die öffentliche Gewalt selbst, um sich mit dieser über die allgemeinen Regeln des Verkehrs in der grundsätzlich privatisierten, aber öffentlich relevanten Sphäre des Warenverkehrs und der gesellschaftlichen Arbeit auseinanderzusetzen" (*Strukturwandel der Öffentlichkeit* 38).

PART 2

The Gaeltacht

Needless to say, it is easier to perceive now, with hind-sight, what should have been done—easier than it would have been 20, 40 or 50 years ago. It was not until 1969–70 that what was needed to save the Gaeltacht was perceived in the Gaeltacht itself, and stated clearly by Gluaiseacht Chearta Sibhialta na Gaeltachta (Gaeltacht Civil Rights Movement) and Iarchonnachta 1985. But by then the clock of Gaeldom stood at five minutes to midnight.

Attempts to stop the erosion of shrinking linguistic minorities are a very new thing, and nowhere yet, to my knowledge, has such an attempt succeeded. Our attempt was the first instance in which a State and its resources were committed to the task. In the circumstances, it was probably inevitable that we would not know how to use these assets, and the language movement, in a successful combination.

—Desmond Fennell, "Why the Gaeltacht Wasn't Saved," *Irish Times*, 4 June 1980 (10)

An Introduction to the Gaeltacht

> In the Gaeltacht, as elsewhere in rural Ireland, after the nadir of despair in the 1950s, the 1960s saw the first serious challenge offered to the defeatism and fatalism of a century. A group of articulate young radicals suddenly found its voice and began demanding policies to arrest the dissolution of and disappearance of its own community. These Gaeltacht radicals were generally well-educated, and like similar groups in Northern Ireland, were part of the global dynamics of youth politics and civil rights movements of the late 1960s. The new movement brought results.
>
> —Gearóid Ó Tuathaigh, "Language, Literature, and Culture in Ireland since the War" (113)

> A synthetic culture is easy. An old culture is remote. We are caught in this tension, yet the forces of growth, the real drives of the expansion, cannot in the end be denied. Already, through many difficulties, there has been growth of a real and valuable kind. But the nature of the expansion warns us that we cannot apply any simple overall test. We have to recognize the contradictions we have been following: between democracy and limited ownership; between genuine extension and the drive to sell. The real history of communications, in showing us the contradictions, shows us also the need to choose between genuinely alternative directions for the future.
>
> —Raymond Williams, *Communications* (35)

On a typically stormy late-fall night in 1987, several residents of the Connemara Gaeltacht put up an unlicensed television transmitter, which they planned to use to stage illegal television broadcasts in Irish Gaelic. "It was erected during a windy and wet October night on the bleak slopes of Cnoc Mórdáin, near Cill Chiaráin," writes Bob Quinn in his autobiography *Maverick*. "Seventeen years previously the Connemara Gaeltacht civil righters had shamed the powers that be into setting up a community radio service, Raidió na Gaeltachta, by use of the same tactic. They called their achievement Saor Radio Conamara [*sic*; Saor-raidió Chonamara (Connemara Free Radio)]. We called ours Teilifís na Gaeltachta and hoped to have the same impact" (23).

This moment, as the transmitter went up and the rain came down, may seem like an innocuous example of some media-savvy community activism-agitation, of pirate TV in the rain. It was that, but it was more than that as well. On that weekend of 2 October, a certain concept of identity was being enunciated, one that had deep roots not only in thought about the Gaeltacht's place in Irish life but in thought about European unification and European identity itself. It seems to me to be a singularly internationalist moment in the history of Irish cultural activism. And it is where the story of North Atlantic broadcast that I have been trying to tell throughout this book ends, where all of its strands come together. I thus want to sketch out some of the political and intellectual lineage of this moment, by way of illustrating how much a product of an Atlanticist world view community activism in the Gaeltacht was. Far from being a parochial or nostalgic movement, this is where Irish politics engaged in sprawling and unpredictable ways with the intersections between the global and the local.

Thus this section attempts to synthesize, via the experience of the Gaeltacht from the 1960s to the 1980s, the themes of North Atlantic broadcast we have seen so far. Intellectually, the Gaeltacht civil rights movement was heavily influenced by the writing and activism of Desmond Fennell. He saw issues around Irish and Gaelic culture generally in a way that was both intensely focused on local issues and constantly but critically looking for international analogies; in this way, his writings share much with the thought of Pierre Perrault, subject of chapter 1. Bob Quinn is indisputably at the centre of the film and television connected to the Gaeltacht civil rights movement. His work, itself influenced by Fennell's ideas, was also rigorously focused on the local, but at the same time it reveals an awareness of international connections and commonalities. Here, though, the connections are more concrete than those between Fennell and Perrault. Quinn's work was explicitly modelled after the NFB's Challenge for Change program, and specifically the Fogo Island project, the subject of chapter 2. Donncha Ó hÉallaithe, the main organizer of the Teilifís na Gaeltachta broadcasts and current custodian of their memory, explicitly presented his work as a locally oriented affair, being cast in the model of community television. And yet, he was inspired by the example of the Faroe Islands, which he visited in 1987 (again influenced by Fennell, who in 1972 wrote a pamphlet called *Take the Faroes for Example*, on which more in chapter 6). When I spoke with him on 29 July 2006 he did not seem to be aware of the only semi-governmental quality of the first broadcasts themselves, the subject of chapter 3, but he was very much aware of the localist idealism that drove that station. Thus the connections between the experiences of the Gaeltacht and their North Atlantic contemporaries become more concrete as this section moves forward. Throughout, though, one thing is clear; the story of Gaeltacht media activism from the 1960s the 1980s is, in abbreviated form, the story of North Atlantic media of that same period. The desire to reconcile internationalism with localism; the focus on collaboration; the mandate to modernize the relationship between language and culture by way of securing autonomy: these are the imperatives of Perrault, of Low, and of the prepublic Faroese television broadcasts. These were the struggles that formed the backbone of the Gaeltacht's efforts to claim their place in the media landscape of the same period.

A Brief Introduction to Gluaiseacht Chearta Sibhialta na Gaeltachta

Before moving to chapters devoted to these three comparisons, I want to sketch the political and intellectual climate of the Gaeltacht in more general terms. This period from the 1960s to the 1980s was rich in terms of activism surrounding bread-and-butter development issues, but it also saw the emergence of a public debate around the relationship between media and culture that was exemplary in its sophistication. The experience of Saor-raidió Chonamara is crucial, and I will spend some time sketching that out. But I also want to show that the ideology of Saor-raidió Chonamara was quite consistent with a number of debates during this period, and was the natural result of a particularly intellectually rich period in Irish life. I think that one would be hard pressed to find another period in Irish life that saw an engagement with localism, internationalism, language, culture, and the hybridity of national identity defined by a comparable rigour or genuine populism.

One crucial element of Gluaiseacht Chearta Sibhialta na Gaeltachta [the Gaeltacht Civil Rights movement] was that its leaders were either uninterested in or explicitly opposed to the nationalist vision of the restoration of the Irish language as the vernacular of the entire country. The movement saw itself as a group of activists trying to make their communities economically and culturally sustainable, not as part of a government plan to transform the nation. "To their emphasis on *teanga* (language), we opposed our emphasis on *pobal* (people or community)," Desmond Fennell wrote in *Beyond Nationalism*, "maintaining that the language would look after itself if the communities which actually spoke it were stabilised through self-government" (141). But this Gaeltacht Civil Rights movement found itself, more than once, in vigorous opposition to the state itself. The march to Dublin to protest the closure of the Kerry Gaeltacht's Irish-medium Dún Chaoin school in April 1971, a protest that was broken up by a baton-wielding riot squad when it reached the General Post Office, is one of the more visceral reminders of this oppositional quality of the movement. An *Irish Times* article of 9 November 1970 about an earlier set of protests around the school quoted Tarlach de Blacán:[1]

> The parents of Dún Chaoin and Montpelier were resisting strongly the imperialism of the system in Dublin. "Usaídim [*sic*] an focal 'impiriúlachas' mar is impiriúlachas atá i gceist í ndúnadh an dá scoil seo" [I use the word "imperialism" because it's a question of imperialism with the closing of these two schools]. The imperialism was of two kinds, he said, cultural and economic. ("Dun Chaoin agitation likely to reopen" 5)

Thus, it is important to realize that although connected closely to nationalism—as Pierre Perrault was, as Colin Low was, and as the television activists of the Faroe Islands were—this was also an insurgent movement, one that was explicit about the degree to which it was engaged in a struggle *against* Dublin, against the neo-colonialism of the metropolitan centre. This sort of insurgent or anti-imperialist rhetoric would become a hallmark of the movement for wider recognition of Irish Gaelic, especially, as we shall see, in the writing of Desmond Fennell, who became the intellectual leader of the movement.

One of the less aggressive examples of Gluaiseacht activism, although clearly the most relevant one for considerations of Irish and North Atlantic media initiatives—was the establishment of Saor-raidió Chonamara in 1970. Iarfhlaith Watson recalls that Desmond Fennell suggested adding a Gaeltacht radio station to the list of demands around the *Quicksilver* protest, a demonstration staged on 18 March 1969 by Gluaiseacht against the filming of an episode of this English-language quiz show in the Gaeltacht (*Broadcasting in Irish* 63). The manifesto for the group Iarchonnachta 1985[2]—started by Fennell and Seosamh Ó Cuaig in 1969—read in part:

> It means a local authority in the region, a national Irish-language newspaper there, a radio station, an airport to send fish to the continent. It means a movie theatre and films in Irish, a regional hospital, a woman's hair salon, butcher shops, printers, laundromats, tailors, cafes, etc. It means a great increase in population for West Connacht.[3]

The radio station (now officially known as RTÉ Raidió na Gaeltachta) is easily the most durable and certainly the most visible (audible, I should say) of all of these Iarchonnachta 1985 dreams; few Gaeltacht areas have laundromats, tailors, or movie theatres (although I discuss Bob Quinn's efforts on that last front in chapter 5), but Irish-language radio is heard in all of them. You would hardly know that it came about after a long series of broken promises. Richard Pine, in his history of Irish radio, traces this to the very beginnings of the state (8–9), although certainly a tipping point came in 1963, with the issue of the report of An Coimisiún um Athbheochan na Gaeilge [the Commission on the Revival of Irish], and the government White Paper in response to that report the year later (in the form of a report titled *Athbheochan na Gaeilge / The Restoration of the Irish Language*).[4] Gearóid Ó Tuathaigh calls this "a lengthy report, the first serious, if rather soft, critical appraisal of the revival policy" (115). But I am struck by the degree to which An Coimisiún's report and the government response are in a kind of strained conversation with one another, with An Coimisiún's report essentially crying, "What is to be done?" and the government saying, "We're doing what we can." What neither document proposed, though, was a radio station for the Gaeltacht, to say nothing of a series of local authorities for the Gaeltacht. Both reports basically assumed that RTÉ (the state-owned broadcaster, which, like the BBC and the CBC, has both television and radio under its umbrella) would be slightly reformed but basically left as it was, just as they assumed that Gaeltarra Éireann (the Gaeltacht development agency) would be slightly reformed but basically left as it was. The Gaeltacht activists, on the other hand, were calling for the creation of new institutions that would be much more local in orientation. But the government's 1969 *White Paper on the Restoration of Irish*, as Niamh Hourigan and Iarfhlaith Watson both recall, did include a recommendation for a Gaeltacht radio station ("A Comparison" 143; *Broadcasting in Irish* 63). Watson goes on to say that, as a result, "In February or March 1969 the government asked RTÉ for a report on the feasibility of a Gaeltacht radio station" (*Broadcasting in Irish* 63).

While these proposals generated little enthusiasm from RTÉ (Watson recalls that the report "complained that it required an increase in the license fee, that a separate channel would be too expensive, but that a Gaeltacht channel would be easier to establish than a national channel" [*Broadcasting in Irish* 64]), then-Taoiseach Jack Lynch was particularly surprising in the degree to which he seemed to endorse the principle of local control of media (Taoiseach is the Irish equivalent of prime minister). "B'Fhearr Stáisiún Raidió Beag i nGach Gaeltacht—An Taoiseach" [A small radio station in each Gaeltacht is preferable—the Taoiseach] was the headline of the Irish-language weekly *Inniu* on 30 January 1970. In this interview, Lynch told *Inniu* that there was an alternative to creating a national station on VHF, which he did not support since "not everyone in the country, nor in the Gaeltacht, has a VHF receiver."[5] He was responding here to RTÉ's proposal that, as Watson recalls, "a segment for the Gaeltacht from 18.45 to 19.45 each evening on the new VHF channel would suffice. This was clearly a half-hearted response—RTÉ had also claimed in the letter that it was awaiting permission to establish a VHF channel and that there were only 50,000 VHF radios in the country" (*Broadcasting in Irish*

64). Lynch also told *Inniu* that he had a different idea. "That is to say putting a small station in each Gaeltacht, like a studio, and employing people from the Gaeltacht there, people who know the Gaeltacht and things like that."[6] In retrospect, this is clearly connected both to the history of government promises about such a station and to the increasing unrest in the Gaeltacht areas. Watson recalls:

> Jack Lynch, who was attending a seminar organised by the Irish Committee of the Munster Branch of Fianna Fáil on 4 April [1969], was approached by a delegation demanding a radio station in Irish for Munster. A report of the meeting appeared in the Irish-language newspaper *Inniu* in which it was claimed that the Taoiseach had agreed to do his utmost to establish a radio and television channel in Irish as soon as possible and that RTÉ would receive an order from Government. This latter statement caused a minor commotion when the Taoiseach denied that he had ever said that RTÉ would receive an order from Government. (*Broadcasting in Irish* 64)

Furthermore, a 1969 film by Pat Kavanagh called *Jack Lynch i gConamara* (which is excerpted in Bob Quinn's 2000 film *Splanc Dheireadh na Gaeltachta*) follows the then-Taoiseach on a campaign tour through the Connemara Gaeltacht and features a sequence where megaphone-wielding activists try to interrupt his speech (one is the activist Seosamh Ó Cuaig, on whom more later). Until that sequence, Lynch had spoken slowly and blandly in Irish at a few campaign stops but mostly chattered with locals in English. When he comes under fire, though, he "comes alive," shooting back in steady Irish that the Gaeltacht is important to Fianna Fáil and will not be forgotten under his government. The film concludes with images that show his motorcade being stopped by nails left in the road; there is a great shot of Lynch smoking his pipe and shooting a camera a look that could stop a train. It isn't difficult to imagine that these experiences in Connemara, or in Munster, coloured Lynch's comments to *Inniu*.

Overall, though, it must have been clear to Lynch that the demand for a radio station was growing and using analogies that must have made his party—officially known as "Fianna Fáil: The Republican Party"—very uncomfortable. Niamh Hourigan recalls that "Bernadette Devlin[7] visited both Galway City and Connemara frequently throughout 1969. Although the immediate object of these visits was to raise money, she also succeeded in raising consciousness levels in Connacht concerning the plight of the Northern nationalist population" ("A Comparison" 125). So far, so good, as far as maintaining the political status quo in Connemara went. But as Hourigan also recalls:

> The underlying message of her speeches, however, threatened political hegemony in Galway West. [In] a predominantly Fianna Fáil constituency, Devlin was a vocal reminder of that party's failure to achieve a United Ireland after almost forty years. PD [People's Democracy] members met with Gaeltacht activists and protest groups during this period and both groups found that they shared considerable common ground. Seosamh Ó Cuaig, a Gaeltacht journalist, forged links with the organization.... Ó Cuaig argues that the prominence of the Northern Civil Rights activists in Galway West created a political opportunity for Gaeltacht activists. It served to underscore the link between political nationalism and the restoration of the Irish language. In doing so, it highlighted Fianna Fáil's failure to achieve either of these objectives. ("A Comparison" 125–26)

This connection had been visible in the lead of an article by Ó Cuaig in the 19 September 1969 issue of *Inniu*, which read "a most remarkable matter of history taking place in the Six Counties for a while now, is a 'free-radio station.'"[8] On 17 October 1969 Ó Cuaig wrote in the *Connacht Tribune* that "it's nothing too difficult; see the mushrooming that has for a while now come from the free-radio station in the Six Counties."[9] Ó Cuaig was referring to Radio Free Derry, a pirate radio station that ran from 1969 to 1970 and during the "Battle of the Bogside"; he recalled in Bob Quinn's 2000 film *Splanc Dheireadh na Gaeltachta* how he had gone to Derry in 1969, had been there for the "Battle of the Bogisde," and was impressed that Radio Free Derry was on the air the entire time. Ó Cuaig told me in a conversation on 29 July 2006 that the pirate radio broadcasts staged by the IRA in the 1940s and 1950s were also important examples for Gluaiseacht Chearta Sibhialta na Gaeltachta, and that they were aware of the radio broadcasts of the Free Wales Army (Ó Cuaig said that the most important European-minority-language connection for Gluaiseacht as a whole was Wales). But the fact that Gluaiseacht Chearta Sibhialta na Gaeltachta saw itself as a southern-Irish equivalent of the civil rights movement in Northern Ireland must have given Jack Lynch pause, especially given the fiery speech that he delivered upon the outbreak of violence in Derry (where he famously pledged that his government would "no longer stand by and see innocent people injured or perhaps worse"). It was becoming clear that the Republic's own embattled minority identified not with the state but with oppressed Northern nationalists whom its government had pledged to defend to the extent that some Unionists feared the Republic would invade Northern Ireland. The late 1960s thus marked the emergence of a movement that identified Irish speakers not as some sort of national essence, but as a minority group, one with the kinds of aspirations and complaints common to such groups worldwide.

One aspect of this newfound minority consciousness was that it was used by some in their efforts to *marginalize* Irish. The clearest example of this is the Language Freedom Movement, which emerged in the early 1960s with the aim of getting Irish removed from leaving-certificate exams (the rough equivalent of A-levels in the British system, or of provincial examinations in the Canadian system). These arguments spilled over into an ongoing debate on RTÉ's enormously popular *The Late Late Show.* In the wake of the release of the government's report *Athbheochan na Gaeilge / The Restoration of the Irish Language*, Garrett FitzGerald (then a senator, later to become Taoiseach) appeared on *The Late Late Show.* Watson describes it thusly:

> Both Fitzgerald and *The Late Late Show* embodied the new ideology. Fitzgerald argued that it was undemocratic for a minority to dictate to the majority. He connected the controversy to Northern Ireland by claiming that there were other minorities in Ireland that were ostracised by national policy, which disseminated and protected an exclusive and homogenous national identity. He linked the controversy to notions of democracy, citizenship, and, within that, minority rights. He expressed the main thrust of the new ideology, in which the Irish language, although remaining of symbolic importance, was of minority interest. Many advocates of Irish, who disagreed with the de-emphasisation within the new ideology, were willing to adopt the minority-rights approach to Irish. (*Broadcasting in Irish* 60–61)

This sense that Irish was unduly dominating the debate about national identity, and more specifically RTÉ's role in that debate, would come up again most vigorously during the debate on "Open Broadcast," which I will discuss shortly. But this slippery sense of who was the aggrieved party—emphasized by the fact that both positions on the language issue claimed Northern Ireland as an analogue—also illustrated the degree to which debates about Irish do not always follow a recognizable minority-rights path. Gluaiseacht Chearta Sibhialta na Gaeltachta was willing to adopt the minority-rights approach, and it's not hard to see why. Irish-speaking areas were almost always underdeveloped economically, they were numerically small, and they existed in the shadow of a much more powerful language. Whatever their opponents may have felt about such a small minority being given undue attention from the state—Article 8 of the constitution recognizing Irish as the first language of the Republic, Irish being required for a leaving certificate, and so on—the movement comprised of actual Irish speakers increasingly emphasized their rebellious, rather than their official, qualities.

One way the movement emphasized this was—in keeping with their longstanding and mostly ignored attempts to get an Irish-language radio station *for the Gaeltacht*—the establishment of what became informally known as a "stáisiún bradach": a stolen station, or pirate station. This was officially known as Saor-raidió Chonamara [Connemara Free Radio], and it began broadcasting on 28 March 1970. Risteárd Ó Glaisne's history of Raidió na Gaeltachta recalls that "despite the *Connacht Tribune*'s publishing a scornful article about 'The Unheard Pirate,' Saor-raidió Chonamara was clearly heard in Ceantar na nOileán, west to Carna, and east as far as Spiddal."[10] That *Connacht Tribune* article asked rhetorically "Did you hear any of the Saor Radio [*sic*] Chonamara—Radio Free Connemara—broadcasts" and went on say that "neither did people in such widely scattered areas as Spiddal, Rossaveal, Lettermullen, Carna, and the Aran Islands. Spot-checks in these Gaeltacht areas failed to locate anyone who had heard the Irish-only 'pirate,' which went off the air voluntarily on Sunday" ("The Unheard 'Pirate'" 1). As the article states, the station shut down fairly quickly, broadcasting from only 28 to 31 March. But it was re-established for Oireachtas na nGael of November 1970, which was itself a sort of "counter-Oireachtas" that was held to protest the holding of the official Oireachtas outside of the Gaeltacht (the Oireachtas, or more grammatically An tOireachtas, is an annual cultural festival celebrating the Irish language). Ó Cuaig reported in *Inniu* on 13 November 1970 that according to a handout for the event, "there will be a debate on matters pertaining to development, co-operatives, politics, and, in particular, on a Gaeltacht authority. There's a good chance the debate will be broadcast on the radio as well."[11] For the Gluaiseacht activists, wherever there was talk of development, co-operatives, politics, and governance, there was almost always talk of media as well.

These pirate efforts essentially embarrassed RTÉ into creating an Irish-language station. As Hourigan recalls, "After the festival [Oireachtas na nGael], George Colley [at that time Minister for Finance] announced officially that Raidio na Gaeltachta would be established" ("A Comparison" 152). Raidió na Gaeltachta (RnaG) went on the air on 2 April 1972, Easter Sunday (the history of debates around the station's governance is found in Watson, *Broadcasting in Irish* 64–66 and in Hourigan, "A Comparison" 170–77). Since its establishment, one of RnaG's highest priorities has always been the maintenance of its community-oriented ethic. Watson recalls that very early on RnaG rejected the policy of allowing news to come from RTÉ in Dublin, preferring to use its own Irish-speaking correspondents both throughout Ireland and internationally (*Broadcasting in Irish* 67). Although it was officially part of RTÉ from the very beginning (as it remains), RnaG wasn't simply an arm of the national media that happened to speak Irish, but an organization based in the Gaeltacht that sought to expand outward into the world. This was also an important aspiration of the Cinegael and Teilifís na Gaeltachta groups; their key members were closely linked both to community activism and internationalization, activities whose minority-rights orientation rather than official or state-sponsored quality was clearly influenced by the writings of Desmond Fennell and just as clearly by the experiences of Gluaiseacht Chearta Sibhialta na Gaeltachta and of Saor-raidió Chonamara.

But before examaining these Gluaiseacht-influenced North Atlantic intellectuals and media activists individually, I want to explain the sophistication of activism around the Irish language vis-à-vis communication theory. The first phase of the movement—the late 1960s—was heavily influenced by Raymond Williams's widely read book *Communications* (1962). This is particularly evident in the controversy around the resignation of several key members of RTÉ's staff (Jack Dowling, Leila Doolan, and Bob Quinn) and the book they produced, *Sit Down and Be Counted* (for which Williams wrote the introduction and which is remarkable for the way that it anticipates the arguments of Williams's 1974 classic *Television*). The second phase—basically the mid-seventies—was heavily influenced by Herbert Schiller's work on cultural domination; we see this most clearly in the arguments between then-minister for Posts and Telegraphs Conor Cruise O'Brien and Irish-language activists over the amendment of the Broadcasting Act and the transmission of the BBC into Ireland (a debate that strongly recalls the arguments around "minority" status so central to the Gluaiseacht period).

Raymond Williams and *Sit Down and Be Counted*

On 23 and 29 May 1969, Jack Dowling and Leila Doolan, respectively, submitted their resignations to RTÉ; Bob Quinn recalls in *Maverick* that "I formally resigned from my staff job at RTÉ in October 1968" (11). They had each been producers there: Quinn had been brought up through the station's trainee programs; Dowling had come from the army to produce news; and Doolan had come from the theatre, first to produce such groundbreaking programs as the serial drama *The Riordans* and the news series *7 Days*, and eventually to become Head of Light Entertainment (many years later she would head up Bord Scannán na hÉireann / Irish Film Board). Their resignation followed months of arguments with management about the direction of the station, and their letters were all lengthy indictments of the way in which the station was being run. "In particular," Dowling wrote, "it seems to me that the progressive dominance of programming by technicians and administrators in radio has been disastrous; sheer quantity dominates everything and everyone" (Dowling, Doolan, and Quinn xxxv–xxxvi).

Their connection to critical communications theory of the 1960s and 1970s is signalled, of course, by the fact that Williams wrote the introduction to *Sit Down and Be Counted* and by the fact that, as that book recalls, he gave a talk to the Television, Radio and Film Guild of Ireland in 1969. *Sit Down and Be Counted* recalls that "in April 1969, the Guild, hoping to give the debate [over the role that RTÉ could play in politics] some purpose, and, thereby, perhaps broaden its own membership to include the technical people, held a public seminar in Dublin on the topic 'Broadcasting—What Can We Do?' Raymond Williams, the Welsh writer and don who had so valuably contributed to communications in Britain, was the guest of honour" (175). *Sit Down and Be Counted* also recalls Williams's argument that "often, television and radio as they are *actually* used, prevent communications. Potentially, they *are* communication" (175). This is the perspective of *Sit Down and Be Counted* overall. The authors go out of their way to point out just how much the management of RTÉ thought of them as a bunch of grouchy, unrepresentative malcontents; they also write, "The [Williams] seminar was regarded by the Director-General as a splinter movement" (175). But in a more ideological sense, it is also the book's overall position that Ireland's elites in politics, business, and the media had sought to use communications technology as a mouthpiece of their ideology and actively resisted anything but a one-way approach. Williams's introduction recalls his time in Dublin and makes his solidarity with RTÉ clear: "I do not know the events from within but I am sure of this: that the voices I heard there, speaking of their own land and of its renewal, are at once Irish and international, in the most authentic senses" (xii). Williams had already recalled the solidarity he felt with these RTÉ producers and, specifically, the degree to which they represented the struggle of public broadcasters against state or commercial forces (struggles that he also saw embodied by disputes in Czechoslovakia and France). As he wrote in his *Listener* column of 12 June 1969,

> I spent some time recently with Radio Telefis Eireann, in Dublin, doing a few programmes and some seminars with producers. I enjoyed it very much, and still think Dublin the only place where I would be asked to give a seminar in the Light Entertainment Department.... Now, in the last two weeks, some of the very best of these people are resigning, after a dispute with the authority about just these issues, and specifically about the effects on programmes of managerial, accounting and commercial pressures. I think they need the urgent support of

all their British colleagues, just as the Czechs and the French did. (*Raymond Williams on Television* 65)

But the deeper Williams–*Sit Down* connection is more theoretical. Williams's treatise *Communications* engages with the complexity of balancing tradition and modernity (previewing his work in *The Country and the City*) as well as dealing with the degree to which television is, like a number of technological practices, complicit in the dilution of democratic life and the replacement of an engaged public with an alienated "mass." These are also recurring critiques offered by *Sit Down and Be Counted*. The Irish book, though, is also highly critical of a purely technological view of television; it argues repeatedly that "a television camera is *not* a mere lump of matter. It is an intelligent organisation of physical components designed to achieve a human purpose. To think of it as dead matter is mere abstraction" (Dowling, Doolan, and Quinn 236). This very precisely follows the arguments that Williams would make five years later in his most widely read book, *Television*.

The way in which *Sit Down and Be Counted* anticipates that book, especially via its rejection of technological determinism, is positively eerie. Midway through, Dowling, Doolan, and Quinn write that "communications-technology is not culturally, socially, or morally negative but ... is, in itself, positive and formative of a cultural and moral attitude of mind and emotion" (233). This is fundamental to their overall objections to the manner in which RTÉ was being run. They struggled not only against the technocratic world view of station management, but also against the degree to which decisions about the nature of the broadcasts were being limited by minds interested only in advancing technical sophistication. In lamenting the degree to which Irish-language programming, literary programming, and arts programming were relegated to "minority" status, they also identify one way that television was being used that was far from neutrally reflecting the facts on the ground. The Irish-language chapter of *Sit Down and Be Counted* opens by pointing out that:

> According to the census of 1961, 716,420 people in this country have some Irish. According to the Department of Post and Telegraphs, there are 444,000 television licenses in the country. According to this there are more people in this country that understand Irish than there are television sets.[12]

The numbers simply did not bear out the idea that Irish was a minority interest. An ideological process was clearly at work here, and that process was clearly born of a desire to construct the Irish mass as uninterested in the Irish language except for a tiny and thus irrelevant minority. But the determining factors leading to this sense of the Irish language as marginal were not neutrally demographic. Williams's *Communications* also rejects this presupposition; Williams longs in that work for a time when "we would have broken out of the social situation in which it is taken for granted that the arts and learning are minority interests, and that the ordinary use of general communications is to get power or profit from the combination of people's needs and their inexperience" (172). Earlier in the book, discussing the way that religious, arts, and Irish-language programs were segregated from the main line of RTÉ, Dowling, Doolan, and Quinn assert that in fact, "the determining factors are, we believe, technological.... It seems to us, therefore, that technology is, *at least* administratively, formative. The pretence that it is neutral is a 'mystification' theory" (234, emphasis theirs). Williams's *Television* is also explicitly opposed to this sort of mystification, seeing it, as the writers of *Sit Down and Be Counted* did, as a way by which ideological or political projects could be concealed as neutral. Williams argues for an interpretation of technological forms such as television that "would allow us to see not only its history but also its uses in a more radical way." He goes on to say that:

> Such an interpretation would differ from technological determinism in that it would restore *intention* to the process of research and development. The technology would be seen, that is to say, as being looked for and developed with certain purposes and practices already in mind. At the same time the interpretation would differ from symptomatic technology in that these purposes and practices would be seen as *direct*: as known social needs, purposes and practices to which the technology is not marginal but central. (7, italics his)

These purposes and practices were not, for either Williams or the *Sit Down and Be Counted* authors, inherently domineering. *Television*, like *Communications*, is devoted in no small part to the ways in which media technology could be used to increase civic, ethical, or aesthetic engagement. But all of these texts are very clear about the degree to which that is not generally the case. Furthermore, all of these texts are determined to make their readers see that this is a decision made by power-holders, a decision made for ideological and political reasons. One of Williams's major contributions to the discourse around media technology is to question the neutrality of that technology; this is a lesson both learned and anticipated by *Sit Down and Be Counted*. The Cuban filmmaker Julio García Espinosa (whose connection to Quinn's work I discuss in more detail in chapter 5) also shared this skepticism towards technical determinism, writing in an essay on film and television schools that "the distance between what we understand by *hardware and software* is today more scandalous than ever."[13] García Espinosa also wrote that "technology now allows education to undo the most mechanical aspects and concentrate on those that reclaim a perspective that is more profound, integrated, and scientific than that of the specialist."[14] These kinds of gaps, between hardware and software, mechanical and integrated approaches, were central to the *Sit Down and Be Counted* authors' sense of the ways in which communications media had been misused and misunderstood by the general public; this was a set of concerns that was very much part of international discourse in the 1960s and 1970s, from Wales to Cuba.[15]

Sit Down and Be Counted also exhibits Williams's hostility towards the notion of the "mass" audience. *Sit Down and Be Counted* recalls, in its coverage of the seminar at RTÉ, that "Williams' main thesis in this discussion was that there are no 'mass' media, for the simple reason that there are no 'masses' but intricately overlapping structures of audience-interest. The whole notion of 'masses,' in his view, was an unconscious conspiracy on the part of manipulative élites. They were an invention that permitted the transmission of controlling ideas in a one-way traffic" (Dowling, Doolan, and Quinn 175). This is a fairly precise restating of the thesis of *Communications*, where Williams outlines his three reasons for rejecting the notion of "mass":

> First, while we go on talking about "the masses" we can have neither the respect for people nor the sense of growth that underlie responsibility. Second, while we go on thinking in a separatist way about "classes"—whether social groupings or such educational groupings as "the academic type," "the technical type," "the operative whose interests are all in his hands"—we cannot have sufficiently flexible ideas about people, and will be constantly tempted to divide our culture into separate areas with no bridges between them. Third, while there is an emphasis on profit, there will be a constant pressure to concentrate on things already known and safe, with never enough effort given to the much longer and more difficult job of trying new things and offering new ideas and experience. (101–2)

This rejection of the concept of "the masses," as well as the sterile and impoverished culture that goes with it, was the real nub of the matter for the *Sit Down and Be Counted* group. In that same passage where the *Sit Down and Be Counted* authors decry the marginalization of arts and Irish-language programming, they also write that RTÉ's "transmission schedule ... is mainly concerned to capture an amorphous 'mass' audience" (Dowling, Doolan, and Quinn 234). They denounce the notion of such an audience a bit later, writing of the sort of mass-marketed productions that RTÉ wanted to focus on,

"This is not popular culture, it is merely popular conditioning. It cultivates nothing, but it manufactures the 'mass'—a hideously commercial product—and identifies it with The People" (273). And again, García Espinosa was just as strongly against the notion of "the mass" as Williams or the *Sit Down and Be Counted* authors, writing in his 1977 manifesto "Por un cine imperfecto" that "mass art (or art for the masses) requires the people to have no taste" ("For an Imperfect Cinema" 30),[16] whereas popular art "needs and constantly tends to develop the personal, individual taste of a people" ("For an Imperfect Cinema" 30).[17] This sort of false populism obscured the real power at work here—elites who benefited from a status quo capitalist approach to broadcasting. And it is the self-perpetuating elites of RTÉ that served as the constant target of *Sit Down and Be Counted*, much as commercial cinema (both Hollywood and Latin American) does for García Espinosa. It is Williams's theories about the mass audience, of course, that most clearly provided the ammunition for the *Sit Down and Be Counted* authors' hostility to the concept, even if he is far less polemical about the damage wrought by the operators of state-owned television stations in *Communications*.

Part of Quinn, Dowling, and Doolan's critique of this false populism was the degree to which RTÉ seemed to ghettoize any attention to regionalism; this is where their defence of Irish-language broadcast can be seen to be consistent with their indictment of the technological determinism in which they believed the station was so invested. Of RTÉ's tendency to embrace a then-emergent global commercial culture, the *Sit Down and Be Counted* group write, "the only defence against this international uniformity of spirit is regional diversity—the greatest possible measure of decentralisation and diversification of control and initiative" (381). Again, the Williams of *Communications* is audible here, specifically his sense that "the way forward is the creation of genuinely independent programme companies," which would circumvent the centralizing and homogenizing quality of BBC programming (157). And it is their call for Gaeltacht television where this desire for decentralization finds its most passionate expression, one that anticipates the calls for local Gaeltacht control that I discuss in chapter 4 as well as the calls for local Gaeltacht television discussed in chapters 5 and 6, and does so in a way that *centralizes* the Irish language in the universe of RTÉ. In the Irish-language chapter of *Sit Down and Be Counted*, the authors dream of a station whose programming includes "musicians, poets, thespians, and various groups looking for airtime."[18] They conclude the chapter with the following:

> We believe that democratic control of this sort will grow naturally in the Gaeltacht. We also believe that it will not be long until the Irish people generally will ask themselves "why don't we have a national station like this?" We believe that the salvation of RTÉ is interwoven with the salvation of Irish at RTÉ and that the salvation of Irish depends on the people of the Gaeltacht.[19]

This passage certainly reflects Fennell's distinction between "pobal" [people or community] and "teanga" [language], a key distinction for Gaeltacht activists generally. But the fíor-ghael [pure laine Gaelic] among my readers will surely hear the echoes in this passage of the famous words of the great Irish-language novelist and activist Máirtín Ó Cadhain: "The Irish language is the recapture of Ireland and the recapture of Ireland is the salvation of Irish. The people's language will save the people."[20] Ó Cadhain made that famous statement as part of a lecture given in Donegal in August 1969; it was published as a pamphlet called *Gluaiseacht na Gaeilge: Gluaiseacht ar Strae* [Irish Language Movement: A Movement Astray]. He argued there that the language movement needed to put itself in the vanguard of Irish life, to fulfill the aspirations of the Irish Revolution. He rejected—as he did throughout all of his work—a Dublin-led revival strategy. Although Ó Cadhain was quite a bit more militant and pessimistic than the *Sit Down and Be Counted* authors (aside from his IRA involvement, it is important to remember that in 1969 he published the very pessimistic report *An Ghaeilge Bheo: Destined to Pass*, about the fate of Irish as a spoken language), he saw, as they did, Irish and the struggles to preserve its *culture* as a key part of the struggle to make a just, independent Irish society. Although *Sit Down and Be Counted* reads in places like an extended grumble about specific conditions of employment (the authors have quite a bit to say about the details of working life at RTÉ), the invocation of Ó Cadhain makes it clear that there was more at stake. It is not hard to see how arguments about the interplay between the remaking or retaking of a post-colonial culture, language, and community are connected to the role of media technology in everyday life. These arguments are indeed, as Williams wrote, at once Irish and international. A few years later this critical internationalism and revived nationalism would once again combine to fight a media-related struggle in the debate about the broadcast of British television in Ireland.

Herbert Schiller and the Debate on Open Broadcast

Arguments about British broadcasting in Ireland were much more explicitly connected to the Irish language than the argument put forward by *Sit Down and Be Counted.* The struggle to prevent this kind of cultural imperialism, though, was similar to the *Sit Down and Be Counted* debate in its connection to communications theory. In place of the ideas and occasionally the physical presence in Ireland of Raymond Williams, we see in this debate about "Open Broadcast" the ideas and at times the physical presence in Ireland of Herbert Schiller.

"Open Broadcast" refers to a series of proposals made in 1974 by Conor Cruise O'Brien, then minister of Posts and Telegraphs for the Irish Labour Party (which was at the time in coalition with the vaguely liberal party Fine Gael). O'Brien's reform project got underway in earnest in February 1974, when he announced that he planned to amend the Broadcast Act by way of reducing RTÉ's imperative to contribute to "the development of the national culture," and, by implication, the development of the Irish language. "I have great respect for the Irish language," he said on 24 February 1974 in a speech announcing the policy. "But I have very little respect for what is called 'the first official language'[21] and I believe that 'the first official language' and the narrow concept of the national culture go hand in dreary hand" ("Policy Reform for Irish" 13). The other controversial element of his reform package was the creation of a second channel of RTÉ, one that would rebroadcast programs from the BBC. Watson summarizes it this way:

> The debate revolved around Cruise O'Brien's proposal to re-broadcast the BBC and opponents who advocated RTÉ-control of a second channel. To a large extent this debate reflected the division in the "Amendment Debate," between the "modern" and earlier ideology. Supporters of re-broadcasting BBC argued that it created competition in the television "market" in the Republic, that it offered viewers choice and that it demonstrated to Northern Protestants that we were not "inward-looking." Opponents argued that the Government would [in the words of then-Senator Mary Robinson] "if not entirely kill RTÉ, certainly reduce RTÉ to a tiny minority viewing programme." (*Broadcasting in Irish* 74)

Both of these efforts ultimately failed (Hourigan writes that O'Brien "had to withdraw the proposal at the end of 1975 and RTÉ was given responsibility for programming on the new channel" ["A Comparison" 136]). But these debates, as Watson makes clear in *Broadcasting in Irish*, were not only joined but also inseparably linked to emerging debates surrounding Irish identity and its place in the wider world. One group of intellectuals—of which O'Brien was arguably the most prominent—believed that a narrow nationalism had too long defined Irish life, and that a sentimental, slavish attention to the Irish language embodied this narrowness. Another group believed that Ireland had not yet fully emerged from being a colonized possession, and that the perilous condition of Irish-speaking communities embodied the degree to which the state had neglected its own fragile culture.

O'Brien's entry into the debate over national identity was very much of a piece with the intellectual territory that he had been staking out. He became famous in the late 1950s and early 1960s for his involvement in Irish foreign affairs and the United Nations, specifically in Katanga during the Dag Hammarskjöld period (this is recounted in his 1962 autobiography *To Katanga and Back*). But in the late 1960s he turned sharply against what he perceived as simplistic nationalism, specifically as it pertained to strife in Northern Ireland. He wrote in a 1969 essay called "The Irish Question" that there was a very real division in the cultural traditions of Ulster, and that "the pretence that this is not so, and that partition is 'artificial' and 'unnatural,' has created the great illusion of the Nationalist tradition" (5). He was allergic, in short, not so much to the idea of Irish independence but to the ways in which nationalism seemed to deny both historical facts and cultural reality. "I reject the idea of Sinn Féin, in the sense of cultural isolationism, the negative and moribund sense," he said in the February 1974 speech. "But in a more philosophical sense ... there was a force in the words. It is proper that we should be interested in ourselves—ourselves as we really are, not as a fantastic image of ourselves" ("Policy Reform for Irish" 13). O'Brien is, in the final analysis, a Burkean; this is borne out not only by his 1992 book *The Great Melody: A Thematic Biography and Commented Anthology of Edmund Burke*, but also by the cool, anti-revolutionary rationalism that O'Brien always seemed to be trying to display.

Maolsheachlainn Ó Caollaí came from the opposite end of the Irish left. He had created a minor controversy in 1970 when, according to the *Irish Times*, he resigned from Comhairle na Gaeilge[22] "as a protest against the government's refusal to take its advice on the means necessary for the restoration of the Irish language" ("O Caollai Resigns from Language Body" 4). The *Irish Times* also pointed out that the tipping point was the threats to close the Irish-language school at Dún Chaoin and the police violence that marred the protest against that closure, which I discussed earlier. Ó Caollaí was better known, though, through his connection to Conradh na Gaeilge (sometimes known as the Gaelic League),[23] of which he was president from 1968 to 1971 and with which he continued to be closely involved thereafter. This was a period when Conradh was both sharply nationalist and keenly interested in broadcasting.

Hourigan writes that "Proinsias Mac Aonghusa cites the entry of young activists such as Maolsheachlainn Ó Caollaí and Ité Uí Chionnaith [*sic*; her name is Íte Ní Chionnaith] as a key factor in the acceleration of the movement's interest in the media.... From this period onwards, some form of media committee existed under a variety of titles" ("A Comparison" 195). Ní Chionnaith, who would become the organization's first female president (1985–89), was very close to Ó Caollaí politically. Hourigan recounts that "from 1977–1985, she constituted one of the most radical voices in Conradh na Gaeilge.... From a Republican background, she became a lecturer in Communications at the Dublin Institute of Technology.... A firm advocate of the separate channel proposal [for Irish Gaelic], she went to prison in 1977 for non-payment of her licence fee" ("A Comparison" 215). Both Ní Chionnaith and Ó Caollaí saw Conradh na Gaeilge as a political-activist organization, one that used the language as a means to advance a more or less nationalist struggle. They were, like the *Sit Down and Be Counted* authors, clearly influenced by Máirtín Ó Cadhain's vision of the Irish language as being key to the retaking of the country from the legacy of foreign colonialism. Ó Caollaí's writing is peppered with discussion of Ireland's neo-colonial status, indicting American capitalist elites but also dwelling on the legacy of British rule. You can almost see Conor Cruise O'Brien rolling his eyes as he read Ó Caollaí's overall assessment that "we are in a neo-colonial relationship with Britain.... The ultimate aim of British imperialism in Ireland has always been to destroy our self-esteem by alienating us from our roots and we have always refused to finally submit" ("Open Broadcasting," *Irish Times* 12; pamphlet 3). Ó Caollaí was writing in explicit opposition to O'Brien's proposals that RTÉ rebroadcast the BBC and de-emphasize the Irish language; the essay was entitled "Open Broadcasting: A Recipe for Extinction." Ó Caollaí made similar points about foreign domination of domestic television in the Irish-language press, where there was a fair bit of coverage of the subject.[24] He took issue in the 13 June 1975 *Inniu* with the government's plan to rebroadcast the BBC, writing of the government that "it is mainly using the most important instruments of neo-colonialism, a new trend that the imperialist countries have used to rob from other countries. It is solely in this context that sense can be made of the policy of rebroadcasting BBC1."[25]

The "Recipe for Extinction" essay first appeared in the *Irish Times* a week after O'Brien's speech (on 4 March 1974), but it was later republished by Conradh na Gaeilge as a pamphlet. Conradh published quite a few pamphlets during this period, many of them focused specifically on television: Ó Caollaí's *Open Broadcasting: An Alternative* and Harri Pritchard Jones's *Wales and*

Ireland: A TV Contrast appeared a bit later in 1974, Ó Caollaí's *Broadcasting and the Growth of a Culture* appeared in May 1975, the anonymous *Teilifís do na Daoine* and its English translation *Television for the People* appeared in March 1977, and Jack Noonan's English-language interview with Ó Caollaí entitled *Issues in Television Broadcasting in Ireland* appeared in 1978. Most of this work is highly polemical, although also quite detailed in terms of its command of the finer points of policy and demographics. But two of those pamphlets had more of a theoretical edge, and they made the stakes of Conradh's investment in broadcasting clearer.

The first one was in English: *New Modes of Cultural Domination*, by Herbert Schiller. It was based on a lecture he gave to Conradh na Gaeilge in Dublin on 2 September 1977, and as its title indicates, it follows strongly from his classic work *Communication and Cultural Domination*, published in 1976. As Ó Caollaí says in the introduction to Schiller's *New Modes of Cultural Domination*, "Dr. Schiller's work played an important inspirational part on the campaign which defeated the Irish government's plan to rebroadcast BBC-1" (5). This goes some way in explaining why the lecture itself, as reprinted in *New Modes of Cultural Domination*, is largely a restating of Schiller's theses about the ways in which elites use communications technology to restrict rather than encourage democratic participation. The important element of Schiller's work in an Irish context was that it served as a polemical backbone, not a detailed policy blueprint. Ó Caollaí complains (a bit grumpily) in his introduction to the lecture that "Dr. Schiller's work is little known in Ireland. This is not surprising since he challenges cultural domination which to the majority of our opinion leaders is perfectly natural and acceptable" (5). But another likely reason that his work is little known in Ireland is that although Schiller had quite a bit to say about South America, Eastern Europe, and Canada in his most widely read book, *Communication and Cultural Domination* (from which the Irish lecture pamphlet took its title), there is nothing there specific to Irish television, and relatively little specific even to British television. In the question period of his Conradh lecture, where he speaks a bit about British imperialism, he speaks about Irish Gaelic so generally that I am left with the sense that he doesn't actually know about the very complex politics of the language:

> Q.: What relevance has the Irish language in regard to cultural domination?
>
> DR. SCHILLER: In their mother tongue the Irish people have a powerful defence mechanism against cultural domination, if they avail themselves of it. Some of the most glaring examples of cultural penetration exist in English-speaking Canada, where the Canadian population is heavily concentrated along the

> U.S.–Canadian boundary. In many Canadian cities and communities the people are far heavier viewers of American than of their own, domestic programming. Of course, there is more than one explanation for this but such a condition would be impossible if a language barrier existed. The Irish language is of priceless value to you. Your society at least has the possibility of organizing defenses, developing initiatives and being able to consider creative alternatives. This, then, is a very powerful asset. In fact, I think it is crucial. (21)

These are words of support to be sure, but they are not much more engaged with sociolinguistic reality than the pleasantries so often mouthed by the Irish government. They certainly give no sense of the complex minority position that Irish occupied in the contemporary state, or of the deep disconnect between that reality and the language's constitutional prominence.

Schiller's importance to the Conradh activists, then, was in the way that he saw communications technology as politics by other means. Most important was his contention that "information and the entire communications process have become key elements in the business of social control" (*Communication and Cultural Domination* 79). Furthermore, a central element of Schiller's *Communication and Cultural Domination* is its tendency to reiterate and expand on elements of Williams's *Television* (which had been published two years earlier), specifically its rejection of technological determinism, a rejection so crucial to the *Sit Down and Be Counted* authors and to Ó Caollaí, who seemed to be following in their footsteps. On that topic, Schiller writes that:

> Technology, which appears mainly, and is almost exclusively understood, as visible machinery and hardware, lends itself admirably to the claim that it is neutral, value free, and employable under *any* social order, for sometimes quite different ends. Moreover, the concept of free flow of information, which holds that benefits accrue to everyone participating in that flow, but which, in reality, is a one-way street for exercising domination by the already-powerful, is extended to technology—with the still greater likelihood of intensifying the dependency of the weaker parties. (50–51)

Schiller's work, then, like that of Williams, was important because it sought to expose the ideology of technological forms and criticized the self-serving tendency of elites to hide the degree to which they were implicated in conscious decisions about the uses of technology. In this way, then, the arguments of the *Sit Down and Be Counted* group and the Ó-Caollaí-led campaigns are very much of a piece theoretically.

The second pamphlet that laid out this theoretical position was in Irish: *Tiarnas Cultúir: Craolachán in Éirinn* [Cultural Domination: Broadcast in Ireland], by Ó Caollaí himself. The title makes the connection to Schiller explicit. Although Schiller's work itself doesn't come up all that often in the pamphlet (Ó Caollaí quotes the Dublin lecture and gets some statistical information from a 1976 article of Schiller's called "Advertising and International Communications" [17]), the way that Ó Caollaí frames the Irish media situation strongly recalls Schiller. Like his American colleague, Ó Caollaí was interested both in Canada and in the Third World as relevant parallels for the Irish situation. Schiller had, however, sung quite a different tune about Canada in *Communication and Cultural Domination* than the pessimistic song of *New Modes of Cultural Domination*, writing in the earlier book that:

> For the new nations which were colonies not so long ago, the effort to create communications-cultural policies for national liberation, and to satisfy the working people's needs for better material conditions of existence is no marginal item.... For nations that were not held in the colonial grip, but for a variety of reasons experience increasing cultural domination, the issues of social integrity and survival are also deeply felt. Canada, for example, a nation of enormous breadth and potential with a history of independence and development, now exhibits a profound and justifiable concern with preserving its own culture and retaining the opportunity to develop it further. (71)

This rejection of a simplistic First World–Third World axis is characteristic of Schiller's work. He was well aware that just because a country was not generally considered part of the Third World didn't necessarily mean that it didn't face comparable issues. Luke Gibbons has famously written that "Ireland is a First World country, but with a Third World memory" (3); sixteen years earlier, Ó Caollaí was trying to enunciate this as well, and Schiller's world view provided a way for him to do that. Explaining the way that West Germany and Belgium were experiencing pressure from American capitalism, Ó Caollaí wrote in *Tiarnas Cultúir* that:

> The story is much worse throughout the *Third World*, and even in Canada, a country that has plenty of indigenous wealth and resources. In 1971 only 28 percent of income from the 70 biggest companies (or advertising agencies) in Canada was from Canadian companies. American companies earned the other 72 percent. Three American companies created the majority of television advertising as well. In Thailand, in 1975, foreign companies had income of $25.3 million and left $1.5 million to Thai companies.[26]

This sounds like a sort of combination of the statements in *Communication and Cultural Domination* and *New Modes of Cultural Domination*, seeing the world not simply as colonial or post-colonial, but instead looking for cultures which have been able, for whatever reason, to assert some cultural independence even as they remain essentially dominated by American-affiliated capitalism. The ease with which Ó Caollaí moves from a Canadian example to a Thai one seems seminally "Schillerian."

What is also Schillerian about Ó Caollaí's position on television, though, is his tendency, in contradiction to the activists of Gluaiseacht Chearta Sibhialta na Gaeltachta, to see matters of linguistic activism and communication technology in *national*, rather than local terms. Schiller wrote in *Communication and Cultural Domination* that "*national* communications policy making may be regarded as a battleground of the contending forces on the social stage" (79). The emphasis there is my own; Schiller's writing always has a certain geopolitical tinge to it, being engaged with the way that weaker nations are exploited by stronger ones via communications technology; there is very little presence of the sort of regionalism that drives the minority-rights influenced discourse of groups like Gluaiseacht. Similarly, Ó Caollaí said in an interview with Jack Noonan (published in 1978 as a pamphlet called *Issues in Television Broadcasting in Ireland*):

> In the present circumstances, I do not favour the idea of a "Teilifís na Gaeltachta" as an alternative to a full service in Irish shared by two national channels. The majority of viewers of Irish-medium programmes live in non-Gaeltacht areas. To set up a Gaeltacht service, under present circumstances, would be to isolate the Gaeltacht and the service in Irish from the majority of Irish-medium viewers whose right to a service in Irish is equally as valid as that of the Gaeltacht. (3)

This is an explicit rejection of the approach of Gluaiseacht, of Fennell's concept of *pobal* over *teanga*. Ó Caollaí, like Conradh generally, sees *national* communications policy as the battleground here, not a policy that empowers Irish-speaking parts of the nation.[27] This is, of course, a reasonable view to take, especially for someone like Ó Caollaí, head of a group whose mandate was specifically *national* and which had no real brief beyond linguistic matters. Community development is not what Conradh was charged with doing or claimed to be expert in, and thus Ó Caollaí knows what his job is and advances a view of language policy consistent with that job. But this view is also consistent with Conradh's reputation among Gaeltacht activists for being a group of urbanites uncomfortable with or uninterested in the rural people who actually populate the Irish-speaking communities. Reg Hindley, writing of the period immediately after the War of Independence, states that in Northern Ireland, "as in the Free State, inherited economic and social structures virtually predetermined that the Gaelic League leadership should derive primarily from the urban and predominantly middle-class learners instead of from the remote and depressed Gaeltachtaí" (40). Very little had happened to change these structures in the 1970s. Thus, it is important to emphasize that while Conradh na Gaeilge and Gluaiseacht were ostensibly committed to the same goal, they saw the television-related struggle in very different ways. Gluaiseacht, as did the *Sit Down and Be Counted* authors, explicitly rejected the very notion of mass media, and thus saw decentralization as a top priority, along with the empowerment of small groups within the state. For Ó Caollaí, it was the state *overall* that needed to be recovered; empowering the small groups just wasn't enough. Ó Caollaí's writing certainly reflects Ó Cadhain's belief that "the Irish language is the recapture of Ireland and the recapture of Ireland is the salvation of Irish." But it did not follow for Ó Caollaí, as it did for the *Sit Down and Be Counted* authors, that "the salvation of Irish depends on the people of the Gaeltacht."[28]

Conclusion

The young, well-educated radicals of which Gearóid Ó Tuathaigh wrote so approvingly did bring results; the establishment of Raidió na Gaeltachta is probably the most concrete of the media-related victories of this period of Gaeltacht activism. But different sorts of results were visible from this period as well: the emergence of a politically and theoretically engaged discussion of the problems facing Irish television. Without doubt, the specifically televisual activism that followed in the 1970s and 1980s was of a different cast than what we see here. Raymond Williams did not influence Bob Quinn's Cinegael project in the same way that he did the *Sit Down and Be Counted* project; Herbert Schiller did not influence the Teilifís na Gaeltachta project in the same way that he did the Conradh na Gaeilge media campaigns. As I will try to show in the next chapters, both Quinn and Ó hÉallaithe's efforts were strongly influenced by the writings of Desmond Fennell, someone who is much more difficult to place politically than the clearly leftist Williams and Schiller (and who is, in this way, typically Irish).[29] But this period did help to enunciate some terms of the debate. Cinegael and Teilifís na Gaeltachta adopted many of the tactics of Saor-raidió Chonamara (such as the staging of low-cost, and sometimes illegal, media production), and also internalized the sense that media needed to be re-centralized and based in vibrant, culturally autonomous communities.

Indeed, groups like Cinegael and Teilifís na Gaeltachta sought, in the words of Irish senator (and later minister for Arts, Culture and the Gaeltacht) Michael D. Higgins, to create "revolutionary art, art that is rooted in social experience" (he made that call during a Seanad Éireann debate on the Broadcasting Authority on 6 May 1975). Higgins was, probably unwittingly, echoing the idealism of Dziga Vertov, an idealism that is such a strong current of North Atlantic media of this period. Media activism around Irish Gaelic has never been simply pragmatic; it has always had a discernibly political and theoretical base. The debates of the 1960s and 1970s showed the activists of the 1970s and 1980s that such a base could, as Ó Tuathaigh wrote, challenge the defeatism and fatalism of a century.

Notes

1 Tarlach de Blacán [*sic*] is identified in the article as the administrator of the Gaelic group at Trinity College Dublin and the chairman of the demonstration; Tarlach de Blácam is now a highly successful sweater designer on Inis Meáin.

2 Iarchonnacht 1985 was meant to rectify a hundred years of underdevelopment in the Gaeltacht regions, especially in West Connacht [Iarchonnacht]. Its manifesto was published in Fennell's booklet *Iarchonnacht Began*. It was an explicitly internationalist movement, having, as that manifesto stated, "gotten examples from Switzerland and Norway" [glacadh sampla ón Eilvéis agus ón Ioruiadh (45)], whose history of decentralized government and successful language revival after breaking away from a larger kingdom, respectively, were an inspiration to Fennell and a frequent topic of his writings on the future of Irish governance. I discuss the internationalism of Fennell's Gaeltacht plans in greater detail in the next chapter.

3 "Ciallaíonn sé údarás áitiúil don réigiún, nuachtán náisiúnta Gaeilge ann, stáisiún raidió, aerfort chun iasc a sheachadadh chun na Mór-roinne. Ciallaíonn sé pictiúrlanna agus scannáin i nGaeilge, ospidéal ceantair, gruagairí ban, búistéirí, clódóirí, tithe níocháin, táilliúirí, caiféanna, srl. Ciallaíonn sé méadú mór ar dhaonra Iarchonnacht." (*Iarchonnacht Began* 45)

4 An Coimisiún's report was published in an Irish-language edition titled *An Coimisiún um Athbheochan na Gaeilge: An Tuarascáil Dheiridh*, with an English-language summary titled *The Restoration of the Irish Language* published simultaneously but in a separate edition. The government's bilingual response was also titled *Athbheochan na Gaeilge / The Restoration of the Irish Language*.

5 "ní gach duine sa tír, ná sa Ghaeltacht, a bhfuil raidió VHF aige" ("B'Fhearr Staisiun Raidio" 2).

6 "Is é sin, stáisiún beag a chur i ngach Gaeltacht, ar nós stiúideo, agus daoine ón nGaeltacht a fhostú ann, daoine a bheadh eolach ar chúrsaí na Gaeltachta agus a leithéidí sin" (2).

7 Bernadette Devlin (b. 1943) is a prominent political activist, immortalized on a giant wall mural in Derry's Bogside neighbourhood because of her role in the Bloody Sunday massacre of civil rights demonstrators on 30 January 1972. She has always identified herself as a socialist, but she split from Official Sinn Féin in the 1970s because it seemed to be abandoning that political mantle (this was a period of numerous splits in the Republican movement, partially along socialist versus nationalist lines). She also rejected Sinn Féin's policy of absenteeism, wherein elected Sinn Féin MPs refused to actually take their seats because they would be required to swear an oath of allegiance to the crown. She sat in Westminster as an MP (starting when she was 21), both as a "Unity" member and as an Independent Socialist.

8 "Gné an-suntasach den stair atá ag tarlú sna Sé Chontae le tamall anuas ná 'saorstáisiúin raidió'" ("'Saorstaisiun Radio' sa Ghaeltacht?" 7).

9 "ní rud é sin atá dó-dhéanta; féach an fás-aon-oíche a thainig faoi na saorstáisiúin raidió sna Sé Chontae tamall ó shin" (3). The *Connacht Tribune* is an English-language daily; this was published as part of their "Colun na Gaeltachta" or Gaeltacht Column. The text is in Irish but without accent marks; in the byline the newspaper also spells Seosamh Ó Cuaig's name "Seosaimh O'Cuaigh." For the sake of legibility I have added accents here; I have also changed "radio" to "raidió."

10 "D'ainneoin an *Connacht Tribune* a d'fhoilsigh alt tarcaisniúil faoi 'The Unheard Pirate,' chualathas Saor-raidió Chonamara go soiléir i gceantar na nOileán, siar go Carna, agus soir chomh fada leis an Spidéal" (29).

11 "beidh díospóireacht ann 'faoi chúrsaí forbartha, comharchumainn, polaitíochta agus, go háirithe, faoin údarás Gaeltachta.' Seans maith go gcraolfar an díospóireacht seo ar an raidió chomh maith" ("Oireachtas na nGael" 3).

12 "De réir daonáireamh na bliana 1961 tá 716,420 duine sa tír a bhfuil Gaeilge acu. De réir an Roinn Poist agus Telegrafa tá 444,000 gléas telefíse ceadúnaithe sa tír. Da réir sin tá níos mó duine sa tír a thuigeann Gaeilge ná mar atá de ghléasanna telefíse" (Dowling, Doolan, and Quinn 291).

13 "La distancia entre lo que conocemos por *hardware y software* es hoy más escandaloso que nunca" (*Una imagen* 69).

14 "La técnica permite hoy que la formación pueda deshacerse de los aspectos más mecánicos y concentrarse en aquellos que reclaman una visión más profunda, integral y científica del especialista" (*Una imagen* 69).

15 This is to say nothing of Dublin. Michael D. Higgins, as I mentioned in the introduction to this book and will discuss in the conclusion, became minister for Arts, Culture and the Gaeltacht in 1993 and was an important voice in that period's arguments about television in Irish (among other initiatives he commissioned the 1995 Green Paper on Broadcasting *Active or Passive? Broadcasting in the Future Tense*, which I discuss in the conclusion). But in 1975 he was a senator, and he lamented in a Seanad Éireann debate on 6 May 1975, "We have avoided any discussion over the years on the relationship between science and technology, a subject discussed by Raymond Williams, for example, in a distinguished fashion in his recent work *Television*. It has also been discussed by a number of recent writers. The questions raised are—Is

the communications network neutral? Should the communications network be useful? Should the communications network be subversive?... I believe it is legitimate in a discussion on communications technology to discuss the uses of communication. For example what particular weight do we give to entertainment, explication, exposition, education or critique in Irish television? These are not petty questions. Neither are they discrete, separate from one another." This is a fascinating and incredibly well-informed debate, with references to communication and political theorists flying fast and furious. It is available, like all the debates that I quote in this book, through the website http://historical-debates.oireachtas.ie/.

16 "El arte de masas o para las masas ... necesita que el pueblo no tenga gusto" (*Una imagen* 7).

17 "necesita, y por la tanto tiende a desarrollar, el gusto personal, individual, del pueblo" (*Una imagen* 7)

18 "ceoltóiri, filí, lucht drámaíochta agus eagraíochtaí éagsúla ag lorg am craolta" (Dowling, Doolan, and Quinn 299).

19 "Creidimid go bhfásfadh stiúradh daonlathach den tsórt seo go nádúrtha sa Gaeltacht [*sic*]. Creidimid chomh maith nárbh fhada go mbeadh muintir na hÉireann i gcoitinne ag cur ceist orthu féin, "cén fáth nach bhfuil a leithéid againn sa tseirbhís náisiúnta"? Creidimid go bhfuil slánú RTÉ fite-fuaite le slánú na Gaeilge ar RTÉ agus go bhfuil slánú na Gaeilge ag braith ar mhuintir na Gaeltachta" (299).

20 "'Sí an Ghaeilge Athghabháil na hÉireann agus is í Athghabháil na hÉireann slánú na Gaeilge. 'Sí teanga na muintire a shlánós an mhuintir" (10). Máirtin Ó Cadhain (1906–70) was one of the most prominent Irish-language writers of the twentieth century; although most of his oeuvre is comprised of short stories, in 1949 he published *Cré na Cille*, widely considered to be the *Ulysses* of Irish Gaelic. He was also a member of the IRA and was interned in the Curragh (in County Kildare) during WWII. He worked for the Government Translation Service after the war and taught at Trinity College Dublin from 1956, becoming Professor of Irish in 1969, the year before he died. He was an important part of Gaeltacht activism, and he gained a reputation as a fiery speaker and a highly principled advocate.

21 Article 8.1 of the *Bunreacht na hÉireann / Constitution of Ireland* reads "Ós í an Ghaeilge an teanga náisiúnta is í an phríomhtheanga oifigiúil í / The Irish language as the national language is the first official language." The English text of Article 8.2 reads "The English language is recognised as a second official language," although the Irish text reads "Glactar leis an *Sacs-Bhéarla* mar theanga oifigiúil eile." The emphasis is mine, as the term "Sacs-Bhéarla" literally means "Saxon English." This term is there partially because "Sacs-Bhéarla" is an archaic usage, and such usage is of course common to documents like national constitutions; part of this, though, seems to be an extra dig at English, a way of trying to link it to a foreign past.

22 Comhairle na Gaeilge, or the Council of Irish, was a semi-state body set up in 1969. It produced short booklets such as *I dtreo polasaí teanga / Towards a Language Policy* (Dublin: Stationary Office, 1971) and *Institiúidí Rialtais Áitiúil agus Forbraíochta don Ghaeltacht* (Baile Átha Cliath [Dublin]: Oifig an tSoláthair, 1971).

23 Conradh na Gaeilge, established in 1893, is the group devoted to the promotion of Irish; at one time its goals were the full restoration of the language as the national vernacular, but this isn't really true of the group today. While some of the membership is committed to language issues in a relatively apolitical sort of way (and thus follow one of the League's founders, Douglas Hyde, who believed that the group should stay out of politics), Conradh has a long history of revolutionary connections, especially via its newspaper *An Claidheamh Solais* (edited by Pádraic Pearse between 1903 and 1909) and via the fact that most of the leaders of the 1916 Easter Rising were members. As the twentieth century progressed, the league developed an image as a national scold and was famously satirized by Flann O'Brien (writing as Myles na gCopaleen) in the novel *An Béal Bocht* (translated into English as *The Poor Mouth*).

24 The 13 June 1975 issue of *Inniu*, for instance, ran a headline story titled "An Dara Bealach: Ráiteas Údarás RTÉ faoin teilifís" [The Second Channel: Statement of the RTÉ Authority on Television]. That issue, which had as its editorial headline "An Dara Bealach Teilifíse" [The Second Television Channel], tried to hedge its bets about whether Irish-language television should be local or national. There we read "Ach más leor roinnt mhaith daoine bheith á éileamh, le go gcuirfeadh an tAire ar fáil dóibh é, nach mó go mór de cheart atá ag muintír na Gaeltachta agus na Gaeilgeoirí eile na tíre seirbhís iomlán teilifíse, a fháil ina teanga féin, is rá go bhfuil sin le fáil ag Béarlóirí uilig na hÉireann" (10) [But if a good number of people are demanding that the Secretary put it into place, then the country's Gaeltacht people and non-native Irish speakers have much more right to receive an entire service in their own language than the English speakers throughout Ireland]. Also see *Inniu* 20 June 1975 and 4 July 1975 for numerous articles on the debate.

25 "Go bhfuil sí in úsáid mar cheann de na gléasanna is tábhachtaí ag an nua-choilíneachas, .i.e. an nós nua atá ag na tíortha impiriúla le húsáid a bhaint as tíortha eile. Is sa chomhthéacs seo amháin is féidir ciall a fheiceáil i bpolasaí athchraolú BBC1" ("Teilifís—Fórsa Láidir inár Saol" 7).

26 "Tá an scéal i bhfad níos measa ar fud an *Tríú Domhain*, agus i gCeanada fiú, tír a bhfuil cuid mhaith saibhris agus maoine dá cuid féin aici. I 1971 ní raibh ach 28% d'ioncam an 70 gníomhaireacht (nó comhlacht fógraíochta) ba mhó i gCeanada, ag gníomhaireachtaí Ceanadacha. Gníomhaireachtaí Meiriceánacha a bhí ag tuilleamh an 72% eile. Trí ghníomhaireachtaí Meiriceánacha a bhí formhór na fógraíochta teilifíse á dhéanamh freisin. I Thailand, i 1975, bhí ioncam de $25.3m ag gníomhaireachtaí eachtrannacha agus an fuíollach de $1.5m ag gníomhaireachtaí Thai" (17, emphasis in original).

27 The key issue in Conradh na Gaeilge's television debates was whether to advocate for more Irish on RTÉ or for the establishment of a second, all-Irish channel. Many in Conradh saw Wales as a model here, which established an all-Welsh channel called Sinael Pedwar Cymru (S4C) in 1982. Hourigan writes of "the formation of the Welsh Language Society (WLS), which began to campaign for a Welsh-language television service in 1966. There was relatively little debate about the model of television sought during the campaign for S4C ... activists were determined that a

separate independent Welsh-language service would be created" (*Escaping the Global Village* 58–59). Conradh was far less united on this question. Discussing the period that followed a conference on media in Celtic countries that was held in the Ráth Cairn Gaeltacht in 1975, Hourigan writes that:

> A number of activists from the Welsh language society spoke of their campaign for a separate television channel.... Íté Uí Chionnaith [*sic*] states that "from then on, I have to admit that I was very strongly of the opinion that we needed a separate channel".... This engendered a split in organization. Former president, Maolsheachlainn Ó Caollaí, and his supporters continued to insist that an increase in the quantity of Irish language programming on RTÉ would fulfill the television needs of the Republic's Irish language speakers.... The row was bitter and divisive.... The debate was resolved at Conradh na Gaeilge's Árd-Fheis at Spiddal in 1980. A motion was passed calling for the establishment of a separate national Irish language television channel and Ó Caollaí's faction was sidelined. ("A Comparison" 195–96).

Yet as I say in the main text, what I want to emphasize here is the difference between the Gluaiseacht position and that of Conradh. Gaeltacht television as such was not on the agenda here, likely because of Conradh's largely urban base of language-learners, as opposed to Gluaiseacht's base of Gaeltacht-based native speakers.

28 Ó Caollaí contributed a short essay called "Cultural Domination in Ireland: The Case of Ireland" to a 1986 Festschrift dedicated to Herbert Schiller, which outlined the history of colonialism and domination in Ireland in very broad terms. The essay has relatively little to say about media technology, and little even to say about the Irish language. However, Ó Caollaí does implicitly indicate his urban, or at least non-Gaeltacht, focus when he writes, "Analyses have shown that the trend is towards secondary bilingualism and away from primary bilingualism, i.e., the increase is a result of English speakers learning Irish. Irish as a first and communal language continues to decline in the Irish-speaking areas" (110). See Ó Caollaí, "Cultural Domination in Europe: The Case of Ireland," in Jörg Becker, Göran Hedebro, and Leena Paldán, eds., *Communication and Domination: Essays to Honor Herbert I. Schiller* (Norwood, NJ: Ablex, 1986), 104–13.

29 Desmond Fennell has written an essay on the slipperiness of left and right in Irish politics (entitled "Left, Right in the New Europe" and found in *Heresy* 178–85), which opens, "In Ireland periodically, people call for a realignment of Irish politics on a 'left/right basis.' It would make things so much clearer, they say. I very much doubt it" (178). Fianna Fáil, which Fennell advised in the 1970s, is ostensibly a centre-right party, but it includes many members whose connections to rural co-operatives or Republican politics place them well to the left of the ostensibly more liberal party Fine Gael (whose base is more urban and which has historically been much less interested in action on Northern Ireland). In that way Fianna Fáil is a sort of mirror image of the Parti Québécois, which is first and foremost a "big tent" nationalist party whose politics are generally social-democratic but which, historically, has had many members whose rural or small-town constituents would identify as small-c conservative.

In some ways, Irish politics also recalls an older version of Canadian politics, where, once upon a time, conservatives could be relied upon to stress communitarian values, Canadian nationalism, and resistance to American interference at the same time that they identified strongly with British Tories; the seminal summary of this tendency in twentieth-century Canada is Charles Taylor's *Radical Tories: The Conservative Tradition in Canada* (Toronto: Anansi, 2006). In this way, Fennell is roughly analogous both to the "Red Tory" Canadian philosopher George Grant and to the American social critic Christopher Lasch; all these intellectuals display strong socialist tendencies and, in equal parts, skepticism of progressive activism. In his book *Maverick*, Bob Quinn, Fennell's friend and collaborator (and the subject of chapter 5), quotes Lasch's *Revolt of the Elites* to explain the degree to which Ireland has produced a class of technocratic managers with no particular attachment to Ireland itself (102–3); the rise of this class has been an ongoing part of Fennell's critique of Irish modernity. Furthermore, Lasch's *The True and Only Heaven: Progress and Its Critics* (New York: Norton, 1991) opens with a chapter called "The Obsolescence of Left and Right," where he decries the rise of Reaganism as a betrayal of real conservatism because of the way that it tried to remove all limits to consumer capitalism, which he saw as the leading threat to tradition and to family life.

4

Desmond Fennell and Pierre Perrault

> I discovered that the language of the country transmitted images of the country, and that the country fashioned the language, invented words likely to translate people, things, jobs, and landscapes that faraway literatures and high-minded dictionaries couldn't manage to describe. The idea occurred to me to navigate this river of language to discover the language of the river.[1]
>
> —Pierre Perrault, *Le mal du nord*

Although he has now shifted his attention to what he sees as a broad and worldwide cultural decline, Desmond Fennell once had, as one of his central intellectual and polemical concerns, the future of the Gaeltacht. Articles, pamphlets, and books that he published in the 1960s until well into the 1980s bore the mark of Gluaiseacht Chearta Sibhialta na Gaeltachta, and frequently took the politics of language and its broader implications for Irish culture as their central concern. Although he didn't have much to say about film or television as such, his ideas about regionalism and internationalism clearly form an intellectual superstructure for the Gaeltacht media activism of the 1970s and 1980s. Niamh Hourigan, in her comparison of the campaigns for Irish-language radio and TV, states that "Des Fennell's advice helped to shape the ideology of Gluaiseacht" ("A Comparison" 297). Furthermore, Fennell's work dovetails with both the cinematic and literary work of Pierre Perrault.[2] Both Perrault and Fennell see the cultural survival of isolated areas as crucial to the survival of minority languages and cultures and thus both have engaged with isolated areas where distinctive languages or language variants remain but are threatened: the Gaeltacht and Irish for Fennell, Charlevoix and its very distinct variant of French for Perrault. Moreover, both used Brittany as an analogy for their own community's struggle against a monopolizing centre, although each had a very different sense of the cultural importance of centre-margin issues. Most importantly, both Fennell and Perrault are heavily invested in philosophical and political approaches to mapping. Thus Fennell's work, like that of Perrault, is also quite close to that of the cartographer, essayist, and land-artist Tim Robinson (most famous for his work on the Aran Islands, and now based in Roundstone, Connemara), whose approach, as I discussed in the introduction, is quite suitable for understanding the way that this North Atlantic work approaches the task of philosophically informed geography.

The most obvious connection between Fennell and Perrault is the degree to which they are engaged with rural areas. Each one has made significant interventions, whether in Ireland or Quebec, but there is a very real way in which Fennell's work is defined by the period from 1968 to 1979, when he lived in and wrote about the Connemara Gaeltacht, just as Perrault's work is arguably defined by the films he made on Charlevoix's Île-aux-Coudres. The themes they developed most explicitly through this work—regionalism, the importance of embattled cultures and their languages, resistance to a homogenizing modernity—were issues that they never really left behind, even once Fennell had moved to Anguillara and Perrault had taken to making work about Abitibi or the high north. For both Fennell and Perrault, these rural areas were the places that brought into sharper focus the crucial issues of renewed nationalism that they both sought.

As I mentioned in chapter 1, Perrault was originally introduced to the Charlevoix region by his wife Yolande Simard, a native of the region, although this place's importance is rarely expressed solely in familial terms; Fennell writes of his own introduction to Gaeltacht politics in a similar way. He begins by recounting personal details, but in short order moves on to the politics that defined his work. In *Beyond Nationalism*, he recalls how "in the autumn of 1968 I moved with my wife and three young children from Dublin to Maoinis." In the next paragraph, he writes that:

> Years later we discovered that in 1968, in West European countries and the USA, a trickle of families and individuals began to move voluntarily from the power-centres to the peripheries. In France, 1968 is looked back to as the year when a resurgence of the depressed cultures on the French periphery—Breton, Occitan, Alsatian and so on—began. In Paris, there was a revival of interest in these cultures, and a drift of young intellectuals and artists from the capital to the regions in question. (130)

As in Perrault's work, what begins with memoir almost immediately moves towards consideration of language, culture, and identity. Yet this passage from Fennell departs from Perrault's recollection in important ways. Fennell's Gaeltacht was not the homeland manqué of Perrault's Charlevoix, but instead a sort of diasporic utopia, one that demanded considerably more linguistic adjustment than the sort of fine tuning that Perrault's ear required when faced with the distinctly non-urban French of Île-aux-Coudres. Learning the meaning of terms like "le frâsil" or getting to understand the unique accents of islanders was no doubt challenging. Yet this sort of linguistic stretching is hardly comparable to what Fennell was calling for; this was the equivalent of a Russian Jew needing to learn Hebrew, which he or she might have remembered from temple but likely had little ability to use as an everyday language.

This analogy is not chosen at random. Fennell's most concrete proposal for a revitalized Gaeltacht was one he published in the 28 February 1969 issue of the Irish-language weekly *Inniu* (and reprinted in his pamphlet *Iarchonnacht Began*) called "Iosrael in Iarchonnachta" [Israel in West Connacht]. "Irish learners, those who have trades and skills, will come to Connemara, and they will make a 'new Israel' there, and will give to the government a development plan run through the authority of the West Connacht Council" (*Iarchonnacht Began* 11).[3] The presence of Gaeilgeoirí—the term for Irish-language learners, as opposed to native speakers—was crucial. Fennell saw outsiders willing to learn Irish as being roughly analogous to displaced Jews anxious to learn Hebrew and build a new state (the Irish-language version of the proposal explicitly, if parenthetically, mentioned kibbutzim as a model: *Inniu* 9; *Iarchonnacht Began* 12). Fennell was only proposing a return to a homeland in the most symbolic way, much as the rhetoric of Zionism relies on imagery of roots in the region mostly on a symbolic level. The modern state of Israel is, clearly, a multicultural community comprised of a majority of relatively recent immigrants. It was once often remarked that Israel is a "young country," and the radicalism that this spirit of youth embodied was clearly inspirational to Fennell and instrumental in shaping his sense of 1968 as the year young intellectuals went to the fringes to help those fringes bloom.[4] This sort of idealism was also well known to Perrault. In the late 1950s he produced a series of radio broadcasts called *Aux portes de la nuit*, which was devoted to song traditions from all over the world. The poetic text[5] he wrote for the "Israël" episode opens:

> only one land was "promised"!
> only one people was "landless"!

this promised land was a desert!
this landless people loved the promise!

Israel! Israel!
where the anxious rocks yearning for a spring
lament the staff of Moses that
did not erase the desert

but the desert speaks in favour of Israel[6]

In the light of present-day Middle Eastern politics, this may all seem quite idealistic; no doubt Fennell would accept that assessment. In the English-language version of the proposal he wrote simply, "Idealists are required, who will take their chance professionally as every other way" ("Language Revival" 8; *Iarchonnacht Began* 8).

This cuts to the core of a key problem of a lot of Gaeltacht activism of the 1960s to 1980s: the role of people not originally from Gaeltacht areas. Of the four main "characters" in this "Gaeltacht section"—Fennell, Seosamh Ó Cuaig, Bob Quinn, and Donncha Ó hÉallaithe—only Ó Cuaig is originally from the area. It is important to see this period of activism as defined not by a desire to liberate the "ethnic Gaels" or those who spoke Irish from the cradle, but to preserve communities who had Irish as their shared language. And like all democratic communities, people from outside could choose to join. Thus the Israel analogy is key; Israel is a multi-ethnic state, comprised of people who come from all over, but including people whose families have been there for hundreds of years—all joined by a common language. That is a very good summary of the sort of community Fennell, Ó Cuaig, Quinn, and Ó hÉallaithe alike were trying to build. Indeed, in addition to Israel, this vision of a diverse, vibrant, and marginalized community is visible in Greenland, at least in the Greenland described so vividly by Gretel Ehrlich in her 2001 book *This Cold Heaven*. There she writes of a Greenlander who recalls to her, "Up north … it is more traditional. The women often go for long periods of time with the men and in the summer they still hunt in kayaks with harpoons. But down here, we have been colonized by the Danes too long. The old ways get mixed up with the new much faster in west Greenland" (93). This little discourse on colonialism and modernity, though, is laid out for Ehrlich by a guy named Hans, who is married to a woman named Arnnannguaq. When he complains of being "colonized by the Danes" he seems not to mean the ethnic group, but a distant, meddling elite based in Denmark whose real interests have little to do with this culturally and linguistically distinct community. In Ehrlich's vision, the struggle in Greenland is hardly ever as simple as Danes versus Inuit; it generally comes in the form of Greenlanders versus Colonists. Thus when Fennell talks about "Gaeltacht agus Impiriúlachas"—Gaeltacht and Imperialism, in an article I will discuss in a moment—he sounds a lot like Ehrlich's friend Hans, as does Ó hÉallaithe when he talks of "those who would like to ethnically cleanse the few remaining Gaeltacht communities from the linguistic landscape" ("Why Was TnaG a Monumental Mistake?" 43). They may not have been born into these struggles, and their "outsider" status might, at first blush, seem to afford them some sort of privilege unavailable to people who *were* born in these marginalized areas. But they are, in Bob Quinn's formulation, immigrants. In informal conversation Quinn always talks about how he had, in essence, decided to immigrate to Connemara, and that going there from Dublin was comparable to going to a different country: it was a radically different lifestyle, they spoke a different language, and so on. And so he, like Fennell, and like Ó hÉallaithe, became an immigrant and eventually a citizen of the place, invested in its future and willing and able to take on positions of leadership, as so many immigrants are.

One of Fennell's more practical (and probably more widely influential) solutions to the problem of an oppressive centre dominating smaller communities such as the one he had chosen to join was a federalist view of Irish governance. Fennell had sketched out plans for a decentralized Gaeltacht government in pamphlets such as *Take the Faroes for Example: The Arguments for Self-government in the Provinces and the Gaeltacht* (1972), which I discuss later in this chapter and in chapter 6. But he was also interested in Sinn Féin's "Éire Nua" [New Ireland] proposals. Fennell writes that "between 1969 and 1972, by a devious route, I came to the conviction that a federally united Ireland, along the lines proposed by Sinn Féin,[7] would be the best solution for the Northern problem" ("Solutions to the Northern Ireland Problem" 1). He wrote this in an article published in the *Canadian Journal of Irish Studies*, and given Canada's internationally known status as a federation, the choice of venue hardly seems accidental. For Fennell, federalism was the path towards Gaeltacht autonomy and away from Dublin's centralizing clutches.

Fennell's hostility towards and sense of exclusion from the Dublin centre was quite consistent with his sense of the Gaeltacht's place in Irish life. This was a good deal more militant than anything that Perrault had to say about his own place, or that of Charlevoix, in Quebec culture. For Fennell, RTÉ often stands in for the Dublin elite—for the Danes, so to speak. But while Perrault, as I discussed in chapter 1, eventually outgrew Radio-Canada, he always spoke of it fondly as a formative experience; as late as 1996 he reminisced to Paul

Warren that his Radio-Canada period "constituted my tape-recorder period, if you will. It was my discovery of the spoken word (Clandfield 172).[8] This gives some sense of the difference in their perspectives on margin-centre issues and what we might take to be the media-based metaphors for such issues; Perrault was as engaged with marginal communities as his counterpart Fennell, but he had far warmer feelings about the media institutions of the centre and their ability to animate and interpret the life of those communities. Now, clearly a big part of Fennell's hostility towards the Dublin elite was a desire to strengthen the autonomy of small communities, but for many years his arguments were phrased in specifically anti-Dublin language. In 1971 he wrote an article for the Irish-language monthly *Comhar* called "Gaeltacht agus Impiriúlachas" [Gaeltacht and Imperialism], an article that, as its title indicates, echoes the insurgent rhetoric of Gluaiseacht that was particularly visible in the protest over the closure of the school at Dún Chaoin that I discussed in the introduction to this section. Fennell argues in that article that once the nineteenth century got under way, "the building of Dublin's empire was at full sail." Fennell uses the made-up place name "Dubhlinn" throughout this article (as well as in his other writing in Irish) rather than the *actual* Irish-language name for Dublin, "Baile Átha Cliath."[9] In part, this seems like a sneering refusal to Gaelicize the name of that Anglo stronghold; it also partially seems a joke about the etymology of the city's name, which literally means "black pool." Either way, it is a clear statement of his sense of the Dublin establishment. The sense that it is an *establishment* is already clear in this early article, as it is in most of Fennell's later writing. Although it does not appear in the English translation of the "Gaeltacht and Imperialism" article, I think it is important to note that Fennell writes, "This elite class is constituted from owners and big-business managers, head officers of state services, managers, and the public tutors of the communication media—the *New Priesthood*."[10] Fennell was determined to resist this priesthood and its patronizing attitudes towards the Gaeltacht; for him, the hope for the survival of the language lay in a community-centred approach to cultural politics. Perrault, by contrast, certainly considered himself and his work marginal, both in general cultural terms and cinematic terms, but, as with the difference in their visions of RTÉ and Radio-Canada, Perrault's is not quite the same sort of marginality as Fennell's. In Jean-Daniel Lafond's 1986 film about Perrault's work (*Les traces du rêve*), Perrault lamented the increasingly commercialized nature of Quebec cinema:

> That fiction cinema is suddenly important in Quebec doesn't concern me. That's its affair and it's normal, since that's how it is elsewhere; it's good for business,

> which doesn't owe me anything. It may be that culture which will bring about our freedom, even if I strongly doubt it. It's maybe more useful than my work. It's maybe the future of Quebec, or of cinema, even if I myself think more of one than the other.[11]

This is a good indication of Perrault's overall sense of these matters. He is as opposed to the creeping crassness of commercial culture as Fennell. Yet it seems clear that he is being semi-ironic, taking for granted the fact that most people understand "utile" [useful] as having an economic, or at least materialistic, etymology. However, it is equally clear that Perrault is far less bitter (or at least less polemical) than Fennell on that matter, self-effacingly wondering if his oddball approach isn't in the end irrelevant.

Fennell had sketched out some plans for a decentralized Gaeltacht government, often using other European cultures as exemplars. His 1972 pamphlet *Take the Faroes for Example: The Arguments for Self-government in the Provinces and the Gaeltacht* was widely read, and it was an inspiration to Donncha Ó hÉallaithe and the Teilifís na Gaeltachta group, who modelled their 1987 pirate TV broadcasts not only after the Saor-raidió Chonamara pirate broadcasts of 1970 but also after the TV station of the Faroe Islands (or at least what they believed it to represent). Fennell's writing is littered with references to multilingual European countries like Switzerland and Belgium, and to European minority cultures generally. His 1988 essay "The Independence of Ireland in the 1990s" (reprinted in *Heresy*) is explicitly engaged with minority cultures in Europe, as is his 2003 essay "A Critical Look at the Charter for Regional and Minority Languages" (reprinted in *Cutting to the Point*). *Beyond Nationalism* also discusses minority cultures frequently and contains short sections called "The Gaeltacht and the Faroes," "Connacht and Iceland," and "Connacht in Switzerland" (210–13). As early as 1969 Fennell (in a lecture given to a community centre in Castlebar) spoke admiringly of Switzerland's success with decentralization, stating that "Switzerland's thinking has been done not in some remote capital city—but in the 22 cantons of Switzerland, each with its own parliament and government, its own laws and budget, all linked together in a federal republic" (*Iarchonnacht Began* 37). And in a paper presented to a 1980 conference on European minority languages, he writes that if the Irish-language revivalist movement "had established its main base in the Gaeltacht, preached its gospel there and founded newspapers there, it would probably have succeeded in transforming the people of the Gaeltacht into something they have never become, namely militant enthusiasts for their language, like the Flemings in Belgium"

("Can a Shrinking Linguistic Minority Be Saved?" 38). Indeed, the example of Flemish appears regularly in Fennell's work. In the *Irish Times* article that contained his Israel proposals, he writes that the aim of the Irish revival movement was "to give Irish something like the same place that Flemish has in Belgian life" ("Language Revival" 8; *Iarchonnacht Began* 3). He also used this as a way into the Northern Ireland conflict in *The Revision of Irish Nationalism*, where he writes how "the acute cultural conflicts between Flemings and Walloons have been defused by institutional measures that allot Flanders to the Flemings, Wallonia to the Walloons, and treat Brussels as a special, mixed area" (54–55).

With his Belgian analogy Fennell's writing evokes to some degree a Flemish writer named Albert Folens, who, according to his 12 September 2003 *Irish Times* obituary, "came to Ireland in 1948 on a 'doctored' passport, having escaped from Allied imprisonment, after finding himself on the wrong side in the second World War.... He was sentenced to 10 years but escaped after 31 months" ("Albert Folens" 8). Once established in Ireland, Folens became a schoolteacher and then began a publishing company specializing in French school textbooks (such as *Folens' French Course*).[12] He also learned Irish and became an advocate for the language (the obituary points out that his first book was "*Nuachúrsa Fraincise*, a French primer using Irish and published by Sáirséal agus Dill"). This interest led Folens to write, in 1958, a short book called *Aiséirí Flóndrais* [Flemish Resurrection], a title that explicitly echoed Arthur Griffiths's famous 1904 defence of Irish nationalism, *The Resurrection of Hungary*. Folens begins his book:

> When the story of the Irish and the story of the Flemish are put alongside each other, this is how people imagine them: that Ireland grew into an independent state but had nearly lost its language, and on the other hand, while Flanders is not yet a state, it seems that it has a secure language that is not in danger today. Thus it would be advantageous for these two groups, the Irish and the Flemish, to be informed about each other's stories.[13]

Folens is far more interested in the idea of an independent Flanders than Fennell ever was; Fennell seems to find Belgium interesting precisely because its communities have been *both* independent and, via the "special, mixed area" that is Brussels, connected. But he would surely agree with Folens' general sense that "it would be advantageous for these two groups, the Irish and the Flemish, to be informed about each other's stories." Folens is not the only person in this Perrault-Fennell connection who was "on the wrong side in the second World War."[14]

Fennell's writing about European culture, federalism, margin-centre issues and Gaeltacht activism took him, at least intellectually, to a place also important to Perrault: Brittany. Perrault made a number of films about Brittany. *Le Règne du jour* (1967), which is also part of one of Perrault's regional cycles of films (it is the second instalment in his Île-aux-Coudres series), has a brief sequence in Saint-Malo, France, and his two-part film *La Grande Allure* (1985) follows a recreation (in reverse) of Cartier's voyage from Saint-Malo (the city is also the subject of its companion film, 1983's *Les voiles bas et en travers*). Two other films, though, deal with Breton politics in more detail. *Un pays sans bon sens!* (1970) has a long section in Brittany and posits Brittany's position in France as roughly analagous to Quebec's in Canada; *C'était un Québécois en Bretagne, madame!* (1977) was part of his cycle of films about Quebec's Abitibi region, and featured that series' main "character," Hauris Lalancette, making a trip to Brittany to connect with his ancestry. *C'était un Québécois en Bretagne, madame!* is thus a sort of companion piece to *Le Règne du jour*, which features the Île-aux-Coudres cycle's main "characters," the Tremblay family, going back to Normandy (and briefly to Brittany) to connect with their ancestry (most pure laine Québécois claim descent from either Normandy or Brittany). Both "regional" films show that even though these Québécois come from areas that are as marginal in France as Quebec is in Canada, the cultural gaps between old and new worlds remain significant, and resistant to a pure laine style of nostalgic nationalism. Bill Marshall, summarizing the analysis that *Le Règne du jour* is making, could also be talking about *C'était un Québécois en Bretagne, madame!* when he states that "the film throws up as many if not more differences between Quebec and France than similarities, and they are articulated between two unstable peripheries rather than between two plenitudes or centres" (79). Something very similar happens in *Un pays sans bon sens!*, which Perrault made in between the production of *Le Règne du jour* and *C'était un Québécois en Bretagne, madame!* It is in *Un pays sans bon sens!* that Perrault wanders most restlessly over different notions of national identity, spending time with a young Franco-Albertan named Maurice Chaillot who is living in Paris, with an older couple from Toronto trying to learn French in Cap-Rouge, Quebec (site of Cartier's first winter encampment and now a suburb of Quebec City), with René Lévesque as he tries to argue for Quebec sovereignty in Manitoba, and with a family of Montagnais Indians as they find it more and more difficult to practise traditional ways of life. He also spends time with a group of slightly depressed Breton nationalists, whose combination of affection and fear for the future of Breton culture seems best described as elegiac. One of them, known in the scenario of the film as *Le mercier* [the haberdasher], is particularly aware of the complexities of the Quebec-Brittany connection. Recalling the visit of General Charles de Gaulle to Montreal and his famous cry "Vive le Québec libre" during a speech on 24 July 1967, Le mercier says:

> Speaking of a "Free Quebec," I thought of one thing ... he spoke for a free Quebec.... That caused some controversy ... we followed it day by day ... minute by minute ... hey!!! Us ... we thought of a free Brittany! But we also thought of a free Czechoslovakia, or Romania, and all the communist satellite states.[15]

This is itself a clear echo of Pierre Trudeau's (minister of Justice at the time of de Gaulle's speech) widely publicized question: how would de Gaulle respond if a Canadian prime minister had shouted "Brittany to the Bretons"? That Perrault would show a Breton nationalist—one who his film was explicitly presenting as an analogue for Quebec nationalists—echoing the words of Trudeau—who was at the time of the film's production prime minster of Canada and who was, to say the least, no friend of Quebec's nationalist intellectuals—shows just how aware Perrault was of the contradictions of national identity. For Perrault, Brittany serves not as a signifier of a simple, neo-colonial / margin-centre relationship, but of a concept of national identity that is equally defined by solidarity and complexity.

This is where Perrault's ideas meet Fennell's ideas about federalism and where he seems to break company with much Quebec nationalist ideology. His film presents us with a sort of federation of small groups, each of whom are looking for recognition. This is not to say that Perrault's model is Canadian federalism as such; he presents separatist premier René Lévesque very positively, shows Chaillot to be someone whose identity as a Francophone is unsustainable in English Canada, and so on. But the clear thesis of this film is that *pays* is understood by all of these people in different ways, and that the threat to self-awareness is a domineering centre (Ottawa for Lévesque, Edmonton for Chaillot, Montreal for the Montagnais, Paris for the melancholic Bretons) and an insufficiently open sense of what constitutes national identity. The dream in *Un pays sans bon sens!* seems to be to achieve "a self-managing, autonomous society: a nation like Iceland, Scotland, The Faroes, Wales, Mann, England, Brittany, and the other nations of the world, from Kirghistan to California" (336). That's not Perrault writing there, though; it's Fennell, dreaming (in his book *Beyond Nationalism*) of a federal Ireland that is itself a part of a federation of small nations. It may be that federalism was what Quebec nationalists, alongside whom Perrault could reasonably be placed, were fighting *against*. But Perrault's films, like Fennell's writing, actually show considerable sympathy for intercultural connections that bear the hallmarks of federation.

Perrault's Brittany films, though, are surprisingly fiery, although this is not immediately evident. Clandfield hints at this political sensibility in his treatment of *C'était un Québécois en Bretagne, madame!*, although he buries it in a footnote. Discussing the way in which Meavenn, the lone female Breton we see in *Un pays sans bon sens!* reappears in *C'était un Québécois en Bretagne, madame!*, Clandfield writes how "she reveals her association with militant Breton nationalism" (82). Then we have a footnote:

> She cites two terrorist acts (the blowing-up of a monument and the dynamiting of rail tracks just before the French premier Édouard Herriot was due to pass). They took place in August and November of 1932. The monument on the front of the city hall in Rennes represented the annexation of Brittany to France. Herriot's later visit was to mark a ceremony celebrating the annexation. Meavenn describes the precautions that were taken to make sure nobody was hurt. The two explosions were actually the work of a secret organization that once carried the name of the Breton flag (Gwenn-ha-Du). Some sources say that Meavenn was a co-founder. By all accounts, the movement of the 1930s was far more clandestine than its counterpart thirty years later. None of this is actually mentioned in the film. (229n20)

It's in the film's outtakes, though. The transcripts of the sound recordings for *C'était un Québécois en Bretagne, madame!* feature considerable discussion of the more violent forms of Breton separatism. During one discussion, Meavenn tells Hauris Lalancette that "you could say that us folks who started the Breton movement, in 1920, just after the war of '14 like everyone eh, we were anti-establishment, absolutely anti-establishment."[16]

That's not all that's not in the film. Jack E. Reece calls Meavann "one of the more curious of all Breton nationalists" and insists that she is on the left of the movement (239n15). Alain Déniel's biographical note for Meavenn (whom he calls "Meaven Fant, de son vrai nom Francoise Rosec") in his book *Le mouvement breton 1919–1945* identifies her simply as "Co-fondatrice de Gwenn ha Du." But he also writes, "In 1944 withdrew to Germany with the Bezenn Perrot."[17] Le Bezenn Perrot was a paramilitary group formed by Célestin Laîné during the Nazi occupation of France; Laîné himself wound up in Ireland after World War II, escaping there through Germany in 1947 and living quietly in the suburbs of Dublin and Galway until his death in 1983.[18] Reece writes that they were a splinter group of the Parti national breton (PNB) and that following the assassination of the Breton nationalist priest Abbé Perrot, a split in the party ensued:

> Laîné then renamed his paramilitary unit the Bezenn Perrot (Formation Perrot), and asked German occupation authorities that he and his men be allowed to wear a special Breton uniform and carry arms freely. The Germans turned down these requests and offered instead to enrol the Bezenn Perrot in the Waffen-SS. In a decision heavy with consequences, Laîné accepted this offer and with his men put on German battle dress. (165)

Earlier on, Reece writes how the history of Gwenn-ha-Du started to come out in the 1960s, and how the memoirs of Olier Mordel revealed that "it had its origins in a small direct action society called Kentoc'h Merval (Plutôt la Mort) created in 1929 by *Célestin Laîné* and Gwilherm Berthou.... After breaking with Berthou in 1930 Laîné recruited several young Breton nationalists who shared his predilection for violence. These included Hervé Delaporte, Robert Le Helloco, *Meavenn*, Jacques de Quélan, Bayer du Kern, and Pierre Denis. With them Laîné late in 1930 reorganized his direct action society under its new name of Gwenn-ha-Du" (127, emphases mine). There is no sense from anything in the film or its sound transcripts that the "nous autres" Meavenn refers to includes the man who would a few years after the period she mentions form a Waffen-SS paramilitary unit, a unit with which Meavenn would then, according to Déniel, withdraw to Germany. You get no sense that the "courant" of contre-courant does, to a certain extent, refer to the Resistance; Reece writes that "Laîné and Guieysse insisted that the PNB should collaborate fully with the Germans against the resistance" (164). There is a telling instance in the sound transcripts for *C'était un Québécois en Bretagne, madame!*, when Hauris Lalancette is talking to two Bretons, Etienne Victor and Leon Martin. Leon Martin tells Hauris, "That was especially a movement for independence during the war."[19] On this transcript, though, the word *pendant* [during] is crossed out, and the word *avant* [before] is handwritten in (see Figure 4.1). The difference, as is evident from Meavann's unspoken connections, is key. Breton nationalism, and especially Breton separatism, is widely regarded in France as a right-wing affair, in no small part because of the ways in which the movement's leaders collaborated with Nazi occupiers during World War II. "Un mouvement pour l'indépendance *pendant* la guerre" is, to many French ears, synonymous with *collaborateur*. Perrault's Quebec-Brittany analogy is fascinating, but there is a sense in the films that pose that analogy that he is failing to deal with a pretty important aspect of the relevant history.

Fennell's work also has connections to Brittany, and they present some of the same problems that they do for Perrault. In *Beyond Nationalism*, Fennell writes:

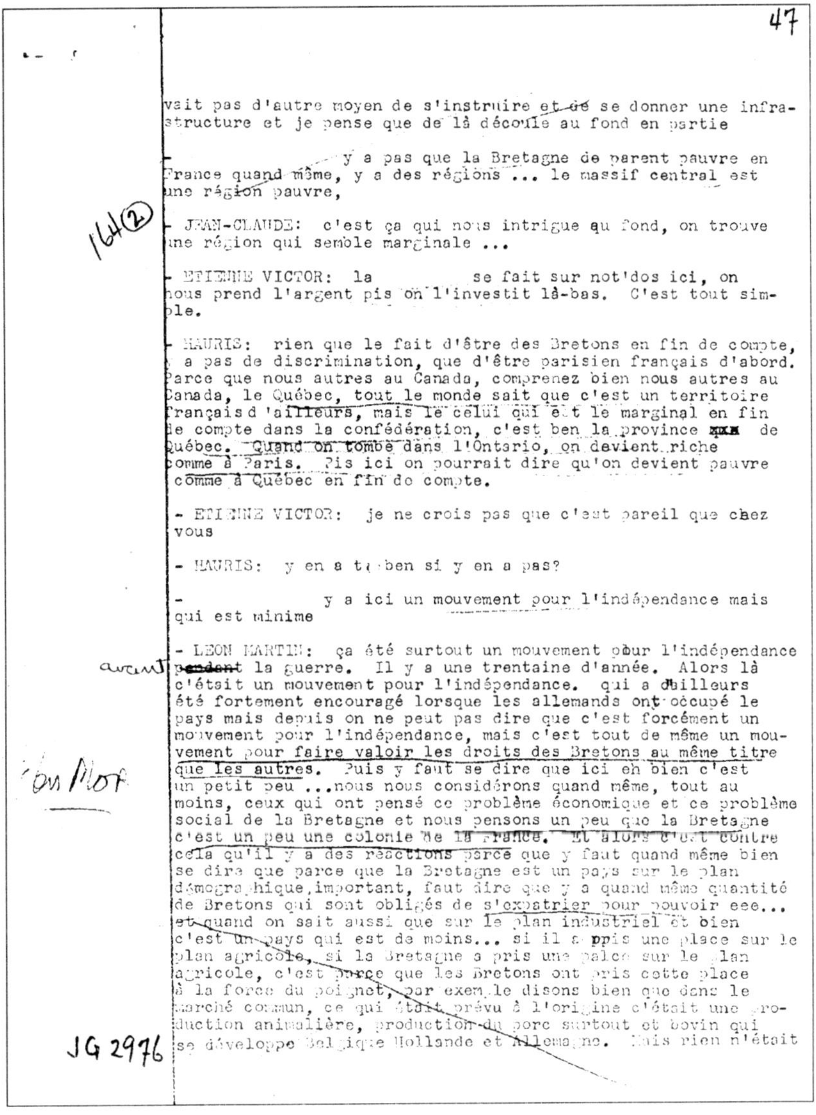

47

vait pas d'autre moyen de s'instruire ~~et de~~ se donner une infra-structure et je pense que de là découle au fond en partie

- y a pas que la Bretagne de parent pauvre en France quand même, y a des régions ... le massif central est une région pauvre,

164②

- JEAN-CLAUDE: c'est ça qui nous intrigue au fond, on trouve une région qui semble marginale ...

- ETIENNE VICTOR: la se fait sur not'dos ici, on nous prend l'argent pis on l'investit là-bas. C'est tout sim-ple.

- MAURIS: rien que le fait d'être des Bretons en fin de compte, y a pas de discrimination, que d'être parisien français d'abord. Parce que nous autres au Canada, comprenez bien nous autres au Canada, le Québec, tout le monde sait que c'est un territoire français d'ailleurs, mais le celui qui est le marginal en fin de compte dans la confédération, c'est ben la province ~~xxx~~ de Québec. Quand on tombe dans l'Ontario, on devient riche comme à Paris. Pis ici on pourrait dire qu'on devient pauvre comme à Québec en fin de compte.

- ETIENNE VICTOR: je ne crois pas que c'est pareil que chez vous

- MAURIS: y en a t'ben si y en a pas?

- y a ici un mouvement pour l'indépendance mais qui est minime

- LEON MARTIN: ça été surtout un mouvement pour l'indépendance ~~pendant~~ avant la guerre. Il y a une trentaine d'année. Alors là c'était un mouvement pour l'indépendance. qui a d'ailleurs été fortement encouragé lorsque les allemands ont occupé le pays mais depuis on ne peut pas dire que c'est forcément un mouvement pour l'indépendance, mais c'est tout de même un mou-vement pour faire valoir les droits des Bretons au même titre que les autres. Puis y faut se dire que ici eh bien c'est un petit peu ...nous nous considérons quand même, tout au moins, ceux qui ont pensé ce problème économique et ce problème social de la Bretagne et nous pensons un peu que la Bretagne c'est un peu une colonie de la France. Et alors c'est contre cela qu'il y a des réactions parce que y faut quand même bien se dire que parce que la Bretagne est un pays sur le plan démographique, important, faut dire que y a quand même quantité de Bretons qui sont obligés de s'expatrier pour pouvoir eee... ~~et~~ quand on sait aussi que sur le plan industriel et bien c'est un pays qui est de moins... si il a pris une place sur le plan agricole, si la Bretagne a pris une palce sur le plan agricole, c'est parce que les Bretons ont pris cette place à la force du poignet, par exemple disons bien que dans le marché commun, ce qui était prévu à l'origine c'était une pro-duction animalière, production du porc surtout et bovin qui se développe Belgique Hollande et Allemagne. Mais rien n'était

Bon Mot

JG 2976

FIGURE 4.1 From the sound transcripts of *C'était un Québécois en Bretagne, madame!* Note that "pendant"—as in "mouvement pour l'indépendance *pendant* la guerre" [independence movement *during* the war]—is crossed out by hand, and replaced with "avant" [before]. Fonds Pierre Perrault, Université Laval (Quebec City), P319/D9,8.

> The publication of *Sketches* [*of the New Ireland*, in 1973] brought me into contact with Yann Fouéré, the Breton writer and political refugee, who had been living for years as a fish-merchant in Cleggan in North Connemara. I read his book *L'Europe aux cents drapeaux* (Europe of the Hundred Flags), which envisages the replacement of the centralised European nation-states by federations of "region-states," and the building of a European federation on this basis. (176)

Fouéré's book (first issued in 1968, reprinted in 1976, and then published in English in 1980 as *Towards a Federal Europe: Nations or States?*)[20] laid out a plan for Europe that, in essence, advocated the breakup of larger nation states in favour of a federation of smaller regions. Fouéré was particularly interested, of course, in Brittany, although he also mentions South Tyrol, the Basque Country, and Flanders frequently. He could have been channelling Fennell (who has always railed against the ravages of consumer capitalism) when he wrote:

> Europe must not be sterilized into a purely materialistic society where production figures would be the only yardstick of progress. Behind the cold exterior of figures and the world of economists, there are human beings and citizens, with the natural communities to which they belong. There is the infinite cultural wealth of Europe which springs from her diversity.[21] (*Federal Europe* 109)

This is the Europe that Fennell sought to protect, what Fouéré calls a "Third Europe." This was in contrast to a "first Europe," which was a Europe of fiefdoms and baronies, and a "second Europe" of large, centralized nation-states. Fouéré summarized the concept this way:

> This has been the guiding idea of this essay. For I have made my choice, together with many other members of some of the oldest European peoples which the nation-states of the second Europe have been trying to destroy. The third Europe must be a Europe of the peoples, not a Europe of the states.[22] (*Federal Europe* xvii)

And thus we approach the nub of the problem. With his notion of "des peuples," Fouéré spoke of a very conservative and I think basically reactionary understanding of "un peuple," one that seems to me, furthermore, inconsistent with Fennell's own sense of "pobal." This notion was crucial for Fennell, since he saw Gluaiseacht's purpose specifically to defend the concept of "pobal," rather than "teanga" [language]. Furthermore, it is important to recall that an essential element of Fennell's "Iosrael in Iarchonnacht" proposals was the movement of "pobail" (plural for people) who had come from *outside*; these proposals were dependent on committed Gaeilgeoirí [Irish-language learners], not just on native-born Irish-speakers. "Nations are the permanent moral reality, the synthesis of the interests and ideals of a people," Fouéré wrote. "They last while the state passes and evolves" (*Federal Europe* 39).[23] Fennell was arguing for a new, reborn sense of Irish identity. He perceived the contours of the state as being fluid and in a state of evolution, but I do not find much evidence in Fennell's writing to suggest that he saw national identity as a "permanent moral reality."

Alas, all of this speaks to Fouéré's own complicated history. Of the period directly following the signing of an agreement on the role of Breton cultural institutions under the occupation, Déniel writes that "of all the signatories of the Jaffrennou plan, Yann Fouéré was the one who played the biggest role in the four years that followed the armistice."[24] Fouéré was imprisoned in France in 1944, shortly after the liberation. He had been imprisoned largely because he was editor of the daily newspaper *La Bretagne*, which he helped to found and which he edited (according to Déniel, the first issue appeared on 20 March 1941 [248]). Fouéré writes of that newspaper, in the second volume of his autobiography *Histoire d'un Breton* (entitled *La Maison du Connemara*) that "we decided to found this journal to try to get administrative and cultural autonomy from the Vichy government, which was at the time invaded and occupied by the German armies."[25] Most historians of the period have seen the matter differently. Déniel writes that in addition to publishing anti-Semitic pieces (which he quotes at length),[26] "the daily followed the corporatist principles defended by Vichy."[27] Hervé Le Boterf is more blunt; in describing Fouéré in volume two of his three-volume history *La Bretagne dans la guerre* he writes, "one man whose Breton patriotism could not be put into doubt decided to play the Vichy collaboration card."[28] Reece, however, sees Fouéré primarily as a pragmatist, writing of Breton federalist/regionalists (as opposed to their more staunchly separatist contemporaries) that:

> In particular they hoped, should Pétain's regime disappear, that untainted by separatism their wartime Breton achievements would remain intact under any succeeding French government. Moderate Breton regionalists like Fouéré also hoped that in such an unpredictable post-Vichy situation they would not be penalized for their Breton action during the German occupation. Events soon showed that these hopes were misplaced. (163)

Fouéré realized that this hope had been misplaced as he left France not long after the liberation ("en cet été de 1946") and under circumstances, as he recalls them in *La Maison du Connemara*, that remarkably echo the *Irish Times*' brief summary of Folens' arrival in Ireland: "My passport and my visa were in order.

They bore my own photo; but they also bore a name that wasn't mine."[29] Fouéré went first to Wales and then to Connemara, eventually settling in Cleggan, where he worked as a fish merchant and as a Gaeltacht correspondent for RTÉ radio. He appealed, in absentia, his conviction on charges of collaboration and was acquitted in 1955.

I recognize that Fennell departs more radically from Fouéré's ideology than he lets on. There's no doubt that Fennell is a cultural conservative, but as I mentioned in note 29 of the introduction to the Gaeltacht section, he is clearly a conservative of the George Grant or Christopher Lasch variety, and was most definitely opposed to the (then-emergent) fundamentalist capitalism of neo-conservatism. This is some distance from the conservatism that we find in Fouéré, which rather than being fundamentalist-capitalist in a neo-conservative way instead tries to bring us, in the words of one of Fouéré's chapter headings, "Vers des régions-États monoethniques" [Towards monoethnic region-states] (*Cent drapeux* 166–68; *Federal Europe* 125–27).

What Fennell was looking for in these proposals was not a sense of the mono-ethnic. Ironically, this seems clear to me from his discussion of Fouéré. Outlining his proposal for a "Federation of Man" (a federated British Isles with a capital on the Isle of Man) in a two-part *Irish Times* article, he notes that the European-federalist quality of his proposal "is in the spirit of my fellow Connemaraman Yann Fouéré, in his book *L'Europe des* [sic] *Cents Drapeaux* (Europe of the Hundred Flags), an essay in Breton nationalism" ("Reorganising the British Isles 1" 8). He seems to have no difficulty thinking of Fouéré's identity as compound, as Irish and Breton; his sense of him as a "fellow Connemaraman" has no whiff of the ethnic at all. This approach to compound national identities becomes clearer when one tries to square his proposals for Gaeltacht activism with his later proposals to reorganize the European Union. Fennell approvingly republished, in his 1988 essay "The Independence of Ireland in the 1990s" (reprinted in his collection *Heresy: The Battle of Ideas in Modern Ireland*), a map by Northcote Parkinson of a revised European Union (see Figure 4.2). It is worth noting that neither the national configuration "Irish" nor the Irish Gaeltacht is indicated on this map. All one can conclude is that within the configurations that do appear on the map—possibly Leinster and Munster, and certainly Connacht and Ulster—Gaeltacht regions would exist, just as the notion of Irish identity would continue to exist in all four. Thus within these new regional configurations *minority* cultures would exist, and a majority culture would not necessarily need to be ensconced in the form of a traditional nation state or even a regional configuration. Furthermore, as Fennell writes about a revived Irish identity, he speaks of Celticism

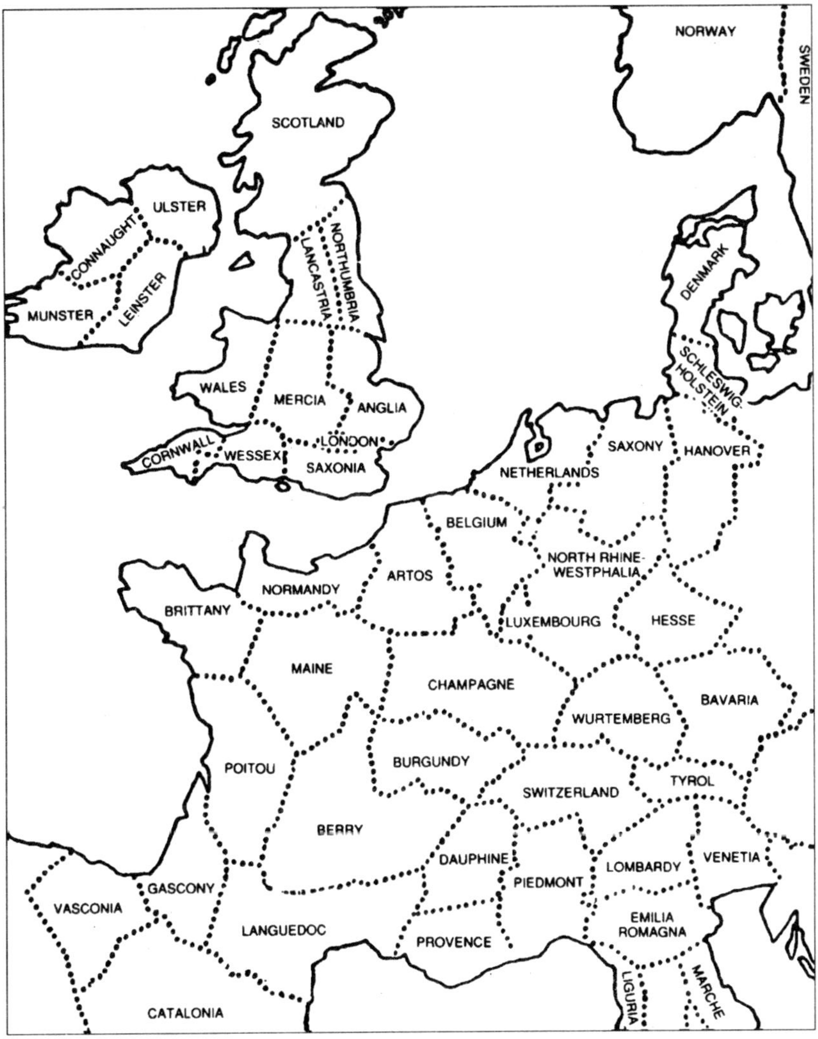

FIGURE 4.2 From Fennell's *Heresy: The Battle of Ideas in Modern Ireland*, p. 79.

not as the essence of Irish identity but as one of its *components*, a component that is especially suited for building connections to other, non-Celtic European cultures. He notes that Ireland's status as a Celtic country should have led to international prominence:

> But since the end of the de Valera era—which was marked by several initiatives towards the other Celtic countries—we have largely ignored the Celtic aspects

> of our Europeanness; and since joining the EC we have ignored, and failed to exploit, the peripheral condition within it that we share with other regions and nations extending from Sicily and Sardinia through Andalusia and Brittany to Scotland and Jutland. (*Heresy* 77)

This is strongly reminiscent of what Perrault went looking for in Brittany. What he sought there was not a sense of Quebec identity based on sentimental notions of a pure laine heritage; not only is this clearly rejected by Perrault's "characters" (who generally find that they do not feel at home in their "homeland"), but by the analogy he posits in *Un pays sans bon sens!* In that film, he shows us not that Quebec = France, as romantic nostalgic nationalism might suggest, but that *Canada* = France. France is not presented here as a longed-for homeland, but as place where marginal cultures have a very hard time. Perrault is arguing in *Un pays sans bon sens!* for a realization of Quebec identity via its impurity, its marginality. That film is pointing out, in essence, that the Québécois "have ignored, and failed to exploit, the peripheral condition ... that we share with other regions and nations," which for Perrault extends from the Montagnais to the Franco-Albertans, from the Bretons he interviews to the Romanians they invoke. Despite his instrumentalist, political connections to Fouéré's desire for a federal Europe, it is Perrault who helps us understand Fennell's ideological investment in the survival of marginal cultures.

Why, then, do neither Perrault nor Fennell acknowledge the far-right legacy of Breton nationalism? It is clear that Fennell is aware of Fouéré's past, since he refers to him as "the Breton writer and *political refugee*" (*Beyond Nationalism* 176, emphasis mine). It is less clear that Perrault is aware of Meavenn's World War II entanglements, although it is hard to imagine that she became his guide to Breton politics purely by chance; she figures in most histories of Breton nationalism, and thus Perrault must have had some idea of who he was getting himself involved with. Oddly, Perrault writes in the section of the *Un pays sans bon sens!* scenario devoted to the Breton nationalists that "whoever claims to master history themselves reclaims power and its exercise. In essence you must deny history the right to arrange people."[30] Fennell wrote something similar in 1989, a propos of the war in Northern Ireland and the place historical writing had in its reconciliation: "History can play that conciliatory social role only if it fulfills history's primary social function, which is to satisfy the history needs of the people whose history it is. That is what the telling of history has always been essentially about, and it can fulfill other social functions only if it performs that one" (*Heresy* 85). I am not trying to argue that Fennell and Perrault ignored historical facts in the service of ideology.

But both men clearly saw history as a tool to understand the present, and specifically to understand the plight of embattled nations such as Ireland or Quebec. It is not entirely surprising, then, that their flexible, politically informed vision of the historical should get the better of them when they are confronted with the intense paradoxes of Breton nationalism. This is especially curious in Perrault's case, since *Le Règne du jour* includes quite a long sequence where Robert Martin, a gamekeeper on a large estate in Normandy and a former Resistance fighter, recalls being arrested and sent to Buchenwald, a sequence that is notable for the way it centralizes the way in which class prejudices seemed to trump national ones even in times of war (the man recalls ruefully how some of the aristocratic Resistance fighters still preferred to talk to the German officers; David Clandfield writes that this "recalls Renoir's *La grande illusion*" [225n36]). Finally, then, I do think that Perrault and Fennell's shared failure to address the World War II legacy of the Breton analogy that they seek compromises the power of that analogy, but it does not erase it entirely. They are both clearly in pursuit of something progressive and exciting in terms of the situation of Brittany and the vision of federalism that situation evokes. That situation's violence and its unanswered questions, though, loom large over the works of both of these writers.

A strong connection between Perrault and Fennell can also be seen in their sense of the meaning of mapping. Fennell makes frequent use of maps in his writing: sometimes geopolitical ones like the one reproduced here as Figure 4.2, and sometimes maps such as Peter Broberg's semi-abstract world map that shows, in Fennell's words in *Beyond Nationalism*, "a world without empires, provinces, or nuclear arms races" (this appeared in *Beyond Nationalism* 174–75 and in *Heresy* 72–73). And one of Fennell's most important contributions to debates around Gaeltacht activism was the Gaeltacht map he published in the 1970s and 1980s. This first appeared in the 21 May 1976 issue of the Gaeltacht-based Irish-language weekly *Amárach*; it was accompanied by an article simply called "Léarscáil na Gaeltachta" [Map of the Gaeltacht]. This map also appeared as part of Fennell's two-part series for the *Irish Times* called "The Last Days of the Gaeltacht" (3 and 4 June 1980), in a TV film called *Last Days of the Gaeltacht* that he made with Bob Quinn in 1980, and in *Beyond Nationalism* (144). The version published in *Amárach* is reproduced here as Figure 4.3. The basic task in all of these manifestations was to attempt to connect the Irish landscape to the Irish language which has historically given it meaning.

The ostensible purpose of publishing the map was fairly clear; Fennell wanted to distinguish between the official Gaeltacht, much of which he saw as being bilingual at best—and the real Gaeltacht, where Irish was a genuine

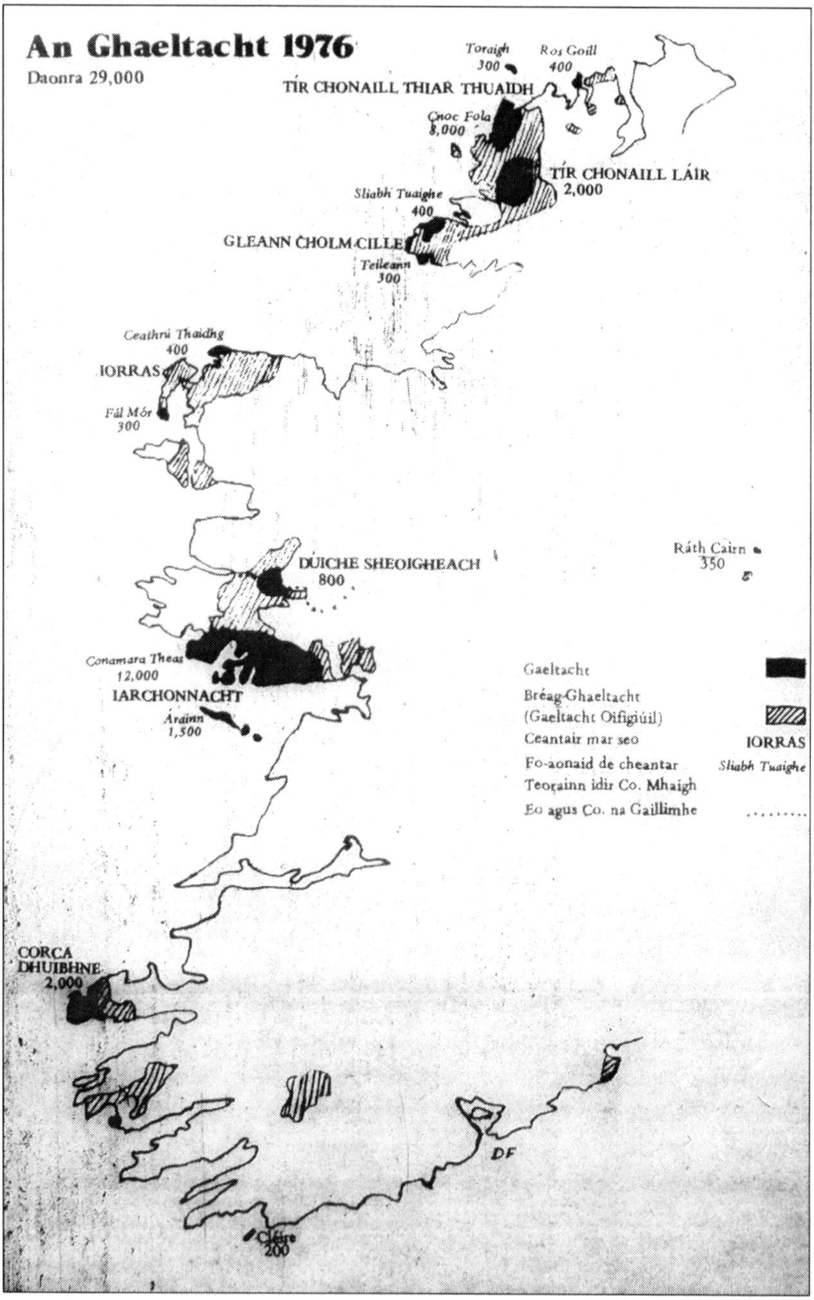

FIGURE 4.3 From Fennell's article "Léarscáil na Gaeltachta," *Amárach*, 21 May 1976, p. 2.

community language. This desire to correct the record was clearly informed by the map of the official Gaeltacht published as part of the government's 1965 White Paper *Athbheochan na Gaeilge / The Restoration of the Irish Language*, itself a response to the 1963 report of An Coimisiún um Athbheochan na Gaeilge [the Commission on the Revival of Irish]. I reproduce that map here as Figure 4.4. By way of introducing the *Amárach* map, Fennell wrote that "the Gaeltacht in the proper sense of the word (and not in the semi-official sense) is my intention with this map."[31] The *Athbheochan / Restoration* map identifies the same regions as Fennell's map, but no indication is given as to how intact Irish is as the community vernacular. Furthermore, the Fennell map uses regional designations unknown in the *Athbheochan / Restoration* report but important for his purposes. "Iarchonnacht" appears on Fennell's map, which is hardly surprising given his investment in that region's development as a sustainable locality. But whereas the *Athbheochan / Restoration* map has only a single designation for "Co. Dhún na nGall" [County Donegal], Fennell uses "Tír Chonaill Thiar Thuaidh" and "Tír Chonaill Láir." "Tír Chonaill" is an older name for the southwest parts of County Donegal (the parts that include the largest and most intact Irish-speaking areas), and this is the name which would generally be used in Irish speech. Thus the uses of Tír Chonaill Thiar Thuaidh [North West Tirconnell] and Tír Chonaill Láir [Central Tirconnell] seem like deliberate attempts to return to place names with some connection both to spoken Irish and to the designation of actual Irish-speaking communities. For the Gaeltacht, the designation Co. Dhún na nGall means very little, given how much of that county is English-speaking; the names Tír Chonaill Thiar Thuaidh and Tír Chonaill Láir evoke a very different history and a very different view of the connection between mapping, language, and community.

This matter of the actual use of the language as a *community* language was crucial for Fennell; it was not enough for him to find a set number of Irish speakers in a given geographical area. He explains this in that same *Amárach* article:

> There are strong *re-Gaelicisation* movements in An Rinn [the Ring Gaeltacht, in County Waterford] and a small part of Muscraí [in west Cork], but the majority opinion of the people in these two places is that there is no *area* surrounding them where Irish is the everyday language. I agree with that view: it's a question of "Irish-speaking households," not a Gaeltacht.[32]

Fennell, who had been strongly skeptical of if not outright opposed to revivalist strategies throughout his career (the title of his article in the *Irish Times* that

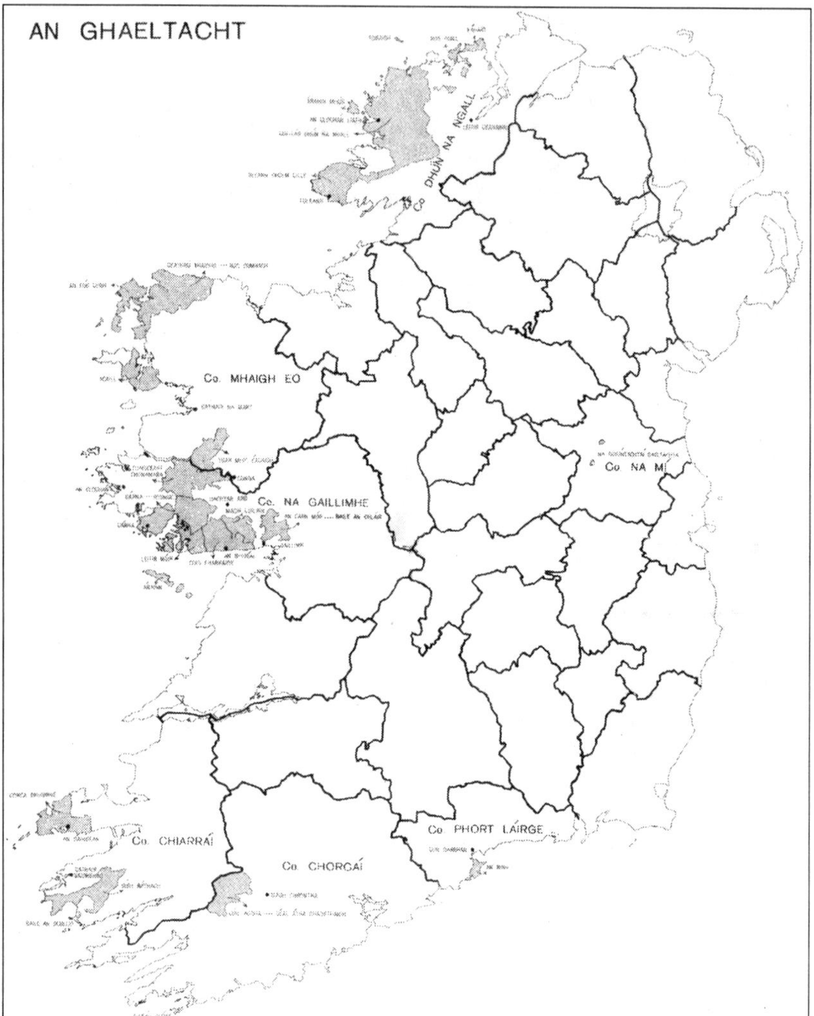

FIGURE 4.4 Map inserted in *Athbheochan na Gaeilge / The Restoration of the Irish Language* (Baile Átha Cliath: Oifig an tSoláthair, 1965).

contained the English-language version of his Israel proposal was "Language Revival: Is It Already a Lost Cause?"; this was clearly a rhetorical question) here identifies the core of his objection. He is not seeking isolated examples of people who can speak Irish, but a territory that still has Irish, a *community* that maintains the connection between the language and the territory. The presence of people who use the language with each other on an everyday basis is indispensable. Fennell makes the point in the film of *The Last Days of the Gaeltacht* that "the land that has been made intelligible by centuries of intimate Gaelic naming will here too [in the Gaeltacht] lose this intelligibility, and become just land." "Just land," shorn of its connections to a natural language spoken as part of everyday life, is of little interest to Fennell. It certainly has nothing to do with the sort of mapping he wants to undertake. "Shouldn't geography, above all, humanise the earth?" asks Pierre Perrault, in an essay called "De la toponymie."[33] This kind of humanization is the sort of mapping that Fennell is striving for, a mapping that has little to do with abstractions but which seeks to illuminate the connections between people and the territory they occupy. And how to illuminate this connection? Again, Perrault has the answer that is present in Fennell's work: "You always return to language."[34]

It is in this return that Perrault and Fennell hook up with that most linguistically ambitious of cartographers, Tim Robinson. Robinson has become justly famous for maps of the Aran Islands and of his current home base of Connemara (he lives in the English-speaking village of Roundstone) that are not only highly detailed in their illustration of geographic formations, but also highly detailed in their attention to place names. The linguistic rewriting that characterized the Ordnance Survey of the 1800s (Dún na nGall into Donegal, etc.) and which has come to serve as a metaphor for the cultural aspect of the British colonial project in Ireland is, in Robinson's hands, reversed in a powerful way. Robinson has written copiously on the subjects of his maps; sometimes this has been in the form of detailed gazetteers that accompany them—as with work on the Connemara landscape—and sometimes it has been in the form of book-length prose companions to previously published maps—as with his two *Stones of Aran* books (subtitled *Labyrinth* and *Pilgrimage*). But he has also written on the subject of mapping generally and with an attention to both the philosophical problems and political meanings of maps. He thus occupies the middle ground between Perrault (who tends to be more interested in the former) and Fennell (who tends to be more interested in the latter). This sense of Fennell and Perrault being joined by Robinson is especially strong in Robinson's 1976 essay "Islands and Images." It is there that he writes:

> In the basic geographic act of mapping I find three conjunctions: that of the place mapped with the one who maps it; that of the mapper with the map itself; and finally that of the map with the mapped—this last a confrontation that tests the worth of the first and the second. (*Setting Foot on the Shores of Connemara* 15)

This third test is the one that Fennell and Perrault are forever struggling to pass. They have both, throughout their work, spun complex networks between territories: Ireland and Europe, Quebec and its various hinterlands, Quebec and France, Ireland and its Gaeltacht. But for both, these projects eventually amble back towards the relationships between the map and the mapped. Fennell engages not with bits on maps that mark Gaeltacht areas but with the fate of Irish-speaking *communities*. Perrault wonders not only about the transatlantic path from Quebec to Brittany but about the degree to which this illuminates the complexities of contemporary national belonging. Fennell wants to "revient toujours au langage," but he does so only to "humaniser la terre."

I dwell on this Perrault-Fennell connection in large part because Fennell's ideas about territory, community, language, and internationalism formed the intellectual superstructure of Gluaiseacht Chearta Sibhialta na Gaeltachta. That movement, of course, had a very strong audiovisual component to it. This came first in radio form, via the raidió bradaíola / Saor-raidió Chonamara pirate broadcasts of 1970, which I discussed in the introduction to the Gaeltacht section. Later it came in cinematic form, via the films of Bob Quinn and the community video projects of his production company Cinegael, which I will discuss in the next chapter. Then it came in a televisual form, via the Teilifís na Gaeltachta pirate broadcasts in 1987, discussed in this book's final chapter. All of this, I would argue, strongly bore the mark of Fennell's ideas. But this may seem incidental; Fennell may have argued for the creation of a Gaeltacht radio station as part of his work with Gluaiseacht Chearta Sibhialta, but he evinced only passing interest in film or TV. What his connection to Perrault can help to illuminate is that these ideas do have a cinematic life. Perrault, whose films and radio programs are some of the most lasting work of post-1960s Quebec cinema and radio, differs from Fennell on some issues, but I do believe they connect in important ways. Perrault is the best filmmaker that the 1970s Gaeltacht movement never had.

Notes

1 "Je découvrais que la langue du pays transmettait des images du pays et que le pays façonnait la langue, inventait des mots susceptibles de traduire les gens, les choses, les métiers, les paysages que les littératures lointaines et les dictionnaires hautains ne parvenaient pas à décrire. L'idée m'est venue de naviguer ce fleuve du langage pour découvrir le langage du fleuve" (26).

2 I argued in a 2002 *Cinema Journal* article that Perrault's films share a great deal with those of Bob Quinn; in the next chapter I connect Quinn with Colin Low instead. This is not because I am backing away from what I still see as a very valid Perrault-

Quinn comparison. But it has become increasingly clear to me that Quinn's cultural-activist work in general—and especially his community TV work through Cinegael—has a clearer connection to the NFB's Challenge for Change program generally and to Low's Fogo Island films specifically. The explicitness of this connection—particularly via Quinn's 1976 film *A Film Board for Ireland?*—probably does trump his Perrault connections (despite strong connections with Perrault via common linguistic interests and aesthetic tendencies). But Quinn is, of course, quite close to Fennell; the two were collaborators on films, and shared many ideas about the place of the Gaeltacht in Irish life. Thus moving from a Perrault–Quinn connection to a Perrault–Fennell one is not really a very significant shift; I have always believed that Perrault and Gaeltacht activists would have had much to say to one another, and I still believe that.

3 "Rachadh Gaeilgeoirí, a raibh chuile cheird agus scil acu, go Conamara," he wrote, "agus dhéanfadh siad 'Israel nua' ann agus chuirfeadh an Rialtas plean forbartha ar siúl faoi údarás Bhord Iarchonnacht" (*Inniu* 9). For "new Israel" Fennell writes "Israel nua" in the version published in *Inniu*, but changes this to "Iosrael nua" in the version reprinted in *Iarchonnacht Began*.

4 The most vivid and aesthetically adventurous example of this sort of idealism that I know of has, as Fennell might guess, a Parisian pedigree. Chris Marker's 1960 film *Description d'un combat* is a film diary of his motorcycle trip all over Israel and is a very vivid document of the way in which the adventure of early Zionism was an inspiration to the intellectual left.

5 This poem is taken from handwritten notes found in the Fonds Pierre Perrault, held at Université Laval (the file number for the *Aux portes de la nuit* folder is P319/C1). The note for P319/C1 in Céline Savard and James Lambert's register states, "There are no indications in these documents concerning the broadcast of these programs. Radio-Canada cannot provide information about this series *Aux portes de la nuit*" [Il n'y a pas d'indications dans ces documents concernant la diffusion de ces émissions. La Société Radio-Canada n'a pu fournir des renseignements sur cette série *Aux portes de la nuit*].

6 "une seule terre fut 'promise'! / un seul peuple fut 'sans terre'! // cette terre promise était un désert! / ce peuple sans terre aimait la promesse! // Israël! Israël! / ou les rochers inquiets en mal de source / regrettent la baguette de Moïse qui / n'a pas effacé le desert / mais le désert parle en faveur d'Israël"

7 Fennell explains in a footnote to "Solutions to the Northern Problem" that he is actually interested in what he calls "Éire Nua (revised version) or Mark Two." The original Éire Nua proposals, published in a pamphlet called *Éire Nua: The Social and Economic Programme of Sinn Féin* (Dublin: Sinn Féin, 1971), called for "not merely the complete overthrow of English rule in Ireland but also the setting up of a Democratic Socialist Republic based on the Proclamation of 1916" (3). No mention of a federation is to be found in that pamphlet. As Fennell writes, "Consequently, when the appendix containing the federal scheme and Draft Charter of Rights was added in a new edition, there were contradictions with the earlier text. These were superficially

resolved in the 'Peace and Justice' leaflet, which ranked thereafter as a summary restatement of *Éire Nua*." (See Fennell, "Solutions to the Northern Problem," 23n7). The revised leaflet Fennell refers to is reproduced in his *Beyond Nationalism* (234).

8 "C'est ma période magnétophone si on peut dire. Ma découverte de la parole" (Warren 36).

9 "Bhí tógáil impireacht Dhubhlinne faoi lántseol" (5). Pádraig Ó Siadhail has suggested to me that the word "Duibhlinn" would be more accurate; I suppose one privilege of making up words, though, is that you get to take some liberties with the grammar.

10 "Bíonn an aicme cheannais comhdhéanta as únaeraí agus bainisteoirí mórghnó, príomhoifigigh na státsheirbhíse, bainisteoirí agus teagascóirí poiblí na meán cumarsáide—an *New Priesthood*" (6).

11 "Que le cinéma de fiction prenne tout à coup l'importance au Québec ne me concerne pas. C'est son affaire et c'est normal puisque c'est ainsi les choses se passent ailleurs; c'est peut-être bon pour le commerce qui ne me doit rien. C'est peut-être ça la culture qui facilitera notre libération même si je le doute fort. C'est peut-être plus utile que mon travail. C'est peut-être l'avenir du Québec ou celui du cinéma même si l'un me préoccupe plus que l'autre" (Lafond, *Les traces du rêve* scenario 70).

12 Folens was, posthumously, the subject of a controversy in 2007 about his time in the Flemish Legion during WWII. The 2006 documentary *Ireland's Nazis* (directed by Keith Farrell), in addition to challenging the Folens' family's version of the nature of his military service, played a tape of a 1985 interview that Folens gave to the *Irish Independent*'s Senan Moloney. *Ireland's Nazis* includes a part of the tape where Folens asks, rhetorically and impatiently, "How come you are going to have any comprehension for what I have done during the war? So how can you understand that we cooperate wholeheartedly with the Germans? We can only get rescue from the Germans." The Folens family brought the filmmakers to the High Court, and although the court concluded that the film was well balanced, the family won the insertion of a voiceover stating that they did not accept that Folens had ever been part of the SS. For media coverage of the controversy see "Amended Folens Interview to be Aired" (*Irish Times*, 15 January 2007) and Ann O'Loughlin, "Folens Family Wins TV Right of Reply" (*Irish Independent*, 16 January 2007); Emmanuel Kehoe critiques the film in "Hidden History: Much Ado about the Nazis" (*Sunday Business Post*, 21 January 2007).

13 "Nuair a cuirtear [*sic*] scéal na hÉireann agus scéal Fhlóndrais i gcomórtas le chéile, seo mar samhlaítear [*sic*] do dhuine iad: gur éirigh le hÉirinn stát neamhspleách a dhéanamh di féin ach gur dhóbair di an teanga bheith caillte aici roimhe sin, agus ar an dtaobh eile dhe, cé nach stát é Flóndras fós, go bhfuil an teanga sábhálta aige ar chuma nach baol di inniu. Mar sin ba bhuntáiste don dá dhream, d'Éireannaigh agus do Pléimeannaigh, eolas a chur ar scéal a chéile" (4).

14 Although this isn't quite the same issue, it is worth noting that Fennell also quotes the work of David Irving, who was jailed in Austria on 20 February 2006 after being convicted of charges connected to Holocaust denial (he was released in December

of the same year). Fennell quotes a passage from Irving's 1963 bestseller *The Destruction of Dresden* in his books *Uncertain Dawn* (Dublin: Sanas, 1996) and *The Postwestern Condition* (London: Minerva Press, 1999), which is basically a shorter, more focused version of *Uncertain Dawn*. Fennell focuses on *The Destruction of Dresden*'s depiction of the reluctance of General Carl F. Spatz, in Irving's words, "to attempt to terrorize the Germans into capitulation." Fennell writes that in this passage "we seem to get a glimpse of American military men making a last-ditch stand for the old humanism before, in the final stages of the war, the giddy slide towards Hiroshima began" (*Uncertain Dawn* 41; *The Postwestern Condition* 77). *The Destruction of Dresden* was widely read upon its release, and it famously influenced Kurt Vonnegut's *Slaughterhouse Five*. Most historians now consider *The Destruction of Dresden* to be discredited. My sense, though, is that the book is in Fennell's work not because of his reliance on the ideology of Holocaust denial, but because of his reliance on popular history; he seems to me a lot closer to Kurt Vonnegut than to David Irving.

15 "En parlant du 'Québec libre' moi j'ai pensé à une chose ... il a parlé pour le Québec libre.... Ça a fait du bruit ... on a suivi ça au jour le jour ... minute par minute ... hien!!! Nous ... on a pensé à la Bretagne libre! mais on a pensé aussi à la Tchécoslovaquie libre, à la Roumanie et à tous ces états satellisés par le communisme" (Perrault, *Un pays sans bon sens!* scenario 93).

16 "On peut dire que nous autres qui avons commencé un mouvement breton, en 1920, juste après la guerre, de 14 comme tout le monde quoi hein, eh bien nous avons été à contre-courant, absolument à contre-courant" (149). These transcripts can be found in the Fonds Pierre Perrault at Université Laval; the file number is P319/D9.8.

17 "En 1944 se replie sur l'Allemagne avec le bezen Perrot" (431).

18 Daniel Leach has written extensively on the matter of far-right minority nationalists seeking asylum in the post-WWII Free State of Ireland (which was neutral during WWII). See his *Fugitive Ireland: European Minority Nationalists and Irish Political Asylum, 1937–2008* (Dublin: Four Courts Press, 2009). On Laîné specifically, see his article "Bezen Perrot: The Breton Nationalist Unit of the SS, 1943–45," *E-Keltoi: Journal of Interdisciplinary Celtic Studies* 4 (2008), 1–38. See also his more general article, "'Repaying a Debt of Gratitude': Foreign Minority Nationalists and the Fiftieth Anniversary of the Easter Rising in 1966," *Éire-Ireland* 43:3–4 (Fall-Winter 2008), 267–89. For more on the Bezen Perrot, see Kristian Hamon's *Le Bezen Perrot: Des nationalistes bretons sous l'uniform allemand* (Le Fouesnant, Fr.: Éditions Yoran Embanner, 2005) and *Les nationalistes bretons sous l'Occupation* (Le Relecq-Kerhuon, Fr.: Éditoins An Here, 2001). *Ireland's Nazis* also deals with Laîné.

19 "Ça été surtout un mouvement pour l'indépendance pendant la guerre" (47).

20 I can't quite tell which edition of the Fouéré book Fennell was reading. I have consulted both the 1968 edition and the 1976 reprint; the passages that I cite are identical in both editions, as is the pagination. It is the 1968 edition that appears in my bibliography. The 1980 translation *Towards a Federal Europe?* appears to have been adapted from the 1968 edition, as its conclusion ends with the date

"October 1963–January 1967" (161); the 1968 edition ends that way, and the 1976 edition does not. *Cent drapeaux* was also revised and reissued in 2007.

21 "On ne doit pas stériliser l'Europe et réduire la construction européenne à l'édification d'une société purement matérielle où l'accroissement des chiffres de la production deviendrait l'impératif premier. Derrière l'impersonnelle froideur des chiffres et du monde des économistes, il y a l'homme et le citoyen, les communautés naturelles auxquelles il appartient, l'infinie richesse culturelle de l'Europe, inséparable de sa diversité" (*Cent drapeaux* 149).

22 "Là est le plan d'objet de cet essai; car pour moi le choix est fait ; il l'est aussi pour des milliers d'autres Européens, membres des plus vieilles nations européennes que la deuxième Europe a cherché à anéantir. La troisième Europe devra être l'Europe des peuples, non l'Europe des États" (*Cent drapeaux* 21).

23 Les nations sont la réalité moral permanente, la synthèse des intérêts et des idéaux d'un peuple. Elles durent, alors que l'État passe, évolue et change" (*Cent drapeaux* 70).

24 "Entre tous les signataires du placet de Jaffrennou, Yann Fouéré fut celui qui joua le plus grand rôle durant les quatre années qui suivirent l'armistice" (247).

25 "Nous avons décidé de fonder ce journal pour tenter d'arracher au gouvernement de Vichy l'autonomie administrative et culturelle de la Bretagne, à l'époque envahie et occupé par les armées allemandes" (13).

26 Déniel recalls some of the more memorable essays found in the pages of *La Bretagne*: "Protesting against the showing of the film *Bécassine*, the regionalist daily proclaimed on 24 March 1941: 'Kick out the Jewish filmmakers and actors.' In June 1942, Olier Gruyon devoted two articles to 'our anti-Semitic tradition,' and welcomed the edict of expulsion that Duke Jean II had promulgated against the Jews at the beginning of the 13th century. The following July, a certain 'Father X' denounced 'the Jewish hold on Christianity'" [Protestant contre la projection du film *Bécassine*, le quotidien régionaliste proclame le 24 mars 1941: "Boutez dehors les cinéastes et acteurs israélites." En juin 1942, Olier Guyon consacre deux articles à "notre tradition antisémite" et se félicite de l'édit d'expulsion que le duc Jean II avait promulgué à l'encontre des Juifs au début du XIIIe siècle. Au mois de juillet suivant, un certain abbé X dénonce "l'emprise juive sur la chrétienté" (249)]. Fouéré has provided his own version of the history of the newspaper, both in his *Histoire d'un Breton* memoirs (1987's *La patrie interdit* and the aforementioned second volume *La Maison du Connemara*) and in the book *L'histoire de quotidien "La Bretagne" et les silences d'Henri Fréville* (Saint-Brieuc: Cahiers de l'Avenir de la Bretagne, 1979), which he co-wrote with Youenn Didro.

27. "le quotidien adhère aux principes du corporatasime défendu par Vichy" (250).

28 "un homme dont le patriotisme Breton ne pouvait être mis en doute, décida de jouer la carte de la collaboration avec Vichy" (123).

29 "Mon passeport et mon visa étaient en règle, ils portaient ma propre photo; mais ils portaient aussi un nom qui n'étaient pas le mien" (*La Maison du Connemara* 13).

30 "Celui qui prétend maîtriser l'histoire réclame à son tour le pouvoir et son exercise. Au fond il faut refuser à l'histoire le droit de disposer les hommes" (87).

31 "An Ghaeltacht sa gcéill cheart seo den fhocal (agus ní sa mbréagchiall oifigiúil) atá i gceist agam sa léarscáil" (2).

32 "Tá gluaiseachtaí bríomhara *athgaelaithe* [*sic*] sa Rinn agus i gcuid bheag de Mhuscraí, ach sé tuairim fhormhór na ndaoine sa dá cheantar sin nach bhfuil *limistéar* ar bith thart orthu inarb í an Ghaeilge an ghnáththeanga. Tagaim leis an tuairim seo: 'teaghlaigh Ghaelacha' atá i gceist, ní Gaeltacht" (2).

33 "La géographie ne doit-elle pas, avant tout, humaniser la terre?" (*De la parole aux actes* 50).

34 "On en revient toujours au langage" (*De la parole aux actes* 50).

5

Cinegael and the Newfoundland Project

> What kept me going was Grierson's perception of the importance of the local. Homer based the *Iliad* on a local squabble. The NFB's Challenge for Change programme inspired me to set up the first closed-circuit TV service in Ireland—perhaps in Europe.
>
> —Bob Quinn, "Recycled Rants," an address first given in Edmonton at the 2000 Canadian Association for Irish Studies and later published in Ireland's *Film West* (27)

> If, finally, TV is our prose (and we'll never speak well enough), cinema has no better chance than in poetry.[1]
>
> —Serge Daney, *Le Salaire du zappeur*

If you want to read about the videos made by Bob Quinn's production group Cinegael, there's no point in going to the standard histories of Irish cinema. Kevin Rockett, Luke Gibbons, and John Hill's 1987 *Cinema and Ireland* doesn't mention these videos at all, nor do more recent books such as Martin McLoone's *Irish Film: The Emergence of a Contemporary Cinema* or Lance Pettitt's *Screening Ireland*, although all three monographs do discuss Quinn's independently produced films, such as *Poitín* (1977), *Budawanny* (1987), and *The Bishop's Story* (1993). The anthologies *Contemporary Irish Cinema* (edited by James MacKillop, 1999) and *Keeping It Real: Irish Film and Television* (edited by Ruth Barton and Harvey O'Brien, 2004) feature no discussion of Quinn's filmmaking at all (in all fairness, Martin McLoone's essay in the MacKillop book gives Quinn's name in a roll call of independent filmmakers, but does not elaborate [51]; Quinn's films are also listed in the book's filmography). Barton's monograph *Irish National Cinema*, a 2004 entry in Routledge's national cinema series, mentions the name Cinegael but identifies it only as the production company for Quinn's films (91); this is also true of Harvey O'Brien's 2004 monograph *The Real Ireland: The Evolution of Ireland in Documentary Film* (185, 187, 195), although O'Brien includes an extended discussion of Quinn's *Atlantean* films (194–203). Lest one think that Quinn's video-based project just wasn't "film-y" enough for these cinephiles, who assumed that the TV people would look after it, Iarfhlaith Watson's invaluable 2003 study *Broadcasting in Irish* makes no mention of Cinegael, and the equally invaluable work of Niamh Hourigan on Irish-language broadcast almost totally ignores it (1998's "A Comparison" mentions it in a footnote),[2] although both scholars discuss Quinn. Robert J. Savage's 1996 book *Irish Television: The Political and Social Origins* makes no mention of Quinn at all, although this is fair enough, since the book ends before Quinn started working at RTÉ.

It should come as no surprise, really, that one place where you can find an explicit—if rather short—explanation of the community TV experiment known as Cinegael is in Risteárd Ó Glaisne's 1982 book *Raidió na Gaeltachta.* Ó Glaisne's last chapter is a sort of appendix called "Agus an Teilifís?" [And Television?]. There we find discussion of Cinegael's overall project, which included *both* video and film: "They made TV progams on videotape and on film, and they sold films they had made of events at Ros Muc's Coláiste na bhFiann and of prize-giving at the Teach Furbo Oireachtais [both places in the Connemara Gaeltacht], to RTÉ."[3] As I'll discuss in the next chapter, we also find in Ó Glaisne's work some discussion of the other forgotten element of the quest for Irish-language television, the example of the Faroe Islands (which is rarely granted more than a sentence in the standard histories of Irish-language media activism). This is no surprise, because Cinegael, like the rest of the work that I have been discussing throughout this book, evolved in a way and existed in a state that would likely be quite unfamiliar to most observers of world cinema (even though Cinegael's prime animator, Bob Quinn, has made films that have enjoyed, as have Low's and Perrault's, considerable exposure in cinematheques and film festivals). It evolved in a way and existed in a state that is, really, much closer to radio. It fits into Risteárd's Ó Glaisne's narrative, into his world view, in a way that it does not fit into that of Ruth Barton or Harvey O'Brien. It follows, in short, what Jan Olsson called "the radio model": a view of television that emphasizes the civic and illustrates what Olsson called "an anti-commercial bias" (256). This "bias" is one line that runs through this North Atlantic cinema, one of the elements that distinguish it from much mainstream filmmaking and most mainstream television.

Another line that runs through this North Atlantic work is a tendency to blur the boundaries between media. This material has strong ties to radio, and those ties are often visible in this material. But this is also because of the ease with which many of these animators move between film and television. Cinegael is the example of the latter par excellence; initiated by a filmmaker, it was ostensibly a community TV experiment, but one that relied on screenings rather than broadcast for dissemination. In conversation, as in the epigraph above, Quinn typically refers to the project as an example of "closed-circuit TV"; but as Quinn indicates in that quote, Cinegael's clearest precursor is a cinematic one: the NFB's Fogo Island project. Quinn has always been explicit about the degree to which the Challenge for Change project generally and the Fogo films specifically influenced his vision, both in conversation and in the films that he made. There is plenty of evidence of this in the Cinegael tapes themselves, which sometimes feature the sort of "feedback" that was so important to Low and Snowden. This feedback, both in the Fogo films and the Cinegael work, frequently appeared in the form of confrontations with government apathy to the consequences of ill-conceived development schemes. Like the Fogo films in Canada, this vision had relatively little impact on the national cinema as a whole. But at least historians of Canadian cinema bother to misrepresent the Fogo films; the Cinegael project is simply absent from Irish cinema studies. But also like the Fogo films, this was an example of a locally rooted and internationally aware experiment in the political use of emerging technology.

As with the Fogo films to which these Cinegael videos are so closely related, I want to sketch some of the historical basics of the project; I also want to explain the way in which it was linked to the Gaeltacht activism that I have been discussing in this section. Furthermore, I want to explain the way in which these videos are the product of innovative ideas about video technology, struggling to enunciate an aesthetic that is not entirely of film or of television, but borrows freely from both forms in search of something new. I have shown how Gaeltacht activism of the 1960s and 1970s sought a renewal heavily invested in modernity, rather than in popular romantic fantasies of rural idylls or popular misperceptions of squalid backwaters; they wanted, echoing the words of Perrault, to de-folklorize the Gaeltacht. As we saw through their interest in issues like broadcasting, European unification, the war in Northern Ireland, and so on, Gluaiseacht Chearta Sibhialta na Gaeltachta and Desmond Fennell were seeking to stabilize Irish-speaking communities through their full integration into an independent, outward-looking Ireland.

Emigrating to Connemara

When we last left Bob Quinn, he was angrily resigning from RTÉ and co-writing the 1969 book *Sit Down and Be Counted: The Cultural Evolution of a Television Station*. "Then I became a dishwasher in London," Quinn recalls in his 2001 book *Maverick*. He eventually found his way to the Connemara Gaeltacht, where his friend Desmond Fennell, whom he knew from their days in Dublin journalism, suggested he might find a welcoming environment. Fennell was active in the emerging Gaeltacht civil rights movement and certainly was a kindred spirit for Quinn. But Fennell had (like Quinn) actually been a newcomer to Connemara (he had been a journalist in Dublin); he quickly became a crucial part of the politics there, but he wasn't really an insider. *Introduction to Fogo Island* introduced Fred Earle by saying that Earle "was born and raised on Fogo Island. He knows, and is known, by all its people." Quinn needed a Fred Earle figure of this kind. He found one in Seosamh Ó Cuaig.

Ó Cuaig was a Gaeltacht activist and a journalist in the Irish-language press (he is currently a member of the Galway County Council and of the board of Údarás na Gaeltachta, "the Gaeltacht authority"). In Robert Quinn's 2004 film *Cinegael Paradiso* (the best source of information about the Cinegael project by a long shot; it is directed by Bob Quinn's son), Bob Quinn recalls how Ó Cuaig was ten years younger than himself but far more sophisticated politically; Ó Cuaig, for his part, recalls that Quinn had both technical know-how when it came to filmmaking and a reputation as a radical. In that film, Quinn also recalls how the name of their scheme to bring televisual images to Connemara was coined by Ó Cuaig:

> He said give me all the words for film, and I gave him all the words I knew for film. And he said, I s'pose we'll have to put in the word Gael somewhere, to say that it's different from RTÉ. And he came up with this very excellent pun: Cine Gael. Which is Irish Cinema; but it also means, "*the race of Irish*."

This story about the naming of the company gives a good sense of the degree to which Quinn's first attempts at media activism outside of RTÉ were completely of a piece with the civil rights movement. Cinegael was about creating images, but it was also in equal parts about helping embattled Irish speakers and about using cinema to help, if not exactly "the race of the Gaels" (a concept I tried hard to reject in the last chapter), then the communities that actually spoke Irish as an everyday language. It seems logical, then, that in addition to Ó Glaisne's history of Raidió na Gaeltachta, another slightly unlikely place where one finds brief but precise discussion of the Cinegael project is Fennell's 1985 book *Beyond Nationalism*, where we read:

> Among the freelancers who came to Iarchonnacht was Bob Quinn, the filmmaker who had resigned from RTÉ. No Gaeilgeoir to begin with, he soon became fluent. He set up a film company, Cinegael, which made a fortnightly videotape of local events that was shown in pubs and halls. By making films of his own in Gaelic, he and his wife Helen (who became an expert in casting and locations) drew other independent filmmakers to the district. Thus, within a space of five or six years, magazine-publishing, radio work, video and film-acting had become part of the life of Gaelic-speaking Connemara, and to these the Cois Fharraige co-op added printing and book-publishing. (142)

As Fennell tells it, then, Quinn's presence here was a precise realization of his "Iosrael in Iarchonnacht" proposals, which I discussed in the last chapter. These proposals imagined skilled Irish people from all over coming to the Gaeltacht, learning Irish, and contributing to the creation of a more sustainable and culturally vibrant set of communities.

Making Cinema Gaelic, Making Gaelic Cinematic

It is difficult to find any criticial discussion of these fortnightly videos. The biography on Quinn's website (http://www.conamara.org/biography.htm) explains the project thusly:

> Cinegael's original intention was to reinforce the identity of this threatened linguistic minority: the group realised that in modern times man's destiny was stated in political terms. Inspired by the National Film Board of Canada's Challenge for Change programme and using pioneering closed-circuit TV techniques it recorded local events and controversies. It mediated successfully between local opinion and public bodies.
>
> Gradually Cinegael began to engage with the larger polity of Ireland. It evolved into a maker of one-off film documentaries and dramas which were all screened on RTE, the Irish Public broadcaster, [as] well as on BBC, Channel Four, SBC etc. and which achieved other international recognition.

This is a pithy summary of the key elements of the project: its place in a minority-rights political struggle; its debt to the NFB's Challenge for Change project; its emphasis on brass-tacks, detail-oriented development, often involving confrontation with state actors; and the emergence of a (slightly better known) production company that made fiction films as well as television documentaries (some conventional, some quite eccentric) based in the Connemara Gaeltacht.

Quinn explained the operational details of Cinegael to me in a conversation at his home in Béal an Daingin, County Galway, on 30 June 2005. He had come to Connemara in 1970, and chastened by his experiences at RTÉ, he said that he "didn't do anything for several years" by way of film production; he had a craft workshop, where he did silkscreening. In 1973 he acquired a then-cutting-edge Portapak video rig (he told me it was an Akai three-quarter-inch video recorder), and he began to tape local people and events (as I discussed in chapter 3, Quinn has kept VHS copies of these tapes at his archives at Béal an Daingin). These included stage plays (on the tapes labelled 2A, 3, and 5A), sporting events (boxing and Gaelic football are on the tape labelled 7), sean-nós singers[4] (on the tapes labelled 4A, 6, and 11), and other traditional musical performances (the tape labelled 6A features a concert by a musical group that includes a Breton lute player), and interviews with young children (the tape labelled 9 features interviews with kids at Indreabhán, Connemara's Scoil Sailearna that were replayed for them twenty years later, in Boston, in Quinn's 1993 film *Pobal i mBoston*). These tapes were circulated rather than broadcast, shown in halls and at community meetings around Connemara (Quinn told me that they had a plan to circulate them via bicycle, and he seemed to be only partly joking). Furthermore, in contrast to the Connemara-centric nature of many Gluaiseacht-related activities, Ó Glaisne also notes that "Cinegael went to Gweedore [in County Donegal], made television films there, and showed them at the Gweedore Theatre on Sundays as a special videotape program."[5] Cinegael videos were also shown before the screenings of movies in the Quinn home.

Those screenings at the Quinns' occurred as part of another important, if slightly contradictory, element of the Cinegael project: the opening of a small movie theatre in Quinn's sprawling home. Writing in *Maverick*, Quinn recalls, "In 1975 in our new home—an old Congested Districts Board factory in Carraroe [An Cheathrú Rua] which we converted into a fleapit cinema—my then wife and I had been showing feature films: films like *Man of Aran*, *Dr. No*, even *Enter the Dragon*" (73). This theatre is also nostalgically recalled in Robert Quinn's *Cinegael Paradiso* as a site of childhood awakening to the wider world. But sentimental recollections of kids acting out Bruce Lee moves at the back of the church aside, the opening of a movie theatre is itself in keeping with the aspirations of Gluaiseacht Chearta Sibhialta na Gaeltachta. Fennell writes specifically that if a revitalized Gaeltacht along these lines was to emerge, "it means a movie theatre, and films in Irish."[6] That wasn't quite what happened at the Cinegael movie theatre at first, but it wasn't long before it did.

The better-known, and certainly more widely discussed, aspect of Cinegael's work was the way in which it acted as the production company for Quinn's independent films. This is something that is present in most of the discourse around Irish cinema; someone reading the general histories of the national cinema would likely find mention of the "small films" that Cinegael produced. But on the surface there would seem to be very little connection between the more local video / "closed-circuit TV" work that Cinegael was doing and the films it was producing. Of course this is not the case at all.

The film that most explicitly illustrates this is Quinn's 1974 short film *Oireachtas na nGael*. This was a documentary about the 1973 Oireachtas na nGael festival,[7] which was held in Tír an Fhia, Corr na Móna, and Cill Chiaráin, three Gaeltacht areas in County Galway. It's a lyrical film, and it gives a sense of intimacy and closeness to the events. One shot of an old man step-dancing is strongly reminiscent of the images of a similar type of dancing in *Children of Fogo Island*, although Quinn shoots his old-timers either from very low angles (from just below the stage) or with close-ups or extreme close-ups of faces and feet. The film's footage of performers (including a number of sean-nós singers), which is mostly in medium shot or close-up, also has a lyrical, intimate sensibility. This is also true of the film's footage of the sporting events; images of boat-racing are shot from within one of the boats, with the rowers often in close-up, giving a sense of immediacy and kinesis. Like the Fogo films, *Oireachtas na nGael* strongly evinces vérité's traditional attachment to the visceral qualities of musical performance; it also evinces vérité's fondness for sporting events (especially evident in the Quebec variant of the genre, in films such as *Les raquetteurs* [Michel Brault and Gilles Groulx 1958] or *Golden Gloves* [Groulx 1961]). That said, the film also makes use of non-synch voice-over, especially at the beginning, where young people speak critically (in English) about the Oireachtas, romanticism about the west, and the general state of life in the Gaeltacht (which one young woman judges to be defined by boredom and a lack of imagination). Quinn's approach to vérité aesthetics in this film is thus very close to Low's agnosticism. Neither filmmaker belongs to the cult of synch sound, even though both seem to basically believe in it; overall they seek fulfillment in cinematic poetry.

The video adjunct of *Oireachtas na nGael*, though, looks very different indeed. This documents a debate held directly following the screening of the film in a community hall, animated and recorded by Cinegael. It is found on the VHS tape in Quinn's archives labelled 4A, and it is partially reproduced in Robert Quinn's film *Cinegael Paradiso* (which identifies it as "*Cill Chiarán* [sic] *Hall 1974*"). The excerpt that Robert Quinn includes in his film features people talking about the film *Oireachtas na nGael*; responses are generally positive, although one man says there was too much of a sense that the festival was all about drinking, and another says there shouldn't have been any English in the film. The full tape opens with an old man singing sean-nós, and then has the animator, Máirtín Davy Ó Coistealbha, taking questions about the film. At one point a man says that he wishes the film would be shown in Dublin, in Belfast, or in Portlaoise prison (a prison in the Republic of Ireland where large numbers of paramilitary prisoners were held), or maybe in the United States. A bit later we can hear Quinn telling the audience that the equipment came from RTÉ and that the film cost £1,000 to produce. He is audible but not visible, because he is operating the camera; he is an active participant in these discussions, though, sometimes interrupting the animator Ó Coistealbha. Seán Bán Breathnach (on whom more later) complains that when the Oireachtas was in Dublin, many people in attendance only had a few words of Irish and that it was mostly devoted to music (the audience applauds at this comment). The discussion is, in short, all over the place, and it is punctuated by numerous silences as Ó Coistealbha keeps asking, "Duine ar bith eile?" [Anyone else?] It is made up of three incredibly long takes (Quinn seems to have had to restart the camera a few times), a sort of aesthetic that is possible only on video. But it is all more or less connected to the film. *Oireachtas na nGael* (1973) and the videotape identified in *Cinegael Paradiso* as "*Cill Chiarán Hall 1974*" are in a sort of symbiotic relationship; they are two separate objects and different in their aesthetic, but it is difficult to understand the meaning or importance of one of them without the other.

This relationship is quite close to the idealism of Serge Daney,[8] who dreamed of a more fully realized, fully conceptualized relationship between film and television. Part of that has to do with the epigraph at the beginning of this chapter, arguing that cinema is our poetry and TV our prose; surely this is a good way of thinking about the relationship between these two Oireachtas-related media productions I have just discussed. As Daney went on to write in *Le Salaire du zappeur*, "The art of cinema has without a doubt consisted of responding in advance to questions that no one yet knew to ask.... In the best case, TV—an adult TV—could maybe take up these questions."[9] This is the Cinegael project to a T, and this is most explicitly illustrated by the *Cill Chiarán Hall 1974* tape, which has, as its primary raison d'être, responding to the questions that the film *Oireachtas na nGael* seems to pose, questions that nobody seems to have asked: questions about the Gaeltacht; questions about the nature of Gaelic culture and its festivals; questions about the connection between forms of state domination, such as the imprisonment of insurgents or the simultaneous predominance and neglect of the minority language.

Daney also longs in *Le Salaire du zappeur* for an engaged, conscious public discourse; this is a televisual challenge that is also at the core of the Cinegael productions. Daney laments that "an 'adult audience' is a utopia that we're still waiting for"[10] and sees television as a key part of this unrealized idealism. He goes on to say that "TV is caught up with ecology because it touches in us the responsible citizen, which is to say, the adult."[11] Cinegael had as one of its primary purposes the enabling of an engaged public, the support of a responsible citizenship. As Seosamh Ó Cuaig said in the film *Cinegael Paradiso*, "Is rud polaitíochta a bhí ann" [It was something political]. Ó Cuaig was referring to a decidedly nuts-and-bolts form of politics, one that Quinn clearly agreed with. These videos were used by Quinn, Ó Cuaig, and others involved with Gluaiseacht as a means to address the serious economic and infrastructural problems that had so long plagued Gaeltacht areas, in both the pre- and post-independence eras. As Quinn recalls in *Cineagel Paradiso*:

> It was quite new to the authorities in the west, like the Western Health Board, Údarás na Gaeltachta,[12] to have people *here* actually recording and getting people's opinions about local issues, and then going to them and showing them the video. And usually, what happened was, we'd ring them up and tell them we want to show you this video about this problem that has arisen. And when we'd go in to show them the video, the problem would have been solved. It was extraordinary.

Quinn says this in *Cinegael Paradiso* in a voice-over accompanying images of an old-timer talking to a government minister; the film identifies the clip as "Peadar Macken interviewing Tom O'Donnell, Minister for the Gaeltacht, 1974." They are discussing how local people are charged £300 to access power poles that are right outside their door; O'Donnell stutters out, "Ah well, problems like this in every Gaeltacht are, are, are ..."[13] Another part of the tape (not in *Cinegael Paradiso*, but on the VHS tape labelled 6A in Quinn's archives) shows O'Donnell speaking (in English) about the creation of a locally based Gaeltacht authority and starting to say that the government has responsibility for the language; a journalist starts to question him (also in English) about local control of communities, and the tape cuts off. This video strongly recalls Fogo films such as *Citizen Discussions*, where in the first half of the film local people talk about the degree to which the government has been unwilling to commit resources or even attention by way of helping to revitalize Fogo or to bring it some sort of locally responsive government, and in the second half

Aiden Maloney, Newfoundland's Minister of Fisheries and Community and Social Development, grouchily and ramblingly answers questions about the way in which these matters have been handled by the Newfoundland government. Quinn and Cinegael were, indeed, trying to create "communication loops between the community and government via film." Clearly he saw the project as "an experiment in the role of communications in social change. As part of this experiment, we filmed local people talking about the problems of a changing community, and played back these films in that community." These are not Quinn's words, of course; they are Colin Low's. The first is from his 1972 report *Fogo Island Communication Experiment*; the second is from the voice-over of the film *Introduction to Fogo Island*. Watching these tapes, particularly in the light of the Fogo Island films, it becomes almost inarguably apparent that Low and Quinn shared the fundamental goal of enabling critical discussion of important issues, and of enabling people to speak of their experience to what Donald Snowden's 1968 report called "the area's 'power' people—whose planning, policies, or neglect affects the lives of the people already on film" (6).

Picking back up on the Daney stream, this is also a very Godardian sensibility for television. Although Jean-Luc Godard is better known as part of the French New Wave, he did quite a bit of work for television and on video, especially in the 1970s and 1980s. This interest was, in 1968, signalled by his visit to small-town Quebec. When he travelled to Montreal in December of 1968, he made a diversion to the small town of Rouyn-Noranda. There he appeared on CKRN-TV, and when he was interviewed, he repeatedly stepped behind the camera, inviting the technicians to participate and wondering why there wasn't more dialogue between these two sides of the frame (this is all recounted in Julie Perron's 2000 film *Mai en décembre: Godard en Abitibi,* which reproduces the audio of the broadcasts accompanied by numerous still photographs; the video track has become illegible). In 1977, the studio Godard ran with Anne-Marie Miéville, Sonimage, was invited to Mozambique to consult on the formation of that country's television service (Godard and Miéville envisioned producing a series of five television documentaries called "Naissance (de l'image) d'une nation," but these were never completed). They travelled to Mozambique in 1978 for meetings and workshops. When Godard and Miéville edited a special issue of the French film magazine *Cahiers du cinéma*, they devoted two substantial appendices to their experiences there, appendices in the form of collages of images and text. One of these features a photograph of a track meet below a photo of a man with a video camera, with the text "Essai d'actualités mozambicains" (94). Another photomontage features, on facing pages, an image of a man behind a video camera with the text "Le droit du regard" and an image of three women with the text "Le droit à la parole" (110–11). These "rights to the gaze" and "to speech" are crucial concerns for Cinegael, as are the evocation of the "actualités" of everyday life that Godard and Miéville wanted to see emerge in Mozambiquean television (Godard and Miéville used shots of a track meet, while Cinegael often shot at boxing matches or Gaelic football games). And Quinn, like Godard in Rouyn-Noranda, was very happy to have the "other side" of the camera involved in dialogue, as he regularly answered questions and sometimes engaged the on-camera animator in discussion about the economics of film production from his own position behind the camera.

But this Godardian connection is largely implicit; Quinn made his Fogo connection, however, explicit in his 1975 film *A Film Board for Ireland?* This is a slightly awestruck documentary portrait of the National Film Board of Canada, one that both opens (over an image of a cigarette-smoking crew filming during an incredibly snowy Montreal winter day) and closes (over a sequence from Norman McLaren's *Pas de deux*) by asking, rhetorically, if Ireland can learn from the Canadian experience. The film has a fairly long sequence on Challenge for Change, one that shows images from *A Memo from Fogo* (Roger Hart, 1972)[14] and *VTR St-Jacques* (Bonnie Sher Klein, 1969), each representing the flagship films of the English-language Challenge for Change and French-language Société Nouvelle,[15] respectively. The film argues that this is key to understanding the role of the film board as a semi-state body charged with filmmaking. At one point the voice-over states that "the strong government hand in the country's film activity might suggest a limitation on freedom of expression. There are many examples to indicate that this is not so, the most outstanding one being the board's 'Challenge for Change' program." Quinn then cuts to an interview with Dorothy Hénaut (an NFB veteran involved in both Challenge for Change and Société Nouvelle) where she states that Grierson wanted the board to be "an inch to the left of the government" and that Challenge for Change represented a return to this goal after a period of "soft" documentaries in the 1950s. What Quinn finds at the NFB, then, is a model liberal state, one that is able not only to tolerate but to fund dissent, a kind of dissent that engages explicitly with the needs of marginalized populations to voice their own view of the world.

Yet, it wasn't always that simple for him. The voice-over of *A Film Board for Ireland?* marvels that "with nineteen different languages spoken and a multitude of ethnic groups making up what they refer to as cultural mosaic, interpreting Canada even to itself was a tall order. From a straightforward propaganda exercise during the Second World War, the Board developed into the most prolific and inventive producer of film documentaries in the world." But in *Sit Down and Be Counted*, we find discussion of how "in September 1967, he [Quinn] was given a generously subsidised leave of absence and spent the winter in a University in Nova Scotia, Canada [he was at St. Francis Xavier University, in Antigonish]. There he attended courses in sociology and read voraciously" (Dowling, Doolan, and Quinn 220). The book also recalls how Quinn discovered that "Canada was described as the second richest country on earth. In the 1961 census it was established that the wages of 47.9 per cent. of the labour force were below the officially-defined poverty level. They had, apparently, learned how to create wealth, but the technique of distributing it evaded them" (221). But it's the notion of "what they refer to as cultural mosaic" that he is most critical of:

> As far as the respect for ethnic and cultural idiosyncrasies implied in the "cultural mosaic" idea was concerned, Quinn saw the French in Quebec so enraged with the situation that they were on the verge of civil war with the Federal Government.
>
> In the same predicament, but reacting differently, were the Indians. The Micmacs were a tribe Quinn visited often. In their school (State-run) there was not a shred of evidence to indicate to the children that they had a group identity quite different to the white man's. They knew nothing of their history and their language was not a formal school subject. After school they watched the television cavalry making mincemeat of their television ancestors. This was on the same programme that carried endless commercials and other items that urged them: "You have no existence as a separate group. Forget your identity, and jump into the melting pot and become white, clean, homogenous consumers like the rest of us." (221)

This is the Quinn who, as Seosamh Ó Cuaig recalled, had the reputation of a radical, someone possessed of a sharply critical vision of consumption-dominated societies and impatience with the pretences of liberalism. How, then, does that square with the more cheerful vision of *A Film Board for Ireland?*

Part of the answer may lie in the complex relationship that Cinegael had with state bodies. Ó Glaisne recalls that "Bob Quinn, Seosamh Ó Cuaig, and Tony Christofides established Cinegael in Connemara in December 1973."[16] He then quotes Quinn's statements to *Inniu* (on 6 September 1974) that "Gaeltarra Éireann helped us, but much more support would be crucial for the business to develop properly."[17] Quinn has said more or less the same thing in English; *Cinegael Paradiso* has him recalling, "Three of us put in £1,000, and with that

£3,000 we went to Údarás na Gaeltachta[18] and proposed to set up a film industry in Connemara. And fair play to them, they matched our funds, and I went off and I bought a 16 mm cinema camera and a small video set-up, with a camera, and a recorder, and a tiny little monitor." So while there was plenty of discussion in Gluaiseacht circles about "Gaeltacht agus Impiriúlachas" [Gaeltacht and Imperialism] (in the words of Desmond Fennell's article of 1971, which I also discussed in the last chapter), Quinn was actually able to work with state bodies and able to recognize when they had done right by him ("fair play to them, they matched our funds"). Furthermore, the position that he sketches out in *Sit Down and Be Counted* is actually not so far from the philosophy of Challenge for Change itself. The explicit purpose of the program, after all, was to make films about poor and marginalized communities and to regionalize the production at the NFB. Although it's not about the Mi'kmaq, the film *PowWow at Duck Lake* (1967), which I briefly discussed in the Fogo Island chapter, dealt quite explicitly with the way that state-run religious residential schools shattered the culture and cohesion of Aboriginal populations (Cree communities in Saskatchewan are the focus there), and did so during a period well before the conditions in residential schools were as widely known and discussed as they are today. Kathleen Shannon's *I Don't Think It's Meant for Us* (1971) was a sharp indictment of the Canadian state and the ways in which "the technique of distributing [wealth] evaded them," via an exposé of the conditions among people receiving public housing support. Quinn would find much in these NFB films that was familiar from his experiences in Nova Scotia; the cheerful tone of *A Film Board for Ireland?* should not be mistaken for a "soft" sensibility towards Canada, along the lines that Hénaut invokes as typical of the 1950s.

So while he has been portrayed in the media, both at the time of his resignation from RTÉ and when his book *Maverick* was released, as an unrealistic malcontent (an image that is, frankly, encouraged by the curmudgeonly tone of much of his writing), Quinn is actually quite rationalist when it comes to the analysis of state and semi-state bodies. He can see when organizations have done well—that despite the shortcomings of Canadian idealism about federations and cultural mosaics, the NFB had become "the most prolific and inventive producer of film documentaries in the world," or that Gaeltarra Éireann had, from time to time, put their money where their mouth was. This rational, flexible sense of the role of the state in no way compromises his reputation as a radical, as a Gaeltacht militant. He does not reject state formations as such, but he does expect that they serve the people of the state, and he is not shy about pointing out when they don't.

This sense of militancy had already been clearly visible in the film that Quinn had made right before *A Film Board for Ireland?* which was *Caoineadh Airt Uí Laoire* (1975). Martin McLoone is quite explicit about the radicalism of this film, writing that it "could operate as a template for the kind of cinema which [Luke] Gibbons has called for, informed by the radical traditions of pre-modern Irish culture" (131). *Caoineadh Airt Uí Laoire* is a fifty-minute work shot on 16 mm, starring local people from around An Cheathrú Rua / Carraroe, and roughly adapted from the famous eighteenth-century poem. Rockett, Gibbons, and Hill, in *Cinema and Ireland*, state that the film was "the first independently produced film in the Irish language and, indeed, was the first major critical indigenous production of the 1970s" (137). Structually it is quite sophisticated, moving in and out of a present-day narrative about a group of Gaeltacht actors (with characters named Art and Eibhlín), staging a version of the *Caoineadh* under the thumb of a pompous English theatre director (John Arden), and the "film version" of that narrative itself (Arden's character sarcastically calls it "our grand new ethnic Gaelic Technicolor epic"). These two diegetic worlds corrupt each other in startling and often comic ways, and the self-consciousness of it all reminds me strongly of the political cinema of the 1970s so often associated with Jean-Luc Godard, especially his Dziga Vertov Group films. This sense of militancy is enhanced by the fact that it was funded by what was then known as Official Sinn Féin, which became the Workers' Party.[19] The film's opponents focused on that fact; recalling how the police had cited him for showing a film without a licence, Quinn writes in *Maverick*, "The garda said that there was the impression abroad that I was showing films to raise money for Sinn Féin!" and was thus engaged in suspicious activities that needed to be curtailed (73). But the film's advocates also focused on its militant, Republican qualities. Bert Hogenkamp, a veteran observer of political cinema, wrote about *Caoineadh Airt Uí Laoire* in the "La vie est à nous"[20] militant cinema column in the French magazine *Écran*, focusing on its Sinn Féin connections. "By way of a symbolic mode," he wrote, "the film evokes the cultural domination of Ireland by England, including its ultimate consequences (for example the question of Ulster)."[21] At one point, Quinn has the director say "just remember, this is just a play, based on something that happened centuries ago; it has no real relevance to what's going on today!"; Quinn's sarcasm is crystal clear there. The poem *Caoineadh Airt Uí Laoire* certainly has a nationalist aspect, since Ó Laoire's troubles begin when he refuses to sell a horse that, under the penal laws, was too valuable for a Catholic to own (Catholics were forbidden to own horses of a military grade). It is not hard to discern, as Hogenkamp does, how this connects to a Republican analysis of the modern-day conflict in Northern Ireland. But the film is acutely aware of the melancholy, futile quality of the resistance depicted by the poem; the character of Art, in both of the film's narratives, is loud, stubborn, and generally a bit obnoxious. Rockett et al. note that "Art's foolish bravado in engaging in a personal fight with the English landlord is seen to be for reasons of personal pique and not part of concerted mass action" (138). They then quote Tomás Mac Giolla, then-president of the Workers' Party, as saying, "Courageous campaigns of resistance, however noble in their inspiration, will fail like the gesture of Art O'Leary if they try to ignore realities.... Romantic acts of heroism or defiance may inspire people but will never organise them" (cited in Rockett, Gibbons, and Hill 138).

Caoineadh Airt Uí Laoire's connections to Bob Quinn's local TV projects, though, are largely absent from these discussions; again Robert Quinn's film *Cinegael Paradiso* is the lone, invaluable exception. But are these roots visible on the screen? What would lead someone who had seen *Caoineadh Airt Uí Laoire* to consider its localist in addition to its nationalist or militant internationalist elements?

Well, one part of this is the film's clear roots in local theatre. All of the film's actors are amateurs except for Arden and Seán Bán Breathnach, and even they weren't really professional actors. Arden was a relatively famous playwright and television/radio scriptwriter, and Rockett et al. point out that he lived in Connemara and worked with the Corrandulla Arts and Entertainment Club (137); Breathnach had worked as a disc jockey for Radio Luxembourg. The ostensible premise of the "real time" narrative is that this is a community-theatre production of a famous Irish work. The condescension of Arden's character seems to be based as much on national chauvinism as it is on the sense that he feels stuck in the back end of nowhere directing a sub-village-pantomime production. He shouts at one point in an exasperated tone, "You all know this effort is being subsidized by a Gaeltacht grant, and as such I have to use Gaeltacht actors!" thus invoking a reality very familiar to residents of Connemara, one which is also a recurring theme of the Fogo films: the degree to which dependence on grant monies perpetuated a sense of inferiority. But the details of staging community theatre, grant-aided and otherwise, would clearly be very familiar to the viewers of Cinegael. Many of those videos documented community theatre productions, and some of them even featured the same actors. The tape labelled 2A in Quinn's archives features footage of an Irish-language production of Brian Friel's *Philadelphia Here I Come!*; the tape labelled 3 features footage of a stage play featuring Seán Bán Breathnach; the tape labelled 5A features images of rehearsals for a stage play, with a director going over blocking; the tape labelled 6A features an extreme close-up of a young woman being made up, followed by footage of play rehearsals. Nobody watching these tapes could miss the importance of local theatre to the life of the community that they document.

Thus *Caoineadh Airt Uí Laoire* is important not only because of its mode symbolique vis-à-vis "what's going on today" in Northern Ireland, but also because of the way in which it evokes and contextualizes the culture of the Gaeltacht. The Irish spoken in the film is Connemara Irish, highly idiomatic and generally baffling to outsiders. Except for Arden its cast is made up entirely of local people. And, crucially, the Irish-language text here—the *Caoineadh* itself—is held at something of a distance, via the insertion of a sort of second narrative level (albeit one that overlaps with the "real-time" narrative). Part of this is no doubt because it is not actually part of Connemara culture: the poem is set in Macroom, County Cork. Indeed, when the "film" of the poem starts and the narrator identifies the setting as Macroom, Art's "real-time" character loudly protests that this is actually Galway that the Ó Laoire character (ostensibly him) is riding through. This feels like a self-deprecating joke on Quinn's part, an acknowledgement of the slightly artificial character of the whole exercise. But he's clear about its relevance to the Gaeltacht, too. Echoing the "Gaeltacht agus Impiriúlachas"-style arguments then current in Gluaiseacht circles, he includes the following exchange (the Irish and the subtitles are not quite identical, so I have reproduced both):

> ARDEN: From now on, unless it's in the script, all comments, and all directions, will be given in English.
>
> ART: Ah, seo aríst é, history repeating itself, mar a déarfá. [Subtitle: Here we go again!]
>
> ARDEN: I'll ignore that, whatever it means.
>
> YOUNG WOMAN: I agree, it's not fair to the director. When in Rome, do what the Romans do! I mean, it's not as if we can't speak English.
>
> ART: Ah, Rome, d'imigh an diabhal ort! Ah, ní hé seo bloody Rome. Ná hiad i bloody Gaeltacht! [Subtitle: To hell with Rome! This is not bloody Rome! It's the bloody Gaeltacht!]

The invocation of Rome—an empire that never conquered Ireland, as any Irish history buff will tell you—is a sharp reminder of the degree to which the Gaeltacht exists in a subjugated state, of the degree to which it has collectively given over to the assimilating power of English. For many Gaeltacht activists, history was repeating itself, with "the English" now replaced with "the English language." The symbolic (and sometimes not-so-symbolic) way in which this repetition is evoked by Quinn's *Caoineadh Airt Uí Laoire* makes it incumbent upon anyone watching the film to deal not only with its status as engaged with the war in Northern Ireland, but also with its intensely localist elements. Asking about the fact that Cinegael's next fiction film, *Poitín*, was also in Irish, Brian McIlroy had the following exchange with Quinn:

> *What about* Poitín? *How important is it for you to make films with Gaelic-speaking actors?*
> It is very important. I don't know why a big thing is made of this because Ray makes them in Indian,[22] Bergman in Swedish ... what is the objection, what is the problem? They can be subtitled. A film is supposed to be about pictures so what's the problem about the words?
>
> *Given the "Northern problem," is it not that people are very conscious about language?*
> It is a response to Dublin more than to the North. I see Dublin as the enemy, not the North! (145)

Aesthetic Considerations

I tried in the chapter to which this discussion is linked, the Fogo Island chapter, to argue that these films needed to be understood not only as examples of community-based activism but also as *film*, as aesthetic objects. It may seem that this is not as relevant a consideration for the Cinegael material, and particularly the videos, which, like *Thoughts on Fogo and Norway*, *Joe Kinsella on Education*, or *Billy Crane Moves Away*, do indeed have a sort of zero-degree quality that it would be easy to ascribe to the project overall. But I do think that the formal character of this material is more complicated than that, although not exactly identical to the aesthetic matters relevant to the Fogo films. Instead of reading the Cinegael material through the aspirations of cinéma vérité (a strategy that is quite relevant for *Oireachtas na nGael*), this is the moment when the writings of Dziga Vertov, and especially his sense of the Radio-Eye, become most central.

I am aware of the historical allowances that need to be made here. Vertov's writings in general, and especially on Kino-Eye and Radio-Ear and -Eye, are awash in a form of Leninism that the word "idealistic" doesn't quite do justice to. Thus I do not think that the Cinegael productions were striving towards "our cherished basic goal—to unite all the workers scattered all over the earth through a single consciousness, a single bond, a single collective will in the battle for communism" (*Kino-Eye* 49).[23] That's how Vertov described the ideals of the kinoks in his 1925 essay "Основное 'Киноглаза'" [The Essence of 'Kino-Eye']. But I do think we can see, in the words of Vertov's 1929 essay "От 'Киноглаза' к 'Радиоглазу'" [From 'Kino-Eye' to 'Radio-Eye'], that, like Vertov's kino-eye workers, Cinegael's participants "did not restrict themselves to the struggle for nonacted cinema; at the same time they tried to meet the transition fully armed, anticipating work within the radio-eye plan, the plan for nonacted sound cinema" (*Kino-Eye* 91).[24] It's just that the transition to which Vertov refers here is from silent to sound cinema; for Cinegael it's from film to video. At any rate, this interest in a non-acted cinema, this desire to create a sound cinema practice that can illuminate the everyday life of ordinary people, is very much the animating spirit of Cinegael; the addition of sound to cinema was a crucial part of that goal. For Vertov, this was more often than not about capturing industrial sounds and making them musical; his was the poetic strategy that Daney, in the epigraph at the beginning of this chapter, associates with film. For Cinegael, at least in its videos, it was about capturing and making cinematic the sound of Connemara Irish; theirs was the strategy of speech, of prose, the strategy that Daney associated with television. But the overall goal is quite similar. That goal is, in the words of Vertov's 1925 essay "'Киноправда' и 'Радиоправда'" [Kinopravda and Radiopravda], "To give the workers of every land the opportunity to see and hear the whole world in an organized form; to see, hear and understand each other" (*Kino-Eye* 56).[25] I'll have reason to quote that same essay, and that same line, in the next chapter, which is on Cinegael's successor, Teilifís na Gaeltachta.

Indeed, the filmmakers around Cinegael, like the filmmakers of Challenge for Change, seem at times like modern-day *kinoks*, Vertov's term for the radical-revolutionary filmmakers he longed for. Yuri Tsivan describes them in this way (and spells their name with a c rather than with a second k):

> The kinocs: a group of documentary filmmakers who declared it their aim to abolish non-documentary filmmaking as such. This achieved, the *kinocs* were supposed to hand over their tools to the people (a planned country-wide network of amateur Kino-Eye circles) and melt into the background. Such, in a nutshell, was the *kinocs*' theoretical agenda, truly anarchist: to de-professionalize filmmaking, and to dismantle the film industry, that is, the very organism within which they were working. (24)

This is close to what Low, in the epigraph that opens chapter 2, describes as Grierson's sense of carrying things too far, and what D. B. Jones sees as an abdication of the artist. As I discussed in that chapter, that's not *actually* what Grierson's NFB charges ended up doing; they did not actually abdicate their role. Nor did the Cinegael artists: they weren't training the people of Connemara to use the camera, they were using the camera to reflect Connemara people's lives.

However, what Cinegael was trying to do, though, more so than the Challenge for Change filmmakers, was "to de-professionalize filmmaking, and to dismantle the film industry." This hostility towards professionalism, towards technical perfection as a goal unto itself, is at the very heart of *Sit Down and Be Counted*. Indeed, the main body of the book ends with "This is the end of our professional participation in these matters. Vale!" (Dowling, Doolan, and Quinn 383). Putting this in more aesthetic terms, Quinn and his co-authors had indicted their technocratic managers in that final chapter by writing that:

> Their enemy will not be uniformity, but amateurism—the Celtic thing. Initially, the quality may be extremely tatty. But this must be risked. Anyway, this is vitally important only when one thinks of television or radio as "show business" or miniature cinema. It is a matter of secondary importance if we regard radio and television as being primarily and essentially communications between members of a culture-community. (381)

By "the Celtic thing" the *Sit Down and Be Counted* authors seem to mean the stereotype of the wild, shaggy Celt, so uncultivated and undisciplined.[26] Niamh Hourigan sums up the position of Meitheal Oibre Theilifís na Gaeltachta—a group headed up by Quinn and Donncha Ó hÉallaithe in the 1980s which I will discuss in the next chapter—by writing that they "despised the ethos of professionalism which informed the work of RTÉ and argued that the Gaeltacht needed a television service which was truly local, open and inclusive. This model was in direct conflict with the proposed Irish language television service which Conradh na Gaeilge had sought during the 1975–1986 period," which I discussed in the introduction to this section (*Escaping the Global Village* 103). That ideal for Teilifís na Gaeltachta clearly grew out of the experience of Cinegael. Furthermore, the tattiness that they seem to easily accept, and which RTÉ and the advocates for a separate Irish-language station would have rejected, sounds quite close to the Cuban filmmaker Julio García Espinosa's notion of "Imperfect Cinema." His essay "Por un cine imperfecto" ["For an Imperfect Cinema"] lays out a case for a rough-hewn filmmaking that is opposed to the smooth, manipulative tendencies of Hollywood especially and realist art in general. García Espinosa writes that imperfect cinema "can be created equally well with a Mitchell or with an 8 mm camera, in a studio or in a guerrilla camp in the middle of the jungle" ("For an Imperfect Cinema" 33).[27] He goes on to say that an artist engaged with imperfect cinema is solely concerned with "how an artist responds to the following question: What are you doing to overcome the barrier of the 'cultured' elite which up to now has conditioned the form of your work?" ("For an Imperfect Cinema" 33).[28] But "For an Imperfect Cinema," written three years before and thousands of kilometres from the world of Gaeltacht activism, is also remarkable for the way that it anticipates Cinegael's own "transition" from film to television. García Espinosa asked:

> What happens if the development of video-tape solves the problem of inevitably limited laboratory capacity, if television systems with their potential for "projecting" independently of the central studio render the ad infinitum construction of movie theatres suddenly superfluous?
>
> What happens then is not only an act of social justice—the possibility for everyone to make films—but also a fact of extreme importance for artistic culture: the possibility of recovering, without any complexes or guilty feelings, the true meaning of artistic activity. Then we will be able to understand that art is one of mankind's "impartial" or "uncommitted" activities. That art is not work, and that the artist is not in the strict sense a worker.[29] ("For an Imperfect Cinema" 28)

What happens, in short, is the end of the sense of cinema—television, film, and video all being invoked by García Espinosa simultaneously—as show business, or as business of any kind. It will cease to become a profession, cease to become work, and be returned to its status as a shared human activity. This is exactly what happened with the Cinegael project, a project based in the development of videotape and its integration into a television system that sought to project the lives of the people of Connemara's Gaeltacht, and explicitly sought to do that independently of the central studio of RTÉ.

Aesthetically, then, the Cinegael films are caught up in a fairly complex confluence of formal patterns. Quinn and his associates, so wary of technical perfection, might scoff at this assessment. But I am struck by Joe Comerford's comments in Robert Quinn's film *Cinegael Paradiso*, which seem to me a very pithy summary of the project:

> We were mostly teaching ourselves how to use, shoot and record. I mean, the sign's on it. We weren't exactly technically accomplished, especially to begin with. But that really wasn't what was carrying the thing. It was really the seed of some sort of local television that can get going, can make something that connects into people's lives.

The sign is indeed on this material. The Cinegael videos are black and white, full of static and *very* grainy; *Caoineadh Airt Uí Laoire* was shot on grainy 16 mm and features choppy editing; Cinegael's next and most widely circulated feature film, *Poitín*,[30] had a similarly rough-hewn visual quality, with sudden zooms in and out substituted for the choppy montages of *Caoineadh Airt Uí Laoire*. But what defined Cinegael was something very close to García Espinosa's sense of popular art. García Espinosa, like the *Sit Down and Be Counted* authors, explicitly rejected the notion of mass art: "Mass art is produced by a minority in order to satisfy the demand of a public reduced to the sole role of spectator and consumer" ("For an Imperfect Cinema" 30).[31] What he favoured was a popular art that "needs and constantly tends to develop the personal, individual taste of a people" ("For an Imperfect Cinema" 30).[32] That tension between individual and collective action runs strongly throughout Vertov's writing as well; whatever their idealism, the *kinoks* were, finally, a group of artists in service of the people. Vertov, as an artist with a very distinctive cinematic voice, never fully melted into the background, any more than Quinn did. Yet Vertov did not give up his desire to create a popular cinema along these lines, and as I mentioned in the chapter on Pierre Perrault, he recalled in his essay "'Киноправда' и 'Радиоправда'" [Kinopravda and Radiopravda] that such a cinema "speaks of radio-eye as eliminating distance between people, as the opportunity for workers throughout the world not only to see, but to hear one another" (*Kino-Eye* 91).[33] The search for that kind of solidarity, that kind of connection into people's lives: that's what was carrying the thing.

Conclusion

It is important to understand that the Cinegael project was cinematic in the way that I discussed in the introduction to this book. Not only is it devoted in equal amounts to film, video, and television, but its productions in each media flow into those other forms. It's hard to really understand films like *Oireachtas na nGael* or *Caoineadh Airt Uí Laoire* without considering their connections to the videos of Cinegael. Without taking these links into account, the films seem like more or less isolated attempts at independent filmmaking, and the videos seem like innocuous, degree-zero-style efforts at documentation. The reality is more complex than that. When Joe Comerford was summarizing Cinegael's project, speaking of what was and wasn't carrying the thing, it's not at all clear if "the thing" he was talking about was a group of videos, *Caoineadh Airt Uí Laoire*, or *Poitín*. And really, it doesn't matter. None of these productions were examples of local TV in the literal sense; the latter two were shot on film, and only *Poitín* was ever broadcast. In Ó Cuaig's words, "Is rud polaitíochta a bhí ann"—it *was* something political, this attempt to merge forms by way of enabling a marginalized population to have some access to moving images of their way of life. *Caoineadh Airt Uí Laoire*'s status as a piece of political cinema is uncontroversial, as is *Poitín*'s; the status of the videos as a form of political cinema should, to my mind, be equally uncontroversial. They are all exemplars of the form of political cinema that I have been arguing emerged in the North Atlantic region from 1958 to 1988, a cinematic practice with philosophical ties to radio that sought, via a renewed sense of aesthetics, to create a form of art that created responsible, affecting, and modernity-oriented images of marginal regions. More than any of the projects I have so far outlined, Cinegael was the very essence of the idea of the Radio-Eye.

Notes

1 "Si enfin la télé est notre prose (et on ne parlera jamais assez bien), le cinéma n'a plus de chance que dans la poésie" (90).

2 That note reads, in full: "Cine Gael made short films about local Gaeltacht issues and these films were then shown to authorities, particularly to Údarás [*sic*; see note 12 below] members. The producers found that the authorities would pre-empt them and solve a problem if they heard a film was being made about it (Bob Quinn, Interview 12 June 1996, Galway)" (252n212). Quinn said something very similar about government officials solving a problem once they heard a video was being made about it in the film *Cinegael Paradiso*.

3 "Chuir siad cláir teilifíse ar video-téip agus ar scannáin, agus dhíol siad le RTÉ scannáin a rinne siad d'imeachtaí Choláiste na bhFiann, Ros Muc, agus de bhronnadh duaiseanna Oireachais i dTeach Furbo, mar shampla" (459).

4 Sean-nós singing is quite important to Quinn, who sees it as a key example of the cultural distinctiveness of Connemara; he has also tried to connect it to traditional forms of music in North Africa and the Middle East. As he writes in his book *The Atlantean Irish*, "It became clear that this form of singing was an artistic response by a highly integrated community to a particular—and precarious—lifestyle in a long-settled environment" (39). Recalling the radio-listening habits of his childhood, he wrote, "In my father's house, sean-nós was switched off. Twenty years later in Conamara I found it was the most popular form of musical expression and, as I learned, the basis of all traditional Irish music.... It defied all the conditions I had been led to believe were essential to enjoy music: it did not easily lend itself to harmony; it had none of the simple rhythms of European classical form, nor the dance rhythms of folk music.... Its closest relation is modern jazz" (38–39).

5 "chuaigh 'Cinegael' go Gaoth Dobhair, rinne scannán teilifíse ann agus thaispeáin é in Amharclann Ghaoth Dobhair, ar an Domhnach mar chuid de chlár speisialta videotéipe" (460).

6 "ciallaíonn sé pictiúrlanna agus scannáin i nGaeilge" (*Iarchonnacht Began* 45).

7 As I mentioned in the introduction to the Gaeltacht section, An tOireachtas is an annual cultural festival celebrating the Irish language. The Oireachtas na nGael of November 1970 was a sort of "counter-Oireachtas" that was held to protest the holding of the official Oireachtas outside of the Gaeltacht (until then it had been held in Dublin); it was revived in the 1980s, and was, as I discuss in the next chapter, the site of the illegal Teilifís na Gaeltachta broadcasts. The official Oireachtas now alternates between a Dublin and a Gaeltacht location. That festival's official name is Oireachtas na *Gaeilge* [the Congress of the Irish Language], reflecting the tension between Gaeilge and Gaeltacht, teanga and pobal, language and community, that runs so strongly throughout the arguments about the future of the Irish language.

8 Serge Daney (1942–92) was an influential French film critic, seen by many (including Dudley Andrew, Jonathan Rosenbaum, and certainly myself) as the intellectual heir to André Bazin. He was editor of the *Cahiers du cinéma* from 1973–81, and then became a full-time film critic for the leftist daily *Libération* until his death. From September to December 1987, he wrote a column for *Libération* called "Le salaire du zappeur" that was devoted to television, a medium that had been a preoccupation of many important figures in French cinema (most notably Jean-Luc Godard and Anne-Marie Miéville, as I discuss briefly in this chapter). Daney's TV columns were collected in a book called *Le Salaire du zappeur* in 1993. On Daney generally, see Jonathan Rosenbaum, "The Missing Image," *New Left Review* 34 (July/August 2005), 145–51. An anthology of Daney's writing has recently been published in English, although it is mostly comprised of a very long interview conducted by Serge Toubiana; see Serge Daney, *Postcards from the Cinema* (Oxford: Berg, 2007).

9 "L'art du cinéma avait sans doute consisté à répondre par avance à des questions que nul ne savait pas encore poser.... Dans le meilleur des cas, la télé—une télé adulte—reprendrait peut-être ces questions" (188).

10 "un 'publique adulte' est une utopie encore à venir" (189).

11 "La télé relevait de l'écologie parce qu'elle touchait en nous le citoyen responsable, c'est-à-dire l'adulte" (189).

12 Údarás na Gaeltachta—the "Gaeltacht Authority"—was established in 1979, replacing Gaeltarra Éireann as the government body primarily responsible for development in the Gaeltacht. Quinn is thus being slightly anachronistic here, since during the period he is discussing they would have been bringing these concerns to Gaeltarra Éireann. The act establishing Údarás and dissolving Gaeltarra Éireann can be found at http://acts.oireachtas.ie/zza5y1979.1.html.

13 "Ah, well, tá, tá, tá faidhbeanna mar sin i ngach Gaeltacht ..."

14 *A Memo from Fogo* was shot four years after the end of the Fogo project, and it was a sort of summary of the project and an attempt to survey what effects filmmaking had had on the communities involved. It was shot in colour (of the original Fogo films, only *Winds of Fogo* was shot in colour), and runs forty-one minutes (*Citizen Discussions* was the longest film in the series, at twenty-eight minutes).

15 Société Nouvelle differed somewhat from Challenge for Change, partially in its greater attachment to videotape (hence the canonical status of *VTR St-Jacques*; VTR is short for video tape recorder) and its tendency to support well-known Quebec auteurs such as Anne-Claire Poirier. See Scott MacKenzie, "Société Nouvelle: The Challenge for Change in the Alternative Public Sphere," *Canadian Journal of Film Studies / Revue canadienne d'études cinématographiques* 5:2 (Fall 1996), 67–83.

16 "i gConamara bhunaigh Bob Quinn, Seosamh Ó Cuaig agus Tony Christofides 'Cinegael' i mí na Nollag 1973" (459).

17 "Tá Gaeltarra Éireann ag cabhrú leo, ach bheadh tacaíocht i bhfad níos mó riachtanach chun an gnó a fhorbairt mar ba chóir" (cited in Ó Glaisne 459–60).

18 See note 12.

19 Sinn Féin split first in 1970, into branches that became known as "Official Sinn Féin," which was more explicitly socialist, and "Provisional Sinn Féin," which was more nationalist. Official Sinn Féin, which was for a brief time known as "Sinn Féin—The Workers' Party," became The Workers' Party in 1977. Provisional Sinn Féin, sometimes called "The Provos," is basically the Sinn Féin we have today. See Joost Augusteijn's entry on "Sinn Féin" in S. J. Connolly, ed., *The Oxford Companion to Irish History* (Oxford: Oxford University Press, 1998), esp. p. 515.

20 *La vie est à nous* was a 1937 film by the great French filmmaker Jean Renoir, sponsored by the Parti Communiste Français. It is seen by many as a sort of ur-text of militant cinema, as it bears strong marks not only of Renoir's naturalist sensibilities but also of the Soviet-style montage and essayistic filmmaking that would be so important to the militant cinema of the 1960s and 1970s; this is made explicit in the article "*La Vie est à nous*, Film Militant," *Cahiers du cinéma* 218 (March 1970), 44–51. The best source in English on the use of film by France's left in the 1930s is Jonathan Buschbaum's *Cinéma Engagé: Film in the Popular Front* (Urbana and Chicago: University of Illinois Press, 1988); on *La vie est à nous*, see pp. 83–184.

21 "Sur un mode symbolique, le film évoque la domination culturelle de l'Irlande par l'Angleterre, y compris dans ses ultimes conséquences (par exemple la question de l'Ulster)" (70).

22 This is actually more of an issue than Quinn suggests. Satyajit Ray's films are in Bengali, and Bengali cinema, although broadly part of "Indian cinema," is very much a distinct industry, and is centered in Calcutta. The Bengali industry stands very far apart, for instance, from "Bollywood," which is a Hindi-language industry centred in Mumbai, to say nothing of the also considerable Telugu- and Tamil-language industries, centred in Hyderabad and Madras, respectively. This is all outlined in Tejaswini Ganti, *Bollywood: A Guide to Popular Hindi Cinema* (London: Routledge, 2004), esp. pp. 2–4 and 45; see also Ashish Rajadhyaksha and Paul Willemen, *Encyclopaedia of Indian Cinema* (London / New Delhi: British Film Institute / Oxford University Press, 1994), esp. pp. 10–12 and 184 (on Ray).

23 "[к] нашей основной и заветной цели—связать всех трудящихся, разбросанных по всему миру, единым сознанием, единой связью, единой коллективной волей к борьбе за коммунизм" (*Stat'i, dnevniki, zamysly* 81).

24 "Но 'киноглазовцы,' не ограничиваясь борьбой за неигровое кино, готовились одновременно и к тому, чтобы во всеоружии встретить ожидаемый нами переход на работу в плане 'радиоглаза,' в плане неигрового звукового кино" (*Stat'i, dnevniki, zamysly* 115).

25 "дать возможность пролетариям всех стран организованно видеть и слышать весь мир, видеть, слышать и понимать друг друга" (*Stat'i, dnevniki, zamysly* 86).

26 Twenty-five years later Colin McArthur would write an article called "The Cultural Necessity of a Poor Celtic Cinema" (119), an expansion of a manifesto he had published in *Sight and Sound* called "In Praise of a Poor Cinema." Asserting that what Celtic Europe needed (he had Scotland in mind specifically) was a low-budget, locally responsive cinema, MacArthur writes in the later version of the essay that this cinema's roots are "discernable in the quasi-artisanal practice of the British documentary movement of the 1930s, in post-war Italian neo-realism, in the French *nouvelle vague*, and, not least, in certain Third World cinematic practices in which distinctions among film-makers, critics and audiences might be eroded" (121). Although he doesn't invoke it directly, McArthur also seems strongly influenced in both essays by the notion of "Imperfect Cinema." See McArthur, "In Praise of Poor Cinema," *Sight and Sound* (August 1993), 30–32, and "The Cultural Necessity of a Poor Celtic Cinema," in John Hill et al., eds., *Border Crossing: Film in Ireland, Britain and Europe* (London/Belfast: British Film Institute / Institute for Irish Studies, 1994), 112–25.

27 "lo mismo se puede hacer con una Mitchell que una cámara de 8 *mm*. Lo mismo se puede hacer en estudio que con una guerrilla en media de la selva" (*Una imagen* 16).

28 "Como responde a la siguiente pregunta: Qué hace para saltar la barrera de un interlocutor 'culto' y minoritario que hasta ahora condiciona la calidad de su obra?" (*Una imagen* 16).

29 "Pero Qué sucede … si la evolución de la técnica cinematográfica (como ya hay señales evidentes) hace posible que ésta deje de ser privilegio de unos pocos, qué sucede si el desarrollo del *video tape* soluciona la capacidad inevitablemente limitada de los laboratorios, si los aparatos de televisión y su posibilidad de 'proyectar' con independencia de la planta matriz, hacen innecesaria la construcción al infinito de salas cinematográficas? Sucede entonces no sólo un acto de justicia social; la posibilidad de rescatar, sin complejos, ni sentimientos de culpa de ninguna clase, el verdadero sentido de la activitas artística. Sucede entonces que podemos entender que el arte es una actividad 'desinteresada' del hombre. Que el arte no es un trabajo. Que el artista no es propiamente un trabajador" (*Una imagen* 2).

30 *Poitín* is Quinn's best-known film, probably due in no small part to two factors. The first is the controversy it aroused when it was broadcast; Brian McIlroy recalls that some calls to RTÉ included assessments such as "'Disgraceful and disgusting,' 'It's a national disgrace,' 'Burn that film and don't let it out of the country'" (68). Further to that last point, I would also point to the fact that a 16 mm print can be rented from the Museum of Modern Art's Circulating Film Library and that this has greatly increased *Poitín*'s visibility in North America. The film is a story of an old Poitín-maker

(Cyril Cusack) and his two treacherous salesmen (Niall Toibín and Donal McCann), and it portrays Connemara as being rife with poverty, alienation, and violence. Most histories of Irish cinema discuss it at least briefly, basically because, as most histories of Irish cinema note, it was the first feature-length narrative film completely in Irish.

31 "Arte para las masas es … la producción desarrollada por una minoría para satisfacer la demanda de una masa reducía al único papel de espectador y consumidora" (*Una imagen* 8).

32 "necesita, y por la tanto tiende a desarrollar, el gusto personal, individual, del pueblo" (*Una imagen* 7).

33 "говорит о 'радиоглазе' как об уничтожении расстояния между людьми, как о возможности для трудящихся всего мира не только видеть, но одновременно и слышать друг друга" (*Stat'i, dnevniki, zamysly* 115).

6

Teilifís na Gaeltachta and the Faroes

The progress made by Raidió na Gaeltachta illustrates the special attraction of a broadcasting service in Irish, not only for the Gaeltacht community but also for people throughout the country, and the effects of this can be seen in the large listening public achieved by Raidió na Gaeltachta. When Raidió na Gaeltachta began in 1972, with 2 hours broadcasting each day, not many people believed that it would be possible to achieve its present position, i.e., in excess of 55 hours per week. Raidió na Gaeltachta has also done excellent work in bonding together diverse Gaeltacht communities with their differing dialects, and also in aiding the Government policy of preserving the status of the Gaeltacht as a community with a special and distinctive language. It is obvious that a similar sized public, at the least, requires an Irish language television service, and it would be difficult to explain why they should not be entitled to it, when a radio service has already been conceded.

—Working Group on Irish Language Television Broadcasting, *Report to the Ministers for the Gaeltacht and Communications* (11)

If we continue to believe in the illusion that Irish can be "revived" or "restored" in communities where it has ceased to be used as a language of the community, then the likelihood is that Irish becomes a language of a dispersed band of well-meaning zealots, like myself, scattered around the country. It will of course continue to be used as a great national symbol of the state; will continue to be used for ornamental and cultural reasons; will continue to be translated to satisfy the Languages Act and will continue to be studied in schools and universities just as Classical Latin and Greek were up to thirty years ago. However, that will not be enough to classify it as a living language, being transmitted organically from one generation to the next.

—Donncha Ó hÉallaithe, "From Language Revival to Language Survival" (184)

On 11 September 1987, the *Connacht Tribune* ran a headline that read "Gaeltacht TV discussion at Oireachtas." That article reported that "the symposium on the possibility of initiating a Gaeltacht television service will be discussed in the light of the service available to the people of the Faroe Islands, which have a population which numbers only half the Gaeltacht population. Mr. Padraig De Bhaldraithe, who was one of a crew of three who sailed to the Faroes some time ago, will outline how the television service works there" (8). One of the other three was Donncha Ó hÉallaithe, a lecturer in Maths at Galway-Mayo Institute of Technology and a prominent Gaeltacht activist. It was Ó hÉallaithe who, with the filmmaker Bob Quinn and the engineer Norbert Payne, had the idea to build a transmitter that could send a TV signal strong enough to be seen throughout the Connemara Gaeltacht. And it was these three who built and mounted that transmitter and who operated the equipment that allowed the pirate TV broadcasts of the weekend of 2 October 1987 as the main event of the Oireachtas na nGael festival, just as the second effort of Saor-raidió Chonamara had been in its day (see Figure 6.1 for a picture of Ó hÉallaithe with the transmitter). Those broadcasts were known as Teilifís na Gaeltachta—Gaeltacht Television.

That's the story with which I opened the Gaeltacht section, and it's the story with which I close this book. That's because it embodies the themes I have been exploring in this book on the North Atlantic's media history. We see in Teilifís na Gaeltachta a deeply committed localism that is explicitly engaged with community-building and the politics of language; a strong resistance to standard models of production and consumption that had become so entrenched even in publicly owned communications technologies; and a formal flexibility that is primarily centred in a non-fictional mode of address but remains open to semi-fictional manipulation, a hallmark of radio practice. Of course, the arguments about the establishment and the future of Teilifís na Gaeltachta were previews of the debates about globalization that so define the discourse surrounding communications media today.

The Faroese Connection

Teilifís na Gaeltachta has very clear connections to the Faroe Islands, although not necessarily to Sjónvarpsfelagið í Havn as such. The Faroes were, for Gaeltacht activists, an important example of a community whose "small language" had been kept intact and whose control over local affairs had been secured; Faroese television was of interest to Gaeltacht activists, but details as to the actual content of its broadcasts rarely come up. The Faroes were a model

FIGURE 6.1 Donncha Ó hÉallaithe with the transmitter used for the Teilifís na Gaeltachta broadcasts in 1987 and 88. The photo was taken in July 2006 at Ó hÉallaithe's home in Aille, Connemara.

for the Gaeltacht in terms of politics and language; its television was a model in much stranger ways.

The Faroese connection with the Gaeltacht was first explicitly explored by Desmond Fennell. He published, in 1972, a pamphlet called *Take the Faroes for Example: The Arguments for Self-government in the Provinces and the Gaeltacht* (which I briefly discussed in chapter 4). The optimistic way that Fennell saw the Faroes is visible literally from the first pages; the work opens with a chapter called "Why Are the Faroes Prosperous?" Recalling that a group from the Shetland Islands had visited the Faroes in 1962, Fennell wrote that:

> The Faroes, in 1962, had a population of 35,000 in an area of 540 square miles. For obvious reasons, the Report produced by the Shetlanders is of interest to the declining districts of similar size in the West of Ireland. In a special way it is of interest to the Gaeltacht communities, for the Faroese speak and write a language of their own—a kind of Danish. (2)

Few Faroese would consider their language "a kind of Danish," although it is part of the Scandinavian language family (it is a West Scandinavian language, on the same branch as Icelandic and Norwegian; Danish and Swedish are East Scandinavian or Mainland Scandinavian languages, and not generally considered mutually intelligible with West Scandinavian languages).[1] At any rate, Fennell is also quite impressed by the Faroes' relatively decentralized government. He goes on to note that:

> Important though [the national Faroese parliament] the Lagting [*sic*] is, its contribution is scarcely greater than that of the district councils (kommunes). About 50 in number, they serve populations which range from 75 to nearly 8,000 (Torshavn).... The existence of self-government to this degree—or anything like it—will surprise most Irish readers. But it is not really unusual by European standards, considering that the Faroes are a group of islands. What is unusual and, indeed, unique is the Irish system of government. (7–8)

He echoes these basic points in *Beyond Nationalism* (210–11). For him the Faroes were an important example of a small region that had assumed control of its own affairs in a way that the Gaeltacht could only aspire to. "In proposing self-government for Connacht," he wrote in *Take the Faroes for Example*, "Comhairle Connacht is suggesting that the 400,000 people of Connacht acquire something like the same control of their own affairs as the 30,000 people of the Faroes acquired more than 30 years ago (there are 38,000 of them today)" (14).

This was very clearly an influential comparison in Gaeltacht activist circles. In the "Agus an Teilifís?" chapter of his 1982 book *Raidió na Gaeltachta*, Risteárd Ó Glaisne discussed a report by the University of Ulster's Antony Alcock and Terence O'Brien on broadcasting in European minority languages such as Basque, Breton, Frisian, and, indeed, Faroese.[2] Ó Glaisne framed this discussion in a way that explicitly referred to Fennell's pamphlet, although Ó Glaisne was wititng in Irish:

> Take the Faroe Islands, for example, islands that have only 30,000 people on them, the same population as the Gaeltacht, according to the estimates made by Desmond Fennell a few years ago. These islands have a radio service of their own, and in the course of these two authors' research permission was given to a private company to make a television service available. A condition of this license was that a public company be established in the future.[3]

"Fennell had shown that it was a good example," Bob Quinn told me in our 30 June 2005 conversation about the birth of the Teilifís na Gaeltachta idea. "Donncha [Ó hÉallaithe] kept it going." He was referring there to the trip that Ó hÉallaithe had made to Faroes in June of 1987. He and Pádraig de Bhaldraithe sailed there in de Bhaldraithe's Galway hooker (a very small boat with a long history in Connemara) over the course of ten days. Ó hÉallaithe told me during a 29 July 2006 conversation that the trip was hard going: "Facing into headwinds, our engine broke down, which meant we were dependent on sail. Sailing against the wind is a slow business." The trip was recalled in more prosaic terms, and terms more immediately relevant to the concerns of this book, in a 1997 issue of the magazine *Pléaráca*:

> In 1986 she [de Bhaldraithe's boat, the *St. Patrick*] completed her historic voyage to America and she sailed to the Faroe Islands in '87. This voyage was connected with the founding of Teilifís na Gaeltachta, as it was in the Faroes that crew members, Donncha Ó hÉallaithe and Pádraig de Bhaldraithe, saw that it was possible to run a television broadcasting channel for a small population in a minority language and in October of the same year both of them were involved in broadcasting Teilifís na Gaeltachta from Ros Muc, during Oireachtas na nGael.[4]

De Bhaldraithe stayed in the Faroes for three days and then sailed back to Galway, but Ó hÉallaithe told me (during our July 2006 conversation) that he stayed an extra week because he wanted to spend more time studying the television service. When the *Irish Times* covered the 1987 pirate television broadcasts of the Teilifís na Gaeltachta group, their reporter Michael Finlan wrote:

> The idea for starting the TV station was inspired by a voyage which a group of young Connemara men made in a Galway hooker to the Danish-owned Faroe Islands earlier this year. They found that the 37,000 Faroese who live on the 17 islands have their own TV service, broadcasting 25 hours a week, which cost only £2 million to launch and £1 million to operate. ("Rosmuc gets its own TV station" 9)

Ó hÉallaithe also told me that upon his return to Ireland, he bumped into Quinn on a train and they got to talking about Gaeltacht TV. "I was madly enthusiastic about this, really fired up," he said. He had seen that the publicly funded Sjónvarp Føroya was being run off of a budget that Ó hÉallaithe recalls being the equivalent of £1 million per year. Could it be done in Connemara, the two wondered. Ó hÉallaithe thought that it could. "Then let's do it," Ó hÉallaithe recalls Quinn saying (he said something very similar to Iarfhlaith Watson; see *Broadcasting in Irish* 85–86).

It's important to note here that Ó hÉallaithe was in the Faroes in 1987, and by that time the public service was well established. The earliest television broadcasts in the Faroe Islands—the experimental "royndarsendingar" or test broadcasts of 1967 and the Sjónvarpsfelagið í Havn project of 1979–83—were basically illegal and basically independent of state control, respectively. These programs strongly resembled what Teilifís na Gaeltachta became, but this appears to have been a coincidence. When I spoke with Ó hÉallaithe in 2006, he did not indicate that he knew of the illegal or independent status of the early broadcasts, saying simply that "at that time it was a legitimate operation." Dairena Ní Chinnéide has written a highly useful article-length history of the push for Irish-language television, wherein she states that the pirate broadcasts of Teilifís na Gaeltachta were "inspirée de l'exemple des Îles Féroé" (30). But again, it's not clear that she means the example of *semi-legal or independent TV* in the Faroes that I discussed in chapter 3. She seems to be speaking generally; "l'exemple des Îles Féroé" seems to be closer to *Take the Faroes for Example* than to a reference to Sjónvarpsfelagið í Havn itself.

A more explicitly televisual Faroese connection also found its way into the debates in the Irish parliament. During a Dáil debate on the renewal of the Broadcasting Act on 30 May 1990, Green Party T.D. [member of parliament] Roger Garland stated, "If the Minister [Fianna Fáil's Denis Lyons] studied the TV service provided by the Faroe Islands he might learn something to his advantage." Garland was reacting there to the report by Údarás na Gaeltachta that stated that a national Irish-language television service would cost upwards of £5 million per year, a figure that he called "ridiculously high" (as I will discuss shortly, the government's Working Group on Irish Language Television Broadcasting had, in 1987, issued a report that similarly argued that an all-Irish television channel would be prohibitively expensive).

I'd like to take Garland up on his suggestion to study the Faroese TV service, because I agree that by doing that we can learn a lot about Irish-language TV. If the minister had rushed home to check the Sjónvarp Føroya TV listings for that day of 30 May of 1990, he might have been discouraged. Sjónvarp

Føroya wasn't broadcasting that day. No matter; they were on the next night. According to the television listings in the *Dimmalætting* of 31 May 1990, SvF came on the air at 7 p.m. and broadcast the following: a sixty-minute program called *Kærleiki og vald* [Love and Power]; the thirty-minute local news show *Dagur og vika* [Day and Week]; two thirty-minute programs called *Á Sýnini* [On Display] and *Peningur* [Money], both of which are of unclear origin; and a Danish movie. Some of this is clearly local, some of it clearly isn't, and some of it is hard to classify. There is not much of it, at any rate; on 31 May 1990, SvF was on the air for four and a half hours altogether. And lest the minister think that 31 May was somehow exceptional, the annual statistical reports published by the Faroese government were, by 1990, being very explicit about the makeup of Sjónvarp Føroya's broadcasts. According to Føroya Landsstýri's *Árbók fyri Føroyar 1991*, SvF broadcast 35 percent Faroese material (3.7 percent of which was subtitled in Faroese), 60.6 percent Danish material, and 4.3 percent foreign material ("Útlendskar sendingar" is the term they use for that category) (388). At this point, SvF had been a fully public television broadcaster, essentially the national television station, for a full six years. And after all this time, just under two-thirds of their broadcast material was being sent out in languages other than Faroese. This does not strike me as a model that minority-language television activists would want to emulate.

The sense that the push for television in the Faroes is similar to the push for television in Irish Gaelic is palatable, until you dig a bit deeper. It's palatable for general reasons, like the ones that Desmond Fennell first identified and which inspired a number of Gaeltacht activists, reasons that have to do with a small society protecting its language, culture, and control over local affairs. Those are the connections that drove Donncha Ó hÉallaithe to travel to the Faroes. But the television service that the militants of the Irish Gaeltacht dreamt of setting up doesn't actually bear much resemblance to Sjónvarp Føroya, or really to Sjónvarpsfelagið í Havn either. In 1987, the year that Donncha Ó hÉallaithe travelled to the Faroes, the *Ársfrágreiðing fyri Føroyar 1987* reported that the total amount of television either in Faroese or subtitled in Faroese accounted for 27.7 percent of SvF's total broadcast year. Ó hÉallaithe told me in our July 2006 conversation that the material he saw was interesting to him because "it was pretty much community TV"; this is the pared-down, low-end aesthetic that I spoke of as being important to the *Sit Down and Be Counted* authors (including Ó hÉallaithe's partner in crime, Bob Quinn) and which was centrally important to the Teilifís na Gaeltachta group. But this micro-budget approach to media making was a very small part of what was actually broadcast on SvF. Just as I wanted to think of programs like

Mykines (1981) or *Flaggskip okkara: Norrøna* (1983) as being somehow central to the project of Sjónvarpsfelagið í Havn, as I spoke with the people involved in that work and got a better a sense of what was actually broadcast, it became clear that this was not really the case. As I'll discuss in the conclusion of this book, the resemblance between television in Faroese and television in Irish actually ended up revealing more about the failure of idealism than it did the links between small language groups.

Teilifís, as Gaeilge

Indeed, it is important to distinguish between "television in Irish"—which has had a number of proposed forms—and Teilifís na Gaeltachta—an experimental set of pirate broadcasts from 1987 that had what seems to me a lamentably small effect on "television in Irish" overall. Thus I will sketch out the basic forms of television in the Irish language that we have seen, hopefully by way of making the discussion of Teilifís na Gaeltachta and its successors a bit easier to follow.

The Irish language has always been at least somewhat present on Irish television. Robert Savage has detailed the ways in which debates around Irish emerged when Irish television was being set up in the 1950s; I will not belabour the details of these debates here, except to say that they are remarkably similar to the 1970s debates around narrow-minded nationalism versus minority rights that I discussed in my introduction to the Gaeltacht section (on the "minority rights" quality of these debates, see Savage 51, 139–44). What actually emerged from these debates was the occasional presence on RTÉ—both radio and television—of the Irish language. The presence was never more than occasional, though. RTÉ would show television documentaries, sometimes produced by Irish-language groups like Gael Linn;[5] interviews with Irish speakers would generally appear unsubtitled (just as Irish speakers would be quoted in untranslated Irish in the *Irish Times* of the period); some broadcasts of Gaelic games (hurling, Gaelic football) would be done in Irish; and occasionally, some entirely Irish-language programs would be produced. Irish-language content hovered well below 10 percent of RTÉ's television broadcasts in the 1960s and 1970s; Iarfhlaith Watson recalls how in 1965, Irish-language material accounted for 6 percent of RTÉ's total broadcast time (radio combined with TV); in 1975 it was 2.5 percent, and in 1985, 2 percent (*Broadcasting in Irish* 50, 52).[6] This tiny amount of Irish was, for the most part, a bone of contention for Irish-language activists, although there was a more positive (some might say Pollyannaish) analysis of this situation as well. While RTÉ management resisted Irish-language hiring requirements,[7] the degree to which the Irish language was widely perceived to be a gateway to the upper middle class meant that many members of staff could speak it at a fair level. Indeed, trying to conjure the exciting, lively early days of RTÉ, the *Sit Down and Be Counted* authors recall a typical day in the life of a staff producer as he bustled from one desk to another and found that "at another desk, another producer would be conducting a telephone conversation in Irish with a shy piper in Kilrush" (Dowling, Doolan, and Quinn 56). Lillis Ó Laoire has recalled how in the 1980s, the visiting Scottish Gaelic TAs at University College Galway "often remarked how pleasantly surprised they were when they heard RTÉ radio announcers turn easily to Irish to make an announcement about Irish programming. Such a thing would have been unheard of in Scotland" (56–57). Irish was present at and on RTÉ in a way that Gaelic never was at the BBC, or Romansch at Schweizer Fernsehen. But you had to seek it out.

And yet, the question of a Gaeltacht television station as such had never really been on the national agenda. Watson recalls that it was brought up in Dáil debates by Ciarán P. Murphy in 1975 and Tom O'Donnell in 1979 (*Broadcasting in Irish* 77), but these were rhetorical gestures that do not seem to have had much impact on the overall discussion. This was despite the rather detailed proposals that *Sit Down and Be Counted* had offered for a Gaeltacht channel in its Irish-language chapter. There they proposed a television channel for the Gaeltacht (they called it a "Bealach na Gaeltachta" [298]); I reproduce the schedule here as Figure 6.2. They stated that this channel would be based on "programs (both talk shows and instructional) provided to the people of the Gaeltacht, and gradually made by themselves."[8] They produced a sample two-day schedule for two networks, a schedule where news and current affairs programming would run at the same time on "Gaeltacht" and "RTÉ" networks, but on Tuesday night the RTÉ network would not compete with the Gaeltacht network's talk shows and instructional programming, and on Friday night RTÉ would show only a half-hour of musical and social programming while the Gaeltacht channel would show a full hour. As far as I can tell, this proposal went nowhere; it is not typical to come across it in the arguments of the 1970s and 1980s about television in Irish.

Those arguments tend to be based in the "Gaeilge versus Gaeltacht" binary that we have come to know so well in this book. These are also the arguments that give shape to the subject of this chapter, the Teilifís na Gaeltachta experiments and their connections with Gluaiseacht Chearta Sibhialta na Gaeltachta, with Cinegael, and with Sjónvarpsfelagið í Havn. And there are *quite a few* of these arguments. Hourigan starts her discussion of "The Campaign for Teilifís

298 ***Sit Down and be Counted***

agus faoi cheannas áitiúil a bheadh an t-iomlán i ngach áit acu. An cuspóir a bheadh acu, tá sé an-simplí: cláracha (idir caidrimh agus teagaisc) a chur ar fáil do mhuintir na Gaeltachta, de réir mar a thograíonn siad féin.

I dtosach na scéime seo ní cóir go mbeadh sé ar an fhoireann léiriúcháin seirbhís iomlán a chur ar fáil. Bheadh sé níos fearr sampla na Danmhairge a ghlacadh agus cupla uair sa tseachtain a chur ar fáil—ach iad bheith go maith. Sé an rud is mó tábhacht ná bealach faoi leith do muintir na Gaeltachta—Bealach na Gaeltachta—bheith ag RTÉ agus na cláracha a bheith ceangailte go ciallmhar le craoladh an ghnáth-Bhealach, mar shampla:

An Mháirt			An Aoine	
Gaeltacht		RTE	Gaeltacht	RTE
8.15			Cúrsaí Reatha	Cúrsaí Reatha
8.45	Nuacht	Nuacht	Nuacht	Nuacht
9.00	Clár Caidrimh	—	Clár Ceoil agus Caidrimh	—
9.30	Clár Teagaisc	—	(uair a chloig)	Clár Ceoil agus Caidrimh

Is léir ón sceideal seo go mbaineann an Mháirt le fadhbanna agus cuspóirí mhuintir na Gaeltachta amháin. Dé hAoine bheadh an sceideal ag plé le cúrsaí reatha agus cúrsaí caidrimh—agus bheadh uair is cúig neomat déag de sin ar fáil ag an gnáthbhealach, ó $1\frac{3}{4}$ uair i niomlán.

Níl amhras ar bith ach go dtabharfadh na huaireanta úd an-spreagadh do na Gaeltachta ach taobh amuigh de sin bheadh buntáistí faoi leith ag gabháil, ní amháin do lucht léiriúcháin RTÉ, ach do shaol cultúrtha an náisiúin.

Ar an gcéad dul síos thabharfadh an córas nua caoi do léiritheoirí bheith ag triall modhanna nua ar chláracha 'beo' telefíse do dhéanamh—agus bheadh smaointe nua ag fás on gcóras féin. Toisc nach mbeadh aon mhaith bheith ag braith ar sceideal foirmiúil ó Bhaile Átha Cliath, is ar na léiritheoirí agus muintir na háite a bheadh na cláracha ag braith. Is léir go mba ionaid chultúrtha na

FIGURE 6.2 The *Sit Down and Be Counted* authors' proposal for a "Bealach na Gaeltachta" or Gaeltacht channel. "An Mháirt" is Tuesday; "An Aoine" is Friday. "Cúrsaí Reatha" is current affairs; "Nuacht" is news; "Clár Caidrimh" is a talk show; "Clár Teagaisc" is an instructional program; "Clár Ceoil agus Caidrimh" is a musical and talk show. From *Sit Down and Be Counted*, p. 298.

na Gaeilge" (which takes up two chapters in her 1998 work) by noting, "The Teilifís na Gaeilge campaign is far more complex than the campaign for Raidió na Gaeltachta. The campaign was of twenty years (1975–1995) duration and a wide variety of organizations were involved" ("A Comparison" 193). I have discussed some of this campaign already in the introduction to this Gaeltacht section. But a number of organizations emerged in the 1980s to build on the work first done by Gluaiseacht Chearta Sibhialta na Gaeltachta (around pirate radio) and Conradh na Gaeilge (around the "Open Broadcast" debate). The turning point here is probably Íte Ní Chionnaith's tenure as president of Conradh na Gaeilge. As I discussed in the Gaeltacht section introduction, the debate on whether Irish should be more present on RTÉ or whether the language needed a "separate channel" was quite divisive in its day. And as I recalled there, Niamh Hourigan writes that "a number of activists from the Welsh language society spoke of their campaign for a separate television channel.... [Conradh na Gaeilge president] Ité Uí Chionnaith [*sic*] states that 'from then on, I have to admit that I was very strongly of the opinion that we needed a separate channel'.... This engendered a split in organization. Former president Maolsheachlainn Ó Caollaí and his supporters continued to insist that an increase in the quantity of Irish language programming on RTÉ would fulfill the television needs of the Republic's Irish language speakers.... The row was bitter and divisive" ("A Comparison" 195–96). But Hourigan also points out how Ní Chionnaith's presidency of Conradh na Gaeilge saw an important ideological shift in these broadcasting debates. She writes, "When Uí Chionnaith [*sic*] became leader of the organization in 1985, her approach to the campaign for Teilifís na Gaeilge changed. Instead of focusing solely on the TnaG campaign, the demand was contextualized in terms of a broader Bill of Rights for Irish speakers. She was the first leader [of the television campaigns] to view the campaign in terms of minority language rights" ("A Comparison" 215–16). That minority rights approach is the animating politics of Teilifís na Gaeltachta, a politics that was highly influenced by the ideology of Gluaiseacht Chearta Sibhialta na Gaeltachta and Desmond Fennell.

Yet what was missing from Conradh's minority-rights discourse was an emphasis on the Gaeltacht itself, and that really was the key element of the Teilifís na Gaeltachta project. Nevertheless, Watson has identified the link between the two groups—Conradh people and Gaeltacht activists—by writing that:

> In 1980, at the same time as Conradh na Gaeilge had decided to demand a separate Irish-language television channel (the Teilifís na Gaeilge model) rather than more Irish-language programmes on RTÉ, "Coiste ar son Teilifís Gaeltachta"

> (Committee for Gaeltacht television—Teilifís na Gaeltachta model) was instituted by Irish-language activists resident in the Gaeltacht, such as Ciarán Ó Feinneadha,[9] Seosamh Ó Cuaig, Seán Ó Drisceoil and Donncha Ó hÉalaithe [*sic*]. They tried to replicate the RnaG [Raidió na Gaeltachta] campaign by setting up a pirate station, but unfortunately a technician died suddenly and the project ended. (*Broadcasting in Irish* 84)

Hourigan identifies Coiste ar son Teilifís Gaeltachta as "the first Gaeltacht/Gaeilgóir [*sic*, Gaeilgeoir] alliance of the campaign" ("A Comparison" 197), which is to say the first time in the campaign for more Irish on Irish television that native speakers based in the Gaeltacht had joined with non-native speakers, most of whom would be presumed to be from outside the Gaeltacht (of course, Quinn, Fennell, and Ó hÉallaithe were all born outside the Gaeltacht).[10] Hourigan has also recalled that this call for an all-Irish television channel came when "At their Spiddal Árd-Fheis [AGM] in 1980, members of Conradh na Gaeilge called for the establishment of 'a separate channel that would broadcast totally in Irish and would be administered through Irish.' This call was initially met with a sceptical response. However, the television channel which began broadcasting Halloween night 1996 is relatively close to the model proposed by Conradh members" ("A Comparison" 242–43). That channel was established as Teilifís na Gaeilge in 1996, and called TnaG for short. As I will discuss in this book's conclusion, Donncha Ó hÉallaithe published an article in the journal *Force 10* called "Why Was TnaG a Monumental Mistake?"; that was in a 1998 special issue edited by Bob Quinn.

It thus is important to differentiate between the positions of Conradh na Gaeilge and Gaeltacht activists, similar though they may sound. Conradh na Gaeilge has a base comprised mostly of urban language-learners; groups such as Coiste ar son Teilifís Gaeltachta or Gluaiseacht Chearta Sibhialta na Gaeltachta had a base comprised almost entirely of Gaeltacht residents. The former saw the matter of Irish-medium television as a national, language-centred movement, the latter saw it as part of a series of movements for greater local control in areas whose community language was Irish. Thus, Conradh's "separate station" proposals were trying to create a *national* Irish-language television station, and that is indeed what Teilifís na Gaeilge became; Gaeltacht activists were looking to create a television station for the Gaeltacht, a station whose language would, naturally, be Irish, and they called their experiments towards that end Teilifís na Gaeltachta. Recall Ó Caollaí's statement in his 1978 interview: "In the present circumstances, I do not favour the idea of a 'Teilifís na Gaeltachta' as an alternative to a full service in Irish shared by two national channels. The majority of viewers of Irish-medium programmes live in non-Gaeltacht areas" (*Issues in Television Broadcasting* 6). Very little changed in the years following, on either side of this split. Hourigan recalls that:

> After an initial spurt of activity, Coiste ar son Teilifís na Gaeltachta, the organization disintegrated in late 1981.... The reasons it fell apart were two-fold. Firstly, the group failed to establish the pirate station and the completion of this project had been the sole purpose of its existence. Secondly, the emerging divisions between Bob Quinn and the Gaeilgóir [*sic*] elements of the organization put paid to attempts to maintain the organizational structure for other purposes. This organization was never revived, suggesting that the dynamic of the movement was linear. However, all of the main participants were subsequently involved in the TnaG campaign, either through FNT [Feachtas Náisiunta Teilifíse] or Meitheal Oibre Teilifís [*sic*] na Gaeltachta. ("A Comparison" 240–41)

It is Meitheal Oibre Theilifís na Gaeltachta specifically, but the idea of a *meitheal* generally, that was central to the first broadcasts of an all-Irish television station in 1987.

Enfin, Teilifís na Gaeltachta

That "station" was the series of illegal broadcasts staged by a group led by Donncha Ó hÉallaithe and Bob Quinn in October 1987. "Seventeen years previously the Connemara Gaeltacht civil righters had shamed the powers that be into setting up a community radio service, Raidió na Gaeltachta," Quinn recalls in his book *Maverick*. "We called ours Teilifís na Gaeltachta and hoped to have the same impact" (23). They hoped to have the same structure, too. By this time, Raidió na Gaeltachta (RnaG) had become well established as the station that connected the various Gaeltacht areas across the country (as the quote from the Working Group that opens this chapter indicates). Although RnaG had a single broadcast, the day was (and still is) shared between stations in the main Gaeltacht areas: the HQ station in Connemara, and smaller stations in Doirí Beaga (Donegal), Baile na nGall (Kerry), and Caisleán an Bharraigh (Mayo), as well as in Dublin (where facilities of RTÉ, ostensibly the umbrella organization for RnaG, were sometime used). Broadcasts from each of these Gaeltacht areas were made in the local dialect, and each dialect (Connemara, Donegal or Ulster, and Munster) was heard at some point during the broadcast day. The balance between national and local was, in short, being rather poetically maintained.

Part of that had to do with the degree to which RnaG maintained its status as a semi-collective entity; while its full-time staff was and continues to be relatively small, there is a strong presence on the air of part-time local people, whose radio work is a part of their ongoing lives. This scenario is familiar to anyone with experience in small-town radio stations; the RnaG headquarters may look like a smaller version of the RTÉ building, but in terms of its operations it seems more like a larger version of KOTO, the radio station of Telluride, Colorado, where it seems like every time you meet someone in that town it turns out they have a show on the station. RnaG is in short, a large, complex operation to which many people contribute in order that it may be maintained. It operates like a *meitheal*, the term that the Teilifís na Gaeltachta group took to designate their organization, which was officially called Meitheal Oibre Theilifís na Gaeltachta. By way of definition, Ó Dónaill's 1977 *Foclóir Gaeilge-Béarla* offers the following: "meitheal, 1. Working party … 2. *Mil.* Party, contingent" (853). But as with the word for the Faroe Islands (see note 3 of this chapter), the more relevant definition comes from the Rev. Patrick S. Dinneen's 1927 *Foclóir Gaedhilge agus Béarla*, which has the following: "meiṫeal,… a gang or party, *esp.* of reapers, a number of men employed at any work, such as haymaking, turf-cutting, *etc.*… in modern times m. seems to include the idea of cóṁar" (737). Dinneen defines "cóṁar" (cómhar) as "co-operation, *esp.* in tillage, mutually borrowed labour" (235); the more modern Ó Dónaill dictionary defines "comhar" simply as "combined work, mutual assistance; co-operation, partnership" (281). This is the way that Donncha Ó hÉallaithe explained the word "meitheal" to me in our July 2006 conversation. He emphasized the word's root in co-operative and often voluntary rural labour, and rejected words like "comharchumann"—usually taken for "co-operative"—which have roots in business relationships. He described the notion of a meitheal as being a group of people who did a job that was too big for a single person, a job that was necessary for the continuance of the community. The Irish government commissioned a report on the viability of a Gaeltacht television station; the group that wrote that report was called the "Working Group on Irish Language Television Broadcasting." It would be easy to think that a loose translation of this might be "Meitheal Oibre Theilifís na Gaeltachta" (*oibre* is the genitive case of *obair*, the word for "work"). But the difference here, actually, was significant. The Working Group came to the opposite conclusion that Meitheal Oibre did. And a meitheal is something very different indeed from a government-formed, Dublin-based working group seeking to impose a solution on a community of which it was not a part.

Indeed, Meitheal Oibre Theilifís na Gaeltachta was quite adamant that they were not seeking a Dublin-based station that happened to be in Irish. A front-page article in the 17 May 1987 issue of the newspaper *Anois* (a Dublin-based Irish-language newspaper) announced a forum on a plan for a Gaeltacht television station: "In this new plan the government will situate the headquarters of Teilifís na Gaeltachta—like Raidió na Gaeltachta—in the Connemara gaeltacht."[11] "We are trying for local television for the people of the Gaeltacht," Donnacha Ó hÉallaithe wrote a letter to that same newspaper on 22 November 1987, explaining that the group which had staged these illegal broadcasts (he identified himself as the treasurer of Teilifís na Gaeltachta) was not trying to create an all-Irish "RTÉ 3." "That's how Raidió na Gaeltachta was gotten."[12] In the fifteen years that had passed since the Saor-raidió Chonamara broadcasts (discussed in the introduction to this Gaeltacht section), RnaG had gone from the status of pirate to the status of a model community media institution.

The activists of Teilifís na Gaeltachta made their connection to Raidió na Gaeltachta even more explicit by deciding to stage a pirate television broadcast at the Oireachtas na nGael, as the pirates of Saor-raidió Chonamara had done at the same event, and in the same town, in 1970. Donncha Ó hÉallaithe told Iarfhlaith Watson that through discreet fundraising, they managed to put together around £5,000 over the course of two weeks or so (*Broadcasting in Irish* 85–86). This was enough to purchase two transmitters. In addition to his work as a math teacher, Ó hÉallaithe also taught electronics at Galway-Mayo Institute of Technology, and as he told Watson, he is also an engineer (*Broadcasting in Irish* 105). Bob Quinn told me (in our June 2005 conversation) that the two of them, working with Norbert Payne (whom Quinn described as a self-taught engineering whiz; he is now based in Copenhagen), put together a small broadcasting facility in Ros Muc's Halla an Phobail, where the Oireachtas na nGael was happening, and they used cameras brought down by Tom Collins of Derry Film and Video (the Channel 4–funded workshop that went on to produce Margo Harkin's *Hush-a-Bye-Baby* in 1990). They also placed a second transmitter on Cnoc Mórdáin, a hill near Cill Chiaráin, along the western coast.[13] Quinn told me that as a result, the broadcasts could be seen throughout Connemara and as far as the island of Árainn (also known as Inishmore): in the words of Risteárd Ó Glaisne on the range of Saor-raidió Chonamara, "clearly in Ceantar na nOileán, west to Carna, and east as far as Spiddal."[14] They sent signals for the duration of the Oireachtas na nGael festival, from 4 to 6 October 1987.

The broadcasts were strongly, although negatively, influenced by the report that had just been released by the government's Working Group on Irish Language Television Broadcasting. Hourigan recalls the degree to which the Teilifís na Gaeltachta project was meant to demonstrate the simple feasibility of a Gaeltacht television service, a feasibility that the government report had called into question:

> The Oireachtas na nGael festival and the pirate broadcasts also cleverly coincided with the publication of the report of the Ministerial Working Group of Teilifís na Gaeilge. The report rejected the notion of establishing a separate channel, arguing that the capital costs of £8.5 million and running costs of £18.5 million per annum would make the cost of their project prohibitive. Therefore, the pirate broadcasts completely changed the campaign. ("A Comparison" 269)

The *Connacht Tribune*, not a newspaper known for its sympathies with Gaeltacht activism, made the matter of the political impact of this government report even more explicit, publishing (on 2 October 1987) a front-page article that read: "People in the Gaeltacht are reported to be angered by the report issued last week by the Government's Working Group on Irish Language television which gave thumbs down to such a venture, pointing out that it would cost £10 million a year for a two hour nightly transmission in Irish" ("Gaeltacht television" 1). That's not quite right; the report states that "a credible dedicated Irish language network would require a minimum of three hours output per night involving capital costs of some £8.5m. and estimated current costs of £15m. per annum" (Working Group 30). At any rate, the paper quickly returns to its grouchy self, saying of the Government report that "it states that no useful purpose would be served by the introduction of a pilot Irish television service" ("Gaeltacht television" 1).

Of course, that's not all the Working Group's report had to say, despite what the *Tribune*'s typically bad-tempered reporting might suggest (recall their skeptical, sarcastic recounting of the Saor-raidió Chonamara broadcasts from the introduction to this section). The quote that opens this chapter gives a good sense of the degree to which the report was in many ways quite supportive of Gaeltacht aspirations. But it is, without a doubt, a typically moderate and cautious government-produced document; there's no reason that Gaeltacht activists should have taken much comfort from it, but no real reason that critics of their activities should have felt very emboldened either. "Evolution rather that revolution should be the motto," the authors write at one point (5), and this is certainly the motto of the report. Overall it radiates a sense that the language activists have a point, and it radiates in equal measure an anxiety about how much addressing that point is going to cost. Furthermore, the authors do not rule out an all-Irish-language channel in the future. Writing of the prospect of increased national bilingualism and friendly feelings towards the language, they state, "If in time—and the Working Group accepts that it could take quite some time—that prospect is fulfilled then it might be appropriate to contemplate a totally discrete and autonomous third channel for Irish programming" (21). But they go on to say that they fear for the ghettoization of the language if this were to happen now, and anxiety about "ghettoization" is pervasive in the report. They write a bit later that "the Working Group would wish to stress that one of the major concerns it has about the conclusions it has reached, is the danger of the language being put into a ghetto" (27).

No doubt this sense that their proposals, indeed their overall world view, threatened the creation of a "Gaelic ghetto" was deeply galling to most Gaeltacht activists. The degree to which the shadow of this report hung over the Teilifís na Gaeltachta broadcasts is quite clear; they seem to have been staged in part as an explicit response to the report's conclusions. And as Hourigan notes, it is also clear that the debates around whether a Gaeltacht station were feasible were radically changed by these broadcasts.

These debates got underway almost as soon as Teilifís na Gaeltachta went off the air. Hourigan recalls that "the low cost of Meitheal Oibre's proposed community service attracted the attention of politicians at the national level. Prime Minister Charles Haughey, an Irish language speaker, was intrigued by the project and allocated £500,000 from National Lottery funds" (*Escaping the Global Village* 104). The eventual outcome of these debates was the establishment in 1996 of Teilifís na Gaeilge, which became TG4 in 1998. That was quite unacceptable as an outcome for the Teilifís na Gaeltachta group, who felt that whatever momentum had been generated by the success of their broadcasts had been dissipated by a push to form a television station with a national, rather than a Gaeltacht, focus.

What is noteworthy, though, is the degree to which the details of the broadcasts themselves are very rarely discussed. This is, of course, a running theme throughout this book; from the Fogo films to the work of Sjónvarpsfelagið í Havn to the Cinegael videos, historians, when they have discussed them at all, have tended to discuss North Atlantic film and broadcast experiments purely in terms of process or institutions (Pierre Perrault being the notable exception to this rule). Most of the studies that mention the Teilifís na Gaeltachta broadcasts give no indication whatsoever of what was actually broadcast. This is true of Iarfhlaith Watson's *Broadcasting in Irish* (86–87) and Niamh Hourigan's *Escaping the Global Village* (104). It is also true of the newspaper coverage both in English and Irish, visible in articles such as Bernie Ní Fhlatharta's "Gaeltacht TV on air again at Christmas" in the *Connacht Tribune*,

Deaglán de Bréadún's "Teilifís bhradach ar ais 'um Nollaig,'" in the *Irish Times*, or Colm Ó Torna's "Teilifís Ghaeltachta á scrúdú ag an Rialtas" in *Anois*. Hourigan's dissertation "A Comparison" is the exception to the tendency in the scholarly literature, although the discussion, like her discussion of the content of the Cinegael videos, is brief. Here it is in full: "Bob Quinn organized programming with the help of local singers, musicians, and actors. The station broadcast a Seán Ó Riada mass, a feature which had also been broadcast on Saor Raidio Connemara [*sic*] in 1971" (268). Michael Finlan's *Irish Times* article is the exception to the tendency in the newspaper coverage. Here is his explanation of what viewers of the broadcast saw, again in full: "They watched a concert of traditional Irish music in the Rosmuc community hall where the TV studio and control booth were located, a symposium discussing the possibility of a full-time Gaeltacht TV station, interviews with local personalities and a number of Irish movies and videos. Yesterday morning [4 October 1987], on the anniversary of Sean O Riada's death, the station carried a live transmission of one of his masses in the church at Rosmuc, sung by the choir that the composer founded in Cuil Aodha, Co Cork, and conducted by his son, Peadar" ("Rosmuc gets its own TV station" 9).

It is not hard to figure out why there is not much detailed discussion of these broadcasts. The archival situation here is, to put it delicately, informal. The work of Pierre Perrault and of the NFB's Newfoundland Project have been very well preserved by the Fonds Pierre Perrault (at Université Laval) and the NFB, respectively. But this Irish-language material (like a lot of the Faroese material), inasmuch as it is still extant at all, tends to be in the file cabinets, basements, or garages of the people who worked on the experiments. Everyone I have spoken with has been very generous indeed about allowing me access, but clearly this is no way to run a navy, as my grandfather used to say. In chapter 3, I connected this informality to the archival problems faced by scholars of early cinema and the possibility of using newspaper reports or listings, as many scholars of pre-1910 cinema often do, to reconstruct what was on the screens of a given period. That was minimally effective in the case of Faroese television; listings in *Sosialurin* and *Dimmalætting* were useful in figuring out the basics of what Sjónvarpsfelagið í Havn was showing (and have been useful in the early part of this chapter, too, as regards Sjónvarp Føroya). Even the illegal "royndarsendingar," or test broadcasts staged in 1967 had listings, published as a letter in the now-defunct Faroese newspaper *14. September*. No comparable resource exists for Teilifís na Gaeltachta; if there is a precise breakdown of what was broadcast when, I have not located it. Furthermore, Donncha Ó hÉallaithe told me (on 29 July 2006) that nothing remains of the first broadcasts: no tapes, no records, nothing. This is not so surprising, really, since this initial Teilifís na Gaeltachta experiment was entirely live, with no pre-recorded material whatsoever in the broadcasts.

Ó hÉallaithe did, however, have a tape of the *second* broadcasts of Teilifís na Gaeltachta, which were not live. That series of transmissions occurred from 28 to 30 December 1988; essentially the group wanted to make one last attempt before the laws around unlicensed broadcasting were revised and strengthened. An *Irish Times* article reported on 31 December 1988 that "most of the nation's illegal radio stations are expected to fall silent today as the provisions of the Broadcast and Wireless Telegraphs Act 1988 come into effect. Fines of up to £20,000 and/or two years imprisonment on conviction are among the penalties" ("Pirates go off the air today" 1). Ó hÉallaithe told me during our July 2006 conversation that they saw this as their last chance to make an impact that would demonstrate the feasibility of a Gaeltacht TV station. In a 30 December 1988 *Irish Times* article titled "Illegal TV broadcasts to Gaeltacht areas," Michael Finlan quotes Ó hÉallaithe as saying that "the principal reason [for the broadcast] is to demonstrate that television programming of a very high quality reflecting the life and quality culture of the Gaeltacht community can be put on the air at very little cost" (9). That article also went into some detail about what was broadcast:

> Yesterday's three-hour transmission, beamed to the Aran Islands, replicated the previous day's broadcast to Connemara. Four video-taped programmes were broadcast, including a documentary on Martin Nee's, a Connemara pub in London and a boat festival in Brittany in which Galway currachs and hookers were prominent. (9)

I have seen this material. Ó hÉallaithe has a copy of it, and as I mentioned in chapter 3, he was very happy to show it to me, although he did not want me to make a copy. What I saw was quite a remarkable combination of local television with forays into idealistic internationalism, all basically with the formal patterns of community television and video, already so familiar from the Cinegael project. This second Teilifís na Gaeltachta broadcast thus quite nicely summarizes the concerns I have been wrestling with throughout this book.

Indeed, the very notion of "the formal patterns of community television and video" brings us back to Vertov, whose writings bear out considerable interest in the kind of media making that activists like those of Cinegael or Teilifís na Gaeltachta would turn to. I spoke in the last chapter of Vertov's interest in "non-acted cinema," and that is certainly an animating idea of the Teilifís na Gaeltachta broadcasts. But as I discussed in chapter 1, Vertov rhapsodized, in his 1925 essay "'Киноправда' и 'Радиоправда'" [Kinopravda and Radiopravda], about the emergent technology of sound recording. He wrote that these devices "record every rustle, every whisper, the sounds of a waterfall, a public speaker's address, etc" (*Kino-Eye* 56).[15] That interest in the everyday, the spontaneous, is easily visible throughout Teilifís na Gaeltachta. Indeed, Vertov saw this as a larger response to the encroachment of artificial, "artistic" cinema. Looking forward to a televisual age, and in a way to Teilifís na Gaeltachta, he wrote in that "Kinopravda and Radiopravda" essay that:

> Technology is moving swiftly ahead. A method for broadcasting images by radio has already been invented. In addition, a method for recording auditory phenomena on film tape has been discovered.
>
> In the near future man will be able to broadcast to the entire world the visual and auditory phenomena recorded by the radio-movie camera.
>
> We must prepare to turn these inventions of the capitalist world to its own destruction.
>
> We will not prepare for the broadcast of operas and dramas. We will prepare wholeheartedly to give the workers of every land the opportunity to see and hear the whole world in an organized form; to see, hear and understand one another.[16] (*Kino-Eye* 56)

Now, as with the Cinegael-Vertov connection, I feel some need to specify that I do not think these videos were based on a desire "to unite all the workers scattered all over the earth through a single consciousness, a single bond, a single collective will in the battle for communism" (*Kino-Eye* 49).[17] What their creators were trying to do, though, is use low-cost technological forms in new ways, ways that were essentially in opposition to a state which was indifferent at best to the community development goals of most Gaeltacht activists. Furthermore, one of the reasons that Vertov didn't come up at all in the chapter on Sjónvarpsfelagið í Havn was that that group, as I discussed there, evinced only passing interest in broadcasting non-commercial, quotidian sorts of images. They were literally preparing for the broadcast of operas and dramas—that is, by and large, the kind of conventional, mainstream material that appeared on Sjónvarpsfelagið í Havn. That is the key distinction between what happened in the Faroes and what happened in the Gaeltacht, the reason that in matters of televisual programming, the Faroes, or at least Sjónvarpsfelagið í Havn, were not much of an example of what Teilifís na Gaeltachta was trying to accomplish. Teilifís na Gaeltachta was, like Cinegael and Challenge for Change and Pierre Perrault before them, looking for an audiovisual form that had several key components. Their practice was formally and structurally flexible (none of these filmmakers limited themselves to linear works of 90 to 120 minutes; only Perrault and Quinn made any films of that description, and they both made plenty of other sorts of films as well). It was not chained down to the idea that film had a story (of all these filmmakers only Quinn has made any narrative films). And perhaps most importantly, their practice was based in the everyday life of the communities they came from. Thus the moments of *Dan Roberts on Fishing* that betray a Vertov-esque musicality, the writings of Perrault on his basis in the tape recorder, Bob Quinn's skepticism towards professionalism—all of this is closely tied to the idealism of Vertov. And all of it is far closer to the spontaneous, unfinished qualities of community television than it is to the workings of classical Hollywood commercial filmmaking.

That said, Teilifís na Gaeltachta's second broadcasts featured some of the small trappings of a standard television station. It had a sort of station logo—designed by Bill Keady, it read "Teilifís na Gaeltachta"—which was used as a test pattern; when that came up on the screen, the music from Marguerite Duras' 1975 film *India Song* would play on the soundtrack. The broadcast opened with Peggy Ní Chonghaile explaining how Teilifís na Gaeltachta had broadcast during the Oireachtas na nGael and was now going to broadcast again, in December 1988. Ní Chonghaile returns throughout the transmission to introduce new programs; she is, in essence, the broadcasts' "anchorwoman."

The first of the programs is a series of interviews with young students at Scoil Sailearna, a primary school in Indreabhán (a small community in the Connemara Gaeltacht, near Spiddal) which was also the site of some Cinegael videos. Donncha Ó hÉallaithe seems to have been especially proud of this program, recalling in a 1991 *Comhar* article on minority language broadcast that "when we began the television campaign in 1987 with the pirate broadcasts in Ros Muc, there wasn't a single Irish-language children's television program on television.... We made our own thirty-minute program at Scoil Sailearna."[18] That program is comprised of interviews with children conducted by Joe Steve Ó Neachtain, a writer, actor, and raconteur also based in the Connemara Gaeltacht. The topics are wide-ranging to say the least; some of the kids talk about their home life, there is some talk of favourite TV shows and movies (these include *Ghostbusters* and *Dempsey's Den*, a children's show on RTÉ 2). There is also quite a bit of musical performance. Some of this looks like a school concert, with all of the kids singing together; other parts are quite accomplished, such as when a few kids perform with accordion and fiddle while another dances, or a bit later still when one of the girls performs a spalpeen[19] song on her guitar. The aesthetic is classic Cinegael: one long take (the sort of which is possible only on video), lots of moving camera, and explicit awareness of the camera on the part of all of the participants (the aesthetic may be vérité, but the film has far more of a sense of self-awareness than is found in a lot of the vérité of this period). That's true of the content too: these students talking about their everyday life, sharing bits and pieces of folk culture, are clearly effected by the mass culture that is all around them, and occasionally—as with the case of the spalpeen song—engage with the combination of these sensibilities that so defines the deeply hybrid culture of the Gaeltacht.

The next program, which Ní Chonghaile calls *Muintir na Gaeltachta* [People of the Gaeltacht], is a similar series of interviews with local people, this time conducted by Seán Ó Domhnaill. We spend some time at a bilingual bingo game, a country music bar, an outdoor dedication ceremony, and so on. Again, these are mostly very long takes. Overall, the program has the look and feel of community television; it is a series of snapshots that are likely to feel very familiar to members of the community, and likely to seem somewhat banal to an audience based in Dublin or even Galway.

Following this program, Teilifís na Gaeltachta broadcasts the aforementioned documentary about Martin Nee's, an Irish pub in London. Ó hÉallaithe is the interviewer here, and the piece is mostly comprised of conversations that he had at the pub (in Irish) with Connemara expatriates. Again the aesthetic is mostly comprised of very long takes, with some hand-held camera work; the sound is very difficult to make out. And again the subject matter is all over the place; there is some talk of immigration, of the ups and downs of the building trade, and of the future prospects of the British Labour Party (Páirtí Oibre—literally worker's party—is the term they use, although it had likely never been referred to that way on television; Ó hÉallaithe confirmed that they were indeed talking about the British Labour Party and not Ireland's Labour Party, whose official name in Irish is Páirtí an Lucht Oibre). Yet there is also a distinctively diasporic sensibility at work here; at one point Ó hÉallaithe sits with a group as they offer greetings to people whom they have, for the time being, left behind in Ireland. Thus, like *Muintir na Gaeltachta*, this might feel slightly banal to an audience in Dublin or Galway. But the tone of familiarity that the program assumes makes it very clear that addressing such an audience was simply not its goal. At this moment, as these youngish and middle-aged drinkers address the camera directly and call out to their families and friends back in the Gaeltacht, the degree to which this is the culmination of a slow move towards a cultural form that can integrate what we would today recognize as globalization becomes clear. As I stated earlier, Arjun

Appadurai writes that "implicit in this book [*Modernity at Large*] is a theory of rupture that takes media and migration as its two major, and interconnected, diacritics"(3). That has been implicit in varying degrees throughout this book as well; it becomes quite explicit at this moment in Teilifís na Gaeltachta.

It becomes more explicit still in the next program on the Teilifís na Gaeltachta docket, one that also hews a bit more closely to the conventions of television documentary than to community television. *Féile na mBád*, a portrait of a 1988 boat festival in Douarnenez, Brittany, is in many ways a straightforward television documentary. It was a mixture of material shot by Pádraig de Bhaldraithe when he sailed that well-travelled Galway hooker of his to Douarnenez to participate in the festival and material from the French television coverage of the event. Throughout, there is a voice-over in Irish that translates the material from French (both French-language voice-overs and on-screen text are translated into Irish), as well as some footage that has only Irish-language voice-over (such as a montage of images of the boats at sea, where an Irish-speaking voice tells us that these boats are from Northern France, Friesland, and so on). In addition to the nautical imagery, there is a fair bit of examination of the cultural aspects of the festival; there is footage of several concerts or informal fêtes, as well as of an outdoor mass and a large communal meal. The emphasis here is clearly on the solidarity of maritime cultures (we see a man who rowed from Norway to France, and a montage of boats from Cornwall, Denmark, Sardinia, Australia, as well as—and I can feel Pierre Perrault smiling down from above—footage of *goelettes*). But the *cultures* are just as important as the maritime aspects. I discussed Bob Quinn's *Atlantean* books in the introduction to this book; *Féile na mBád* is as effective an example of a cultural production coming out of Connemara that makes it clear just how much that culture was preoccupied by international connections and the search for forms of solidarity that sidestepped national identity.

The broadcast concludes with a poetry recitation from Tom Sailí Ó Flaithearta and Eibhlín Ní Chualáin and then some polemical statements. The polemics centre on the need for a Gaeltacht television station. Ní Chonghaile speaks to the camera about the origins of the TV experiment; this was followed by a montage of footage from the original Teilifís na Gaeltachta broadcast, including images of sean-nós singers and Galway hookers. We then return to Ní Chonghaile, who talks about how Gaeltacht people make their home in the United States, Britain, and Dublin; this is followed by a montage of (presumably diasporic) people calling for programs that are not only in English. Then we return to Ní Chonghaile again, who reads from the Gluaiseacht

Chearta Sibhialta na Gaeltachta manifesto about the need for a radio station; she then says that the people of the Gaeltacht now face the same situation with television. This is followed by a sequence with Joe Steve Ó Neachtain talking to people on the beach about television, the Irish spoken in Dublin, and how they use Raidió na Gaeltachta (which was, of course, the station that grew out of that Gluaiseacht Chearta Sibhialta na Gaeltachta manifesto). Then we return to Ní Chualáin again, who talks about the need for a *local* television service ("seirbhís áitiúil na teilifíse" is the term she uses); by way of example we cut to images of the Faroe Islands: first of Tórshavn, then of a map showing where the Faroes are located, and then images from Sjónvarp Føroya. The program—and the broadcast—concludes with clip of an interview with Seosamh Ó Cuaig, from the Irish-language program *Cúrsaí*. There is a brief return to the Teilifís na Gaeltachta logo, and then the broadcast ends.

Thus the program concludes with fairly explicit attempts to connect all of this to ongoing projects of Gaeltacht activism, right on back to the 1960s. The presence of Ó Cuaig, of the Gluaiseacht Chearta Sibhialta na Gaeltachta manifesto, of the reality of the economic migration out of the Gaeltacht, of the Faroes as model: this was a sort of roll call of the last two decades of *local* activism, a local activism which was always looking outward for examples and context. It is also, of course, a summary of the goals of the broadcast overall, which illuminated both local and international concerns, all of them joined by a sensitivity for the connections to the culture of the Connemara Gaeltacht. All of this is without question in the form of a "seirbhís áitiúil na teilifíse," but none of it is provincial. In Desmond Fennell's 1985 critique of Irish culture, *Beyond Nationalism: The Struggle against Provinciality in the Modern World*, he sketched out just this sort of inward-outward duality as a replacement for an Irish-obsessed, neurotic provincialism. Recalling a speech he gave in 1969, he insisted that the way forward was a combination of the local and the global that truly emphasized both in equal measure:

> Connacht, I told my audience, was held down, and prevented from realising itself, by its habit of seeing itself, its resources, its place in the world and so on, through Dublin's eyes. Look at Iceland, with its disadvantageous location, its resources less than Connacht's, its population less than half of Connacht's, and what it has made of itself! Look at Switzerland—or half of it, which would be about the size of Connacht! Those countries had succeeded economically because they looked at themselves through their own eyes, and therefore had a real view of their economic possibilities. Let Connacht follow their example! (151)

Thus Teilifís na Gaeltachta called for local television, but they looked to the Faroes for an example. They called for a base in the culture of the Gaeltacht, and to find that they went to Scoil Sailearna and to bingo halls, but they also went to Brittany and London. This was consistent with a call made by Seosamh Ó Cuaig in an article published between the two Teilifís na Gaeltachta broadcasts. Writing in the May 1988 issue of *Comhar*, he said that "the new station must be local and international, as is the Gaeltacht itself."[20]

This form of globalization strikes me as far more progressive than much of what has emerged since. Teilifís na Gaeltachta was part of a project of localist activism, one that was determined to create communities that were self-sustaining, both economically and culturally, and communities which were integrated into modern Irish life and not left off as some sort of museum- or national-park-like curiosity. From this local origin came complex, sometimes flawed international connections. Quebec, Newfoundland, and the Faroes, but also Brittany, Wales, Switzerland, Cuba, and the Soviet Union—these places have all been directly relevant in figuring out the complex cultural situation of Gaeltacht media activism, a media activism that maintained its localist sensibilities to the very end, rejecting a national TV service and insisting on community TV from the last moments of its final pirate broadcasts. I think it is difficult to find a part of the cultural activism of twentieth-century Ireland that is more alive to the connections between the international and the local. I also think that, despite the failures I will now outline in the conclusion, it is hard to find a period of media history more connected to the paradoxes of localism, globalism, and modernity than the experimental productions of the North Atlantic from the end of the 1950s to the end of the 1980s.

Notes

1 Tom Nauerby has traced the degree to which Faroese and Danish are linguistically, politically, and historically intertwined. He writes of Faroese that "the development of the spoken language had removed it considerably from Icelandic and pushed it much closer to Danish. This was compensated for by the written form's conscious orientation towards the past and towards Icelandic. The written and spoken language thus pull, quite literally, in opposite directions, threatening to deform the language even more than before" (83). I take Nauerby's point here. Given the fact that almost all Faroese are bilingual (since Danish is taught in the school system from a very early age because the Danish constitution mandates that all Danish citizens be schooled to speak Danish at a good level), it is quite unsurprising that there are many Danish elements in contemporary spoken Faroese. But anyone who has spent time in the company of Faroese and Icelanders has also seen the degree to which they can more or less understand each other; this is not the case with people

speaking Faroese and Danish to each other. The organization of the language tree—West Scandinavian (Icelandic, Faroese, and Norwegian) versus Mainland Scandinavian (Swedish and Danish)—bears out this anecdotal experience.

2 The report is actually not very precise about the Faroes. Alcock and O'Brien write, "Permission has been given to a private company to start television broadcasting pending the establishment of a public company. To date [the report is dated June 1980], it is understood, there is no television station in operation" (5.0210). But as I discussed in chapter 3, Sjónvarpsfelagið í Havn was broadcasting at that time; according to Føroya Landsstýri's *Ársfrágreiðing 1980* they broadcast a total of 990 hours in the year that Alcock and O'Brien were writing.

3 "Tóg oileáin Faró, mar shampla, oileáin nach bhfuil ach 30,000 duine orthu, an líon céanna daoine atá sa nGaeltacht, de réir an mheastacháin a rinne Deasún Fennell cúpla bliain ó shin. Tá seirbhís raidió dá gcuid féin acu ar na hoileáin sin agus le linn don bheirt údar a bheith ag cur a gcuid taighde le chéile bhí cead tugtha do chomhlacht príobháideach seirbhís teilifíse a chur ar fáil. Cuireadh de choinníoll leis an gceadúnas go mbunófaí comhlacht poiblí amach anseo" (461–62). Ó Glaisne uses the term "oileáin Faró" for Faroe Islands, but there is a word in Irish for the Faroes: Na Scigirí. That is the word that Donncha Ó hÉallaithe used with me in our correspondence and conversation. It is not found in Niall Ó Dónaill and Tomás de Bhaldraithe's 1977 *Foclóir Gaeilge-Béarla*, which is the dictionary I have been using throughout this work; there we find only "Faróch" the word for "Faroese," on page 519. It is, however, found in the Rev. Patrick S. Dinneen's 1927 *Foclóir Gaedhilge agus Béarla*; on page 971 we find an entry for "Scıʒıɲe, pl., with *art.*, the Faroe Islands, Ey-Keggiar."

4 "I 1986 rinne siad [Bád Chonroy] an turas cáiliúil go Meiriceá agus chuaigh sí go hOileáin Faroe in' 87. Bhí baint ag an turas seo le bunú TnaG mar is sna Faroes a chonaic Donncha Ó hÉallaithe agus Pádraig de Bhaldraithe go bhféadfaí stáisiún teilifíse a reachtáil i mionteanga do dhaonra beag agus mí Dheireadh Fómhair na bliana céanna bhí baint acu le Teilifís na Gaeltachta a chur ar an aer ó Ros Muc, le linn Oireachtas na nGael." The Irish and English-language versions here are both taken from the website of Cumann hÚicéirí na Gaillimhe / Galway Hooker Association at http://www.galwayhookerassociation.ie. The boat is known as the *St. Patrick* in English but as *Bád Chonroy* (Conroy's boat) in Irish because it was originally owned by relatives of de Bhaldraithe's named Conroy. Ó hÉallaithe told me that the boat had once carried Pádraig Pearse to Árainn (the main island of the Aran Islands).

5 The language organization Gael Linn had made a series of proposals for an Irish television station in the late 1950s; theirs were among many competing proposals for the first Irish station. Recounting the foundation of Irish television as it struggled between commercial and public imperatives, the *Sit Down and Be Counted* authors note sardonically, "Perhaps a review of the proposals put before the Government by foreign and domestic enterprises may have helped it make up its mind. We understand that a novel and modest proposal put forward by Gael-Linn was set aside" (Dowling, Doolan, and Quinn 13). See Savage 181–90 and

193–210 for a narrative of that period, which includes detailed discussion of the Gael Linn proposals.

6 Watson has described the Irish-language programming on RTÉ, and on Radio Éireann before it, in great detail. On Radio Éireann see *Broadcasting in Irish* 21, 26, 34, 50; on RTÉ's 1965 Irish-language television lineup see *Broadcasting in Irish* 50.

7 Savage notes that as RTÉ television was being established, "The Joint Committee [of Gaelic Bodies] argued that the television service should be staffed, initially, by Irish speakers. It admitted that initially exceptions might have to be made in order to recruit qualified technicians" (141). The *Sit Down and Be Counted* authors, however, give the distinct sense that this went nowhere, writing of an internal RTÉ document on language usage that "it said, simply, that jobs which required bilingualism should be carried out by bilingualists, even if they had to equip themselves after recruitment" (Dowling, Doolan, and Quinn 73).

8 "cláracha (idir caidrimh agus teagaisc) a chur ar fáil do mhuintir na Gaeltachta, de réir mar a thograíonn siad féin" (298).

9 Pádraig Ó Siadhail tells me that Ciarán Ó Feinneadha, an active member of Conradh na Gaeilge, enjoyed some minor celebrity during this period for climbing up RTÉ's tower in Donnybrook in order to protest their lack of Irish-language programming.

10 Hourigan also writes that Coiste ar son Teilifís Gaeltachta "was dominated by representatives from Gaelscoileanna and Gaeltacht blow-ins" ("A Comparison" 197). She is referring to people involved in Irish-medium schools, collectively called Gaelscoileanna, and to people who had moved to the Gaeltacht from outside. The terms "blow-in" and "Gaeilgóir" are usually used pejoratively. But it is worth noting that most of the prime animators here fit both descriptions. Desmond Fennell, Bob Quinn, and Donncha Ó hÉallaithe, in addition to being born outside the Gaeltacht and moving there as adults, learned Irish as a second language, not as a mother tongue.

11 "Faoi phlean nua seo an Rialtais beidh ceanncheathrú Theilifís na Gaeltachta suite—fearacht Raidió na Gaeltachta—i nGaeltacht Chonamara" ("Cuirfidh Teilifís" 1).

12 "Táimid ag iarraidh teilifís áitiúil don phobal Gaeltachta. Sin mar a fuarthas Raidió na Gaeltachta" ("Teilifís na Gaeltachta" 6).

13 The *Irish Times* tells it slightly differently. Michael Finlan's article about the pirate broadcasts states that "a Dubliner, Norbert Payne, built the transmitter in a fortnight and was given technical assistance by Josie McDonagh from Carraroe and Tommy Collins from Derry" ("Rosmuc gets its own TV station" 9).

14 "go soiléir i gceantar na nOileán, siar go Carna, agus soir chomh fada leis an Spidéal" (29).

15 "записывают каждый шорох, каждый шепот, шум водопада, речь оратора и т.д." (*Stat'i, dnevniki, zamysly* 86).

16 "Техника быстро шагает вперед. Уже изобретен способ передачи изображений по радио. Кроме того, найден способ записи слуховых явлений на кинопленку. В ближайшее время человек сможет записанные радиокиноаппаратом зрительные и слуховые явления одновременно

передавать по радио всему миру. Мы должны подготовиться к тому, чтобы эти изобретения капиталистического мира обратить ему же на погибель. И не к демонстрации опер и драм мы будем готовиться. Мы будем усиленно готовитсья к тому, чтобы видеть и слышать весь мир, видеть, слышать и понимать друг друга" (*Stat'i, dnevniki, zamysly* 86).

17 "связать всех трудящихся, разбросанных по всему миру, единым сознанием, единой связью, единой коллективной волей к борьбе за коммунизм" (*Stat'i, dnevniki, zamysly* 81).

18 "Nuair a thosaigh muid an feachtas teilifíse i 1987, leis an gcraoladh bradach i Ros Muc, ní raibh aon chlár do ghasúir i nGaeilge ar an teilifís.… Rinneamar féin clár 30 noim. i Scoil Shailearna" ("An Teilifís agus Teangacha Mionlaigh" 26).

19 Spalpeen (*spailpín* in Irish) is a term for a migrant labourer; it generally refers to a migrant worker, and often specifically to someone who has left Ireland to go to England to work construction. One of the most accomplished evocations of the plight of the spalpeen is *I Could Read the Sky*, a 1997 book with text by Timothy O'Grady and photos by Steve Pyke (London: Harvell, 1997); it was made into a film by Nichola Bruce in 2001, with music by Iarla Ó Lionáird, who has also released a CD of that music with additional songs that are closely related to the material. I have written on the complexity of this work elsewhere; see "*I Could Read the Sky* and an Irish Avant-Garde," *Film Criticism* 28:3 (Spring 2004): 37–51.

20 "Caithfidh an stáisiún nua a bheith áitiúil agus idirnáisiúnta mar atá an Ghaeltacht féin" ("Gan Teilifís Ghaeltachta, Gan Ghaeilge" 8).

Conclusion

This is no longer an old-stock Quebec of the porpoise hunt, the water-craft, and the musk-oxen of Pierre Perrault's films. This is a Quebec that is colourful, mixed, polymorphous, urban.... Finally I am saying that the mythic country that he gave to us as a gift so that the world might continue has in a way gone with him.[1]
—Nathalie Petrowski, "Pour la suite du monde," in *La Presse*, 29 June 1999

According to Ronald Dick, Colin Low, who developed regionalization for the NFB, felt that English-Canadian film-makers at the board emphasized the totality of a pan-Canadian cinema at the expense of the diverse "parts that made the whole meaningful."
—The analysis of the work of Colin Low, *in its entirety*, in Christopher Gittings's 2002 book *Canadian National Cinema* (89)

That status of this as a foundation is not clear; it's not clear how the television associations, with 50 percent Danish material and 50 percent material from other sources, can be a Faroese alternative.[2]
—Jørgen Poulsen, interview in *Sosialurin*, 27 March 1980

I switched to [the Irish-language television channel] TG4 last week and watched a film starring John Wayne. But he was not speaking Irish.
—Michael Ring, T.D., during a debate on the Broadcasting Bill, Dáil Éireann, 10 November 1999

I said I ended the main body of this book with Teilifís na Gaeltachta because it represented something of a culmination of the Radio-Eye idea. But I ended there for another reason too; the success of Teilifís na Gaeltachta was mixed, and its philosophical and political positions were either rejected or forgotten by its successors. This, alas, has been the case with quite a bit of the North Atlantic media that I have been discussing. Quebec cinema did not follow the example of Pierre Perrault, Canadian Cinema did not follow the example of the Fogo Island project, Faroese television looks very different than the model put forward by Sjónvarpsfelagið í Havn, and Cinegael (like Bob Quinn's work generally) remains a very marginal part of Irish cinema. Nobody likes to end a book on a negative note, and there seems to me little doubt that this part of the North Atlantic's media history—1958 to 1988—was an exceptional period which showed an alternative path for film and video. But this example was not, by and large, followed.

For while Quebec has seen the emergence of a highly distinctive cinematic culture, it does not, as a whole, bear much resemblance to the work or ideals of Pierre Perrault. Perrault saw this quite clearly, and was openly indifferent to conventional cinema. This was not so much because of a hostility to the narrative form of "cinéma de fiction," which is, after all, not so far from the manipulated, often highly constructed documentaries like *Pour la suite du monde*, but to the commercial essence of the project. Just because "c'est bon pour le commerce," as Perrault told Jean-Daniel Lafond, doesn't necessarily meant that it is good for culture, and culture was Perrault's primary concern. "It's maybe the future of Quebec, or of cinema," he went on to say in that same conversation (which I quoted in chapter 4), "even if I myself think more of one than the other."[3] He clearly meant Quebec rather than cinema to have pride of place in his thoughts since cinema was, as I discussed in chapter 1, one of many media that he worked in. Quebec is frequently cited in discussions of Canadian cinema as a success story, not least because Quebec productions frequently account for as much as 25 percent of Quebec's annual box office returns; such a proportion for domestic productions would be unthinkable in English Canada, where the annual figure is usually below 5 percent.[4] But those films which have such a prominent presence are popular films, often based in Hollywood-influenced genres such as melodrama, slapstick comedy, and so on. Bill Marshall has placed this conflict in specifically Perrault-centric terms, writing in his chapter on popular cinema in *Quebec National Cinema* that:

> In Perrault, we have seen, despite the elements of invention and becoming, the "people" are linked to notions of authenticity which in turn depend on putting

> reworkings of traditional practices into discourse. However, this is not a viable approach for a wider Quebec cinema in a modernizing society, still less for a cinema wishing to reach mass audiences. In this chapter I shall take "popular cinema" to mean those attempts in Quebec cinema at reaching a mass rather than a merely *cinéphile* audience. "Popular" thus slides into "mass" here, but the reality of contemporary capitalist culture is to do just that, to link together, transform, and rearticulate elements of traditional society for the purposes of commodification. (172)

This slide from "popular" into "mass," could be seen, in the words of Julio García Espinosa, as the difference between art that "needs and constantly tends to develop the personal, individual taste of a people" ("For an Imperfect Cinema" 30)[5] and "production by a minority to satisfy the demand of a mass reduced to the sole role of spectator and consumer" ("For an Imperfect Cinema" 30).[6] Perrault was a popular artist, although not in the way that "popular cinema" is being used by Marshall to discuss Quebec (a use that is certainly consistent with the general usage of the term "popular cinema"). Quebec cinema since the 1980s has undoubtedly seen the rise of a newer generation of filmmakers in the Perrault model, filmmakers interested in finding new ways to cinematically meditate on Quebec as a culture or a landscape: Catherine Martin and Lucie Lambert spring to mind most readily; their films—such as *Océan* (2002) or *Paysage sous les paupières* (1996), respectively—are formally innovative meditations on landscape and culture. But they are exceptions, and they are very rarely discussed by critics or scholars. The filmmakers more at the core of critical discussion, however formally or politically ambitious they may be, tend to be artists closer to pop cinema than to the model of Perrault: Denys Arcand, Robert Lepage, Manon Briand. Their films basically cohere to the feature-narrative model, and while they are all formally eccentric and variably successful at the box office, they have little problem fitting into the conventional production-distribution-consumption model that so defines classical cinema and which Perrault's films, like all of the media work I have been discussing in this book, utterly flummox.

There is an argument to be made that this is as much a cultural matter as a cinematic one; this is certainly the argument advanced by Nathalie Petrowski in the epigraph that opens this conclusion. Petrowski was writing just as Perrault had died, and as she says in the passage I quote, her basic argument is that his Quebec has died, too, and has been replaced by a new, more urban and cosmopolitan country. This seems to me simplistic in the extreme, although it is certainly a widely held opinion. Marco de Blois responded to Petrowski's column and similar posthumous attacks on the contemporary meaning of Perrault's imagery in a brief article in *24 Images*, scoffing at the ahistorical piety that dismissals of Perrault's work seemed to embody. "Ah! la bonne conscience!" he sarcastically wrote. He also asserted that "if you do a quick skim through the writing on cinema in the local media, then it seems that the notion of *métissage* in the cinema was invented around 1995.... But there is surely as much 'métissage' in a film by Michka Saäl, Arto Paragamian, Robert Morin, Jacques Leduc, or Pierre Perrault."[7] This brief list of Quebec filmmakers, who have dealt with Quebec's Middle Eastern community (Saäl, *La Position de l'escargot* [1999]), its English-speaking community (Paragamian, *Because Why* [1993], *Two Thousand and None* [2000]), and people with multiple identities (Leduc, *La Vie fantôme* [1992]), and who have also made formally eccentric, bilingual, semi-narrative, semi-fake-documentary videos which also use footage shot on film (Morin, *Yes Sir Madame!* [1994]), indicates that de Blois has a much broader and more open sense of what *métissage* in cinema can be. The kind of métissage that Perrault embodies is both formal and cultural. It is a form of métissage that illuminates Quebec's current condition and challenges conventional ideas about the constituent elements of both tradition and modernity. It seems to me (and to de Blois too) much too easy to latch on to the ostensibly nostalgic elements of Perrault's cinema. What he is showing his viewer throughout is the flexibility of formal patterns (fiction mixes freely with documentary), of cultural identity (whale hunts mix with modernity, Bretons and Normans with Québécois, all the while their connections made as clear as their differences), and of cinema itself (television mixes with film mixes with radio). This sort of flexibility, and this sort of openness, is also part of what Petrowski is trying to identify as typical of contemporary Quebec culture. Her dismissal of the relevance of Perrault's oeuvre, and of the world that gave birth to it, seems to me to display a very superficial understanding of that work; it also seems to me typical of the way that Perrault, and Quebec cinema along with him, is currently widely understood.

Much the same is true of the way in which Low has been remembered and discussed in a contemporary context. Gittings's book, which vaguely remembers Low as part of long-gone regionalist and pan-Canadian idealism, is typical of the way in which Low is now basically seen as a marginal figure with little to tell us about Canadian cinema as a whole. Lest anybody think that the Gittings book is exceptional, allow me to quote Jim Leach's analysis of Low's work in his 2006 book *Film in Canada*, again *in its entirety*: "Its [Challenge for Change's] greatest success came with a series of films made in 1968 by Colin Low with the inhabitants of Fogo Island, Newfoundland" (16). This is at least concluded with a footnote leading readers to Janine Marchessault's essay on Challenge for Change. The name "Colin Low" does not appear at all in George Melnyk's *One Hundred Years of Canadian Cinema*, published in 2004.

Part of this is no doubt because of the way that Low's films embody a kind of high Griersonianism (despite his disagreements with "Dr. Grierson" himself), a philosophy of documentary that emphasizes not only realism but the civic uses of cinema. Writing specifically about his experiences in Canada and denying that the principles he laid out in the 1930s were of mere historical interest, Grierson wrote in 1942 that "the materials of citizenship today are different and the perspectives wider and more difficult; but we have, as ever, the duty of exploring them and waking the heart and will in regard to them. That duty is what documentary is about. It is, moreover, documentary's primary service to the State" (*Grierson on Documentary* 215). That sense of cinema being connected to civic and state-bound duty, a sense that seems so central to the Newfoundland films, has come under enormous fire in both Britain and Canada in the last few decades. In Canada, Peter Morris got the ball rolling in 1986 by writing that "Grierson's ideology shares, at least, common ground with neo-conservative ideology and a body of elitist aesthetics influential in Europe before the Second World War" (47).[8] Joyce Nelson's 1988 book *The Colonized Eye: Rethinking the Grierson Legend* was an indictment of a figure she saw as basically ineffectual and pro-establishment. Nelson writes there that "this reformist effort was devoted to changing the attitudes of the viewing public and working people, not to reforming any of those industrial, commercial and scientific forces that were reshaping the world" (36). The British critic Brian Winston has a similar problem with Grierson: "Grierson and his school could take government and industrial money for the making of liberal films selling the existing order and its capacity for gradual social amelioration" (36). This sense of Grierson, and "his school," as being government men—so to speak, state-funded tools—has certainly led to a widespread critical and scholarly turning away from Canadian traditions of socially engaged documentary and towards narrative cinema, work that tends to be both more widely seen and more clearly amenable to both formal analysis and forms of cultural criticism that illuminate broad shifts and currents in Canadian society.

Much the same tendency has been visible in the discussions of Bob Quinn, who really is a singularly peculiar figure in Irish cinema. In one way, he is inarguably central to the national cinema. He was at the centre, via his co-authored book *Sit Down and Be Counted*, of an important national debate about the role of television in Irish life. Nine years later, he won the Arts Council of Ireland's first script award for his film *Poitín*, the first feature film entirely in Irish (see Rockett, Gibbons, and Hill 129). His film *Budawanny* (1987) and its 35 mm "remake" *The Bishop's Story* (1993) were widely screened, and as Kathleen Murphy's program notes for the Film Society of Lincoln Center's 1994 Irish cinema retrospective assert, "This often silent film, shot in black-and-white, recalls Bergman's early tough purity" (13–14). He was the first filmmaker to be elected to Aosdána, Ireland's most elite assembly of artists and writers (Seamus Heaney, Brian Friel, and Neil Jordan are all members). But recent work on Irish cinema relegates Quinn to the fringes of the national cinema. Most book-length studies mention him briefly and might offer a bit about the roughness of *Poitín*, but there is very little sense that he is even approximately as important as Irish-Hollywood transients such as Neil Jordan or Jim Sheridan, or as important as the legacy of British or American representations of the violence in Northern Ireland. The fact that Ruth Barton and Harvey O'Brien's 2004 anthology *Keeping It Real: Irish Film and Television* (which grew out of a 2002 conference on Irish film) does not mention Quinn at all is an indication of how the discourse around Irish film has evolved. In this way—and in many other ways—Quinn is very much like Colin Low. The fact is that most people knowledgeable about Irish or Canadian cinema know the films of Quinn or Low, and most would acknowledge the two filmmakers as "senior statesmen." Both have received plenty of tributes; in 2000 Low was feted by the NFB on the occasion of the fiftieth anniversary of his hiring there, and in 2001 Quinn received the Irish Film Institute's Lifetime Achievement Award. Both have been the subject of biographical films; in 2000 Low released his autobiographical film *Moving Pictures*, and Quinn's son Robert's 2004 film about his father's exhibition and community TV work, called *Cinegael Paradiso*, was shown both on the Irish-language station TG4 and in film festivals worldwide. So they are very far from being unknown figures. However, there is an overwhelming sense in histories of both national cinemas that the really important material is work in feature-length narrative. David Cronenberg is generally taken to be important to Canadian cinema in a way Colin Low can never be; likewise with Neil Jordan and Bob Quinn.

A very different problem has plagued the Faroese television service, Sjónvarp Føroya (SvF), the fully publicly funded successor to the independent television projects like Sjónvarpsfelagið í Havn. This is an institution that is surely central to the country's cultural life, and the frequency with which it comes up in general discussion about the Faroes bears this out. Recall that the article I quoted by Jóhan Hendrik W. Poulsen at the end of chapter 3 was actually about Danish interference, in the linguistic sense, in Faroese speech, not really about television at all. As Poulsen recalled in that article, SvF, throughout its existence, has never been an all-Faroese service. Poulsen was very clear about how SvF "has neither the money nor the personnel to fill out the whole range of programmes with Faroese material. It therefore resorts to a considerable degree to showing cheap or even free Danish programmes, also for children, often without furnishing them with Faroese subtitles or speech" (255); that was written in 1994, twelve years after the legislation establishing SvF was passed.

But SvF has faced other sorts of problems as well. "DR1 í oktober" [Danish television in October] was the banner headline of the Faroese newspaper *Dimmalætting* on 3 August 2004; the poster for the paper that day (reproduced here as Figure C.1) was more expansive, screaming in huge type "Sjónvarp Føroya sendir DR1 1.oktober" [SvF will broadcast Danish television on 1 October]. This fear that SvF would have to start simply rebroadcasting Danish television within a month or two was brought on by a financial crisis at the station, one whose sources were not entirely clear. Furthermore, Sonja J. Jógvansdóttir's *Dimmalætting* article that reported on the impeding rebroadcast agreement also noted how serious a problem the linguistic makeup of the station was becoming; referring to the law that governed SvF, she wrote that:

> According to article 17, section 2, a third of the total Sjónvarp Føroya broadcast material should, as of 1 January 2001, be Faroese.
>
> In 2002 Sjónvarp Føroya broadcast 627 hours of Faroese television. That represented 23 percent or less than a fourth of the total of 2,739 hours broadcast in 2002.[9]

The situation that I discussed in the early parts of this book, then, had scarcely changed at all by the turn of the century, and showed no sign of changing with a defacto Danish television takeover now looming. In the end the takeover did not occur; SvF continued to broadcast and produce Faroese material more or less as it had in the past. What did change was institutional. SvF is now part of Kringvarp Føroya, or Faroese Broadcasting, a semi-governmental organization that governs both SvF and the radio station Útvarp Føroya. SvF remains in the same location that it has been in since its foundation. Thus the station's recent history has been marked by crises and rearrangements; what has remained consistent is its inability to produce much material in Faroese, an inability that, at this stage, is in contravention of Faroese law.

The situation of Irish-language television did not evolve in quite such a grim way, but there is nevertheless a comparable sense of lost possibility among the activists who advocated for its creation, especially Meitheal Oibre Theilifís na Gaeltachta and Donncha Ó hÉallaithe himself. The details of this

Figure C.1 The poster (put in shop windows, etc.) for the 3 August 2004 issue of the Faroese newspaper *Dimmalætting*, which covered the impending rebroadcast of Danish TV on Sjónvarp Føroya. The text reads "No delay: Faroese television to broadcast DR1 [Danish television], 1st of October."

activity are laid out in Iarfhlaith Watson's *Broadcasting in Irish*, and so I will not repeat them here (on the political manoeuvring leading up to the establishment of an all-Irish channel, see *Broadcasting in Irish* 88–115 and Hourigan's "A Comparison" 280–99). Suffice it to say that the immediate aftermath of the first Teilifís na Gaeltachta seemed to be defined by some real government action on the issue of an all-Irish channel. As I mentioned in the last chapter, Niamh Hourigan has recalled how then-Taoiseach Charles Haughey "allocated £500,000 from National Lottery funds for the development of Gaeltacht television" (*Escaping the Global Village* 104). Haughey was going out on a limb there, since the report from the government's Working Group on Irish Language Television Broadcasting had concluded that a Gaeltacht service would, as I noted in the last chapter, be prohibitively expensive and likely to ghettoize the language.[10] But Watson writes that "after all the promises and advisory bodies, the National Lottery funds which Haughey had vaguely 'earmarked' for the Irish-language television services were directed to the state coffers and later that year (1991) Haughey said on Raidió na Gaeltachta that due to financial constraints he was uncertain as to whether or not the television channel would be established" (*Broadcasting in Irish* 94). This push and pull between what seems to be quite sincere and often engaged government interest and a difficulty with follow-though defines the institutionalization of Irish-language television, as it defines Irish-language policy generally.

One of the reasons that Haughey fell off the Irish-broadcast map (as Watson notes on page 94 of *Broadcasting in Irish*) was that he soon lost the leadership of Fianna Fáil (in February 1992), a party which itself lost the government to what became known as the "Rainbow Coalition" of Fine Gael, Labour, and Democratic Left (which was formed in December 1994). Michael D. Higgins became minister for Arts, Culture and the Gaeltacht in the Fianna Fáil government of 1993, as part of the 27th Dáil. That was a Fianna-Fáil-led government that had for a while included the Irish Labour Party (of which Higgins was a member) as a coalition partner; Labour left that coalition at the end of 1994, Higgins stood down from his ministerial post, and future-Taoiseach Bertie Ahern took the portfolio briefly. When Fianna Fáil became the opposition, Labour became part of the "Rainbow Coalition" and Higgins returned to the Arts, Culture and the Gaeltacht portfolio in 1994 (this was still the 27th Dáil; the Fianna Fáil government collapsed and Fine Gael stood forward to form a new coalition in December 1994). During Higgins's time as minister, matters related to Irish-language broadcast began to look up a bit. As I mentioned in the introduction, Higgins was once a lecturer in politics and sociology at University College Galway (now National University of Ireland / Galway). At the time of his election to the Dáil, his constituency was (and still is) Galway West, which includes the Connemara Gaeltacht; he speaks fluent Irish (and is also known as Micheál D. Ó hUigínn) and has long had a keen interest in media issues. Indeed, as I mentioned in note 15 of the introduction to the Gaeltacht section, Higgins was also a reader of Raymond Williams, going so far as to invoke *Communications* in a debate in Seanad Éireann on 6 May 1975. And in 1990, he had vigorously argued for the establishment of an Irish-language television channel, saying in the Dáil, "What we are now witnessing is a total abandonment of the right of the people of the Gaeltachts to have a television station located in the Gaeltacht which meets their own needs and provides a national service for anyone interested in the language" (cited in Watson, *Broadcasting in Irish* 93–94). Thus it was no surprise when he took to the cinematic portions of his portfolio with gusto. Part of this gusto was his re-establishment of Bord Scannán na hÉireann / Irish Film Board in 1993. It had been established in 1981 but then deactivated in 1987 (both actions by Fianna Fáil), essentially because the films it produced had made very little money. Higgins's reactivation seemed to signal that the Bord's remit would be a cultural rather than an economic-development one. Again, the details of the Bord's history are well documented elsewhere (on the Bord's first incarnation, see Rockett, Gibbons, and Hill 114–22; on its second, see Barton 104–12).

Higgins's enthusiasm for the full-scale reform of Irish broadcasting can also be seen in his department's issuing of a Green Paper on Broadcasting; published in a bilingual edition, it was called *Gníomhach nó Fulangach? Fáthmheas ar an Réimse Craolacháin / Active or Passive? Broadcasting in the Future Tense.* While Jürgen Habermas's name does not actually appear in the document, his ideas about the public sphere clearly influence its aspirations. Chapter 3 is titled "Na Meáin Chumarsáide agus an Réimse Poiblí / Media and the Public Sphere" and goes so far as to invoke the political clubs and coffee houses so beloved of Habermas (27/145). But this influence is made most explicit in chapter 10, "An Ghaeilge agus an cultúr sa chraoladh / Irish Language and Culture in Broadcasting":

> It can be argued that to deprive the Irish-speaking community of the means of public debate in its own first language is, in effect, to deny its existence, since it is constituted as a community through the Irish language and its culture is carried largely by the language. To deny the legitimacy of an Irish language public sphere is to relegate this community to the position of a cultural ghetto, useful only for providing to the English-speaking sphere a sense of cultural continuity with the past and a feeling of cultural reassurance in an uncertain, globalised world.[11] (205)

The Irish-language public sphere, in short, needed to belong to and serve the needs of people who actually spoke Irish; to have it organized around the needs of an English-speaking, globalization-fearing majority, a majority who, by and large, constituted the state authorities, was unacceptable. This follows Habermas quite closely, as he was adamant about the public sphere's need to be at some distance from state authorities. He wrote elsewhere in *Strukturwandel der Öffentlichkeit* that as the seventeenth century wore on, "the now emerging *public sphere of civil society* ... developed to the extent to which the public concern regarding the private sphere of civil society was no longer confined to the authorities, but was considered by the subjects as one that was properly theirs" (*Structural Transformation* 23; italics in the translation).[12] For the Higgins report, it was crucial that Irish speakers come to recognize this Irish-language public sphere as "properly theirs," and not the result of a nationalist desire to appropriate their language for the purposes of asserting distinctiveness.

But it is the specific constitution of this public sphere that has lead to skepticism from analysts of Irish-language media as to its genuinely democratic, or even genuinely Habermasian, nature. Muiris Mac Conghail, as part of a forum published in *Irish Communications Review* called "After the Green Paper, What Next for Broadcasting in Ireland?" wrote that "the references to Habermas, the German philosopher, and his notions of the public sphere, are fundamental to the Minister's concerns" (80). Noting that this sphere needed to be free of state control but still protected by that state, Mac Conghail continued, "To accept this state protection but to separate the process out from the government of the day is a major task of the legislators and broadcasters" (80). Mac Conghail went on to be more sharply critical on these sorts of matters, writing two years later and in Irish that "certainly Habermas' ideas and the Minister's are not comparable."[13] That was in an article called "Teilifís na Gaeilge: Teilifís ar Strae?" [Irish-language Television: Television Astray?], again explicitly connecting the struggle for Irish-language broadcast to the insurgent legacy of Máirtín Ó Cadhain, as the *Sit Down and Be Counted* authors had done via their invocation of Ó Cadhain's seminal 1969 speech *Gluaiseacht na Gaeilge: Gluaiseacht ar Strae* [Irish-Language Movement: A Movement Astray]. And as he had in English, Mac Conghail argued there that the difference between Habermas and O'Higgins lay in the place they saw for the state and its officials, specifically its ministers: "I was anticipating that the minister's paper would create such a project within the public sphere, answerable to him, if it could not come about from the State. I wonder if the minister got tired of his plan to bring broadcasting to the people in such a way that they would be active in the process."[14] This basic paradox—a public sphere that is created by a minister of the state—does indeed seem to have a very tenuous relationship with Habermas' conception of the public sphere.

Mac Conghail's Irish-language essay differs from his English-language one not only because of its presumed audience, but because when he is writing in Irish, Mac Conghail is writing *after* the establishment of an Irish-language station. "If we really value our Constitution's designation of Irish as the first national language," the *Irish Times* editorialized on 31 October 1996, "we should wholeheartedly welcome the first broadcast from Teilifís na Gaeilge today" ("Teilifís na Gaeilge" 10). The creation of Teilifís na Gaeilge (TnaG) was indeed not welcomed by everybody; it was most definitely not welcomed by the Teilifís na Gaeltachta group. "I am deeply concerned about the type of service about to be established," Donncha Ó hÉallaithe writes in 1994, just as the institutional apparatus for Teilifís na Gaeilge was being finalized ("Longstanding Gaeltacht TV activist" 18). Decrying the fact that this would be a national service with a Dublin-based governing body, he writes in that same article that "the Gaeltacht is faced with the prospect that the service to be established, as a result of the campaign for a Gaeltacht community television service, will have a 'Dublin 4'[15] rather than a Gaeltacht bias to it" (18). He also had concerns about whether people living in the Gaeltacht would actually be able to receive the service, worrying that "people along the West Coast from Donegal down to Kerry will be unable to receive the new service, unless they go to the trouble and expense of buying and installing a new UHF aerial. This is the kind of Dublincentric mentality that is behind the planning of the new service, unfortunately" (18). Ó hÉallaithe is not invoking Habermas directly here, but he is clearly annoyed that Teilifís na Gaeilge ("a name which is not acceptable to the Gaeltacht communities," he added in that same article) is also being set up to fail as a public sphere. He writes there that its institutional details—a base of operations in Dublin, an advisory board where "not one of them could be described as being involved in Gaeltacht Community affairs to any extent"—were clearly going to be, in the words of the Páipéar Glas ar Chraolachán / Green Paper on Broadcasting, "useful only for providing to the English-speaking sphere a sense of cultural continuity with the past and a feeling of cultural reassurance in an uncertain, globalised world." Seeing the service in action hardly changed Ó hÉallaithe's mind on this; in 1998 he wrote a short essay called "Why Was TnaG a Monumental Mistake?" for a special issue of the journal *Force 10* that was guest-edited by Bob Quinn. As I mentioned in chapter 4, he stated there that "TnaG should reinvent itself as Teilifís na Gaeltachta, and attempt to satisfy the demand in the Gaeltacht for community TV in

Irish. However I can well imagine that the above approach would prove to be impossible in the prevailing cultural climate, dominated by those who would like to ethnically cleanse the few remaining Gaeltacht communities from the linguistic landscape" (43).

TnaG did indeed reinvent itself, but not at all in the way Ó hÉallaithe suggested in *Force 10*. After two years, the station was rechristened TG4. *Irish Times* media reporter Jackie Bourke found this slightly puzzling, writing that "less than a year after the station was launched, the head of TnaG, Cathal Goan, said more people were watching it than any other minority-interest channel, including Sky News, Eurosport and MTV.... Why, then, has TnaG had to undergo a major image overhaul?... The explanation from TG4 is that the name change is a bid to have the station shifted further up the spectrum of stations on cable services" (10). But this was much more than a name change. As the *Times*' Irish-language editor Pól Ó Muirí noted on the same day, "TnaG—the Irish-language station—is dead and TG4—a bilingual station—is born. The chances are that if you tune in, you are as likely to see a programme in English as Irish. The station makes a virtue of this vice, arguing that English-language material is needed to improve the audience figures and, hopefully, stay tuned and follow the Irish-language programmes" (10). By this logic Michael Ring T.D. is, as one of the quotes that open this chapter indicates, something of a perfect viewer; brought in by a John Wayne film, he ends up giving the station free publicity in the Dáil. Indeed, the station shows Hollywood westerns quite frequently, and has become well known for that. As I am writing this I check the TG4 schedule for 27 November 2007; sure enough, *The Virginian* is showing at 13:05. Other programs for 27 November 2007 include *France 24* (a twenty-four-hour news show from Paris), *Homes Under the Hammer* (a British show about real estate auctions), *What I Like About You* (an American sitcom), *Pimp My Ride* (an American reality show), *Stíl na Réalt: Gwen Stefani* (a version of the program *Style Star*, this one a broadcast of a concert from an American pop star), *The People vs. Larry Flynt* (an American movie from 1996), *Curb Your Enthusiasm* (an American sitcom), and *France 24* again.

So even though TG4 is now based in the Connemara Gaeltacht community of Baile na hAbhann, it represents the complete abandonment of the community television model put forward by the Teilifís na Gaeltachta group. A recent anthology of essays—*TG4@10: Deich mBliana de TG4* [Ten Years of TG4], edited by Eithne O'Connell, John Walsh, and Gearóid Denvir—celebrated the emergence and stabilization of the channel, and certainly there is much to celebrate. But that book is notable in part for the fact that the Teilifís na Gaeltachta experiments are basically absent. Íte Ní Chionnaith, in her memoir of her resistance to RTÉ's neglect of Irish (as I mentioned in the Gaeltacht section introduction, she went to prison in 1977 for refusing to pay for her television licence), gives a roll call of the organizations involved in agitation for Irish-language television that includes Meitheal Oibre Theilifís na Gaeltachta, and also mentions the "stáisiún bradach teilfíse i Ros Muc" [the pirate television station in Ros Muc] in passing (31). Emer Ní Bhrádaigh, in her analysis of TG4 from the standpoint of entrepreneurship, also mentions the "stáisiún bradach" and that this was done with the inspiration of the Faroe Islands' station ["le hinspioráid ó stáisiún sna hOiléain Fharo"], and that the initiatives were led by Bob and Helen Quinn, Seosamh Ó Cuaig, Donncha Ó hÉallaithe, and Gluaiseacht Chearta Sibhialta na Gaeltachta (140). But details or analysis of the broadcasts are basically absent. Indeed, the sharpest recollection of the Teilfís na Gaeltachta perspective comes from Niall Mac Eachmharcaigh, who doesn't actually mention the pirate broadcasts, when he mockingly writes about the change of name from Teilifís na Gaeilge to TG4: "Four! Ar *Dublin 4* atá siad ag díriú a n-airde" [Four! It's on Dublin 4 that they're focusing their attention] (163) (italics in the original; I reproduce this in Irish in the main text to draw attention to the linguistic switching). This strongly recalls Donncha Ó hÉallaithe's 1994 statement about Dublin 4 mentioned above. However, the fact that this most *explicit* evocation of these arguments comes in the book's most bitter essay (Mac Eachmharcaigh's essay is largely a complaint about the difficulties he had working as an independent producer for TG4) gives a different sort of sense of just how far from the workings of TG4 the idealism of Teilifis na Gaeltachta really is.

Breandán Delap's 2008 essay on "Irish and the Media" follows a similar line. The words "Teilifís na Gaeltachta" do not appear in his article, although he does recall how their pirate broadcasts were modelled after Saor-raidió Chonamara and how "having bravely defied the authorities for several days the pirate broadcast finally came unstuck when a sharp gust of wind felled the makeshift transmitter on Cnoc Mordáin" (157). But overall he is vagely dimissive of the entire project: "The story has far outgrown the event, however, and it sometimes seems that as many people claim to have been instrumental in the campaign as those who claimed to have been in the GPO in 1916" (157). As I have tried to show, though, the cast of characters in these pirate broadcasts is not at all difficult to trace; furthermore, a simple comparison between the amount written about the GPO in the scholarly history of Irish insurgency and the amount written about Teilifís na Gaeltachta in the scholarly history of Irish media should give a sense of just how spurious this (admittedly tongue-in-cheek) comparison is. Delap also echoes the position of *TG4@10*, praising the new, reconstituted station's combination of internationalism and localism, recalling how on the death of Yasser Arafat, "Nuacht RTÉ/TG4 ran a story on how his family and the Palestinian Authority had taken out shares in the Canadian parent company of Bioniche in Indreabhán" (160). I take the point here, and it is clear that this admirable example of TG4 making the local and the international speak to one another is indeed a valuable reform of televison-news conventions. But Teilfís na Gaeltachta, as I have recalled, also featured a program of interviews with school children in Indreabhán, as did Cinegael ten years earlier. These programs were radical rejections of television-news formats, an example of using low-end television to give voice to people who had genuinely been absent from mainstream media. News about multinational corporations such as Bioniche hardly fits that description.

It is this seemingly inevitable shift towards a more-or-less conventional, consumption-driven model of television that is at the centre of both Watson's and Hourigan's rejection of the Habermasian public sphere as a reasonable way to understand Irish-language broadcast. The degree to which broadcasting tends to conflate consumption with participation is at the core of both of these scholars' critiques. Watson, in a 1998 article titled "Teilifís na Gaeilge as a Public Sphere," is quite sympathetic to TnaG's aspirations towards a publicly oriented remit. He also argues in that article that the station's aspiration towards "polysemy" demonstrates "a limited freedom within the transformed public sphere" (75). He writes at one point that "polysemy is also central in the Green Paper on Broadcasting and TnaG's structure.... Within TnaG itself, polysemy is reflected in its commissioner/broadcaster role which it is hoped will produce a polysemy of texts" (75). A less semiotically inflected version of this sense was at the centre of independent producers' longstanding gripe that RTÉ was unfriendly to independent producers; TnaG, and TG4 after it, did seem to address this complaint by relying very heavily on external production companies rather than making most programs in-house. But polysemy, for Watson, is not enough. He concludes that 1998 article by saying that although "TnaG plays a critical role providing consumer products in Irish, a consumer is not a citizen. Active participation in the public sphere cannot be equated with the 'right to withhold acclamation' or with a polysemy of consumer products" (78). He reiterated a similar critique five years later in *Broadcasting in Irish*, writing of the pro-TnaG argument that "Irish speakers as Irish citizens had the right to choose to be informed and entertained in Irish.... A major flaw in this 'postmodern' ideology is that it has a very passive notion of citizenship, which almost equates the citizen to the consumer" (91). Hourigan rejects the Habermasian analysis completely; as she writes in *Escaping the*

Global Village, "The public sphere model is particularly unsuitable for the analysis of minority language media.... Television is a hierarchical medium where there is a substantial power disparity between the audience and the program-maker. It is clear that although some radio and television programs attempt to create channels of access through new technology, television is still a closed medium where the general public does not have either high levels of access or control" (48–49). High levels of access and control on the part of Gaeltacht communities was, of course, the number one priority of the Teilifís na Gaeltachta group. They were also hoping to have, as Habermas wrote in *Structural Transformation of the Public Sphere*, "claimed the public sphere regulated from above against the public authorities themselves, to engage them in a debate over the general rules governing relations in the basically privatized but publicly relevant sphere of commodity exchange and social labor" (27).[16] Indeed, the Teilifís na Gaeltachta followed this model quite closely. Their broadcasts were illegal, and thus they tried to retake the sphere of broadcast from the state-sanctioned, and indeed state-owned, authorities; they insisted that their station remain separate from the semi-state body that is RTÉ; and they engaged in a vigorous debate about the cost and sustainability of non-commercial local television, debating directly and vigorously the positions put forward by the reports of the government's Working Group on Irish Language Television Broadcasting or of the semi-state body Údarás na Gaeltachta. Their complete marginalization and alienation from the Irish-language television stations that actually emerged is but one indicator of the degree to which the notion of Irish-language television did indeed fail to achieve the status of a public sphere.

This is entirely consistent with the North Atlantic experience. This period in the region's media history—1958 to 1988—was, as I have tried to demonstrate in this book, remarkable for the emergence of media projects—some by individuals, some by semi-state bodies, some by individuals working together in varying degrees of opposition to the state—which explicitly engaged with community-building, the politics of regionalism and/or minority nationalism, and the politics of language, and which did so quite outside of the commercial, production-consumption model that defines conventional media production. These experiments were quite idealistic in terms of aesthetics—which often reinvented cinema in significant ways, especially in the case of Perrault and the Newfoundland Project—and in terms of politics—which were often remarkable for their simultaneous and equally rigorous engagement with localism and internationalism, especially in the case of the Gaeltacht media experiments. And they were all very free about integrating the lessons of other forms, especially those of radio. They were, in short, previews of the arguments that would define globalization. How can marginal societies survive while reconciling tradition and modernity? How can communications media be used in new ways to help answer this question? How can the breaking down of barriers between media make the work more fertile? That these projects are now mostly forgotten, with the media of the region tending to move off in very different directions, is a real loss for our understanding of the ways in which communities have used cinema in order to express their collective sense of reality. To rediscover this media history is to realize just how long the questions of globalization have been with us, and to realize that radical, innovative answers to those questions have already been offered, and are still waiting for responses.

Notes

1 "Ce n'est plus le Québec pure laine de la pêche au marsouin, des voitures de l'eau, et des bœufs musqués des films de Pierre Perrault. C'est un Québec coloré, métissé, polymorphe, urbain.... Je dis enfin que ce pays mythique dont il nous a fait cadeau pour la suite du monde, en quelque sorte est parti avec lui" (B5).

2 "Tað er í hesari grundgevingini ikki greitt, hvussu sjónvarpið hjá sjónvarpfelagnum við 50 prosentum av donskum og 50 prosentum av tilfari úr øðrum londom kann vera eitt føroyskt altenativ" ("Pirat.sendarar ..." 4).

3 "C'est peut-être l'avenir du Québec ou celui du cinéma même, si l'un me préoccupe plus que l'autre" (70).

4 On this matter of domestic box office revenues for Canadian films, journalist Kate Taylor writes in the *Globe and Mail* ("Hooray for Hollywood and Other Bad Telefilm Ideas," 24 September 2005), "It's official: The Federal film policy isn't working.... The goal was for Canadian films, never popular with Canadian audiences, to earn a meagre 5 per cent of the domestic box office so utterly dominated by Hollywood. Many in the industry said it couldn't be done and have been proved more or less right" (R4). She goes on to observe that the situation in Quebec is far better, since Quebec films account for around 25 percent of the province's box office.

5 "necesita, y por la tanto tiende a desarrollar, el gusto personal, individual, del pueblo" (*Una imagen* 7).

6 "la producción desarrollada por una minoría para satisfacer la demanda de una masa reducía al único papel de espectador y consumidora" (*Una imagen* 8).

7 "Si on fait un survol rapide de ce qui s'est écrit sur le cinéma dans les médias d'ici, la notion de métissage dans les films aurait été inventée vers 1995.... Alors qu'il y a sûrement autant de 'métissage' dans un film de Michka Säal, d'Arto Paragamian, de Robert Morin, de Jacques Leduc, de Pierre Perrault" (27).

8 This paper was presented at a joint conference of the Film Studies Association of Canada and the Association québécois d'études cinématographiques, held at Université Laval

in 1986. That was the year Perrault had gotten an honorary degree from Laval, and Michael Dorland has recalled how this led Thomas Waugh to remark during the conference's wrap-up session, "We demystified one of our great men; you sanctified one of yours." Cited in Michael Dorland, "Beyond Shame and Glory," in Dorland, Mario Falsetto and Pierre Véronneau, eds., *Dialogue* (Montreal: Médiatexte / Cinémathèque québécoise, 1986), 316.

9 "Sambært grein 17, stk 2. so er málið hjá Sjónvarpi Føroya at 1. januar 2001, skuldi ein triðjingur at øllum sendum tilfari verið føroyskt. Í 2002 vóru 627 tímar føroyskir tímar sendir í Sjónvarp Føroya. Hetta svarar til 23 prosent ella minnið enn ein fjórðingur av teimum tilsams 2739 tímunumm, ið sendir vóru í 2002" (5). That law, known as Kringvarpslóg, can be found at http://www.svf.fo/UserFiles/File/Skjol/Kringvarpslog .doc. Article 17, section 2 reads, in part: "The television should produce or allow to be produced sufficient Faroese material so that the measure is, on 1 January 2001, required to be one-third of broadcast hours being Faroese productions" ["Sjónvarpið skal framleiða ella lata framleiða so nógv føroyskt tilfar sum tilber og málið er, at 1.januar 2001 skal 1/3 av senditíðini verða føroysk framleiðsla"].

10 During this period the government had also asked Údarás na Gaeltachta (the Gaeltacht Authority) to prepare a report on the feasibility of Gaeltacht television; Watson wrote in 2003 that the report "is still unpublished" (*Broadcasting in Irish* 92). Hourigan writes of the Údarás report, "Much to the chagrin of Meitheal Oibre activists, the Údarás 1990 report, researched in conjunction with KPMG, recommended the establishment of a *national* television service. Quinn's model of community television did not interest them, possibly because of the small number of jobs it would create" ("A Comparison" 282).

11 "Is féidir a rá gurb ionann an cumas díospóireachta poiblí ina chéadteanga [*sic*] féin a choinneáil ón bpobal Gaeilge agus, déanta na fírinne, a marthain a cheilt air, ós rud é go bhfuil sé bunaithe mar phobal tríd an nGaeilge agus gurb í an teanga sin cuid mhór a iompraíonn a chultúr. Is ionann dlisteanacht réimse poiblí na Gaeilge a shéanadh agus an pobal seo a chur ina gheiteo cultúrtha, gan úsáid ach amháin chun mothú leanúnachais chultúrtha leis an am atá imithe thart a thabhairt don réimse Béarla chomh maith le mothú dearfachta cultúrtha i saol neamhchinnte domhanda" (87–88).

12 "der nun entstehenden *bürgerlichen Öffentlichkeit* ... entwickelt sich nämlich in dem Maße, in dem das öffentliche Interesse an der privaten Sphäre der bürgerlichen Gesellschaft nicht mehr nur von der Obrigkeit wahrgenommen, sondern von den Untertanen als ihr eigens in Betracht gezogen wird" (*Strukturwandel der Öffentlichkeit* 34; italics his).

13 "Go deimhin ní hionann tuairim Habermas agus gníomh an aire" ("Teilifís na Gaeilge: Teilifís ar Strae?" 23).

14 "Bhíos ag súil go gcuirfeadh Páipéar an aire tús lena leithéid laistigh den réimse poiblí faoi dhídean an aire mura bhféadfaí í a thionól faoi dhídean agus coimirce an stáit. Níl a fhios agam ar bhuail tuirse na gaibhne an t-aire maidir lena phlean chun scéal an chraolacháin a chur i láthair an phobail, 's go mbeidís rannpháirteach sa ngnó ar fad" (23).

15 "Dublin 4" is the postal code for the southern suburbs of Dublin, which include institutions such as RTÉ (located in Donnybrook) and University College Dublin (located in Belfield). The term has become a kind of shorthand for the "cultural elite" of Ireland. Desmond Fennell (who was raised in the more working-class north side of Dublin) has written a bitterly scathing essay on the topic, "Getting to Know Dublin 4." He writes of the postal code's population: "Seeing themselves as 'enlightened' (their word) and therefore truly rational (really human) and morally good (sensitive, compassionate, requiring strict honesty from the powerful, deeply appalled by evil actions), they regard people who disagree with them as mentally darkened and morally delinquent (irrational, ignorant, uneducated, blinkered, brainwashed, crooked, fanatical, bigoted, hating the light—all this with the suggestion of inhuman)" (205). The essay is found in *Heresy*, pp. 186–212. In note 29 of the Gaeltacht introduction, I suggested that Fennell is quite close to the late Christopher Lasch; this is especially true, as I mentioned in that note, in the case of their shared dislike of this particular demographic. Writing of the American liberal intelligentsia in his posthumously published *Revolt of the Elites* (New York: Norton, 1996), Lasch follows Fennell very closely indeed, claiming, "When confronted with resistance to these initiatives, they betray the venomous hatred that lies not far beneath the smiling face of upper-middle-class benevolence. Opposition makes humanitarians forget the liberal virtues they claim to uphold. They become petulant, self-righteous, intolerant. In the heat of political controversy, they find it impossible to conceal their contempt for those who 'just don't get it,' in the self-satisfied jargon of political rectitude" (28).

16 "reglementierte Öffentlichkeit alsbald gegen die öffentliche Gewalt selbst, um sich mit dieser über die allgemeinen Regeln des Verkehrs in der grundsätzlich privatisierten, aber öffentlich relevanten Sphäre des Warenverkehrs und der gesellschaftlichen Arbeit auseinanderzusetzen" (*Strukturwandel der Offentlichkeit* 38).

BIBLIOGRAPHY

A Film Board for Ireland? Dir. Bob Quinn. Cinegael / RTÉ, 1976.

"Albert Folens: Flemish Patriot Found Home in Ireland." *Irish Times* 12 Sept. 2003: 8.

Alcock, Antony, and Terence O'Brien. *Policies to Support Radio and Television Broadcasting in the Lesser Used Languages of the European Community*. Coleraine, Northern Ireland: University of Ulster, 1980.

Allio, René. "Cinéma du réel et cinéma de la fiction: vraie ou fausse distinction? Dialogue entre Pierre Perrault et René Allio." Gauthier and Véronneau 42–57.

An Coimisiún um Athbheochan na Gaeilge: An Tuarascáil Dheiridh. Baile Átha Cliath [Dublin]: Oifig an tSoláthair, 1963.

An Coimisiún um Athbheochan na Gaeilge: Summary, in English, of Final Report, 13th July 1963. Dublin: Stationary Office, 1963.

Andreassen, Eyðun. *Folkelig offentlighed: En undersøgelse af kulturelle former på Færøerne i 100 år*. Tórshavn / København [Copenhagen]: Føroya Fróðskaparfelag / Museum Tusculanums Forlag, 1992.

Andreassen, Henry. "Sjónvarp—ja ella nei." *Sosialurin* 1 Apr. 1978: 7.

Appadurai, Arjun. *Modernity at Large: Cultural Dimensions of Globalization*. Minneapolis: University of Minnesota Press, 1996.

Arge, Jógvan. "Hvør ráðgevur landsstýrinum í sjonvarpsspurninginum?" Sosialurin 18 Apr. 1978: 6.

Athbheochan na Gaeilge / The Restoration of the Irish Language: Arna leagan ag an Rialtas faoi bhráid gach Tí den Oireachtas, Eanáir, 1965. Baile Átha Cliath [Dublin]: Oifig an tSoláthair, 1965.

Augaitis, Daina, and Dan Lander. Introduction. *Radio Rethink: Art, Sound and Transmission*. Ed. Augaitis and Lander. Banff, AB: Walter Phillips Gallery, 1994. 1–10.

Bailyn, Bernard. *Atlantic History: Concepts and Contours*. Cambridge, MA: Harvard University Press, 2005.

Barnouw, Eric. *Documentary: A History of the Non-Fiction Film*. Oxford: Oxford University Press, 1974.

Barton, Ruth. *Irish National Cinema*. London: Routledge, 2004.

Barton, Ruth, and Harvey O'Brien, eds. *Keeping It Real: Irish Film and Television*. London: Wallflower Press, 2004.

"B'Fhearr Staisiun Raidio Beag i nGach Gaeltacht—An Taoiseach." *Inniu* 30 Jan. 1970: 1, 6.

Blake, Raymond. *Canadians At Last: Canada Integrates Newfoundland as a Province*. Toronto: University of Toronto Press, 2004.

Boelhower, William. "'I'll Teach You How to Flow': On Figuring Out Atlantic Studies." *Atlantic Studies* 1.1 (2004): 28–48.

Bonneville, Léo. *Le cinéma québécois par ceux qui le font*. Montréal: Éditions Paulines, 1979.

Boulais, Stéphane-Albert, ed. *Le cinéma au Québec: Tradition et modernité*. Saint-Laurent, QC: Fides, 2006.

Bourke, Jackie. "Súil eile?" *Irish Times* 13 Oct. 1999: 10.

Brögger, Chris. *Kvikmyndin*. Reykjavík: Iðunn, 1980.

Brûlé, Michel. *Pierre Perrault ou un cinéma national*. Montréal: Les Presses de l'Université de Montréal, 1974.

Bruzzi, Stella. *New Documentary: A Critical Introduction*. New York/London: Routledge, 2000.

Buhler, Jean. *Sur les routes de l'Atlantique*. Lausanne: Payot, 1951.

Butel, Paul. *The Atlantic*. London: Routledge, 1999.

———. *Histoire de l'Atlantique: De l'antiquité à nos jours*. Paris: Perrin, 1997.

"Býráðið í Havn vil hava sjónvarp." *14. September* 11 Feb. 1978: 3.

"Býráðið vil hava sjónvarp í Havnini." *Sosialurin* 11 Feb. 1978: 1.

Cadbury, William, and Leland Pogue. *Film Criticism: A Counter-Theory*. Ames: Iowa State University Press, 1982.

Cinegael Paradiso. Dir. Robert Quinn. Distinguished Features / TG4, 2004.

Cinéma Vérité: Defining the Moment. Dir. Peter Wintonick. National Film Board of Canada, 1999.

Clandfield, David. *Pierre Perrault and the Poetic Documentary*. Bloomington / Toronto: Indiana University Press / Toronto International Film Festival Group, 2004.

Comolli, Jean-Louis. "L'île, ou l'exemplarité d'un cinéma de combat." *Cahiers du cinéma* 194 (October 1967): 56–58.

Compton, Margaret A. "The Archivist, the Scholar, and Access to Historical Television Materials." *Cinema Journal* 46.3 (2007): 129–33.

Conley, Tom. *Cartographic Cinema*. Minneapolis: University of Minnesota Press, 2007.

Cowie, Peter. *Scandinavian Cinema*. London: Tantivy Press, 1990.

Crocker, Stephen. "The Fogo Process: Participatory Communication in a Globalizing World." *Participatory Video: Images that Transform and Empower*. Ed. Shirley A. White. London: Sage, 2003. 122–41.

"Cuirfidh Teilifís na Gaeltachta Olc ar Dhá Eite." *Anois* 17 May 1987: 1, 4.

Dahl, Tormóður. "Um sjónvarp, Goethe, at mjólka heilagum kúm og okkurt annað forvitnisligt." *Sosialurin* 15 Apr. 1978: 6, 7.

———. "Um sjónvarp, Goethe, at mjólka heilagum kúm og okkurt annað forvitnisligt." *Sosialurin* 22 Apr. 1978: 6, 7, 13.

———. "Um sjónvarp, tey gomlu á bygd, lættisoppar og onnur fyribrigdi." *14. September* 18 Feb. 1978: 7.

Daney, Serge. *Le Salaire du zappeur*. Paris: P.O.L., 1993.

Danielsen, Dánjal Pauli. "Tað nyttar ikki at bera seg undan í sjónvarpsspurninginum." *Sosialurin* 25 Feb. 1978: 7.

de Blois, Marco. "Métissé(e)." *24 Images* 105 (Winter 2001): 27.

de Bréadún, Deaglán. "Teilifís bhradach ar ais 'um Nollaig.'" *Irish Times* 7 Oct. 1987: 6.

Delap, Breandán. "Irish and the Media." *A New View of the Irish Language*. Ed. Caoilfhionn Nic Pháidín and Seán Ó Cearnaigh. Dublin: Cois Life, 2008. 152–63.

Deleuze, Gilles. *Cinéma 2: L'image-temps*. Paris: Éditions de Minuit, 1985.

———. *Cinema 2: The Time-Image*. Trans. Hugh Tomlinson and Robert Galeta. Minneapolis: University of Minnesota Press, 2003.

Déniel, Alain. *Le mouvement breton: 1919–1945*. Paris: François Maspero, 1976.

de Ville, Barry. *Distributive Targets for the Fogo Island Films*. Report for the National Film Board of Canada. August 1972. [Held at archives of National Film Board of Canada, Fogo Island box]

Dowling, Jack, Lelia Doolan, and Bob Quinn. *Sit Down and Be Counted: The Cultural Evolution of a Television Station*. Dublin: Wellington, 1969.

"Dun Chaoin agitation likely to reopen." *Irish Times* 9 Nov. 1970: 5.

Ehrlich, Gretl. *This Cold Heaven: Seven Seasons in Greenland*. New York: Pantheon, 2001.

Éire Nua: The Social and Economic Programme of Sinn Féin. Dublin: Sinn Féin, 1971.

"Eitt alment føroyskt sjónvarp nýtist ikki at skula kosta nógv." *Sosialurin* 14 Feb. 1981: 1.

Evans, E. Estyn. *Ireland and the Atlantic Heritage: Selected Writings*. Dublin: Lilliput Press, 1996.

Evans, Gary. *In the National Interest: A Chronicle of the National Film Board of Canada from 1949 to 1989*. Toronto: University of Toronto Press, 1991.

Extension Service, Memorial University of Newfoundland. *Community Television Conference Report: June 20–22, 1982*. St. John's: Memorial University of Newfoundland, 1982. [Held at Centre for Newfoundland Studies, Memorial University of Newfoundland]

Feldman, Seth. "Vertov after Manovich." *Canadian Journal of Film Studies / Revue canadienne d'études cinématographiques* 16.1 (2007): 39–50.

Fennell, Desmond. *Beyond Nationalism: The Struggle against Provinciality in the Modern World*. Dublin: Ward River Press, 1985.

———. "Can a Shrinking Linguistic Minority Be Saved?" *Minority Languages Today*. Ed. E. Haugen, J. D. McClure, and D. S. Thomson. Edinburgh: Edinburgh University Press, 1981. 32–39.

———. *Cutting to the Point: Essays and Objections 1994–2003*. Dublin: Liffey, 2003.

———. "Gaeltacht agus Impiriúlachas." *Comhar* 30.6 (June 1971): 5–8.

———. *Heresy: The Battle of Ideas in Modern Ireland*. Belfast: Blackstaff Press, 1993.

———. *Iarchonnacht Began*. Cill Chiaráin, Ire.: Iarchonnachta 1985, 1969.

———. "Iosrael in Iarchonnachta." *Inniu* 28 Feb. 1969: 9.

———. "Language Revival: Is It Already a Lost Cause?" *Irish Times* 29 Jan. 1969: 8.

———. "The Last Days of the Gaeltacht." *Irish Times* 3 June 1980: 12.

———. "Léarscáil na Gaeltachta." *Amárach* 21 May 1976: 2.

———. "Reorganising the British Isles 1: A New Look at Federation." *Irish Times* 23 Mar. 1974: 8.

———. "Reorganising the British Isles 2: The Federation of Man." *Irish Times* 25 Mar. 1974: 8.

———. *The Revision of Irish Nationalism*. Dublin: Open Air Press, 1989.

———. "Solutions to the Northern Ireland Problem: A Federal Ireland and Other Approaches." *Canadian Journal of Irish Studies* 21.1 (1995): 1–24.

———. *Take the Faroes for Example: The Arguments for Self-government in the Provinces and the Gaeltacht*. Dublin: Pobal Teoranta, 1972.

———. "Why the Gaeltacht Wasn't Saved." *Irish Times* 4 June 1980: 10.

Finlan, Michael. "Illegal TV broadcasts to Gaeltacht areas." *Irish Times* 30 Dec. 1988: 9.

———. "Rosmuc gets its own TV station." *Irish Times* 5 Oct. 1987: 9.

Fiske, John. *Television Culture*. London/New York: Routledge, 1995.

Fjallstein, Martin. "Sjónvarpið—eitt luksus." *Sosialurin* 4 Mar. 1978: 6.

———. "Sjónvarpsmálið aftur á tingborð." *14. September* 25 Jan. 1978: 8.

Fogo Island Film and Community Development Project. Report for the National Film Board of Canada. May 1968. [Held at archives of National Film Board of Canada, Fogo Island box]

Fogo Process in Communication: A Reflection on the Use of Film as an Inter-Community Communication. St. John's: Memorial University of Newfoundland Extension Service, 1972. [Held at archives of National Film Board of Canada, Fogo Island box]

Folens, Albert. *Aiséirí Flóndrais*. N.p.: self-published, 1958.

Forchhammer, Jette. *Børn med tv*. København [Copenhagen]: Nordisk Ministerråd, 1998.

Føroya Landsstýri. *Ársfrágreiðing 1979*. Tórshavn: Føroya Landsstýri, 1980.

———. *Ársfrágreiðing 1980*. Tórshavn: Føroya Landsstýri, 1981.

———. *Ársfrágreiðing 1981*. Tórshavn: Føroya Landsstýri, 1982.

———. *Ársfrágreiðing 1982*. Tórshavn: Føroya Landsstýri, 1983.

———. *Ársfrágreiðing fyri Føroyar 1983*. Tórshavn: Føroya Landsstýri, 1984.

———. *Ársfrágreiðing fyri Føroyar 1984*. Tórshavn: Føroya Landsstýri, 1985.

———. *Ársfrágreiðing fyri Føroyar 1985*. Tórshavn: Føroya Landsstýri, 1986.

———. *Ársfrágreiðing fyri Føroyar 1987*. Tórshavn: Føroya Landsstýri, 1988.

———. *Árbók fyri Føroyar 1990*. Tórshavn: Føroya Landsstýri, 1991.

———. *Árbók fyri Føroyar 1991*. Tórshavn: Hagstova Føroya, 1992.

"Føroyingur fingið halva mill. kr. til at kanna árinið av sjónvarpinum." *Sosialurin* 4 Aug. 1979: 3.

Fouéré, Yann. *L'Europe aux cent drapeaux: Essai pour servir à la construction de l'Europe*. Paris: Presses d'Europe, 1968.

———. *La Maison du Connemara: Histoire d'un Breton 2*. Rennes, Fr.: Coop Breizh, 1995.

———. *Towards a Federal Europe: Nations or States?* Trans. H. Le Helloco. Swansea, UK: Christopher Davies, 1980.

"Gaeltacht television ready to broadcast." *Connacht Tribune* 2 Oct. 1987: 1.

"Gaeltacht TV discussion at Oireachtas." *Connacht Tribune* 11 Sept. 1987: 8.

García Espinosa, Julio. "For an Imperfect Cinema." Trans. Julianne Burton. *Twenty-five Years of the New Latin American Cinema*. Ed. Michael Chanan. London: British Film Institute / Channel 4, 1983. 28–33.

———. *Una imagen recorre el mundo*. Ciudad de la Habana [Havana]: Editoriales Letras Cubanas, 1979.

Gauthier, Guy, Philippe Pilard, and Simone Suchet. *Le documentaire passe au direct*. Montréal: VLB éditeur, 2003.

Gauthier, Guy, and Pierre Véronneau, eds. *Écritures de Pierre Perrault: Actes du colloque 'Gens de paroles,' 24–28 mars 1982, Maison de la culture de La Rochelle*. Dossiers de la Cinémathèque 11. Montréal: Cinémathèque québécoise, 1983.

Gibbons, Luke. *Transformations in Irish Culture*. Field Day Essays 2. Cork: Cork University Press, 1996.

Gilroy, Paul. *The Black Atlantic: Modernity and Double Consciousness*. Cambridge, MA: Harvard University Press, 1993.

Gittings, Christopher. *Canadian National Cinema*. New York/London: Routledge, 2002.

Glissant, Édouard. *Caribbean Discourse: Selected Essays*. Trans. J. Michael Dash. Charlottesville: University Press of Virginia, 1989.

———. *Le discours antillais*. Paris: Gallimard, 1997.

———. *Introduction à une poétique du divers*. Paris: Gallimard, 1996.

Gníomhach nó Fulangach? Fáthmheas ar an Réimse Craolacháin / Active or Passive? Broadcasting in the Future Tense. Baile Átha Cliath [Dublin]: Oifig an tSoláthair, 1995.

Godard, Jean-Luc, and Anne-Marie Miéville, eds. *Cahiers du cinéma* 300, numéro special (1979).

Godtfred, Boði. "Fjernsyn på Færøerne." MA thesis. Danmarks Journalisthøjskole, 1980.

Golfman, Noreen. "Imagining Region: A Survey of Newfoundland Film." *North of Everything: English Canadian Cinema Since 1980*. Ed. William Beard and Jerry White. Edmonton: University of Alberta Press, 2002. 46–59.

Gould, Glenn. *The Latecomers. Glenn Gould's Solitude Trilogy: Three Sound Documentaries*. Toronto: CBC Records, 1992. [First broadcast November 1969]

Grierson, John. *Grierson on Documentary*. Ed. Forsyth Hardy. New York: Harcourt, Brace, 1947.

Gwyn, Sandra. *Cinema as Catalyst*. Report on the seminar "Film, Video and Social Change." St. John's: Memorial University of Newfoundland Extension Service, 1972. [Held at archives of National Film Board of Canada, Fogo Island box, and at Centre for Newfoundland Studies, Memorial University of Newfoundland]

Habermas, Jürgen. *The Postnational Constellation: Political Essays*. Trans. Max Pensky. Cambridge, MA: MIT Press, 2001.

———. *Die postnationale Konstellation: Politische Essays*. Frankfurt am Main: Suhrkamp, 1998.

———. *The Structural Transformation of the Public Sphere: An Inquiry into a Category of Bourgeois Society*. Trans. Thomas Burger. Cambridge, MA: MIT Press, 1999.

———. *Strukturwandel der Öffentlichkeit. Untersuchungen zu einer Kategorie der bürgerlichen Gesellschaft*. Neuwied am Rhein/Berlin: Hermann Luchterhand, 1965.

Hansen, Annette Schäfer, and Ulrik Schack. *Sjónvarp Føroya: TV'et, der snublede til starten*. København [Copenhagen]: Institut for Filmvidenskab, 1984.

"Hava fingið loyvi at sjónvarpa á Tvøroyi." *Sosialurin* 15 Sept. 1979: 4.

Hendy, David. "Radio's Cultural Turns." *Cinema Journal* 48.1 (2008): 130–38.

Hilmes, Michelle. "Rethinking Radio." *The Radio Reader: Essays in the Cultural History of Radio*. Ed. Michelle Hilmes and Jason Loviglio. New York: Routledge, 2002. 1–19.

Hindley, Reg. *The Death of the Irish Language: A Qualified Obituary*. London: Routledge, 1990.

Hjálmarsson, Vilhjálmur. "Ræða við setningu kvikmyndahátíðar í Reykvavík 1978." *Tímínn* 5 Feb. 1978: 6–7.

Hogarth, David. *Documentary Television in Canada: From National Public Service to Global Marketplace*. Montreal / Kingston: McGill-Queen's University Press, 2002.

Hogenkamp, Bert. "La vie est à nous: Irlande." *Écran* 66 (1978): 69–70.

Højgaard, Andrias. "Sjónvarp." *Sosialurin* 20 May 1978: 6.

Højgaard, J. Karter. "Latið okkum fara undir regluligar sjónvarpssendingar við føstum senditíðum og undir eftirliti skjótast gjørligt." *Sosialurin* 11 Mar. 1978: 6.

Hourigan, Niamh. "A Comparison between the Campaigns for Raidió na Gaeltachta and Teilifís na Gaeilge." Diss. National University of Ireland, Galway, 1998.

———. *Escaping the Global Village: Media, Language and Protest*. Lanham, MD: Lexington Books, 2004.

Jacobs, Lewis, ed. *The Documentary Tradition*. 2nd ed. New York: Norton, 1971.

Jarvie, Ian. *Hollywood's Overseas Campaign: The North Atlantic Movie Trade, 1920–1950*. Cambridge: Cambridge University Press, 1992.

Joensen, Árni. "Sjónvarpsfelagið." *Sosialurin* 11 Feb. 1968: 6.

Joensen, Dagny. "Ikki bert spurningur um pening." *Sosialurin* 17 May 1984: 16.

———. "Leggið dent á barnasjónvarpið." *Sosialurin* 24 May 1984: 8–9.

Jógvansdóttir, Sonja J. "Sjónvarpið í óvissuni." *Dimmalætting* 3 Aug. 2004: 5.

Jones, D. B. *Movies and Memoranda: An Interpretive History of the National Film Board of Canada*. Ottawa: Deneau / Canadian Film Institute, 1981.

Kernan, Michael. "A Way of Social Change through Film." *Washington Post* 2 Mar. 1969: 4.

Konigsberg, Ira. *The Complete Film Dictionary*. New York: Meridian, 1987.

Lacasse, Germain. "L'accent aigu du cinéma oral." Boulais 47–60.

Lacroix, Yves. "À l'écoute." *Image et Son* 256 (January 1972): 29–36.

———. "Petite misère du scripteur radiophonique." *Voix et images du pays* 4 (1971): 53–97.

Lafond, Jean-Daniel. *Les traces du rêve, ou, Il était une fois Pierre Perrault, cinéaste, poète, et Québécois*. Montréal: Éditions de l'Hexagone, 1988.

"Landsstýrið givið Sjónvarpsfelagnum sendiloyvi." *14. September* 9 Nov. 1978: 4.

Leach, Jim. *Film in Canada*. Oxford: Oxford University Press, 2006.

Le Boterf, Hervé. *La Bretagne dans la guerre: Tome II, 1941*. Paris: Éditions France-Empire, 1970.

Lefebvre, Jean Pierre. "Colin Low, poète de la survivance." *Objectif* 22–23 (October-November 1963): 24–38.

Lindberg, Halgir, and Árni C. Joensen. "Royndarsjónvarp." *14. September* 2 Sept. 1967. 1.

Lippmann, Walter. [Unsigned] "The Defense of the Atlantic World." *New Republic* 17 Dec. 1917: 59–61.

"Løgmaður steðgar royndarsjónvarpinum." *14. September* 2 Dec. 1967: 1.

Loiselle, André. *Cinema as History: Michel Brault and Modern Quebec*. Bloomington / Toronto: Indiana University Press / Toronto International Film Festival Group, 2007.

———. *Le cinéma de Michel Brault: À l'image d'une nation*. Paris: L'Harmattan, 2005.

Low, Colin. "*Capitale de l'or* et *Île Fogo*: Le documentaire comme outil de communication et catalyseur de changement social." *Le Documentaire: Contestation et propagande*. Ed. Catherine Saouter. Montréal: XYZ Éditeur, 1996. 63–73.

———. *The Fogo Island Communication Experiment*. Report for the National Film Board of Canada. 5 July 1972. [Held at archives of National Film Board of Canada, Fogo Island box]

———. "Grierson and Challenge for Change." *John Grierson and the NFB*. Ed. John Grierson Project. Toronto: ECW Press, 1984. 111–19.

———. Untitled report on Fogo Island project. Report for the National Film Board of Canada. 22 January 1968. [Held at archives of National Film Board of Canada, Fogo Island box]

Mac Conghail, Muiris. Contribution to the forum "After the Green Paper: What Next for Broadcasting in Ireland?" *Irish Communications Review* 5 (1995): 79–81.

———. "Teilifís na Gaeilge: Teilifís ar Strae?" *Comhar* 56.5 (1997): 22–25.

Mac Eachmharcaigh, Niall. "Guth Aduaidh ó Lios na Sí." O'Connell, Walsh, and Denvir 162–63.

MacKillop, James, ed. *Contemporary Irish Cinema*. Syracuse, NY: Syracuse University Press, 1999.

Mac Murchaidh, Ciarán ed. *"Who Needs Irish?" Reflections on the Importance of the Irish Language Today*. Dublin: Veritas, 2004.

Mai en décembre: Godard en Abitibi. Dir. Julie Perron. Office national du film du Canada, 2000.

Manovich, Lev. *The Language of New Media*. Cambridge, MA: MIT Press, 2001.

Marchessault, Janine. "Reflections on the Dispossessed: Video and the 'Challenge for Change' Experiment." *Screen* 36.2 (Summer 1995): 131–46.

Marcorelles, Louis. *Living Cinema: New Directions in Contemporary Film-Making*. Trans. Isabelle Quigley. New York: Praeger, 1973.

Marks, Laura U. *The Skin of the Film: Intercultural Cinema and the Senses*. Durham, NC: Duke University Press, 2000.

Marshall, Bill. *Quebec National Cinema*. Montreal / Kingston: McGill-Queen's University Press, 2001.

Marsolais, Gilles. *L'aventure du cinéma direct revisitée*. Saint-Laurent, QC: 400 Coups, 1997.

McIlroy, Brian. *World Cinema 4: Ireland*. Trowbridge, UK: Flicks Books, 1988.

McLoone, Martin. *Irish Film: The Emergence of a Contemporary Cinema*. London: British Film Institute, 2000.

Melnyk, George. *One Hundred Years of Canadian Cinema*. Toronto: University of Toronto Press, 2004.

Moretti, Franco. *Atlas of the European Novel, 1800–1900*. London: Verso, 1998.

Morris, Peter. "Re-Thinking Grierson: The Ideology of John Grierson." Véronneau, Dorland, and Feldman 21–56.

Mortensen, Johann. "Annaðhvørt alment sjónvarp—ella einki!" *Sosialurin* 18 Mar. 1978: 3.

Murphy, Kathleen. [Unsigned] Program notes for "In the Name of the Nation: Celebrating Irish Filmmaking, 1910–1994." New York: Film Society of Lincoln Center, 1994.

"Næstan annaðhvørt hús sjónvarp." *Sosialurin* 13 Feb. 1980: 5.

Nauerby, Tom. *No Nation Is an Island: Language, Culture and National Identity in the Faroe Islands*. North Atlantic Monographs 3. Aarhus, Den.: Aarhus University Press, 1996.

Nelson, Joyce. *The Colonized Eye: Rethinking the Grierson Legend*. Toronto: Between the Lines, 1988.

"Neyvan rætt at loyva lýsingar í sjónvarpinum." *Sosialurin* 29 Apr. 1981: 5.

Ní Bhrádaigh, Emer. "TG4@10: An Léargas Fiontraíochta." O'Connell, Walsh, and Denvir 137–54.

Ní Chinnéide, Dairena. "Telifís na Gaeilge: Une chaîne de télévision en langue irlandais." *Mercator Media Forum* 1 (1995): 29–35.

Ní Chionnaith, Íte. "Fíorú Aislinge: Cuimhní Cinn agus Smaointe Feachtasóra." O'Connell, Walsh, and Denvir 27–50.

Ní Fhlatharta, Bernie. "Gaeltacht TV on air again at Christmas." *Connacht Tribune* 9 Oct. 1987: 1.

Nielsen, Greg. *Le Canada de Radio-Canada*. Collection Theoria 4. Toronto: Éditions du Gref, 1994.

"Norröna í Sjónvarpinum." *Sosialurin* 21 June 1983: 1.

O'Brien, Conor Cruise. "The Irish Question—1969." *Irish Times* 29 Jan. 1969: 5.

O'Brien, Harvey. *The Real Ireland: The Evolution of Ireland in Documentary Film*. Manchester: Manchester University Press, 2004.

Ó Cadhain, Máirtín. *Gluaiseacht na Gaeilge: Gluaiseacht ar Strae*. Baile Átha Cliath [Dublin]: Misneach, 1970.

Ó Caollaí, Maolsheachlainn. *Issues in Television Broadcasting in Ireland*. Dublin: Conradh na Gaeilge, 1978.

———. "Open Broadcasting: A Recipe for Extinction." *Irish Times* 4 Mar. 1974: 12. [Also published by Conradh na Gaeilge as a pamphlet, 1974]

———. "Teilifís—Fórsa Láidir inár Saol." *Inniu* 13 June 1975: 7.

———. *Tiarnas Cultúir: Craolachán in Éirinn*. Baile Átha Cliath [Dublin]: Conradh na Gaeilge, 1980.

"O Caollai Resigns From Language Body." *Irish Times* 11 Nov. 1970: 4.

O'Connell, Eithne, John Walsh, and Gearóid Denvir, eds. *TG4@10: Deich mBliana de TG4*. Indreabhán [Inveran], Ire.: Cló Iar-Chonnachta, 2008.

Ó Cuaig, Seosamh. "Colun Na Gaeltachta." *Connacht Tribune* 17 Oct. 1969: 8.

———. "Gan Teilifís Ghaeltachta, Gan Ghaeilge." *Comhar* 47.5 (May 1988): 8–9.

———. "Oireachtas na nGael." *Inniu* 13 Nov. 1970: 3.

———. "'Saorstaisiun Radio' sa Ghaeltacht?" *Inniu* 19 Sept. 1969: 7.

Ó hÉallaithe, Donncha. "From Language Revival to Language Survival." Mac Murchaidh 159–92.

———. "Longstanding Gaeltacht TV activist Donncha OhEallaithe explains his fears for the future of the new channel." *Film Ireland* April/May 1994: 18.

———. "An Teilifís agus Teangacha Mionlaigh." *Comhar* 50.3 (1991): 24–28.

———. "Teilifís na Gaeltachta." Letter. *Anois* 22 Nov. 1987: 6.

———. "Why Was TnaG a Monumental Mistake?" *Force 10* no. 10 (1998): 43.

Ó Glaisne, Risteárd. *Raidió na Gaeltachta*. Indreabhán [Inveran], Ire.: Cló Chois Fharraige, 1982.

Ó Laoire, Lillis. "Níl Sí Doiligh a Iompar! / No Load to Carry: A Personal Response to the Current Situation of Irish." Mac Murchaidh 46–63.

Olsson, Jan. "One Commercial Week: Television in Sweden Prior to Public Service." *Television after TV: Essays on a Medium in Transition*. Ed. Lynn Spigel and Jan Olson. Durham, NC: Duke University Press, 2005. 249–69.

Ó Muirí, Pól. "Tay Gay Four: The Case Against." *Irish Times* 13 Oct. 1999: 10.

O'Reilly, William. "Genealogies of Atlantic History." *Atlantic Studies* 1.1 (2004): 66–84.

Ó Torna, Colm. "Teilifís Ghaeltachta á scrúdú ag an Rialtas." *Anois* 15 Nov. 1987: 2.

Ó Tuathaigh, Gearóid. "Language, Literature and Culture in Ireland since the War." *Ireland 1945–1970: The Thomas Davis Lectures*. Ed. J. J. Lee. Dublin: Gill and MacMillan, 1979.

Pageau, Pierre. "Colin Low et Pierre Perrault: Points de convergence." Véronneau, Dorland, and Feldman 139–51.

———. "Colin Low, un anglophone au Québec." Boulais 257–69.

Perrault, Pierre. *De la parole aux actes: Essais*. Montréal: Éditions de l'Hexagone, 1985.

———. "Discours sur la parole." *Cahiers du cinéma* 191 (June 1967): 26–33.

———. *Le mal du nord*. Hull, QC: Vents d'ouest, 1999.

———. *Un pays sans bons sens!* Montréal: Éditions Lidec, 1972.

———. *Toutes isles: Récits*. Montréal: Éditions de l'Hexagone, 1963.

Petrowski, Nathalie. "Pour la suite du monde." *La Presse* 29 June 1999: B5.

Pettitt, Lance. *Screening Ireland: Film and Television Representation*. Manchester: Manchester University Press, 2000.

"Philips byrjar framsýning við sjónvarpstólum í dag." *Sosialurin* 7 Apr. 1979: 4.

Pine, Richard. *2RN and the Origins of Irish Radio*. Dublin: Four Courts, 2002.

"Pirates go off the air today." *Irish Times* 31 Dec. 1988: 1.

"Pirat.sendarar ..." *Sosialurin* 27 Mar. 1980: 4.

Pogue, Leland. "Leland Pogue Replies to Robert Self's 'Robert Altman and the Theory of Authorship.'" *Cinema Journal* 25.3 (Spring 1986): 76–80.

"Policy Reform for Irish on RTE: O'Brien to Amend Broadcasting Act." *Irish Times* 25 Feb. 1974: 1, 13.

Poulsen, Jóhan Hendrik W. *Mál í Mæti*. Tórshavn: Føroya Fróðskaparfelag, 2004.

Poulsen, Jørgen. *TV og den færøske kulturs fremtid*. Tórshavn / Aalborg, Den.: Føroya Fróðskaparfelag / Aalborg Universitetsforlag, 1980.

Quinn, Bob. *Atlantean: Ireland's North African and Maritime Heritage*. London / New York: Quartet, 1986.

———. *The Atlantean Irish: Ireland's Oriental and Maritime Heritage*. Dublin: Lilliput, 2005.

———. *Maverick: A Dissident View of Broadcast Today*. Dingle, Ire.: Brandon, 2001.

———. "Recycled Rants." *Film West*, October 2000. 26–30.

Rawlyk, G. A. *The Atlantic Provinces and the Problems of Confederation: Report to the Task Force on Canadian Unity*. St. John's, Nfld.: Breakwater, 1979.

Reece, Jack E. *The Bretons against France: Ethnic Minority Nationalism in Twentieth-Century Brittany*. Chapel Hill: University of North Carolina Press, 1977.

Rhodie, Sam. *Promised Lands: Cinema, Geography, Modernism*. London: British Film Institute, 2001.

Riendeau, Roger. *A Brief History of Canada*. Markham, ON: Fitzhenry and Whiteside, 2000.

Robinson, Tim. *Setting Foot on the Shores of Connemara and Other Writings*. Dublin: Lilliput, 1996.

———. *Stones of Aran: Labyrinth*. New York: NYRB Classics, 2009.

———. *Stones of Aran: Pilgrimage*. New York: NYRB Classics, 2008.

Rockett, Kevin, Luke Gibbons, and John Hill. *Cinema and Ireland*. Syracuse, NY: Syracuse University Press, 1987.

Savage, Robert. *Irish Television: The Political and Social Origins*. Cork, Ire.: Cork University Press, 1996.

Savard, Céline, and James Lambert. *Répertoire numérique détaillé du Fonds Pierre Perrault (P319)*. Sainte-Foy, QC: Université Laval, Division des archives, 1994.

Schiller, Herbert. *Communication and Cultural Domination*. White Plains, NY: International Arts and Sciences Press, 1976.

———. *New Modes of Cultural Domination*. Dublin: Conradh na Gaeilge, 1977.

Self, Robert. "Robert Self Replies." *Cinema Journal* 25.3 (Spring 1986): 80–83.

"Sendið lýsingar í sjónvarpinum og keypið útgerð fyri pengarnar!" *Sosialurin* 11 Apr. 1981: 5.

"Sjónvarp sendi nú reguliga." *Sosialurin* 11 Apr. 1979: 1, 5.

"Sjónvarpsfelagið vil hava sendiloyvi. " *Sosialurin* 11 Jan. 1978: 3.

"Sjónvarpsfundur." *Sosialurin* 13 Dec. 1967:1.

"Sjónvarpsmálið lagt fyri landsstýrið í hesi tingsetuni." *Sosialurin* 11 Jan. 1978: 1.

"Sjónvarpssendarin kemur 20. apríl!!" *Sosialurin* 7 Mar. 1979: 2.

"Sjónvarpssendarin kemur um hálvan." *Sosialurin* 7 Feb. 1979: 3.

"Sjónvarpssendingar í Klaksvík." *14 September* 11 Mar. 1978: 11.

"Sjónvarp til eysturoyingar og norðoyingar—prísurin 100.000 kr." *Sosialurin* 21 Apr. 1979: 3.

"Skulu vit hava danskt fjarsýn?" *14. September* 18 Mar. 1967: 1.

Snowden, Donald. *Film and Community Development*. Report for the Office of Economic Development, Washington DC. September 1968.

Splanc Dheireadh na Gaeltachta. Dir. Bob Quinn. TG4/Gael Media, 2000.

Story, G. M., and W. Kirwin. "The Dictionary of Newfoundland English: Progress and Promise." *Regional Language Studies Newfoundland* 5 (1974): 15–17.

Story, G. M., W. Kirwin, and J. D. A. Widdowson. *The Dictionary of Newfoundland English*. Toronto: University of Toronto Press, 1982.

Sveinsson, Erlendur, ed. *Kvikmyndir á Íslandi: 75 ára*. Reykjavík: Kvikmyndasafn Íslands, 1981.

"Teilifís na Gaeilge." *Irish Times* 31 Oct. 1996: 10.

Teodoro, José. "*Cartographic Cinema.*" *Film Comment* 43.2 (2007): 79.

Thompson, Kristin. *Exporting Entertainment: America in the World Film Market, 1907–1934*. London: British Film Institute, 1985.

Tsivan, Yuri. *Lines of Resistance: Dziga Vertov and the Twenties*. Sacile, It.: Le Giornate del Cinema Muto, 2004.

"The Unheard 'Pirate.'" *Connacht Tribune* 10 Apr. 1970: 1.

Untitled report on the Film Unit of Memorial University of Newfoundland's Extension Service and their involvement with the National Film Board. 6 January 1970. [Held at archives of National Film Board of Canada, Fogo Island box]

Véronneau, Pierre. "Le Québec: De la fiction, dirent-ils. Des origines à 1960." *Les Cinémas du Canada*. Ed. Sylvain Garel and André Paquet. Paris: Centre Georges Pompidou, 1992. 35–49.

Véronneau, Pierre, Michael Dorland, and Seth Feldman, eds. *Dialogue: Cinéma canadien et québécois / Canadian and Quebec Cinema*. Montréal: Médiatexte / Cinémathèque québécoise, 1986.

"Verðurfastir í Mykinesi—stytta um tíðina við sjónvarpi." *Sosialurin* 28 Jan. 1981: 1.

Vertov, Dziga. *Kino-Eye: The Writings of Dziga Vertov*. Ed. Annette Michelson. Trans. Kevin O'Brien. Berkeley: University of California Press, 1984.

———. *Stat'i, dnevniki, zamysly*. Moskva [Moscow]: Iskusstvo, 1966.

Warren, Paul. *Pierre Perrault: Cinéaste de la parole*. Montréal: Éditions de l'Hexagone, 1996.

Watson, Iarfhlaith. *Broadcasting in Irish: Minority Language, Radio, Television and Identity*. Dublin: Four Courts, 2003.

———. "Teilifís na Gaeilge as a Public Sphere." *Irish Communications Review* 7 (1998): 69–80.

Waugh, Thomas. "Challenge For Change / Société Nouvelle: Two Case Studies in Textual Analysis." Paper presented at the annual meeting of the Film Studies Association of Canada. York University, Toronto. 28–30 May 2006.

Williams, Raymond. *Communications*. Rev. ed. London: Chatto and Windus, 1966.

———. *Raymond Williams on Television: Selected Writings*. Ed. Alan O'Connor. Toronto: Between the Lines, 1989.

———. *Television: Technology and Cultural Form*. London: Routledge, 2003.

Williamson, H. Anthony. *The Fogo Process: User-Oriented Communications Systems and Social Development*. Summary of presentation at UNESCO meeting on the Planning and Management of New Communications Systems, 8–12 October 1972, Paris. [Held at Centre for Newfoundland Studies, Memorial University of Newfoundland]

Wimsatt, W. K. *The Verbal Icon: Studies of Meaning of Poetry*. Lexington: University Press of Kentucky, 1954.

Winston, Brian. *Claiming the Real: The Documentary Film Revisited*. London: British Film Institute, 1995.

Wollen, Peter. *Readings and Writings: Semiotic Counter-Strategies*. London: Verso, 1982.

Working Group on Irish Language Television Broadcasting. *Report to the Ministers for the Gaeltacht and Communications*. Dublin: Stationary Office, 1987.

Wylie, Jonathan. *The Faroe Islands: Interpretations of History*. Lexington: University Press of Kentucky, 1987.

INDEX

C

D

M

N

U

V

W

Books in the Film and Media Studies Series
Published by Wilfrid Laurier University Press

Image and Identity: Reflections on Canadian Film Culture / R. Bruce Elder / 1989 / [2006] paperback https://www.wlupress.wlu.ca/Books/B/ Beyond-Bylinesedition 2012 / xviii + 484 pp. / ISBN 978-1-55458-469-7

Image and Territory: Essays on Atom Egoyan / Monique Tschofen and Jennifer Burwell, editors / 2006 / viii + 418 pp / photos / ISBN 978-0-88920-487-4

The Young, the Restless, and the Dead: Interviews with Canadian Filmmakers / George Melnyk, editor / 2008 / xiv + 134 pp. / photos / ISBN 978-1-55458- 036-1

Programming Reality: Perspectives on English-Canadian Television / Zoë Druick and Aspa Kotsopoulos, editors / 2008 / x + 344 pp. / photos / ISBN 978-1-55458-010-1

Harmony and Dissent: Film and Avant-garde Art Movements in the Early Twentieth Century / R. Bruce Elder / 2008 / xxxiv + 482 pp. / ISBN 978-1-55458-028-6

He Was Some Kind of a Man: Masculinities in the B Western / Roderick McGillis / 2009 / xii + 210 pp. / photos / ISBN 978-1-55458-059-0

The Radio Eye: Cinema in the North Atlantic, 1958–1988 / Jerry White / 2009 / xvi + 284 pp. / photos / ISBN 978-1-55458-178-8

The Gendered Screen: Canadian Women Filmmakers / Brenda Austin-Smith and George Melnyk, editors / 2010 / x + 272 pp. / ISBN 978-1-55458-179-5

Feeling Canadian: Nationalism, Affect, and Television / Marusya Bociurkiw / 2011 / viii + 184 pp. / ISBN 978-1-55458-268-6

Beyond Bylines: Media Workers and Women's Rights in Canada / Barbara M. Freeman / [2011] paperback edition 2015 / xii + 328 pp. / photos / ISBN 978-1-55458-303-4

Canadian Television: Text and Context / Marian Bredin, Scott Henderson, and Sarah A. Matheson, editors / 2011 / xvi + 238 pp. / ISBN 978-1-55458- 361-4

Cinema and Social Change in Germany and Austria / Gabriele Mueller and James M. Skidmore, editors / 2012 / x + 304 pp. / photos / ISBN 978-1- 55458-225-9

DADA, Surrealism, and the Cinematic Effect / Bruce Elder / 2013 / viii + 766 pp. / ISBN 978-1-55458-625-7

Two Bicycles: The Work of Jean-Luc Godard and Anne-Marie Miéville / Jerry White / 2013 / x + 204 pp. / ISBN 978-1-55458-935-7

The Legacies of Jean-Luc Godard / Douglas Morrey, Christina Stojanova, and Nicole Côté, editors / 2014 / photos / xxvi + 244 pp. / ISBN 978-1- 55458-920-3

Detecting Canada: Essays on Canadian Crime Fiction, Film, and Television / Jeannette Sloniowski and Marilyn Rose, editors / 2014 / xxiv + 318 pp. / ISBN 978-1-55458-926-5

Reverse Shots: Indigenous Film and Media in an International Context / Wendy Gay Pearson and Susan Knabe, editors / 2014 / xii + 372 pp. / ISBN 978-1-55458-335-5

Making Feminist Media: Third-Wave Magazines on the Cusp of the Digital Age / Elizabeth Groeneveld / 2016 / xiv + 206 pp. / ISBN 978-1-77112-120-0

Stan Brakhage in Rolling Stock, 1980–1990 / Jerry White / 2018 / xii + 372 pp. / ISBN 978-1-77112-303-7